# BUSING U.S.A.

**Also by Nicolaus Mills . . .**

*Comparisons: A Short Story Anthology*
*American and English Fiction in the Nineteenth Century*
*The Great School Bus Controversy*
*The New Journalism: A Historical Anthology*

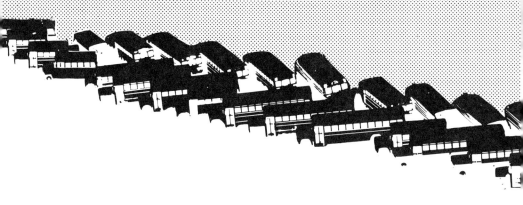

Teachers College, Columbia University
New York and London  1979

# BUSING
# U.S.A.

NICOLAUS MILLS, Editor

Sarah Lawrence College

For
Marvin Frankel
Elizabeth and John Hallowell

Published by Teachers College Press, Teachers College,
Columbia University, 1234 Amsterdam Avenue,
New York, NY 10027.

Library of Congress Cataloging in Publication Data

Main entry under title:

Busing U.S.A.
   Includes index.
   1.  School children—United States—Transporta-
tion.  2.  School children—Transportation—Law
and legislation—United States—Cases.  I.  Mills,
Nicolaus.
LC214.5.B88    371.8'7'0973    78–31327
ISBN 0–8077–2554–4

Designed by
Romeo M. Enriquez
1 2 3 4 5 6 7 8      84 83 82 81 80 79
Manufactured in the U.S.A.

*Cover photo: United Press International Photo*

# Contents

# Introduction

## NICOLAUS MILLS

In the early 1970s, when the busing controversy first reached fever pitch, it seemed, like so much else that was going on at the time, a reaction to the unresolved turmoil of the 1960s. An America that had lost faith in the programs of Lyndon Johnson's Great Society and was no longer sympathetic to the expectations produced by the civil rights movement was now saying enough. It wanted political breathing space, and it did not want its children saddled with problems that adult society had failed to answer.

A Harris Survey released before the 1972 elections showed that 73 percent of the public opposed busing for racial balance, but even with this kind of popular support, it was not clear that the antibusing movement could keep going once the anger and political backlash it fueled itself on ran out. To begin with, there were the facts of the case. In 1972 only three percent of the children in the country (now in 1978 an estimated seven percent) were being bused to school as a result of court orders; while 42 percent (now over 50 percent) were riding the school bus for reasons having nothing to do with desegregation. More important, opposition to the antibusing movement rested on a solid base. In the Senate, men like Walter Mondale, Chairman of the Select Committee on Equal Educational Opportunity, did not hesitate to confront the issue head on. "Busing is one means—and at times the only means—by which segregation in public education can be reduced," Mondale argued. The same hard core of resistance was true in academic circles, where sociologists like Thomas Pettigrew of Harvard, principal author of the 1967 Civil Rights Commission report, *Racial Isolation in the Public Schools*, maintained, "To our knowledge there is actually no evidence whatsoever that 'busing' for desegregation harms children." Above all, there was the Supreme Court, which, despite its Nixon-appointed Judges, observed in its 1971 *Swann* decision requiring desegregation for Charlotte, North Carolina, "Bus transportation has been an integral part of the public education system for years" and continues to be "a normal and accepted tool of educational policy."

By 1974 it was clear, however, that the busing crisis had reached a new stage, and antibusing forces now had every reason to believe that they were in the driver's seat. For the first time in 20 years, the Supreme Court backed off the path it had followed since its historic *Brown* decision, when it held that "separate but equal" has no place in public education. Ruling on a desegregation case, *Milliken v. Bradley,* for the city of Detroit, the Court said that despite the presence of *de jure* segregation within Detroit schools and despite the fact that "state agencies did participate in the maintenance of the Detroit system," a metropolitan or interdistrict remedy was not in order. For Detroit, with a school system more than 80 percent black, the decision meant the end of meaningful desegregation. But in the political climate of 1974, the thrust of the Court's ruling went far beyond Detroit. To the rest of the country the message of *Milliken* was unmistakable. If you lived in the North, if you could afford a house in a suburb that had its own school system, there was little likelihood of busing ever being a problem for you.

A crisis that might have been solved if the entire country— North as well as South, middle class as well as poor—felt called upon to act was now no longer a truly national problem. The consequences were not what they might have been if President Nixon had gotten his much publicized Constitutional amendment against busing passed, but they were close to it. Up to this point, the Supreme Court had always been a dike against antibusing sentiment. Now it was a dike with a gaping hole, and what followed over the next two years was a flood of antibusing feeling and legislation.

In Boston, capital of the only state in the country to vote for George McGovern, the antibusing forces were able to portray themselves as victims, and white resistance to a desegregation plan that failed to include such nearby suburbs as Brookline and Newton quickly turned the city into a Northern Little Rock. The mood in Washington was no different. Liberal Senators such as

Delaware's Joseph Biden, under pressure from antibusing forces in their home states, found the busing crisis a "domestic Vietnam," and by the end of 1975 Congress had passed a bill forbidding the Department of Health, Education, and Welfare from ordering school districts to bus children beyond their neighborhood schools for the purposes of desegregation. Even the new President found the antibusing mood impossible to resist, and in election year 1976, President Ford issued a memorandum (quickly made public) to his Attorney General asking that he "look for an appropriate and proper case" in which to ask the Supreme Court to "re-examine" busing as a desegregation tool.

The pressure on those who in the past had defended the usefulness of busing was overwhelming. Blacks, who in the early 1970s had favored busing by a slim margin, now began tilting the other way, and a 1975 Harris Survey showed 47 percent of them opposed to busing and only 40 percent of them in favor of it. Even in the academic community, which ever since Kenneth Clark's famous doll studies on the effects of prejudice had always supplied the courts with reasons to desegregate, there was a swing to the right. When James Coleman, principal author of the massive 1966 government study, *Equality of Educational Opportunity*, came out against busing, the newspapers rushed to report his findings, and Coleman became an instant celebrity, making an hour-long television appearance in Boston and addressing a national conference on alternatives to busing in Louisville, Kentucky.

It is this second stage in the national busing battle that this anthology, a sequel to an earlier book, *The Great School Bus Controversy*, seeks to capture. In section one, "The Courts and the Law," the focus is on the Detroit school bus case, *Milliken v. Bradley*, in light of the Supreme Court's two-decade history of desegregation rulings. The section begins with a long introductory essay in which Yale University Law Professor Owen M. Fiss first traces the path the Supreme Court followed to get to *Milliken v. Bradley* and then concludes that, as a result of the legal uncertainty created by the *Milliken* decision, "Consistency can only be achieved if we abandon the illusory search for the incidents of past discrimination and address in a direct and explicit way the hard question—Is a segregated pattern of student attendance harmful, and if so, how harmful?" The heart of this section is not, however, analysis of the Supreme Court's landmark desegregation rulings but the rulings themselves, and Professor Fiss's essay, "School Desegregation: The Uncertain Path of the Law," is followed by three cases from the Warren Court—*Brown I, Brown II,* and *Green v. New Kent County*—and three cases from the Burger Court—*Swann v. Charlotte-Mecklenburg, Keyes v. Denver School District No. 1,* and *Milliken v. Bradley.* The cases appear here in chronological order, but what is so striking about that order is that up to the *Milliken* decision it shows the Supreme Court widening the scope of its desegregation rulings—demanding in *Brown II* that schools eliminate segregation with "all deliberate speed," insisting on immediate compliance by *Green,* ordering district-wide busing in *Swann,* and in *Keyes,* its first major Northern case, asserting that racial segregation in a significant proportion of a school district creates the presumption that the entire district is contaminated.

In section two, "The Social Scientists and White Flight," the focus shifts to the demographic reaction to school desegregation and to the analysis of "white flight" that the academic community has provided. The essays in this section are, however, anything but merely academic in their implications. Like Kenneth Clark's doll studies, which along with the work of other sociologists, prompted the Supreme Court to observe in its 1954 *Brown* decision that separating school children solely on the basis of race "may affect their hearts and minds in a way unlikely ever to be undone," these studies have also had an impact on the courts and on the media. The opening essay in this section is an article in which James Coleman, chief author of *Equal Educational Opportunity,* a government report most often cited to justify desegregation orders, surveys school desegregation trends from 1968 to 1973 and concludes that the loss of white students in this process means, "Ironically, 'desegregation' may be increasing segregation." To stop this white flight Coleman urges a halt to the "full-scale" busing remedies courts have ordered and in their place the use of the kinds of plans that would allow "each child in a metropolitan area to attend any school in that area so long as the school to which he chose to go had no higher proportion of his race than his neighborhood school." Coleman's report is followed by an extensive critique of his research and policy recommendations by Professor Thomas Pettigrew of Harvard and Professor Robert Green of Michigan State. Then there is an exchange in which Coleman reasserts his claim that "current desegregation policies are having serious long-term demographic effects" and Green and Pettigrew amplify their major counter-charges: 1) Coleman "ignores the fact that separation of the races between suburbs and central cities has been under way throughout this century"; 2) "Racial desegregation of schools has not been proven to *cause* so-called 'white flight' in any rigorous sense." The concluding essays in this section—the first by Professor Christine Rossell of Boston University, the second by Professor Diane Ravitch of Columbia's Teachers College—continue the Coleman-Green-Pettigrew debate but in a way that makes them far more than partisan position papers. For in the end Rossell and Ravitch bring us back to what is too easily forgotten in the white flight controversy: namely, that in the academic community all sides have been concerned with what is the best way to end racial separation in America's schools.

In section three, "National and Local Politics," the emphasis shifts again: first to how Congress and the President have responded to the busing crisis of the middle seventies and then to how local communities have dealt with the same problem. The section opens with Gary Orfield's account of "The President, Congress, and Antibusing Politics," which takes us from 1964 to the Carter administration. Next come reports from four cities—three of which have undergone highly publicized court-ordered busing plans. In the case of Charlotte, North Carolina, which as a result of the Supreme Court's 1971 *Swann* decision, began a city-county busing program, we see a Southern community successfully coping with busing. As *Charlotte Observer* reporter Mark Nadler points out, Charlotteans may not like busing, but in a school system approximately two-thirds white and one-third black, they have accepted it and made it work. In Detroit, on the other hand, we see what happens when the Court limits busing to the inner city and inner city schools are basically one-race schools. As *Detroit Free Press* education writer William Grant notes, little has changed in Detroit since *Milliken v. Bradley*, except for a slight increase in the percentage of blacks in white schools. Approximately half the schools in the city's system remain 90 percent black. The surprise story in this section is Boston, which in 1974 became the embodiment of Northern resistance to court-ordered busing. Howard Husock, staff reporter for *The Boston Phoenix*, shows how Boston changed in three years' time so that by 1977 not only would two busloads of white students voluntarily go from South Boston to an innovative new high school in black Roxbury, but the city electorate would defeat an entire slate of antibusing school board candidates. As in Mark Nadler's account of Charlotte, Husock's report shows what happens when local leadership asserts itself and ignores the temptation to exploit busing as a political issue. The final report is from Chicago, which, despite massive segregation in its school system, has not had to deal with court-ordered busing. In this story David Moberg, a reporter for the weekly, *In These Times,* shows how resistance to a limited black-white busing plan designed to relieve overcrowding in Southwest Chicago has aroused violent feelings, and his account closes by raising the question implicit throughout this anthology: What have those cities that have not experienced court-ordered busing learned from its history, and how will they react if it comes their way?

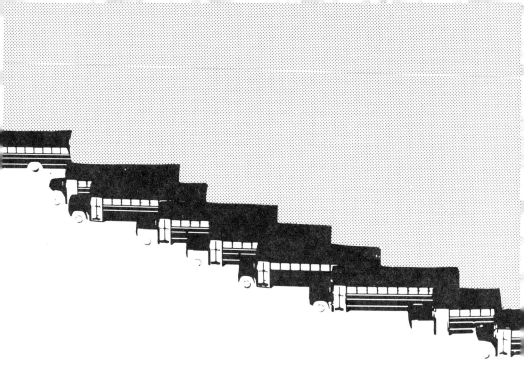

# The Courts
# and the Law

*In this essay Owen M. Fiss, Professor of Law at Yale University and a specialist on the relationship between law and race, traces the rulings of the Supreme Court from the Brown decision of 1954 to the Detroit school bus case, Milliken v. Bradley, in 1974. He concludes that the Court's decision to deny cross-district busing in the Detroit case "does not make sense in practical terms" nor "is it rooted in any inexorable principle of logic or constitutional law."*

# School Desegregation:
# The Uncertain Path of the Law

OWEN M. FISS

The most pressing and yet most elusive dimension of school desegregation law has been that relating to students. In order to understand it a distinction must be drawn between two phenomena. The first is a process or activity—assigning students to schools on the basis of race (racial assignment). The second is a demographic pattern—all the white students are in one school and all the black students are in another (segregation).[1]

In *Brown v. Board of Education* the Supreme Court was confronted with the traditional dual school system in which both phenomena were present and, more importantly, were causally related.[2] Students were assigned to schools on the basis of their race and the demographic pattern was one of racial segregation. Racial assignments produced the segregated schools. There was

Owen M. Fiss, "School Desegregation: The Uncertain Path of the Law," *Philosophy and Public Affairs* 4, no. 1 (Fall 1974). Copyright © 1974 Princeton University Press. Reprinted by permission.

thus no occasion for the Court to draw a sharp distinction between the two phenomena, to determine whether the principal vice was the racial assignment or the segregated schools. The Court simply held the dual school system unlawful. This was an acceptable, indeed probably a commendable, mode of decision. But at the same time it left unresolved whether either of these phenomena standing alone would constitute a denial of equal protection. This ambiguity accounts for the hesitant, uncertain, and sometimes illogical path of Supreme Court doctrine over the last two decades.

### THE PERMISSION QUESTION:
### MAY STUDENTS BE ASSIGNED TO SCHOOLS ON THE
### BASIS OF RACE IN ORDER TO ACHIEVE INTEGRATION?

For the first decade, the principal task facing the Court was reaffirming its commitment to *Brown* and obtaining compliance with the forms of the law—ending open defiance. Then the task became one of defining what desegregation would actually entail. One of the first questions raised was whether racial assignment could be used to achieve integration.

It was then argued that the fatal vice of the dual school system was racial assignment and that it made no difference whether the racial assignment was used to achieve integration rather than segregation. A blanket ban on racial assignment was sought, and in support of that position Justice Harlan's aphorism in his dissent in *Plessy v. Ferguson* that "our Constitution is color-blind" was invoked.[3] This argument was advanced in part to halt voluntary attempts by school boards to integrate, but it was principally used to limit the reach of the desegregation orders of the judiciary. The theory was that if racial assignments were deemed per se unlawful, even when used to achieve integration, the courts would have no option but to permit the local boards to use such student assignment criteria as freedom of choice or geographic proximity. Given prevailing prejudices and segregated residential patterns, these criteria would tend to leave a large residue of segregation. (There was little prospect that random assignments would be required.)

By the late 1960s this argument was rejected by the lower courts, and in 1971 its death knell was formally sounded by the Supreme Court. In *Swann v. Charlotte-Mecklenburg Board of Education*, the Court declared that when racial assignment is linked to integration rather than segregation, it is constitutionally permissible.[4] Segregation is not a constitutionally permissible goal, but integration is; and racial assignment is well suited to achieve this goal. Our understanding of *Brown* was thus sharpened: if it was the racial assignment rather than the demographic pattern that was the principal vice of the dual school system, it was not racial assignment alone but *racial assignment that produced segregation.*

Today, some three years later, *Swann* remains good law. It is established doctrine that racial assignment to achieve integration at the elementary and secondary level is constitutionally permissible. A challenge to that practice would be readily dismissed. But at the same time, during this past Term, the Court had considerable difficulty with the *DeFunis* case.[5] The question now arises as to why the Court saw this case to be so much more difficult than *Swann.*

At issue in *DeFunis* was the use of race by a state law school, the University of Washington Law School, in its admission process.[6] The law school's preferential admission of blacks (and some other minorities, e.g., Chicanos) had the effect of curtailing the number of places available to others. Suit was brought by a rejected white claimant, DeFunis, and it was assumed that DeFunis would have been admitted but for the preferential policy. The Court decided to hear the case but, after it had been fully briefed and argued, dismissed it as moot because DeFunis, who had been admitted to the law school as a form of interlocutory relief, was now about to graduate. There was thus no decision on the merits. Yet the very grant of certiorari and the mootness disposition itself, in this instance indicative of deep division in the Court,[7] suggest that the Court perceived *DeFunis* as a difficult case, a harder one than *Swann.* Why?

The absence of past racial discrimination by the law school in *DeFunis* does not strike me as the factor that distinguished the cases for the Court. The permission to make racial assignments to achieve integration at the elementary and secondary level has not been confined to school systems that operated on a dual basis in the recent past. True, *Swann* involved a North Carolina school system, and the integration there was constitutionally mandated on the theory (to be explored in detail later) that the present segregation was a vestige of past discrimination. But a consistent line of lower court cases sustained the practice even when it was assumed that the integration was not constitutionally mandated. Indeed, on the very same day that the Court decided *Swann,* it summarily affirmed a three-judge federal district court invalidating New York's antibusing law, which prohibited local school boards from assigning students to schools on the basis of race and thus interfered with the power of the local school boards to make racial assignments to achieve integration.[8] In the context of New York, it is not fair to assume that the integration goal would be designed for the most part to correct past discrimination and thus (under prevailing doctrine) constitutionally mandated. In that context no more can be said than that integration was a constitutionally permissible or favored goal and that goal makes race an appropriate criterion for assignment.[9] Of course, the permissibility of the integration goal may have some roots in the special place of blacks in our society, a place defined by the unique historical treatment of that minority in America over the last three centuries. But if such a generalized notion of past discrimination can be the predicate of the permission to use racial assignment at the elementary and secondary school level, then past discrimination is neither a limiting nor a distinguishing factor. It could be found anywhere, including *DeFunis.*

For these reasons, I do not believe past discrimination to be the key to the *Swann* permission. Nor do I perceive how the presence of past discrimination in *DeFunis* would have fundamentally altered the situation or made the preferential policy of the law school less troublesome and thus as acceptable as the racial assignment in *Swann.* Assume that there was past discrimination by the University of Washington Law School; would that make any difference? There are two theories that would appear to give an affirmative answer to that question. One is a theory of compensation—preferential admissions compensate for past wrongdoing. The problem with this theory is that there is a misperception of who is paying the compensation. Conceivably, some part of it might be paid by the wrongdoer (the law school), but surely the brunt of the policy is felt by today's rejected nonblack applicants, the DeFunises, those who were not implicated in the earlier assumed discrimination of the law school and received no benefit from it in any direct or immediate sense. (Some of the price might also be paid by future consumers—those who might obtain less capable lawyers because of the preferential policy— and also by those educational institutions below the law school level, which might find it more difficult to motivate students if law school admission policies became unrelated to past performance.) Past injustices to blacks may require compensation, but it is hard to justify this particular policy of preferential law school admission as a form of compensation when the compensation is largely paid by innocent third parties. Second, there is the pump-priming theory—past discrimination by the law school discourages blacks from applying to the law school today (they feel they will not be treated fairly in the admission process and are not welcome at the law school). Thus the preferential admission policy is a means of increasing the flow of black applicants by serving as an encouragement to apply. But this is a case of overkill —there are alternate ways of increasing black applicants, e.g., black recruitment programs. Although such programs may involve greater dollar expenses for the law school, they do not localize all the costs on the applicants who must be rejected because of the preferential policy. Hence, I do not think that a finding of past discrimination by the law school would have made *DeFunis* less difficult a case, nor do I think that it was the absence of a finding of past discrimination in *DeFunis* that made the Court view *DeFunis* as a harder case than *Swann*.

I believe the distinguishing factor is scarcity. It made *DeFunis* appear to be a case of *racial preference*, while the Court could conceive of *Swann* as a case of *racial assignment*. In *DeFunis* a scarce good, admission to law school, was being allocated. A place given to one cannot be given to another. The fact that DeFunis might have been (and in fact was) able to get into another law school does not eliminate the problem of scarcity; for it is fair to assume, perhaps from the very existence of the preferential policy, either that the opportunities elsewhere are of a lesser quality or that there are more law school applicants than there are law school openings. If the total number of places are limited and if DeFunis is forced to go to some other law school, another applicant will be rejected and DeFunis could be viewed as his proxy.

But at the elementary and secondary school level, this form of scarcity does not predominate. Every student will attend some school; it is just a question of which one. Sending an individual to some particular school (because of his color) does not deny another the opportunity to go to school; the student merely attends another school in the system. Conceivably, the resource at the elementary and secondary school level could have been defined in such a way as to make scarcity predominate: the resource could have been defined, not as "going to some school," but rather as "going to a particular school," for example, the neighborhood school or the school with the best reputation. But in fact the resource at the elementary and secondary school level was not so perceived by the Court in *Swann*. Instead it was perceived in such a way as to de-accentuate the element of scarcity, that is, all the schools were viewed as on a parity. Ironically, this perception might be traced to the "separate but equal" slogan, to the claims of those who defended the dual school system on the ground that, not withstanding the segregation, all the schools in each system were equal. These are claims that the Court had to listen to for more than half a century. Or the perception may reflect the Court's own judgment that, despite parental preferences, one school in the system was in fact not better than another; that the Court could not afford to treat one as better than another (because it would then be acknowledging another form of inequality); or that the parents' perceptions of the differences in quality were tied up with racial prejudices, feelings that the Court should not or could not afford to honor.

This element of scarcity—the limitation on the total number of educational opportunities—thus seems to be the central distinguishing fact of *DeFunis* and accounts for two important ethical differences between *DeFunis* and *Swann*. First, scarcity introduces an element of individual unfairness. Scarcity makes the paradigm in *DeFunis* a competitive one—a situation where a group of applicants is being judged and someone will be chosen from that group for the last place in the law school. When a preference is given to a black because of his color, the nonblack applicant whose place is taken can claim that he is being treated unfairly because an inappropriate criterion is being used as a basis for the choice among the applicants. This claim of individual unfairness is not a constitutionally impenetrable barrier, one that can never be transgressed; [10] it is an unpleasantness, a grievance present in *DeFunis* and not in *Swann*, and thus a factor that makes *DeFunis* a more difficult case.

Inappropriateness is a relative concept. A purpose must be specified, for the critical question is: Appropriate for what? The color black is not inappropriate if the postulated purpose is, for example, to increase the number of black lawyers (which in turn might sustain minority aspirations and insulate the minority from hostile attacks by the majority in the future). If that is the purpose to be served, then the color black is an appropriate admission criterion. On the other hand, the purpose could be conceived in terms that would make the color black inappropriate. For example, if the purpose is to choose the candidate who most deserves the place (because of his past efforts) or the one who is likely to be most intellectually productive, then the color black becomes inappropriate.

In *Swann* the purpose is integration and in order to achieve that goal it is appropriate to make a distinction among individuals on the basis of color. But a second group of purposes—those that make meritocratic criteria appropriate and color inappropriate—is present in *DeFunis* and, perhaps what is most important, cannot be eliminated by unilateral fiat. A simple declaration by the law school that its purpose is to increase the number of black lawyers does not set or fix the purpose in such a way as to preempt all other purposes and to dissolve the claim of inappropriateness or individual grievance. These purposes inhere in the situation. A scarce educational opportunity is being allocated, and, regardless of what the law school *says*, the place in the school can be perceived as a reward for past effort or as a training opportunity, not just a passport. It is this intractable fact that morally entitles one outside the ruling hierarchy of the institution—the rejected applicant, for example—to insist that an inappropriate criterion is being used to choose among the applicants and that also forces us to listen to him. (Talk about mixed purposes does not eliminate the claim of inappropriateness, for the proportions of the mixture also cannot be unilaterally determined.)

Just as the inappropriateness of the color black cannot be eliminated by fiat, it cannot be eliminated by default—by the inadequacy of other criteria. Charges have been leveled against the (partial or exclusive) use of LSAT scores and grade-point averages in the law school admission process on the ground that they are not accurate predictors of future performance and are particularly misleading for blacks. But even if this is true, it means only that they are also inappropriate for the purpose of allocating a scarce educational opportunity. The inappropriateness of such meritocratic criteria does not make the color black appropriate for the purpose served by those criteria. What is called for is the development of more refined meritocratic criteria that are accurate for all groups (or to make adjustments to eliminate the bias against blacks). If that project is totally hopeless, then the law school committed to avoiding or minimizing the individual unfairness can disavow any intent to pick the best candidate in the meritocratic sense and instead institute a lottery.

Random selection would be as ill-suited as race for picking the best candidate in the meritocratic sense. But it would at least formally and openly acknowledge the hopelessness of finding accurate meritocratic criteria; that acknowledgment would constitute some proof of the sincerity of the declaration of default. It would also provide all applicants with the assurance that they have an equal chance. The applicants might be willing to exchange their claimed right to be judged on the basis of meritocratic criteria, which the law school says cannot in any event be fulfilled because there are no such criteria, for the right to an equal chance. Race is ill-suited for meritocratic purposes and has the additional fault of not providing all applicants—who at the time they are being judged know their race—with an equal chance.

Second, scarcity not only introduces an element of individual unfairness but also tends to affect the appeal of the goal to be served by the use of race. At the elementary and secondary school level, the goal to be achieved by racial assignment is integration. Long familiar to the courts, this goal is linked to the furtherance of many objectives that cluster around the idea of equality—assuring an equal distribution of resources among the schools of the district, eliminating the badge of inferiority imposed by placing blacks in separate schools, furthering the social contacts between racial classes, and reducing the educational achievement gap between whites and blacks by placing blacks in a setting dominated by the educational advantages and aspirations of the majority class. That is why integration is conceptualized as a means of insuring equality of educational opportunity. Indeed, the connection between the idea of equality and integration may be so firm as to make integration not only a constitutionally permissive goal but also a constitutionally favored or required one. This can be seen from the doctrine to be examined later requiring local school boards to integrate and also from the companion cases to *Swann* invalidating the state antibusing laws of North Carolina and New York.[11] These cases must mean that integration is in such a constitutionally favored position that states will be denied the power to enact laws restricting the method of achieving that goal—i.e., laws forbidding the local boards to make racial assignments for that end.

On the other hand, the goal to be served by the preferential policy of the law school can be perceived only faintly as integration (e.g., as a means of diversifying the student body). Rather, it must be justified as a means of increasing the supply of black lawyers so as to increase the number of minority-group members who are in positions of power and prestige. This goal is concrete, appealing, and, like integration, in some ultimate sense related to the ideal of equality. But because of the very fact that it necessarily involves a redistribution—every gain to blacks is matched by a loss to nonblacks—the link with equality is more attenuated and there is a natural tendency to scrutinize it with greater care. One tends to be less tolerant of imperfections than one is with the integration goal; there is no suggestion, at least today, that the goal that might be served by the law school preferential admission policy—to increase the supply of black lawyers—is constitutionally favored.

The ultimate purpose of elementary and secondary school integration may be to improve the *relative* position of blacks—to lessen the social and economic gap between whites and blacks. But the means does not include redistribution—nothing is being taken from whites. Rather the improvement in relative position is supposed to occur from the elimination of a condition that otherwise impairs the schooling of blacks. The theory of integration is that it seeks to make certain that the educational opportunity given to blacks is equal to that afforded whites. On the other hand, the opportunity afforded the admitted black in *DeFunis* is denied to some nonblack. Moreover, although we are beginning to realize that the achievement of integration may be costly, perhaps more costly than a law school preferential admissions policy, the costs are not localized. They are distributed among all those within the public school system (although as we will see later, groups insulated from the costs can be created through the definition of the relevant geographic area). It is like a tax rather than a direct transfer of funds from one group to another. This is why the Court might have perceived the integration goal —which it has been working with for several decades and which is so closely linked to the ideal of equality—as more appealing and as capable of shouldering more, including the practice, long deemed questionable, of using race as a criterion.

Although the emphasis has been on the distinction between *Swann* and *DeFunis* arising from the element of scarcity, one important similarity between the two cases should be noted: the use of race in both cases is free from the element of insult. In the dual school system, race was used to segregate blacks. So used, it conveyed a dehumanizing message—"We don't want your kind to go to school with us." The message was perceived by the Court and was one predicate for the *Brown* decision. Similarly, in the classic case of law school discrimination, the black excluded or rejected on the basis of his color is being insulted— he is once again being told, "We don't want your kind." His self-esteem is at stake. (This harm to his dignity probably explains in part why the color black would not be a permissible criterion for purposes of exclusion or segregation even if it were statistically relevant to some permissible goal, e.g., ability grouping.) But that insult is not present when race is used for purposes of integration, as it was in *Swann*. Nor is it present in *DeFunis*.

In the *DeFunis* case there is no direct exclusion. Rather the exclusion takes place through a two-step process: (1) we want more blacks and thus (2) due to the problem of scarcity, we (unfortunately) cannot take as many nonblacks. It is not just that the *DeFunis* exclusion takes place with regret (there is no animus against the excluded), but that the excluded class has no identity. It is multiracial and includes persons of both sexes, all religions, all national origins, and all social levels—to list the categories by which people naturally tend to identify themselves. The defining characteristic of the excluded class in *DeFunis*—those who would have been admitted under the meritocratic system but for the preference for blacks—is not one that is today used as the basis of individual identity, nor is it likely to be so used in the near future. (I think this would be true even if the identifying characteristic of the class excluded was "smartness.") For this reason the two-step exclusionary process of *DeFunis*, like the racial assignment in *Swann*, does not entail the element of insult inherent in the classic case of racial discrimination (the direct exclusion of blacks) and in that sense could be considered a more benign use of race even when viewed from the perspective of the person excluded.

## THE OBLIGATION QUESTION:
## MUST THE SCHOOLS BE INTEGRATED?

With the permission question, the focus has been on one particular method or way of achieving integration—racial assignment. In order to sustain the practice of making racial assignments for integration, it first had to be posited that integration was a constitutionally permissible goal. But that was not a matter of much controversy. The debate instead raged over one way in which that goal could be achieved, although it was understood that if the method of racial assignment were denied the school boards, then achievement of the goal would become difficult, perhaps extremely difficult. With the obligation question, the constitutional status of the goal itself becomes the center of the controversy, and the issue is whether school boards are obligated to take appropriate steps (which may include racial assignment) toward the achievement of that goal.

Does the Constitution require integration? The question of obligation is often stated in this way, but usually by those who wish a negative answer. For the natural, intuitive retort is that of *Briggs v. Elliott*: "The Constitution . . . does not require integration. It merely forbids discrimination." [12] And, like Harlan's color-blind aphorism, regardless of how many times the *Briggs v. Elliott* retort is formally repudiated, the thought still lingers. It refuses to die.

It is the starkness of the question that gives power to the *Briggs v. Elliott* retort. Movement toward an affirmative answer to the question of obligation becomes possible only if the question is reformulated. In order to do that a distinction must first be drawn between *violation* and *remedy*, where segregation, the denial of equal protection, would be the violation and integration the inescapable remedy. The question that should be asked first is whether the maintenance of segregated schools violates the Constitution. If so, then what would be required is the elimination of that segregation or integration.

### The Violation: Does the Constitution Forbid Segregation?

In *Brown* two phenomena were present—segregation and racial assignment—and in answering the permission question, we saw that the Court refused to construe *Brown* to forbid racial assignment per se. Now we are concerned with the other half of the combination, the segregated pattern. The issue now is one of determining whether the segregation alone—that is, without regard to the basis of assignment—is unlawful. The issue arises because segregation can exist even when students are not assigned to schools on the basis of race, as was true in the dual school system, but rather on the basis of some seemingly innocent criterion, such as geographic proximity.

The constitutional argument against the segregated pattern has two parts. The first is that the segregation is particularly harmful to blacks because it gives rise to the inequality, to the claim that their educational opportunity is unequal. The theory is that, regardless of the method of assignment, the segregation stigmatizes the blacks, deprives them of educationally significant contacts with the socially and economically dominant group, and creates the danger that their schools will be given fewer resources simply because they are attended only by members of the minority group.

The second part of the argument is to establish the school board's responsibility for the segregated pattern. The Fourteenth Amendment is not a general guarantee of equality; it provides that "No State shall . . . deny . . . the equal protection of the laws." Under the dual school system, racial assignments produced the racial segregation, and thus school board responsibility for the segregation was unmistakable. When nonracial criteria are used, reliance must be placed on another theory of responsibility, one that holds a government entity responsible for the foreseeable and avoidable consequences of its action. I refer to this theory as a nonaccusatory one because it does not charge the board with an intentionally wrongful act, such as racial assignment. Rather the emphasis would be on the fact that the segregation is the wrong and that the school board chose the criterion of student assignment that results in the segregation. Given the prevailing residential pattern, segregation is the foreseeable consequence of the decision to assign students to schools on the basis of geographic criteria.[13] Admittedly, this theory depends on two factual assumptions. The first is that the residential pattern is not truly voluntary (otherwise the responsibility might be shifted to those choosing to live in a segregated fashion), and the second is that the segregation is avoidable, i.e., that there are "reasonable" steps the school board could take to avoid or to reduce the school segregation. But in the generality of cases both assumptions would be well founded, and whenever they hold, the school board could be deemed responsible for the segregation even though it was not produced by racial assignment.

Both parts of this argument have considerable force, and yet there has been a reluctance on the part of the courts to embrace wholeheartedly the argument against the segregated pattern. This reluctance in large part stems from the uncertainty surrounding the central empirical proposition upon which the first part of the argument rests, namely, that a segregated pattern of student attendance itself leads to inferior education for blacks—an uncertainty that has persisted for the last twenty years, not in spite of but rather because of the state of social science data. The reluctance stems also from a concern about the costs inherent in any order designed to eliminate the segregation. Despite the logical integrity of the violation/remedy distinction, a judge looks at both dimensions at once, either as a practical matter or because the nonaccusatory theory of responsibility analytically requires some consideration of the alternatives open to the school board to avoid the segregation. Accordingly, in determining whether there is a violation, a judge usually looks ahead to the remedy that might be required if a violation is found, and it is the specter of the remedial costs that causes him to hesitate in finding a violation.

If the vice is deemed racial assignment, or even segregated patterns directly produced by racial assignment, the needed remedy is obvious and relatively cheap—stop making racial assignments. The costs consist only of the frustration of the associational desires of those insisting upon the racial assignments and served by them. But if the court decides that the segregated patterns themselves are unlawful, even when produced by a nonracial criterion, such as geographic proximity, the costs of the remedial order will be great. The court realizes that before long it would probably have to insist upon an attendance plan that, in order to eliminate the segregation, entails not only transportation of students for substantial distances but possibly even racial assignments. Such a remedial order would probably divert considerable resources (time and money); it would impose on children and parents the burdens inherent in any bus trip to school; and it would frustrate the intense associational desires of large parts of the community.

The costs of a remedial order will be further magnified if the focus narrows to a situation where the segregation consists of the maintenance of integrated schools on the one hand and all-black schools on the other. Traditionally, segregation was understood to mean that all the white students are in one set of schools and all the blacks are in another. But segregation may also exist when the predominantly white schools are sprinkled with some blacks and a substantial portion of the blacks still attend all-black schools. In that situation—probably the typical urban situation today—the remedial order must either disperse the blacks and bus them to the white areas (one-way integration), or, unless the physical plants of the former all-black schools are abandoned, bus whites to the black areas and vice versa (two-way integration). In either case the costs involved, from the perspectives of both the blacks and the whites, are enormous and may even lead families to leave the community or to withdraw from the public school system altogether. Since these options are probably more available to the financially able, to more whites than blacks, they would make the elimination of segregation extremely difficult.

Despite these considerations, the Court did not reject outright the constitutional argument against the segregated pattern and take a position that made racial assignment the critical flaw of the dual school system of *Brown* (a position that might even have made racial assignment impermissible for purposes of integration). Nor did the Court take the intermediate position that segregation is prohibited when it is produced (in some direct and current sense) by racial assignment. Rather it seems committed to a result-oriented approach to school cases—one that minimizes, but does not eliminate, the link with racial assignment and that tends to emphasize the segregated pattern.

The turning point occurred in 1968 in *Green v. New Kent County.*[14] There the Warren Court, in an opinion by Justice Brennan, held that a violation may exist even when the segregation is not produced in a current and direct sense by racial assignments. This approach was reaffirmed and extended in the first two major school cases of the Burger Court, *Swann v. Charlotte-Mecklenburg Board of Education* (1971)[15] and *Keyes v. District No. 1, Denver, Colorado* (1973).[16] The concept of past discrimination (past racial assignment) invoked in these cases to bring the segregation within the ban of the Constitution; but it seemed that the segregation was the critical factor and that the past discrimination was used for purposes of appearance—to make it seem that these decisions were merely implementations of *Brown*. Then this past term in the Detroit school case, *Milliken v. Bradley* (1974),[17] a narrowly divided Court took a step in a different direction.

### Green v. New Kent County

*Green* involved a former dual school system, where freedom of choice was substituted for racial assignment. Under the school board's plan, no student was assigned to a school on the basis of his race. Instead, each student, black and white, was assigned on the basis of his choice. The result was that some blacks attended the formerly all-white school, most blacks remained in the black school, and no whites attended the black school. The Court declared that in the school system before it, freedom of choice was an impermissible basis for assigning students to schools. The Court expressed this by saying that there had not been a sufficient conversion from a dual school system to a unitary one.

The *Green* decision did not embrace the argument that made the segregated pattern the fatal flaw nor did it say that a student assignment plan would be deemed constitutionally acceptable only when it produced an integrated pattern of student attendance, i.e., when it eliminated the all-black school. But *Green* started to move in that direction. This was implicit in the Court's decision to hold the student assignment plan unconstitutional even though it was willing to assume that the plan was free from racial assignment. This assumption is evidenced by the Court's deliberate and explicit decision in *Green* not to rest its ruling on the assertion that the segregation was the product of threats or that procedural irregularities of the plan interfered with the exercise of true free choice.

### Swann and Keyes

In *Swann* and *Keyes* the Court reaffirmed *Green*'s rejection of the view that *Brown* forbade only the use of race, although it did so in a different and more important context. The basis of assignment in *Swann* and *Keyes* was not the strikingly odd freedom-of-choice criterion of *Green* but rather the more commonplace one of geographic proximity—students were assigned to schools nearest their homes. In both, the Court held that there was a denial of equal protection even though assignments were made on the nonracial basis of geographic proximity. It is important to emphasize, however, that, as in *Green,* the Court did not say that the segregated pattern itself violated the Equal Protection Clause. It was "segregation plus," and in *Swann* and *Keyes* we got some indication, not present in *Green,* what the "plus" might be—past discrimination.

### The Swann Model: Segregated Pattern Plus Overt Racial Assignment in the Past

*Swann* involved a North Carolina school district, a former dual school system. The Court was willing to assume that the immediate, present cause of the segregated pattern of student attendance was not racial assignment, that students were in fact assigned on the basis of geographic proximity. But at the same time the Court saw a causal connection between the board's admitted past discrimination and present segregation. The past discrimination was a nonimmediate cause but nonetheless a cause, and nonimmediate causes are, the Court reasoned, a sufficient basis of classifying the segregation as "state-imposed," a type of segregation all would concede is unlawful.

Two types of nonimmediate causal connections between past discrimination and present segregation were hypothesized in *Swann.* (a) The past discriminatory conduct of a school board might have contributed to the creation and maintenance of segregated residential patterns which, when coupled with the present use of geographic proximity as the basis for assignment, produce segregated patterns of student attendance. The assumption is that under the dual system, schools were racially designated as "white" or "black" and were located in different geographic areas, and that in the past, racial groups chose to live near "their" particular schools. That choice might have been motivated by the desire of families to live close to the schools which their children attended, or it might have reflected the belief that the racial designation of a school also racially designated the residential area. (b) Prior decisions by a school board regarding the location and size of schools might in part explain why assigning students to the schools nearest their homes would result in racially homogeneous schools. Under the dual school system, school sites were selected and the student capacity of schools determined with a view toward serving students of only one race. These past policies are important because assignment on the basis of geographic proximity will not result in a racially homogeneous school unless, in addition to the existence of residential segregation, the school is so small that it serves only a racially homogeneous area or so situated that it is the closest school to students of only one race.

These nonimmediate causal connections between past discrimination and present segregation are no more than theoretical possibilities. Obviously, the question still remains whether the past discrimination was *in fact* the cause or one of the causes of the present segregation—there are many alternative causal hypotheses to explain the segregation. The Court was aware of this, and in *Swann* announced an evidentiary presumption that in effect resolved all the uncertainties against the school board. The Court was willing to presume the existence of these conjectured connections from the mere presence of the segregation.[18]

This presumption is rebuttable. The school board is given the opportunity to show that the segregated pattern was not in fact caused by its discriminatory action. But the burden of rebuttal is a most difficult one. It cannot be discharged simply by showing that the school segregation is produced, given the segregated residential pattern, by assigning students on the basis of geographic proximity. The school board will also have to show that its past discriminatory conduct—including racial designation of schools, site selection, and determination of school size—is not a link in the causal chain producing the segregation. To be sure, there is a comforting statement in *Swann* to the effect that the presumption might be overcome by the mere passage of time— that over a period of time the connection between the past discrimination and the present segregation might become so attenuated as to be incapable of justifying judicial intervention; but there is no indication as to when that point might be reached.

*The Keyes Model: Segregated Pattern Plus Covert Racial
Assignment in the Past in Some Meaningful Portion of the
System*

*Keyes* involved the Denver school system, not a former dual school system as in *Swann*. Hence the talk, largely liturgical, in *Green* and *Swann* about "converting" and "dismantling" the dual school system had to be abandoned. But that was of little moment. The conceptual apparatus of Swann, with its focus on past discrimination, could still be used. Only two requirements of the Swann model had to be relaxed. First, in Keyes the Court held that past discrimination need not be overt, as it was in the dual school system. It is sufficient if it is covert. The covert/overt distinction goes only to the difficulty of proof. In the dual school system the racial assignments are overt, and thus, in dealing with a former dual system, the past discrimination is admitted. Under an alleged unitary system, the racial assignments are covert—a form of cheating—and thus there is no admission to ease plaintiff's burden. The plaintiff must prove this covert past discrimination, and that may be a heavy burden to shoulder. But that is no reason for not letting the plaintiff try.

Second, in Keyes the Court had to deal with the fact that the past discrimination may have occurred in only part of the school system. Under the dual school system the discrimination is not only overt but presumably also systemwide. That is not generally true in nondual school systems, where the residential pattern is segregated and students are purportedly assigned on the basis of geographic proximity. Then the discrimination, in covert form, usually takes place along the borders of the ghetto. This pattern is reflected in Keyes. There was a finding of past covert discrimination in the Park Hill area of the system, which the Court emphasized was a substantial or meaningful portion of the Denver system; but the trial court refused to make a similar finding with respect to the core-area schools.[19] However, the Court refused to be stymied, and in Keyes constructed two elaborate theories to broaden this finding of past discrimination. Then, once broadened, Swann was used to bring all the segregation of the system within the reach of the Equal Protection Clause.

*The Spread Theory*  As a touchstone for this theory the Court approvingly quoted a statement by Judge Wisdom: "Infection at one school infects all schools."[20] The thought was that the discrimination in the Park Hill area could have an effect in other areas—and in that sense spread beyond the immediate confines of the Park Hill area and indeed reach the core-area schools.

The Court first explained how the germ might spread to *nearby* schools—how racial assignment in the Park Hill portion of the system could affect the racial composition of the nearby schools.

(a) Putting all the blacks in one school on the basis of race will keep other nearby schools all white, even though the white students are assigned to those schools on the basis of geography. (b) Past decisions with respect to the location and size of one school have an effect on the racial composition of other nearby schools. For example, if the board decides that a new school should be a black school and located in a black area and sized to serve only the students in that area, then the other nearby schools will be white.

Second, the Court tried to show how the germ might spread beyond the nearby schools to all the other schools throughout the system. To do this the Court considered not only student assignment and school construction practices, but also pointed to the other facets of the educational system (e.g., the use of mobile classrooms, student transfer programs, transportation programs, faculty assignments). The Court treated all of these programs and policies as though they were based on race, and as having the effect of "earmarking" schools in the Denver system as either white or black.

Third, the Court shifted gear—from an explanation as to how the germ *might* have spread to a conclusion that the germ had *in fact* so spread, not only to nearby schools but throughout the school system. The shift was brought about by a judicially created presumption that placed the burden on the school board to establish that the germ had not spread.

Fourth, the presumption is almost impossible to overcome. Great uncertainty surrounds the propositions that the board would have to establish, and in addition the Court stipulated that the board could overcome the presumption only by showing that the portion of the school system in which the past discrimination occurred was "a separate, identifiable, and unrelated unit." The Court also indicated that these terms would be interpreted in the most stringent sense; for in *Keyes* itself the Court set aside a finding by the trial court that a six-lane highway sufficiently confined or isolated the past discrimination of Park Hill so as to prevent its spread throughout the system. The Court declared that "a major highway is generally not such an effective buffer between adjoining areas" as to meet the newly articulated requirement that the discrimination occur in "a separate, identifiable, and unrelated unit."

Fifth, establishment of this spread means that past discrimination has existed throughout the system. Then the *Swann* theory of nonimmediate causation is plugged in—we shall presume that the past discrimination played a causal role in the residential segregation and that it is in part responsible for the present school segregation. Hence, under the spread theory of *Keyes,* there is a double presumption—first to establish the horizontal spread and then to establish the link over a period of time between the past discrimination and the present segregation.

*The Repetition Theory*   It seemed unlikely that the school board could ever shoulder the burden cast by the spread theory, and thus the segregated pattern in the core schools would be brought within the ban of the Equal Protection Clause. But in *Keyes* the Court did not stop at that point. Instead it went on to construct an alternative theory for attacking the segregated pattern. This theory postulates that the board is likely to have repeated itself, i.e. that if there was discrimination in the practices of the board with regard to one portion of the system, then it is fair to presume that its practices with respect to the other portions of the system were of a like character, also discriminatory.

The initial premise is that the board, despite its announced policy of assigning students on the basis of geography, may have assigned them to schools on the basis of race. All agree that this occurred in the Park Hill area, and the only question is whether it also occurred in the core area. The Court realizes that this will be a very difficult factual question to resolve and that the allocation of the burden of proof will be near decisive. Having made this point, the Court then decides to place on the school board the burden of proving that it has not cheated on its announced nonracial policy in the core area. This reallocation from the plaintiff to the defendant is based on the plaintiff's success in showing that there was past discrimination in one substantial portion of the system, the Park Hill area. The Court is willing to infer that the board repeated its pattern of behavior: if there were racial assignments in one portion of the system, then it is fair to presume that its use of geographic criteria elsewhere was a facade and that race was the real basis of assignment.

If the board cannot overcome this presumption (the presumption of cheating), then a second presumption (the *Swann* presumption of nonimmediate causation) will come into play, linking the past discrimination and the present segregation. As the Court put it, "At that stage, the burden becomes the school authorities' to show that the current segregation is *in no way* the result of those past segregative acts." [21] Hence, as with the spread theory, the theory of repetition in *Keyes* involves a double presumption triggered by a finding of past discrimination in one portion of the system. (a) If there is past discrimination in one substantial portion of the system, then we will presume that there is past discrimination throughout the system. (b) Once we know that there is past discrimination in all the portions of the system, then we will presume that this past discrimination played some role in causing the present segregated residential patterns in all parts of the system and that this residential segregation is in part responsible for the school segregation throughout.

It is obvious that both the spread and repetition theories of *Keyes* build on *Swann,* and that both theories and *Swann* itself are attempts to find a link between the segregated pattern and the racial assignment. Unable to find present racial assignment, the Court becomes satisfied with past racial assignment. This link does not permit the conclusion that the Court has severed the connection between racial assignment and the segregated pattern, that school desegregation law has reached a point where the segregated pattern itself deemed a violation of the Equal Protection Clause. But I think it is fair to say that *Swann* and *Keyes* brought us close to that point.

The link with past discrimination was viewed in *Swann* and *Keyes* as a basis for attributing to the school board responsibility for the segregation, for rejecting the claim that the segregation was "adventitious." But the Justices were aware of alternative theories for attributing responsibility which do not rely on past discrimination. Indeed, in *Keyes* two Justices from widely divergent wings of the Court, Justice Douglas and Justice Powell,[22] indicated their willingness to embrace the approach to school segregation that dispensed with the requirement of past discrimination. This was a first. And, perhaps more importantly, Justice Brennan, who wrote the Court's opinion in *Keyes,* an opinion joined by Justices Marshall, White, Stewart, and Blackmun, carefully indicated that, while the past discrimination was a sufficient condition for bringing the segregated pattern within the reach of the Equal Protection Clause, it might not be a necessary condition. Justice Brennan carefully reserved that question.

In addition, there is implicit evidence that what moved the Court in *Swann* and *Keyes* was the segregated pattern, and that the reliance on past discrimination was dressing designed to improve the acceptability of its decisions by making them appear to be direct descendants of *Brown*. Part of this evidence consists of the willingness of the Court to create presumptions in both these cases. Even if these presumptions can individually be justified as a reflection of natural probabilities, their cumulative effect cannot be. The creation of this set of presumptions as a set can only be explained in terms of a determination by the Court to bring the segregation within the reach of the Equal Protection Clause. The artificial and stringent conditions the Court imposes for overcoming these presumptions reinforce this impression. Finally, the reach of the remedy is revealing. In neither *Keyes* nor *Swann* does the Court make an attempt to limit the remedy to that portion of the present segregation that could in all fairness be attributed to the past discrimination. This refusal is explicit in *Keyes,* where the past discrimination in some portion of the school system is used to bring the segregated pattern of the whole system within the ban of the Equal Protection Clause. It is also present in *Swann*. There the Court moved from (a) the undisputed existence of past discrimination to (b) the possibility or likelihood that the past discrimination played some causal role in producing some of the segregation to (c) an order requiring the elimination of segregation throughout the entire system. The reach of the remedy can be explained only if the segregation itself is viewed as the evil and the past discrimination is viewed as the triggering mechanism.

### Milliken v. Bradley

Thus far we have been concerned with segregation within a single district. But in recent years the focus is shifting to large city school districts which have become increasingly all-black, a development requiring that we broaden our concern. We must now talk both about a segregated pattern within a single school district (within-district segregation), and also about a segregated pattern that emerges when all the school districts in a metropolitan area are viewed as a group (cross-district segregation). The schools of an all-black school district would not be regarded as segregated if we look only into that district; for segregation is a form of separation and the demographic pattern within the district is not one of separation with blacks in one set of schools and whites in another. It is one of racial homogeneity. But if the schools of the black school district are viewed in the context of the surrounding ones, the white suburban districts, then there would be a demographic pattern of separation—blacks are in one set of schools and whites are in another, in this instance divided by the district line.

Both types of segregation were present in the Detroit school case, *Milliken v. Bradley*. Detroit is a predominantly black system surrounded by predominantly white suburban systems. In 1970 the ratio of black/white student population in Detroit was about 64/36; in the surrounding suburbs it was 13/87. There was also within-district segregation in Detroit (the core schools were all black). The trial judge applied a *Keyes*-like theory and concluded that because of the past discrimination of the Detroit school board (in which the state played a role) the within-district Detroit segregation was unlawful and had to be remedied. Then he sought to fashion the remedy. Because the Detroit district was predominantly black and because a remedy confined to Detroit would only accelerate that trend, he developed a plan that used cross-district busing. A desegregation area consisting of the Detroit system and fifty-three suburban systems was delineated; within that area fifteen clusters were established, each containing part of the Detroit system and two or more suburban districts; and students within each cluster were to be assigned to schools so that the proportion of whites and blacks in each school (or grade or classroom) would not substantially deviate from the proportion of whites and blacks in the overall pupil population.

The Supreme Court held that the district court erred not because it found the Detroit within-district segregation unlawful,[23] but rather because the cross-district busing was not called for under applicable remedial principles requiring that the remedy should "fit" the violation. The violation consisted of the within-district segregation, and the plan did more than cure that violation. It eliminated the cross-district segregation—the pattern of black Detroit schools and white suburban schools.

From this perspective *Milliken* seems to have only the remedial implication that cross-district busing cannot be used to cure within-district segregation. But I believe this appearance is misleading. For one thing, the principle used for interpreting Keyes and Swann is applicable here—the scope of the remedy gives you an insight into the nature of the wrong. In Keyes and Swann, the refusal to limit the remedy to that portion of the segregation that in all fairness could be deemed related to past discrimination suggested that what was of utmost concern to the Court was the segregation, not the past discrimination. Conversely, the decision to limit the remedy in Milliken in such a way as to leave most of the Detroit schools predominantly black and the suburban systems white suggests that the segregation is not at the center of the Court's concern. If this segregation was perceived to be the evil (because of stigmatization and the preclusion of educationally significant contacts) the Supreme Court could have found ways to uphold the district court's desegregation plan even if it were to be conceived as a means of correcting the within-district segregation—the segregation that is unlawful under established principles (Keyes).[24]

Furthermore, the Court in Milliken must be saying something substantive about the cross-district segregation. The remedy decreed by the trial judge clearly would not be inappropriate if the cross-district segregation were held unlawful; then the remedy and the violation would be a perfect "fit." But the Court rejects that possibility, and it does so by postulating first, that the cross-segregation is unlawful only if government is responsible for it and second, that for these purposes government responsibility can be established only on the basis of an accusatory theory— one predicated on wrongful acts (discrimination) by the state, past or present, that can be said to be causally related to the cross-district segregation.[25] Racial gerrymandering of the districts by the state, or past discrimination by the white suburban districts, neither of which have been established in this case, might suffice. But past discrimination by the Detroit board, and involvement by the state in that activity would not.[26] For the horrible fact is that such conduct probably retarded white flight to the suburbs, and thus tended to reduce the cross-district segregation. Thus, although the Court leaves open the possibility of declaring cross-district segregation unlawful in future cases, it also holds unacceptable a theory that would make the state responsible for the cross-district segregation because (a) the state determines the geographic boundaries of the school districts, and (b) the cross-district segregation is the foreseeable and avoidable result of maintaining the present boundaries.[27]

In rejecting this nonaccusatory theory for purposes of holding the state responsible for the cross-district segregation, the Court may also be read as rejecting a similar theory for use with the within-district segregation—the theory which holds the local board responsible for the segregation that results from its decision to use geographic criteria for student assignment since, in the context of residential segregation, school segregation is the foreseeable and avoidable consequence of that decision. It is hard to see why a nonaccusatory theory should have more force with one type of segregation rather than another. Such an interpretation of *Milliken* is reinforced by the language of the Court's opinion by Chief Justice Burger. That language emphasizes the importance of the past discrimination in rendering the Detroit within-district segregation unlawful. In contrast to Justice Brennan's measured language in *Keyes*, there is no effort to reserve the question whether the presence of past discrimination is necessary for holding that segregation is unlawful. School segregation itself is referred to by the Chief Justice as a "condition," a word that suggests that without the past or present racial assignments government is not responsible for it.

A rejection of the nonaccusatory theory of responsibility for within-district segregation might ultimately lead the Court to draw back on *Keyes* and *Swann*; for, in my judgment, these cases are explicable only in terms of such a theory for attributing governmental responsibility. But there is also reason to believe that *Milliken* is not a prelude to retrenchment. Two of the five Justices in the majority in *Milliken* would probably resist the move. In *Keyes* Justice Powell indicated his willingness to subscribe to a result-oriented approach to school desegregation at the within-district level. His decision to join the majority opinion in *Milliken* is puzzling, but I doubt that he is prepared to withdraw the views he expressed in *Keyes.* Justice Stewart wrote a separate concurrence in *Milliken* to emphasize that "the Court does not deal with questions of substantive constitutional law." Finally, all of the Justices who formed the majority in *Milliken* are sensitive about public reactions: a perceptible step backward in the area of school desegregation would probably expose the Burger Court to the kind of public criticism it wishes to avoid. Hence, in the final analysis, even though *Milliken* should not be read as a purely remedial case, it should not be read as an assault on *Swann* and *Keyes*. It should be viewed as a stopping point. The movement toward a result-oriented approach to school desegregation, one that emphasizes the demographic pattern (segregation) and severs the link with the activity (racial assignment), began in *Green*, it continued through *Swann* and *Keyes*, and now in *Milliken* it has been brought to a halt.

### Integration as a Remedial Obligation

Once it is established that the segregated pattern is constitutionally impermissible, then the question of the appropriate remedy must be faced. An order merely prohibiting racial assignment would be beside the point if it is the segregated pattern that is the wrong; this is true even if the segregation is linked to past racial assignments, for that activity by definition is already at an end. Nor can the remedial duty be conceptualized as one of substituting nonracial methods of assignment for the racial method of the past. This substitution might not have the effect of eliminating the segregation. Given the prevailing level of prejudice, the substitution of freedom of choice would clearly not have that effect. Nor would the substitution of geographic proximity where there are segregated residential patterns. This is the rule rather than the exception in urban areas, and thus, in those cases at least, the task of eliminating the school segregation would have to be faced more directly. The remedial obligation would have to be conceptualized as a duty to integrate—a duty to eliminate the segregation.[28]

The Court has in fact so conceptualized the remedial obligation but it has avoided the use of the word "integration," probably because of the term's emotive impact. Instead, a series of code words have been used. In *Green*, the Court talked in terms of racial identifiability: the evil to be remedied is the "racial identification of the system's schools";[29] the goal is "a system without a 'white' school and a 'Negro' school, but just schools."[30] In *Swann* the critical phrase became "actual desegregation,"[31] and the emphasis was on the word "actual."

The Court's first impulse was to set the remedial obligation in the most stringent of terms: integration at any cost. In *Swann* the Court declared that "the greatest possible degree of actual desegregation" must be achieved. The desegregation plan approved in that case involved racial assignment and required a massive, long-distance transportation program. Students living closest to inner-city schools were to be assigned to suburban ones and students living closest to suburban schools were to be assigned to inner-city ones. Similarly, in a companion case to *Swann,* one involving Mobile, Alabama, the Supreme Court refused to be stymied by a major highway that divided the metropolitan area.[32] For the lower courts the highway had constituted a sufficient practical barrier to permit some all-black schools to remain in operation since, in order to integrate, students would have to be assigned across that highway. The Supreme Court remanded because "inadequate consideration was given to the possible use of bus transportation and split zoning." [33] These same sentiments were echoed in *Keyes,* where the Court spoke of "all-out desegregation." The practicalities of the situation must, of course, also be taken into account, but in these cases the Court made clear that if there is a conflict between integration and other values, integration will generally prevail. Every *possible* step had to be taken to produce integration.

But now *Milliken* has set one important limitation on the remedial obligation. Although the duty is to integrate, the school board's obligation is to produce only that level of integration possible by within-district busing. The school district is to be viewed as a self-contained unit. The students to be mixed are only those living within the district. (Cross-district busing is only permissible if the cross-district segregation is found unlawful.)

Although the desire to impose some limits on the remedial obligation is understandable, I fail to see the basis for the restriction set in *Milliken.* First, *Milliken* means that we may have to live with all-black school systems. From the perspective of the district, an all-black school system may be indicative only of racial homogeneity, not segregation. But from the metropolitan perspective it represents ordinary segregation and poses the same threat to the educational opportunities of blacks that moved the Court in *Swann* and *Keyes.*

Second, the limit set in *Milliken* to the remedial stringency seems artificial. The district line is not an accurate measure of the total social costs incurred in integration because: (a) A cross-district bus trip may be as long as within-district bus trips (the school district of Charlotte-Mecklenburg was 550 square miles;

that of Mobile 1248 square miles; and that of Detroit 140 square miles). (b) Within-district busing may frustrate associational preferences as much as would cross-district busing, for people express their associational preferences in schools not just by moving out of a school district, but also by moving to neighborhoods feeding certain schools. (c) Although cross-district busing may introduce a set of administrative problems not present with the within-district remedy, these problems are not different in kind than those created by a within-district busing plan, and they are probably not the ones people truly care about.

Third, the *Milliken* limitation creates an insulated position for suburbanites. They are relieved of the burdens of integration, yet there is no rational basis for treating them differently than those who still remain within the school district. The in-district dweller is bused, not because he has committed a wrong nor because he is in any direct sense a beneficiary of the past discrimination of the school board, but rather because that is the only way of integrating the schools. (Even if individual fault were the predicate of busing, it would be difficult, if not impossible, to differentiate between the two classes of citizens on that basis.) Furthermore, this special status of the suburbanite, the *Milliken* immunity, creates the wrong incentives. It might well reinforce white exodus from the cities and intensify segregation—cross-district segregation.

In sum, the *Milliken* limitation in the remedial obligation, i.e., no cross-district busing, does not make sense in practical terms. Nor is it rooted in any inexorable principle of logic or constitutional law. Cross-district busing could have been permitted on either of two theories. The first, advanced by the dissenters, is that cross-district busing is an appropriate remedy for a within-district violation because the harm inherent in segregation stems from having blacks attend all-black schools. The harm remains if within-district racial homogeneity persists—the school a black child would be attending would still be all black. The second theory, a more sensible one for the Court to have embraced, is the nonaccusatory theory of government responsibility (used in the reapportionment cases) that deems the cross-district segregation unlawful. Then the wrong to be corrected would have been the cross-district segregation, and cross-district busing clearly would have been suited to that purpose.

Such a disposition would have been in accord with *Swann* and

*Keyes.* The common predicate would have been that segregation is harmful—it impairs the educational opportunities of blacks. In *Swann* and *Keyes* there are incidents of past discrimination; but no one truly believed they were of much significance—they were merely dressing. In truth, responsibility was attributed to the school board for the segregation because that demographic pattern was a foreseeable and avoidable consequence of using geographic criteria for student assignment. Only this theory could fully explain the Court's actions in *Swann* and *Keyes.* Another version of it could be used in the cross-district segregation cases.

A judicial decision eschewing reliance on the incidents of past discrimination, and explicitly adopting a nonaccusatory theory of responsibility (for both within-district and cross-district segregation) might result in some relaxation of the remedial obligation fashioned in *Swann* and *Keyes.* The remedial stringency of *Keyes* and *Swann*—requiring the board to take all possible steps to eliminate the segregation—may be rooted in the notion of past discrimination. Past discrimination has the aura of intentional wrongdoing, and those cases may reflect the same sentiment that underlies the tort rule which holds an intentional wrongdoer accountable for *all* the consequences of his actions. The alternative tort rule, applicable to a nonintentional wrongdoer, holds an individual accountable only for the *proximate* consequences of his action, and it may govern in the school area if a nonaccusatory theory of responsibility is adopted: government will be required to take all *reasonable,* rather than all *possible,* steps to eliminate the segregation. This across-the-board relaxation of the remedial stringency may raise some problems of judicial administration, but it makes much more sense to me than the artificial situation resulting from the juxtaposition of *Keyes* and *Swann,* on the one hand, and *Milliken* on the other. The most stringent of obligations is now imposed on those within the city district, while the suburbanites are granted immunity.

## THE PROBLEM OF EMPIRICAL UNCERTAINTY

To return to the original distinction between racial assignment (the activity) and segregation (the demographic pattern), the development of school segregation law over the last two decades can be summarized by saying that of the two phenomena, segregation has become the more important factor. This can be seen from four propositions that define the present state of the law: (1) racial assignment to produce segregation is not permissible; (2) racial assignment to eliminate segregation is permissible; (3) within-district segregation produced by nonracial assignment is not permissible, provided the local board has made racial assignments in the past; and (4) cross-district segregation is permissible unless it can be shown that it is produced by racial assignments, past or present.

From this perspective the evaluation of segregation is of the utmost importance. Is segregation harmful? Is it particularly harmful to blacks? How harmful is it? These seem like purely empirical questions, susceptible to the methodology of the social scientists.[34] But the truth of the matter is that these questions have not been answered with the kind of clarity one might hope for when the task is justifying a judicial license to the school boards to make racial assignments for the purpose of eliminating the segregation, or when the task is justifying a judicial order coercing the school boards into taking appropriate steps to eliminate the segregation.

More empirical research is needed, but it will take considerable time. Meanwhile, what do the courts do? How is the judicial system to live with empirical uncertainty?

One strategy may be for the courts to eschew any doctrine that places reliance upon empirical propositions clouded by so much controversy. The theory would be (a) the promulgation of doctrine resting on unproven empirical propositions impairs the integrity of judicial law-making; (b) the good purportedly to be achieved by the promulgation of the doctrine has to be discounted because of the uncertainty surrounding the empirical propositions (the good might not be that good); and (c) the loss to judicial integrity would be greater than whatever good might be achieved by the doctrine to be promulgated. However, the Supreme Court refused to accept that theory. It also rejected the intermediate escape route by refusing to say that there is enough certainty to justify the permission to integrate (even through the use of racial assignments) but not enough to justify a judicially imposed obligation to integrate. This refusal is probably in part based on the fear that a concession on the obligation issue might undermine its position on the permission issue. If the Court were to announce that there was no legal obligation to integrate, there would be little likelihood that the school boards would take advantage of the permission granted to do so—part of the incentive and part of the argument would be gone.

The Court chose neither of these strategies. Rather it answered both the permission and obligation questions in the affirmative, despite empirical uncertainty. The Court probably reasoned that there is enough evidence to suggest that segregation might hurt the underclass, and that the risk of such harm is a sufficient predicate for the remedial efforts. Nevertheless, it also sensed the need to say something more. At first racial assignment served this purpose. Whenever the empirical propositions concerning segregation came under attack, the judiciary could talk about the moral repugnancy of "state-imposed" segregation (as an interference with liberty) or the unfairness or insult involved in denying blacks access to the white schools on the basis of their race. That worked for about fifteen years, during which time the exclusive concern was with the movement away from the dual school system. But once that phase passed and students began to be assigned to schools, not on the basis of race but rather on the basis of nonracial criteria, such as geographic proximity, something else was needed. The Court then employed a new concept—past discrimination. If the present segregation was linked with past racial assignment, then almost the same moral pressure to correct the segregation would seem present. This moral pressure tends to eclipse the uncertainty surrounding the assertions that segregation is harmful, that it is particularly harmful to blacks, and that it is so harmful as to justify expensive remedial measures. Initially, the theory of past discrimination was applied to the former dual school system (*Swann*) and then to a system (*Keyes*) whose past practices are similar to those of most other urban systems. What emerged from this use of the concept of past discrimination was an approach to school desegregation that virtually embraced the nation and that preserved the continuity with *Brown*. The Court was thus able to require the elimination of segregation, and at the same time safeguard its institutional position.

This strategy seemed to work. But there are two problems with it. First, the concept of past discrimination compounded the empirical uncertainty. Once past discrimination became central, another set of empirical propositions were introduced. These propositions generalized the past discrimination throughout the school system and linked it to the present school segregation. Because they seem as open to doubt as the ones relating to the harmful effects of segregation, an additional ingredient of empirical uncertainty is introduced and it may further impair the integrity of judicial law-making. Second, the use of this concept of past discrimination has left the Court in an awkward position. The Court is committed to decreeing the most extensive within-district integration and at the same time leaving cross-district segregation intact. The concept of past discrimination was not the "cause" of the Detroit school case, but it provided the doctrinal apparatus which made that move possible. It made it possible for some of the five Justices—for example, Justice Stewart—to join *Milliken* and also to say that the Court was still committed to *Swann* and *Keyes*.

Because of the empirical uncertainty, one can justifiably be skeptical about the judicial efforts to coerce the elimination of segregation, especially when it involves enormous social costs. One can also justifiably insist that there be limits. But it is hard to understand why the line should be the one the Supreme Court set in *Milliken*. That line might please the suburbanites, but it will remain inexplicable to the citizens of Denver and Charlotte-Mecklenburg, all of whom are subject to extensive busing decrees. It is a line that limits the practical import of *Brown* and its progeny for the predominantly black urban systems and it is a line that creates all the wrong incentives—those hastening white flight to the suburbs. Empirical uncertainty about segregation may require caution, hesitancy, modesty—not inconsistency. Consistency can only be achieved if we abandon the illusory search for the incidents of past discrimination and address in a direct and explicit way the hard question—Is a segregated pattern of student attendance harmful, and if so, how harmful?

## REFERENCES

1. Part of the difficulty in understanding school desegregation law stems from the fact that the term "segregation" can refer to either the activity (e.g., "The school board has engaged in segregation") or the demographic pattern (i.e., the segregated pattern of student attendance). In this paper it is used exclusively to refer to the latter phenomenon.

2. 347 U.S. 483 (1954); 349 U.S. 294 (1955).

3. 163 U.S. 537, 559 (1896).

4. 402 U.S. 1 (1971); see also United States v. Montgomery Board of Education, 395 U.S. 225 (1969) (faculty assignments).

5. DeFunis v. Odegaard, 94 S. Ct. 1704 (1974), vacating as moot, 82 Wash. 2d 11, 507 P.2d 1169 (1973).

6. I have tried to distinguish racial assignment at the elementary and secondary school level from the uses of race in noneducational contexts, such as jury selection, housing, and elections, in an earlier article, "Racial Imbalance in the Public Schools: the Constitutional Concepts," 78 *Harv. L. Rev.* 564, 578 n.14 (1965). The NAACP's elementary and secondary school litigation program, which reached fruition in *Brown*, was launched by a series of successful attacks on law school admission policies. See Missouri ex rel. Gaines v. Canada, 305 U.S. 337 (1938); Spinel v. University of Oklahoma Board of Regents, 332 U.S. 631 (1948); Sweatt v. Painter, 339 U.S. 629 (1950). Thus it would be ironical if *De-Funis* undid some of the post-*Brown* doctrinal advances.

7. The strained quality of the mootness disposition is suggested by several factors. First, it was well known at the time certiorari was granted that DeFunis was to graduate at the end of that year, and it is hard to believe that the Court granted certiorari to decide the mootness issue. Further, DeFunis' admission to the law school had been procured through interlocutory relief; and, since the law school intended (as the Court acknowledged) to pursue its preferential policy in the future, hardship obviously would be incurred by other similarly rejected applicants forced to run DeFunis' gauntlet.

8. Chropowicki v. Lee, 402 U.S. 935 (1971). See also North Carolina Board of Education v. Swann, 402 U.S. 43 (1971), invalidating a North Carolina antibusing law.

9. More may be required for invalidating a state antibusing law. It is not totally clear why the federal Constitution would invalidate a state law that prohibited racial assignment for integration if integration were nothing more than a constitutionally permissible goal.

10. In Morton v. Mancari, 94 S. Ct. 2474 (1974), the Supreme Court unanimously upheld a federal statute giving Indians (or more precisely "members of federally recognized tribes") a preference for employment in the Bureau of Indian Affairs (BIA). The non-Indian employees of the BIA had a grievance in some respects similar to that of DeFunis; the Court nevertheless sustained the statute on the ground that the preference is "reasonably designed to further the cause of Indian self-government and to make the BIA more responsive to the needs of its constituent groups." Id., at 2484. The Court, in an opinion by Justice Blackmun, stressed that this was a "non-racially based goal" and that the preferred group is not a racial one. The opinion reads: "The preference is not directed towards a racial group of Indians; instead, it applies only to members of 'federally recognized tribes.' This operates to exclude many in-

dividuals who are racially to be classified as 'Indians.' In this sense, the preference is political rather than racial in nature." Id., n.24. Justice Blackmun was obviously writing with an eye toward the *DeFunis* case. But why did he think the nonracial character of the preferred group was significant? I think that there are two possible answers to this question. (1) There is a rule against racial preferences that is not applicable to preferences for other groups. (2a) The self-government rationale is a satisfactory explanation for the preference only if the preference is limited to those subject to the BIA, and (2b) that is the only rationale that is offered or that the Court is willing to accept. The first answer is not based on the language of the applicable constitutional provisions (the Fifth Amendment), though it may be rooted in the language of federal statutes prohibiting racial discrimination in employment, one of which was invoked (along with the Constitution) by the non-Indian BIA employees.

11. See fn. 8 above.

12. 132 F. Supp. 776, 777 (E.D.S.C. 1955).

13. Responsibility for the school segregation may also be predicated on governmental involvement in the creation and maintenance of the segregated residential patterns. This may occur because of governmental involvement in the housing area (such as the location of public housing on a racially discriminatory basis). In that case the school board, as one agency of government, would be called on to help eliminate wrongs created by another governmental agency. The mere use of geographic criteria by the school board may also implicate government in the creation of segregated residential patterns. By rigidly adhering to geographic criteria over a long period of time, a school board assures the white parent who does not want his children to go to school with blacks that this desire can be fulfilled by a change of residence. Both these theories of responsibility, as well as the one set forth in the text, are elaborated in two earlier articles of mine, the one cited in fn. 6 above and "The Charlotte-Mecklenburg Case—Its Significance for Northern School Desegregation," 38 *U. Chi. L. Rev.* 697 (1971). See also Comment, "School Desegregation After Swann: A Theory of Government Responsibility," 39 *U. Chi. L. Rev.* 421 (1972).

14. 391 U.S. 430 (1968).

15. 402 U.S. 1 (1971).

16. 413 U.S. 189 (1973).

17. 94 S. Ct. 3112 (1974).

18. The critical passage reads: "Where the school authority's proposed plan for conversion from a dual to a unitary system contemplates the continued existence of some schools that are all or predominantly of one race, they have the burden of showing that such school assignments are genuinely nondiscriminatory. The court should scrutinize such schools, and the burden upon the school authorities will be to satisfy the

court that their racial composition is not the result of present or past discriminatory action on their part." 402 U.S., at 26.

19. This bifurcation may be attributed to the litigative strategy of the plaintiffs. They first brought suit attacking the Park Hill portion, won on that, and then sought to expand their suit to include the whole system, including the core area.

20. United States v. Texas Education Agency, 467 F.2d 848, 888 (5th Cir. 1972).

21. 413 U.S., at 211, n. 17. Emphasis added.

22. This is the view expressed in that portion of Justice Powell's opinion in *Keyes* that is a concurrence. He is determined to have a single nationwide school desegregation law, not one that tends to disfavor the South, as might be the case if past discrimination were not only a sufficient but also a necessary condition. The other portion of his opinion is a dissent predicated on the view that the remedy is excessive.

23. Fn. 18 of the Court's opinion starts by saying that the issues of the within-district violation are not before it (because they were not tendered in the petitions seeking review). But then, probably in exchange for some Justice's vote, the footnote ends by saying that under *Keyes* "the findings appear to be correct."

24. Justice White tries to formulate such a theory: ". . . had the Detroit school system not followed an official policy of segregation throughout the 1950's and 1960's, Negroes and whites would have been going to school together. There would have been no, or at least not as many, recognizable Negro schools and no, or at least not as many, white schools, but 'just schools,' and neither Negroes nor whites would have suffered from the effects of segregated education, with all its shortcomings. Surely the Court's remedy will not restore to the Negro community, stigmatized as it was by the dual school system, what it would have enjoyed overall or most of this period if the remedy is confined to present day Detroit; for the maximum remedy available within that area will leave many of the schools almost totally black, and the system itself will be predominantly black and will become increasingly so." 94 S. Ct., at 3144.

25. For the within-district segregation, there was no analytic gap between the past discriminatory practices of the local school board and the present segregation, only a factual one. It is hard to believe that the past discriminatory practices were the cause for all of the residential or the school segregation within the district. But this factual gap does not stop the Court in the within-district cases in the way that the analytic gap stops the Court in the cross-district cases. In *Swann* and *Keyes* the factual gap is closed by another judicial creation, presumptions. Once past discriminatory practices are found in a meaningful portion of the system, government is presumed responsible for all the school segregation within the district.

26. For the Detroit school board, the discriminatory practices, all in the past, consisted of the use of optional zones; drawing the boundaries of school attendance areas in a north/south, rather than an east/west direction; a discriminatory transportation system where, for example, blacks were bused past white schools; and a discriminatory school construction and site selection policy. For the state the record was even more limited: the enactment of the state law of April 7, 1970, rescinding a voluntary desegregation plan affecting about half of Detroit's high schools; state approval of an arrangement in the late 1950s whereby students for a black suburban district were educated in a predominantly black high school in Detroit; and involvement by the state in the discriminatory school construction and site selection actions of the Detroit board. None of these acts are causally related to the cross-district segregation. The financing practices of the state that enabled the suburban districts to make larger per pupil expenditures despite less tax effect might be related; for they made the suburban districts more attractive, and those with greater residential mobility (whites) took advantage of this opportunity. But the Supreme Court failed to perceive this analytic connection and seemed to suggest that, in any event, these financing practices were not discriminatory and hence not a sufficient basis for attributing responsibility. Discriminatory practices by the suburban school boards and involvement by the state in those practices may also be causally related to the cross-district segregation: blacks stayed out of those districts and remained in Detroit. But the record was deficient on that score. Finally it is not clear whether discriminatory acts by government in the housing field would suffice for attributing responsibility for school segregation. The district court alluded to discriminatory practice of government agencies in the housing area that may have caused segregated residential patterns; but the Court of Appeals expressly noted that "we have not relied at all upon testimony pertaining to segregated housing." On the basis of this disclaimer the Supreme Court concluded, in fn. 7 of its opinion: "Accordingly, in its present posture, the case does not present any question concerning possible state housing violations." See fn. 13 above.

27. The critical passage reads: "Specifically, it must be shown that racially discriminatory acts of the State or the local districts, or of a single school district have been a substantial cause of inter-district segregation." 94 S. Ct., at 3127. Later the Court adds: "The boundaries of the Detroit School District, which are coterminous with the boundaries of the city of Detroit, were established over a century ago by neutral legislation when the city was incorporated; there is no evidence in the record, nor is there any suggestion by the respondents, that either the original boundaries of the Detroit School District, or any other school district in Michigan, were established for the purpose of creating, maintaining or perpetuating segregation of the races." Id., at 3129.

28. If the emphasis is on the link with past discrimination, then the segregation may be viewed as a "vestige" of unlawful activity, rather than unlawful itself. But I doubt whether anything turns on these alternative conceptualizations of the segregation; a remedy is supposed to eliminate both a wrong and its vestiges.

29. 391 U.S., at 435.

30. 391 U.S., at 442.

31. 402 U.S., at 26.

32. Davis v. Board of School Commissioners, 402 U.S. 33 (1971).

33. Id., at 38.

34. I am not certain whether the "how harmful" question is purely empirical. The point of asking the question is to determine whether the harm is sufficient to justify the remedial costs, that is, those costs involved in eliminating the segregation. I doubt whether a purely quantitative answer would shed much light on that ulterior question. Even if the answer is "a little," costly remedial measures may be justified, either because one believes that every little bit counts or because one believes that no other measure would have a better cost-benefit relationship.

*In the Brown case the Supreme Court ruled that segregating public school children solely on the basis of race was illegal under the equal protection of the laws guaranteed by the Fourteenth Amendment. The Warren Court's decision changed race relations in America and two decades later culminated in the busing crises of the 1970s. Here, and in the Supreme Court cases that follow, the text is unchanged except for the deletion of certain footnotes and purely technical references.*

# Brown v. Board of Education–I

(MAY 17, 1954)

Mr. Chief Justice Warren delivered the opinion of the Court.

These cases come to us from the States of Kansas, South Carolina, Virginia, and Delaware. They are premised on different facts and different local conditions, but a common legal question justifies their consideration together in this consolidated opinion.

In each of these cases, minors of the Negro race, through their legal representatives, seek the aid of the courts in obtaining admission to the public schools of their community on a nonsegregated basis. In each instance they had been denied admission to schools attended by white children under laws requiring or permitting segregation according to race. This segregation was alleged to deprive the plantiffs of the equal protection of the laws under the fourteenth amendment. In each of the cases other than the Delaware case, a three-judge Federal district court denied relief to the plaintiffs on the so-called separate but equal doctrine announced by this Court in *Plessy v. Ferguson.* Under that doctrine equality of treatment is accorded when the races are provided substantially equal facilities, even though these facilities be separate. In the Delaware case, the Supreme Court of Delaware adhered to that doctrine, but ordered that the plaintiffs be admitted to the white schools because of their superiority to the Negro schools.

The plaintiffs contend that segregated public schools are not "equal" and cannot be made "equal," and that hence they are deprived of the equal protection of the laws. Because of the obvious importance of the question presented, the Court took jurisdiction. Argument was heard in the 1952 term, and reargument was heard this term on certain questions propounded by the Court.

Reargument was largely devoted to the circumstances surrounding the adoption of the fourteenth amendment in 1868. It covered exhaustively consideration of the amendment in Congress, ratification by the States, then existing practices in racial segregation, and the views of proponents and opponents of the amendment. This discussion and our own investigation convince us that, although these sources cast some light, it is not enough to resolve the problem with which we are faced. At best, they are inconclusive. The most avid proponents of the post-war amendments undoubtedly intended them to remove all legal distinctions among "all persons born or naturalized in the United States." Their opponents, just as certainly, were antagonistic to both the letter and the spirit of the amendments and wished them to have the most limited effect. What others in Congress and the State legislatures had in mind cannot be determined with any degree of certainty.

An additional reason for the inconclusive nature of the amendment's history, with respect to segregated schools, is the status of public education at that time. In the South, the movement toward free common schools, supported by general taxation, had not yet taken hold. Education of white children was largely in the hands of private groups. Education of Negroes was almost nonexistent, and practically all of the race were illiterate. In fact, any education of Negroes was forbidden by law in some States. Today, in contrast, many Negroes have achieved outstanding success in the arts and sciences as well as in the business and professional world. It is true that public school education at the time of the amendment had advanced further in the North, but the effect of the amendment on northern States was generally ignored in the congressional debates. Even in the North, the conditions of public education did not approximate those existing today. The curriculum was usually rudimentary; ungraded schools were common in rural areas; the school term was but 3 months a year in many States; and compulsory school attendance was virtually unknown. As a consequence, it is not surprising that there should be so little in the history of the fourteenth amendment relating to its intended effect on public education.

In the first case in this Court construing the fourteenth amendment, decided shortly after its adoption, the Court interpreted it as proscribing all State-imposed discriminations against the Negro race.[1]

The doctrine of "separate but equal" did not make its appearance in this Court until 1896 in the case of Plessy v. Ferguson, supra, involving not education but transportation.[2] American courts have since labored with the doctrine for over half a century. In this Court, there have been six cases involving the "separate but equal" doctrine in the field of public education. In Cumming v. County Board of Education, 175 U.S. 528, and Gong Lum v. Rice, 275 U.S. 78, the validity of the doctrine itself was not challenged. In more recent cases, all on the graduate school level, inequality was found in that specific benefits enjoyed by white students were denied to Negro students of the same educational qualifications. . . . In none of these cases was it necessary to reexamine the doctrine to grant relief to the Negro plaintiff. And in Sweatt v. Painter, supra, the Court expressly reserved decision on the question whether Plessy v. Ferguson should be held inapplicable to public education.

In the instant cases, that question is directly presented. Here, unlike Sweatt v. Painter, there are findings below that the Negro and white schools involved have been equalized, or are being equalized, with respect to buildings, curricula, qualifications and salaries of teachers, and other "tangible" factors. Our decision, therefore, cannot turn on merely a comparison of these tangible factors in the Negro and white schools involved in each of the cases. We must look instead to the effect of segregation itself on public education.

In approaching this problem, we cannot turn the clock back to 1868 when the amendment was adopted, or even to 1896 when Plessy v. Ferguson was written. We must consider public education in the light of its full development and its present place in American life throughout the Nation. Only in this way can it be determined if segregation in public schools deprives these plaintiffs of the equal protection of the laws.

Today, education is perhaps the most important function of

State and local governments. Compulsory school attendance laws and the great expenditures for education both demonstrate our recognition of the importance of education to our democratic society. It is required in the performance of our most basic public responsibilities, even service in the armed forces. It is the very foundation of good citizenship. Today it is a principal instrument in awakening the child to cultural values, in preparing him for later professional training, and in helping him to adjust normally to his environment. In these days, it is doubtful that any child may reasonably be expected to succeed in life if he is denied the opportunity of an education. Such an opportunity, where the State has undertaken to provide it, is a right which must be made available to all on equal terms.

We come then to the question presented: Does segregation of children in public schools solely on the basis of race, even though the physical facilities and other "tangible" factors may be equal, deprive the children of the minority group of equal educational opportunities? We believe that it does.

In *Sweatt v. Painter, supra,* in finding that a segregated law school for Negroes could not provide them equal educational opportunities, this Court relied in large part on "those qualities which are incapable of objective measurement but which make for greatness in a law school." In *McLaurin v. Oklahoma State Regents, supra,* the Court, in requiring that a Negro admitted to a white graduate school be treated like all other students, again resorted to intangible consideration: ". . . his ability to study, to engage in discussions and exchange views with other students, and, in general, to learn his profession." Such considerations apply with added force to children in grade and high schools. To separate them from others of similar age and qualifications solely because of their race generates a feeling of inferiority as to their status in the community that may affect their hearts and minds in a way unlikely ever to be undone. The effect of this separation on their educational opportunities was well stated by a finding in the Kansas case by a court which nevertheless felt compelled to rule against the Negro plaintiffs:

> Segregation of white and colored children in public schools has a detrimental effect upon the colored children. The impact is greater when it has the sanction of the law; for the policy of separating the races is usually interpreted as denoting the inferiority of the

Negro group. A sense of inferiority affects the motivation of a child to learn. Segregation with the sanction of law, therefore, has a tendency to [retard] the educational and mental development of Negro children and to deprive them of some of the benefits they would receive in a racial[ly] integrated school system.

Whatever may have been the extent of psychological knowledge at the time of *Plessy v. Ferguson,* this finding is amply supported by modern authority.³ Any language in *Plessy v. Ferguson* contrary to this finding is rejected.

We conclude that in the field of public education the doctrine of "separate but equal" has no place. Separate educational facilities are inherently unequal. Therefore, we hold that the plaintiffs and others similarly situated for whom the actions have been brought are, by reason of the segregation complained of, deprived of the equal protection of the laws guaranteed by the fourteenth amendment. This disposition makes unnecessary any discussion whether such segregation also violates the due process clause of the fourteenth amendment.

Because these are class actions, because of the wide applicability of this decision, and because of the great variety of local conditions, the formulation of decrees in these cases presents problems of considerable complexity. On reargument, the consideration of appropriate relief was necessarily subordinated to the primary question—the constitutionality of segregation in public education. We have now announced that such segregation is a denial of the equal protection of the laws. In order that we may have the full assistance of the parties in formulating decrees, the cases will be restored to the docket, and the parties are requested to present further argument on questions 4 and 5 previously propounded by the Court for the reargument this term.⁴ The Attorney General of the United States is again invited to participate. The attorneys general of the States requiring or permitting segregation in public education will also be permitted to appear as *amici curiae* upon request to do so by September 15, 1954, and submission of briefs by October 1, 1954.

### REFERENCES

1. *Slaughter-House Cases,* 16 Wall. 36, 67–72 (1873); *Strauder v. West Virginia,* 100 U.S. 303, 307–308 (1880):

"It ordains that no State shall deprive any person of life, liberty, or property without due process of law, or deny to any person within its jurisdiction the equal protection of the laws. What is this but declaring that the law in the States shall be the same for the black as for the white; that all persons, whether colored or white, shall stand equal before the laws of the States, and, in regard to the colored race, for whose protection the amendment was primarily designed, that no discrimination shall be made against them by law because of their color? The words of the amendment, it is true, are prohibitory, but they contain a necessary implication of a positive immunity, or right, most valuable to the colored race,—the right to exemption from unfriendly legislation against them distinctively as colored,—exemption from legal discriminations, implying inferiority in civil society, lessening the security of their enjoyment of the rights which others enjoy, and discriminations which are steps towards reducing them to the condition of a subject race."

2. The doctrine apparently originated in *Roberts v. City of Boston,* 59 Mass. 198, 206 (1850), upholding school segregation against attack as being violative of a state constitutional guarantee of equality. Segregation in Boston public schools was eliminated in 1855. But elsewhere in the North segregation in public education has persisted in some communities until recent years. It is apparent that such segregation has long been a nationwide problem, not merely one of sectional concern.

3. K. B. Clark. Effect of Prejudice and Discrimination on Personality Development (Midcentury White House Conference on Children and Youth, 1950); Witmer and Kotinsky, Personality in the Making (1952), c. VI; Deutscher and Chein, The Psychological Effects of Enforced Segregation: A Survey of Social Science Opinion, 26 J. Psychol. 259 (1948); Chein, What are the Psychological Effects of Segregation Under Conditions of Equal Facilities?, 3 Int. J. Opinion and Attitude Res. 229 (1949); Brameld, Educational Costs, in Discrimination and National Welfare (MacIver, ed., 1949), 44–48; Frazier, The Negro in the United States (1949), 674–681. And see generally Myrdal, An American Dilemma (1944).

4. "4. Assuming it is decided that segregation in public schools violates the Fourteenth Amendment

"(a) would decree necessarily follow providing that, within the limits set by normal geographic school districting, Negro children should forthwith be admitted to schools of their choice, or

"(b) may this Court, in the exercise of its equity powers, permit an effective gradual adjustment to be brought about from existing segregated systems to a system not based on color distinctions?

"5. On the assumption on which questions 4(a) and (b) are based, and assuming further that this Court will exercise its equity powers to the end described in question 4(b)

"(a) should this Court formulate detailed decrees in these cases;

"(b) if so, what specific issues should the decrees reach;

"(c) should this Court appoint a special master to hear evidence with a view to recommending specific terms for such decrees;

"(d) should this Court remand to the courts of the first instance with directions to frame decrees in these cases, and if so what general directions should the decrees of this Court include and what procedures should the courts of first instance follow in arriving at the specific terms of more detailed decrees?"

*Having ruled in Brown I that the doctrine of "separate but equal" had no place in public education, the Supreme Court then had to face the problem of how its decision should be implemented. In Brown II it ruled that district courts and local school officials must act with "all deliberate speed" to eliminate racial discrimination in the public schools.*

# Brown v. Board of Education–II

## (MAY 31, 1955)

Mr. Chief Justice Warren delivered the opinion of the Court.

These cases were decided on May 17, 1954. The opinions of that date, declaring the fundamental principle that racial discrimination in public education is unconstitutional, are incorporated herein by reference. All provisions of Federal, State, or local law requiring or permitting such discrimination must yield to this principle. There remains for consideration the manner in which relief is to be accorded.

Because these cases arose under different local conditions and their disposition will involve a variety of local problems, we requested further argument on the question of relief. In view of the nationwide importance of the decision, we invited the Attorney General of the United States and the attorneys general of all States requiring or permitting racial discrimination in public education to present their views on that question. The parties, the United States, and the States of Florida, North Carolina, Arkansas, Oklahoma, Maryland, and Texas filed briefs and participated in the oral argument.

These presentations were informative and helpful to the Court in its consideration of the complexities arising from the transition to a system of public education freed of racial discrimination. The presentations also demonstrated that substantial steps to eliminate racial discrimination in public schools have already been taken, not only in some of the communities in which these cases arose, but in some of the States appearing as *amici curiae,* and in other States as well. Substantial progress has been made in the District of Columbia and in the communities in Kansas and Delaware involved in this litigation. The defendants in the cases coming to us from South Carolina and Virginia are awaiting the decision of this Court concerning relief.

Full implementation of these constitutional principles may require solution of varied local school problems. School authorities have the primary responsibility for elucidating, assessing, and solving these problems; courts will have to consider whether the action of school authorities constitutes good faith implementation of the governing constitutional principles. Because of their proximity to local conditions and the possible need for further hearings, the courts which originally heard these cases can best perform this judicial appraisal. Accordingly, we believe it appropriate to remand the cases to those courts.

In fashioning and effectuating the decrees, the courts will be guided by equitable principles. Traditionally, equity has been characterized by a practical flexibility in shaping its remedies and by a facility for adjusting and reconciling public and private needs. These cases call for the exercise of these traditional attributes of equity power. At stake is the personal interest of the plaintiffs in admission to public schools as soon as practicable on a nondiscriminatory basis. To effectuate this interest may call for elimination of a variety of obstacles in making the transition to school systems operated in accordance with the constitutional principles set forth in our May 17, 1954, decision. Courts of equity may properly take into account the public interest in the elimination of such obstacles in a systematic and effective manner. But it should go without saying that the vitality of these constitutional principles cannot be allowed to yield simply because of disagreement with them.

While giving weight to these public and private considerations, the courts will require that the defendants make a prompt and reasonable start toward full compliance with our May 17, 1954, ruling. Once such a start has been made, the courts may find that additional time is necessary to carry out the ruling in an effective manner. The burden rests upon the defendants to establish that such time is necessary in the public interest and is consistent with good faith compliance at the earliest practicable date. To that end, the courts may consider problems related to administration, arising from the physical condition of the school plant, the school transportation system, personnel, revision of school districts and attendance areas into compact units to achieve a system of determining admission to the public schools on a nonracial basis, and revision of local laws and regulations which may be necessary in solving the foregoing problems. They will also consider the adequacy of any plans the defendants may propose to meet these problems and to effectuate a transition to a racially nondiscriminatory school system. During this period of transition, the courts will retain jurisdiction of these cases.

The judgments below, except that in the *Delaware* case, are accordingly reversed and the cases are remanded to the district courts to take such proceedings and enter such orders and decrees consistent with this opinion as are necessary and proper to admit to public schools on a racially nondiscriminatory basis with all deliberate speed the parties to these cases. The judgment in the *Delaware* case—ordering the immediate admission of the plaintiffs to schools previously attended only by white children—is affirmed on the basis of the principles stated in our May 17, 1954, opinion, but the case is remanded to the Supreme Court of Delaware for such further proceedings as that court may deem necessary in light of this opinion.

In Green v. New Kent County *the Supreme Court moved to stop delays in the desegregation process it had begun a decade earlier. It emphasized the "affirmative duty" once-segregated school systems had to eliminate racial discrimination "root and branch." "The burden on a school board today," the Court said, "is to come forward with a plan that promises realistically to work, and promises realistically to work now."*

# Green v. New Kent County

## (MAY 27, 1968)

Mr. Justice Brennan delivered the opinion of the Court.

The question for decision is whether, under all the circumstances here, respondent school board's adoption of a "freedom-of-choice" plan which allows a pupil to choose his own public school constitutes adequate compliance with the board's responsibility "to achieve a system of determining admission to the public schools on a non-racial basis . . ." (*Brown II*).

Petitioners brought this action in March 1965 seeking injunctive relief against respondent's continued maintenance of an alleged racially segregated school system. New Kent County is a rural county in eastern Virginia. About one-half of its population of some 4,500 are Negroes. There is no residential segregation in the county; persons of both races reside throughout. The school system has only two schools, the New Kent school on the east side of the county and the George W. Watkins school on the west side. In a memorandum filed May 17, 1966, the district court found that the "school system serves approximately 1,300 pupils, of which 740 are Negro and 550 are white. The school board operates one white combined elementary and high school [New Kent], and one Negro combined elementary and high school [George W. Watkins]. There are no attendance zones. Each school serves the entire county." The record indicates that 21 school buses—11 serving the Watkins school and 10 serving the New Kent school —travel overlapping routes throughout the county to transport pupils to and from the two schools.

The segregated system was initially established and maintained under the compulsion of Virginia constitutional and statutory provisions mandating racial segregation in public education. . . . These provisions were held to violate the Federal Constitution in *Davis v. County School Board of Prince Edward County,* decided with *Brown v. Board of Education, (Brown I).* The respondent School Board continued the segregated operation of the system after the *Brown* decisions, presumably on the authority of several statutes enacted by Virginia in resistance to those decisions. Some of these statutes were held to be unconstitutional on their face or as applied. One statute, the Pupil Placement Act, Va. Code (1964), not repealed until 1966, divested local boards of authority to assign children to particular schools and placed that authority in a State Pupil Placement Board. Under that act, children were each year automatically reassigned to the school previously attended unless upon their application the State board assigned them to another school; students seeking enrollment for the first time were also assigned at the discretion of the State board. To September 1964, no Negro pupil had applied for admission to the New Kent school under this statute, and no white pupil had applied for admission to the Watkins school.

The school board initially sought dismissal of this suit on the ground that petitioners had failed to apply to the State board for assignment to New Kent school. However, on August 2, 1965, 5 months after the suit was brought, respondent school board, in order to remain eligible for Federal financial aid, adopted a "freedom-of-choice" plan for desegregating the schools. Under that plan, each pupil may annually choose between the New Kent and Watkins schools and, except for the first and eighth grades, pupils not making a choice are assigned to the school previously attended; first and eighth grade pupils must affirmatively choose a school. After the plan was filed, the district court denied petitioner's prayer for an injunction and granted respondent leave to submit an amendment to the plan with respect to employment and assignment of teacher and staff on a racially nondiscriminatory basis. The amendment was duly filed and on June 28, 1966, the district court approved the "freedom-of-choice" plan as so amended. The Court of Appeals for the Fourth Circuit, en banc, affirmed the district court's approval of the "freedom-of-choice" provisions of the plan but remanded the case to the district court for entry of an order regarding faculty "which is much more specific and more comprehensive" and which would incorporate in addition to a "minimal, objective timetable" some of the faculty provisions of the decree entered by the Court of Appeals for the Fifth Circuit in *United States v. Jefferson County Board of Education.* Judges Soboloff and Winters concurred with the remand on the teacher issue but otherwise disagreed, expressing the view "that the district court should be directed . . . also to set up procedures for periodically evaluating the effectiveness of the [board's] 'freedom of choice' [plan] in the elimination of other features of a segregated school system." We granted certiorari, 389 U.S. 1003.

The pattern of separate "white" and "Negro" schools in the New Kent County school system established under compulsion of State laws is precisely the pattern of segregation to which *Brown I* and *Brown II* were particularly addressed, and which *Brown I* declared unconstitutionally denied Negro schoolchildren equal protection of the laws. Racial identification of the system's school was complete, extending not just to the composition of student bodies at the two schools but to every facet of school operations—faculty, staff, transportation, extracurricular activities and facilities. In short, the State, acting through the local school board and school officials, organized and operated a dual system, part "white" and part "Negro."

It was such dual systems that 14 years ago *Brown I* held unconstitutional and a year later *Brown II* held must be abolished; school boards operating such school systems were required by *Brown II* "to effectuate a transition to a racially nondiscriminatory school system." It is of course true that for the time immediately after *Brown II* the concern was with making an initial break in a long-established pattern of excluding Negro children from schools attended by white children. The principal focus was on obtaining for those Negro children courageous enough to break with tradition a place in the "white" schools. . . . Under *Brown II* that immediate goal was only the first step, however. The transition to a unitary, nonracial system of public education was and is the ultimate end to be brought about; it was because of the "complexities arising from the transition to a system of public education freed of racial discrimination" that we provided for "all deliberate speed" in the implementation of the principles of *Brown I*. Thus we recognized the task would necessarily involve solution of "varied local school problems." In referring to the "personal interest of the plaintiffs in admission to public schools as soon as practicable on a nondiscriminatory basis," we also noted that "[t]o effectuate this interest may call for elimination of a variety of obstacles in making the transition . . ." Yet we emphasized that the constitutional rights of Negro children required school officials to bear the burden of establishing that additional time to carry out the ruling in an effective manner "is necessary in the public interest and is consistent with good faith compliance at the earliest practicable date." We charged the district courts in their review of particular situations to—

> . . . consider problems related to administration, arising from the physical condition of the school plant, the school transportation system, personnel, revision of school districts and attendance areas into compact units to achieve a system of determining admission to the public schools on a nonracial basis, and revision of local laws and regulations which may be necessary in solving the foregoing problems. They will also consider the adequacy of any plans the defendants may propose to meet these problems and to effectuate a transition to a racially nondiscriminatory school system.

It is against this background that 13 years after *Brown II* commanded the abolition of dual systems we must measure the effectiveness of respondent school board's "freedom-of-choice" plan to achieve that end. The school board contends that it has fully discharged its obligation by adopting a plan by which every student, regardless of race, may "freely" choose the school he will attend. The Board attempts to cast the issue in its broadest form by arguing that its "freedom-of-choice" plan may be faulted only by reading the 14th amendment as universally requiring "compulsory integration," a reading it insists the wording of the amendment will not support. But that argument ignores the thrust of *Brown II*. In the light of the command of that case, what is involved here is the question whether the board has achieved the "racially nondiscriminatory school system" *Brown II* held must be effectuated in order to remedy the established unconstitutional deficiencies of its segregated system. In the context of the State-imposed segregated pattern of long standing, the fact that in 1965 the board opened the doors of the former "white" school to Negro children and of the "Negro" school to white children merely begins, not ends, our inquiry whether the Board has taken steps adequate to abolish its dual, segregated system. *Brown II* was a call for the dismantling of well-entrenched dual systems tempered by an awareness that complex and multi-faceted problems would arise which would require time and flexibility for a successful resolution. School boards such as the respondent then operating State-compelled dual systems were nevertheless clearly charged with the affirmative duty to take whatever steps might be necessary to convert to a unitary system in which racial discrimination would be eliminated root and branch. . . . The constitutional rights of Negro school children articulated in *Brown I* permit no less than this; and it was to this end that *Brown II* commanded school boards to bend their efforts.[1]

In determining whether respondent school board met that command by adopting its freedom-of-choice plan, it is relevant that this first step did not come until some 11 years after *Brown I* was decided and 10 years after *Brown II* directed the making of a "prompt and reasonable start." This deliberate perpetuation of the unconstitutional dual system can only have compounded the harm of such a system. Such delays are no longer tolerable for "the governing constitutional principles no longer bear the imprint of newly enunciated doctrine." . . . Moreover, a plan that at this late date fails to provide meaningful assurance of prompt and effective disestablishment of a dual system is also intolerable. "The time for mere 'deliberate speed' has run out." . . . The burden on a school board today is to come forward with a plan that promises realistically to work, and promises realistically to work *now*.

The obligation of the district courts, as it always has been, is to assess the effectiveness of a proposed plan in achieving desegregation. There is no universal answer to complex problems of desegregation; there is obviously no one plan that will do the job in every case. The matter must be assessed in light of the circumstances present and the options available in each instance. It is incumbent upon the school board to establish that its proposed plan promises meaningful and immediate progress toward disestablishing State-imposed segregation. It is incumbent upon the district court to weigh that claim in light of the facts at hand

and in light of any alternatives which may be shown as feasible and more promising in their effectiveness. Where the court finds the board to be acting in good faith and the proposed plan to have real prospects for dismantling the State-imposed dual system "at the earliest practicable date," then the plan may be said to provide effective relief. Of course, where other, more promising courses of action are open to the board, that may indicate a lack of good faith; and at the least it places a heavy burden upon the board to explain its preference for an apparently less effective method. Moreover, whatever plan is adopted will require evaluation in practice, and the court should retain jurisdiction until it is clear that State-imposed segregation has been completely removed.

We do not hold that freedom of choice can have no place in such a plan. We do not hold that a freedom-of-choice plan might of itself be unconstitutional, although that argument has been urged upon us. Rather, all we decide today is that in desegregating a dual system a plan utilizing freedom of choice is not an end in itself. As Judge Sobeloff has put it—

> "Freedom of choice" is not a sacred talisman; it is only a means to a constitutionally required end—the abolition of the system of segregation and its effects. If the means prove effective, it is acceptable, but if it fails to undo segregation, other means must be used to achieve this end. The school officials have the continuing duty to take whatever action may be necessary to create a "unitary, nonracial system."

Although the general experience under freedom of choice to date has been such as to indicate its ineffectiveness as a tool of desegregation,[2] there may well be instances in which it can serve as an effective device. Where it offers real promise of aiding a desegregation program to effectuate conversion of a State-imposed dual system to a unitary, nonracial system there might be no objection to allowing such a device to prove itself in operation. On the other hand, if there are reasonably available other ways, such for illustration as zoning, promising speedier and more effective conversion to a unitary, nonracial school system, freedom of choice must be held unacceptable.

The New Kent school board's freedom-of-choice plan cannot be accepted as a sufficient step to "effectuate a transition" to a unitary system. In 3 years of operation not a single white child has chosen to attend Watkins school and although 115 Negro children enrolled in New Kent school in 1967 (up from 35 in 1965 and 111 in 1966) 85 percent of the Negro children in the system still attend the all-Negro Watkins school. In other words, the school system remains a dual system. Rather than further the dismantling of the dual system, the plan has operated simply to burden children and their parents with a responsibility which *Brown II* placed squarely on the school board. The board must be required to formulate a new plan and, in light of other courses which appear open to the board, such as zoning,[3] fashion steps which promise realistically to convert promptly to a system without a "white" school and a "Negro" school, but just schools.

The judgment of the court of appeals is vacated insofar as it affirmed the district court and the case is remanded to the district court for further proceedings consistent with this opinion.

## REFERENCES

1. "We bear in mind that the court has not merely the power but the duty to render a decree which will so far as possible eliminate the discriminatory effects of the past as well as bar like discriminations in the future." *Louisiana v. United States,* 380 U.S. 145, 154. Compare the remedies discussed in, e.g., *NLRB v. Newport News Shipbuilding & Dry Dock Co.,* 308 U.S. 241; *United States v. Crescent Amusement Co.,* 323 U.S. 173; *United States v. Standard Oil Co.,* 221 U.S. 1. See also *Griffin v. County School Board,* 377 U.S. 218, 232–234.

2. The views of the United States Commission on Civil Rights, which we neither adopt nor refuse to adopt, are as follows:

"Freedom of choice plans, which have tended to perpetuate racially identifiable schools in the Southern and border States, require affirmative action by both Negro and white parents and pupils before such disestablishment can be achieved. There are a number of factors which have prevented such affirmative action by substantial numbers of parents and pupils of both races:

"(a) Fear of retaliation and hostility from the white community continue to deter many Negro families from choosing formerly all-white schools;

"(b) During the past school year [1966–1967], as in the previous year, in some areas of the South, Negro families with children attending previously all-white schools under free choice plans were targets of violence, threats of violence and economic reprisals by white persons and Negro children were subjected to harassment by white classmates notwithstanding conscientious efforts by many teachers and principals to prevent such misconduct;

"(c) During the past school year, in some areas of the South public officials improperly influenced Negro families to keep their children in Negro schools and excluded Negro children attending formerly all-white schools from official functions;

"(d) Poverty deters many Negro families in the South from choosing formerly all-white schools. Some Negro parents are embarrassed to permit their children to attend such schools without suitable clothing. In some districts special fees are assessed for courses which are available only in the white schools;

"(e) Improvements in facilities and equipment . . . have been instituted in all-Negro schools in some school districts in a manner that tends to discourage Negroes from selecting white schools."

3. "In view of the situation found in New Kent County, where there is no residential segregation, the elimination of the dual school system and the establishment of a 'unitary, non-racial system' could be readily achieved with a minimum of administrative difficulty by means of geographic zoning—simply by assigning students living in the eastern half of the county to the New Kent School and those living in the western half of the county to the Watkins School. Although a geographical formula is not universally appropriate, it is evident that here the Board, by separately busing Negro children across the entire county to the 'Negro' school, and the white children to the 'white' school, is deliberately maintaining a segregated system which would vanish with non-racial geographic zoning.

In the Swann case the Supreme Court, now under Chief Justice
Warren Burger, held that "all awkwardness and inconvenience
cannot be avoided in the interim period when remedial adjustments are being made to eliminate the dual school systems."
Busing, the Court insisted, was an appropriate tool to use in desegregating the Charlotte-Mecklenburg schools.

# Swann v. Charlotte-Mecklenburg

## (APRIL 20, 1971)

Mr. Chief Justice Burger delivered the opinion of the Court.

We granted certiorari in this case to review important issues as
to the duties of school authorities and the scope of powers of
federal courts under this Court's mandates to eliminate racially
separate public schools established and maintained by state action. *Brown v. Board of Education* (1954).

This case and those argued with it arose in states having a long
history of maintaining two sets of schools in a single school system
deliberately operated to carry out a governmental policy to separate pupils in schools solely on the basis of race. That was
what *Brown v. Board of Education* was all about. These cases
present us with the problem of defining in more precise terms
than heretofore the scope of the duty of school authorities and
district courts in implementing *Brown I* and the mandate to eliminate dual systems and establish unitary systems at once. Meanwhile district courts and courts of appeals have struggled in
hundreds of cases with a multitude and variety of problems under
this Court's general directive. Understandably, in an area of
evolving remedies, those courts had to improvise and experiment
without detailed or specific guidelines. This Court, in *Brown I*,
appropriately dealt with the large constitutional principles; other
federal courts had to grapple with the flinty, intractable realities

of day-to-day implementation of those constitutional commands. Their efforts, of necessity, embraced a process of "trial and error," and our effort to formulate guidelines must take into account their experience.

## I

The Charlotte-Mecklenburg school system, the 43d largest in the Nation, encompasses the city of Charlotte and surrounding Mecklenburg County, North Carolina. The area is large—550 square miles—spanning roughly 22 miles east-west and 36 miles north-south. During the 1968–1969 school year the system served more than 84,000 pupils in 107 schools. Approximately 71% of the pupils were found to be white and 29% Negro. As of June 1969 there were approximately 24,000 Negro students in the system, of whom 21,000 attended schools within the city of Charlotte. Two-thirds of those 21,000—approximately 14,000 Negro students—attended 21 schools which were either totally Negro or more than 99% Negro.

This situation came about under a desegregation plan approved by the District Court at the commencement of the present litigation in 1965, . . . based upon geographic zoning with a free transfer provision. The present proceedings were initiated in September 1968 by Petitioner Swann's motion for further relief based on *Green v. County School Board* and its companion cases. All parties now agree that in 1969 the system fell short of achieving the unitary school system that those cases require.

The District Court held numerous hearings and received voluminous evidence. In addition to finding certain actions of the school board to be discriminatory, the court also found that residential patterns in the city and county resulted in part from federal, state, and local government action other than school board decisions. School board action based on these patterns, for example by locating schools in Negro residential areas and fixing the size of the schools to accommodate the needs of immediate neighborhoods, resulted in segregated education. These findings were subsequently accepted by the Court of Appeals.

In April 1969 the District Court ordered the school board to come forward with a plan for both faculty and student desegregation. Proposed plans were accepted by the court in June and August 1969 on an interim basis only, and the board was ordered to file a third plan by November 1969. In November the board moved for an extension of time until February 1970, but when that was denied the board submitted a partially completed plan. In December 1969 the District Court held that the board's submission was unacceptable and appointed an expert in education administration, Dr. John Finger, to prepare a desegregation plan. Thereafter in February 1970, the District Court was presented with two alternative pupil assignment plans—the finalized "board plan" and the "Finger plan."

## THE BOARD PLAN

As finally submitted, the school board plan closed seven schools and reassigned their pupils. It restructured school attendance zones to achieve greater racial balance but maintained existing grade structures and rejected techniques such as pairing and clustering as part of a desegregation effort. The plan created a single athletic league, eliminated the previously racial basis of the school bus system, provided racially mixed faculties and administrative staffs, and modified its free transfer plan into an optional majority-to-minority transfer system.

The board plan proposed substantial assignment of Negroes to nine of the system's 10 high schools, producing 17% to 36% Negro population in each. The projected Negro attendance at the 10th school, Independence, was 2%. The proposed attendance zones for the high schools were typically shaped like wedges of a pie, extending outward from the center of the city to the suburban and rural areas of the county in order to afford residents of the center city area access to outlying schools.

As for junior high schools, the board plan rezoned the 21 school areas so that in 20 the Negro attendance would range from 0% to 38%. The other school, located in the heart of the Negro residential area, was left with an enrollment of 90% Negro.

The board plan with respect to elementary schools relied entirely upon gerrymandering of geographic zones. More than half of the Negro elementary pupils were left in nine schools that were 86% to 100% Negro; approximately half of the white elementary pupils were assigned to schools 86% to 100% white.

## THE FINGER PLAN

The plan submitted by the court-appointed expert, Dr. Finger, adopted the school board zoning plan for senior high schools with one modification: it required that an additional 300 Negro students be transported from the Negro residential area of the city to the nearly all-white Independence High School.

The Finger plan for the junior high schools employed much of the rezoning plan of the board, combined with the creation of nine "satellite" zones.* Under the satellite plan, inner-city Negro students were assigned by attendance zones to nine outlying predominately white junior high schools, thereby substantially desegregating every junior high school in the system.

The Finger plan departed from the board plan chiefly in its handling of the system's 76 elementary schools. Rather than relying solely upon geographic zoning, Dr. Finger proposed use of zoning, pairing, and grouping techniques, with the result that student bodies throughout the system would range from 9% to 38% Negro.

The District Court described the plan thus:

> Like the board plan, the Finger plan does as much by rezoning school attendance lines as can reasonably be accomplished. However, unlike the board plan, it does not stop there. It goes further and desegregates all the rest of the elementary schools by the technique of grouping two or three outlying schools with one black inner city school; by transporting black students from grades one through four to the outlying white schools; and by transporting white students from the fifth and sixth grades from the outlying white schools to the inner city black school.

Under the Finger plan, nine inner-city Negro schools were grouped in this manner with 24 suburban white schools.

On February 5, 1970, the District Court adopted the board plan, as modified by Dr. Finger, for the junior and senior high schools. The court rejected the board elementary school plan and adopted the Finger plan as presented. Implementation was partially stayed by the Court of Appeals for the Fourth Circuit on March 5, and this Court declined to disturb the Fourth Circuit's order.

On appeal the Court of Appeals affirmed the District Court's order as to faculty desegregation and the secondary school plans, but vacated the order respecting elementary schools. While agreeing that the District Court properly disapproved the board plan

---

* A "satellite zone" is an area that is not contiguous with the main attendance zone surrounding the school.

concerning these schools, the Court of Appeals feared that the pairing and grouping of elementary schools would place an unreasonable burden on the board and the system's pupils. The case was remanded to the District Court for reconsideration and submission of further plans. This Court granted certiorari, and directed reinstatement of the District Court's order pending further proceedings in that court.

On remand the District Court received two new plans for the elementary schools: a plan prepared by the United States Department of Health, Education, and Welfare (the HEW plan) based on contiguous grouping and zoning of schools, and a plan prepared by four members of the nine-member school board (the minority plan) achieving substantially the same results as the Finger plan but apparently with slightly less transportation. A majority of the school board declined to amend its proposal. After a lengthy evidentiary hearing the District Court concluded that its own plan (the Finger plan), the minority plan, and an earlier draft of the Finger plan were all reasonable and acceptable. It directed the board to adopt one of the three or in the alternative to come forward with a new, equally effective plan of its own; the court ordered that the Finger plan would remain in effect in the event the school board declined to adopt a new plan. On August 7, the board indicated it would "acquiesce" in the Finger plan, reiterating its view that the plan was unreasonable. The District Court, by order dated August 7, 1970, directed that the Finger plan remain in effect.

## II

Nearly 17 years ago this Court held, in explicit terms, that state-imposed segregation by race in public schools denies equal protection of the laws. At no time has the Court deviated in the slightest degree from that holding or its constitutional underpinnings. None of the parties before us challenges the Court's decision of May 17, 1954, that

> in the field of public education the doctrine of "separate but equal" has no place. Separate educational facilities are inherently unequal. Therefore, we hold that the plaintiffs and others similarly situated . . . are, by reason of the segregation complained of, deprived of the equal protection of the laws guaranteed by the Fourteenth Amendment. . . .

Because these are class actions, because of the wide applicability of this decision, and because of the great variety of local conditions, the formulation of decrees in these cases presents problems of considerable complexity. *Brown v. Board of Education.*

None of the parties before us questions the Court's 1955 holding in *Brown II,* that

> School authorities have the primary responsibility for elucidating, assessing, and solving these problems; courts will have to consider whether the action of school authorities constitutes good faith implementation of the governing constitutional principles. Because of their proximity to local conditions and the possible need for further hearings, the courts which originally heard these cases can best perform this judicial appraisal. Accordingly, we believe it appropriate to remand the cases to those courts.
>
> In fashioning and effectuating the decrees, the courts will be guided by equitable principles. Traditionally, equity has been characterized by a practical flexibility in shaping its remedies and by a facility for adjusting and reconciling public and private needs. These cases call for the exercise of these traditional attributes of equity power. At stake is the personal interest of the plaintiffs in admission to public schools as soon as practicable on a nondiscriminatory basis. To effectuate this interest may call for elimination of a variety of obstacles in making the transition to school systems operated in accordance with the constitutional principles set forth in our May 17, 1954, decision. Courts of equity may properly take into account the public interest in the elimination of such obstacles in a systematic and effective manner. But it should go without saying that the vitality of these constitutional principles cannot be allowed to yield simply because of disagreement with them.

Over the 15 years since *Brown II,* many difficulties were encountered in implementation of the basic constitutional requirement that the State not discriminate between public school children on the basis of their race. Nothing in our national experience prior to 1955 prepared anyone for dealing with changes and adjustments of the magnitude and complexity encountered since then. Deliberate resistance of some to the Court's mandates has impeded the good-faith efforts of others to bring school systems into compliance. The detail and nature of these dilatory tactics have been noted frequently by this Court and other courts.

By the time the Court considered *Green v. County School*

*Board* in 1968, very little progress had been made in many areas where dual school systems had historically been maintained by operation of state laws. In *Green*, the Court was confronted with a record of a freedom-of-choice program that the District Court had found to operate in fact to preserve a dual system more than a decade after *Brown II*. While acknowledging that a freedom-of-choice concept could be a valid remedial measure in some circumstances, its failure to be effective in *Green* required that

> The burden on a school board today is to come forward with a plan that promises realistically to work . . . *now* . . . until it is clear that state-imposed segregation has been completely removed.

This was plain language, yet the 1969 Term of Court brought fresh evidence of the dilatory tactics of many school authorities. *Alexander v. Holmes County Board of Education* restated the basic obligation asserted in *Griffin v. School Board* (1964) and *Green, supra,* that the remedy must be implemented *forthwith*.

The problems encountered by the district courts and courts of appeals make plain that we should now try to amplify guidelines, however incomplete and imperfect, for the assistance of school authorities and courts. The failure of local authorities to meet their constitutional obligations aggravated the massive problem of converting from the state-enforced discrimination of racially separate school systems. This process has been rendered more difficult by changes since 1954 in the structure and patterns of communities, the growth of student population, movement of families, and other changes, some of which had marked impact on school planning, sometimes neutralizing or negating remedial action before it was fully implemented. Rural areas accustomed for half a century to the consolidated school systems implemented by bus transportation could make adjustments more readily than metropolitan areas with dense and shifting population, numerous schools, congested and complex traffic patterns.

## III

The objective today remains to eliminate from the public schools all vestiges of state-imposed segregation. Segregation was the evil struck down by *Brown I* as contrary to the equal protection guarantees of the Constitution. That was the violation sought to be corrected by the remedial measures of *Brown II*. That was the basis for the holding in Green that school authorities are "clearly charged with the affirmative duty to take whatever steps might be necessary to convert to a unitary system in which racial discrimination would be eliminated root and branch."

If school authorities fail in their affirmative obligations under these holdings, judicial authority may be invoked. Once a right and a violation have been shown, the scope of a district court's equitable powers to remedy past wrongs is broad, for breadth and flexibility are inherent in equitable remedies.

> The essence of equity jurisdiction has been the power of the Chancellor to do equity and to mould each decree to the necessities of the particular case. Flexibility rather than rigidity has distinguished it. The qualities of mercy and practicality have made equity the instrument for nice adjustment and reconciliation between the public interest and private needs as well as between competing private claims. Hecht Co. v. Bowles (1944).

This allocation of responsibility once made, the Court attempted from time to time to provide some guidelines for the exercise of the district judge's discretion and for the reviewing function of the courts of appeals. However, a school desegregation case does not differ fundamentally from other cases involving the framing of equitable remedies to repair the denial of a constitutional right. The task is to correct, by a balancing of the individual and collective interests, the condition that offends the Constitution.

In seeking to define even in broad and general terms how far this remedial power extends it is important to remember that judicial powers may be exercised only on the basis of a constitutional violation. Remedial judicial authority does not put judges automatically in the shoes of school authorities whose powers are plenary. Judicial authority enters only when local authority defaults.

School authorities are traditionally charged with broad power to formulate and implement educational policy and might well conclude, for example, that in order to prepare students to live in a pluralistic society each school should have a prescribed ratio of Negro to white students reflecting the proportion for the district as a whole. To do this as an educational policy is within the broad discretionary powers of school authorities; absent a finding of a constitutional violation, however, that would not be within the authority of a federal court. As with any equity case, the nature of the violation determines the scope of the remedy. In default by the school authorities of their obligation to proffer acceptable remedies, a district court has broad power to fashion a remedy that will assure a unitary school system.

The school authorities argue that the equity powers of federal district courts have been limited by Title IV of the Civil Rights Act of 1964. The language and the history of Title IV show that it was not enacted to limit but to define the role of the Federal Government in the implementation of the *Brown I* decision. It authorizes the Commissioner of Education to provide technical assistance to local boards in the preparation of desegregation plans, to arrange "training institutes" for school personnel involved in desegregation efforts, and to make grants directly to schools to ease the transition to unitary systems. It also authorizes the Attorney General, in specific circumstances, to initiate federal desegregation suits. Section 2000c (b) defines "desegregation" as it is used in Title IV:

"Desegregation" means the assignment of students to public schools and within such schools without regard ot their race, color, religion, or national origin, but "desegregation" shall not mean the assignment of students to public schools in order to overcome racial imbalance.

Section 2000c–6, authorizing the Attorney General to institute federal suits, contains the following proviso:

nothing herein shall empower any official or court of the United States to issue any order seeking to achieve a racial balance in any school by requiring the transportation of pupils or students from one school to another or one school district to another in order to achieve such racial balance, or otherwise enlarge the existing power of the court to insure compliance with constitutional standards.

On their face, the sections quoted purport only to insure that the provisions of Title IV of the Civil Rights Act of 1964 will not be read as granting new powers. The proviso in § 2000c–6 is in terms designed to foreclose any interpretation of the Act as expanding the *existing* powers of federal courts to enforce the Equal Protection Clause. There is no suggestion of an intention to restrict those powers or withdraw from courts their historic equitable remedial powers. The legislative history of Title IV indicates that Congress was concerned that the Act might be read as creating a right of action under the Fourteenth Amendment in the situation of so-called "de facto segregation," where racial imbalance exists in the schools but with no showing that this was brought about by discriminatory action of state authorities. In short, there is nothing in the Act which provides us material assistance in answering the question of remedy for state-imposed segregation in violation of *Brown I*. The basis of our decision must be the prohibition of the Fourteenth Amendment that no State shall "deny to any person within its jurisdiction the equal protection of the laws."

## IV

We turn now to the problem of defining with more particularity the responsibilities of school authorities in desegregating a state-enforced dual school system in light of the Equal Protection Clause. Although the several related cases before us are primarily concerned with problems of student assignment, it may be helpful to begin with a brief discussion of other aspects of the process.

In *Green*, we pointed out that existing policy and practice with regard to faculty, staff, transportation, extra-curricular activities, and facilities were among the most important indicia of a segregated system. Independent of student assignment, where it is possible to identify a "white school" or a "Negro school" simply by reference to the racial composition of teachers and staff, the quality of school buildings and equipment, or the organization of sports activities, a *prima facie* case of violation of substantive constitutional rights under the Equal Protection Clause is shown.

When a system has been dual in these respects, the first remedial responsibility of school authorities is to eliminate invidious racial distinctions. With respect to such matters as transportation, supporting personnel, and extracurricular activities, no more than this may be necessary. Similar corrective action must be taken with regard to the maintenance of buildings and the distribution of equipment. In these areas, normal administrative practice should produce schools of like quality, facilities, and staffs. Something more must be said, however, as to faculty assignment and new school construction.

In the companion *Davis* case, the Mobile school board has argued that the Constitution requires that teachers be assigned on a "color blind" basis. It also argues that the Constitution prohibits district courts from using their equity power to order assignment of teachers to achieve a particular degree of faculty desegregation. We reject that contention.

In *United States v. Montgomery County Board of Education,* the District Court set as a goal a plan of faculty assignment in each school with a ratio of white to Negro faculty members substantially the same throughout the system. This order was predicated on the District Court finding that

> The evidence does not reflect any real administrative problems involved in immediately desegregating the substitute teachers, the student teachers, the night school faculties, and in the evolvement of a really legally adequate program for the substantial desegregation of the faculties of all schools in the system commencing with the school year 1968–69.

The District Court in *Montgomery* then proceeded to set an initial ratio for the whole system of at least two Negro teachers out of each 12 in any given school. The Court of Appeals modified the order by eliminating what it regarded as "fixed mathematical ratios" of faculty and substituted an initial requirement of "substantially or approximately" a five-to-one ratio. With respect to the future, the Court of Appeals held that the numerical ratio should be eliminated and that compliance should not be tested solely by the achievement of specified proportions.

We reversed the Court of Appeals and restored the District Court's order in its entirety, holding that the order of the District Judge

> was adopted in the spirit of this Court's opinion in *Green* . . . in that his plan "promises realistically to work, and promises realistically to work *now.*" The modifications ordered by the panel of the Court of Appeals, while of course not intended to do so, would, we think, take from the order some of its capacity to expedite, by means of specific commands, the day when a completely unified, unitary, nondiscriminatory school system becomes a reality instead of a hope. . . . We also believe that under all the circumstances of this case we follow the original plan outlined in *Brown II* . . . by accepting the more specific and expeditious order of [District] Judge Johnson. . . .

The principles of *Montgomery* have been properly followed by the District Court and the Court of Appeals in this case.

The construction of new schools and the closing of old ones is one of the most important functions of local school authorities and also one of the most complex. They must decide questions of location and capacity in light of population growth, finances, land values, site availability, through an almost endless list of factors to be considered. The result of this will be a decision which, when combined with one technique or another of student assignment, will determine the racial composition of the student body in each school in the system. Over the long run, the consequences of the choices will be far reaching. People gravitate toward school facilities, just as schools are located in response to the needs of people. The location of schools may thus influence the patterns of residential development of a metropolitan area and have important impact on composition of inner city neighborhoods.

In the past, choices in this respect have been used as a potent weapon for creating or maintaining a state-segregated school system. In addition to the classic pattern of building schools specifically intended for Negro or white students, school authorities have sometimes, since *Brown,* closed schools which appeared likely to become racially mixed through changes in neighborhood residential patterns. This was sometimes accompanied by building new schools in the areas of white suburban expansion farthest from Negro population centers in order to maintain the separation of the races with a minimum departure from the formal principles of "neighborhood zoning." Such a policy does more than simply influence the short-run composition of the student body of a new school. It may well promote segregated residential patterns which, when combined with "neighborhood zoning," further lock the school system into the mold of separation of the races. Upon a proper showing a district court may consider this in fashioning a remedy.

In ascertaining the existence of legally imposed school segregation, the existence of a pattern of school construction and abandonment is thus a factor of great weight. In devising remedies where legally imposed segregation has been established, it is the responsibility of local authorities and district courts to see to it that future school construction and abandonment is not used and does not serve to perpetuate or reestablish the dual system.

When necessary, district courts should retain jurisdiction to assure that these responsibilities are carried out.

## V

The central issue in this case is that of student assignment, and there are essentially four problem areas:

1. to what extent racial balance or racial quotas may be used as an implement in a remedial order to correct a previously segregated system;
2. whether every all-Negro and all-white school must be eliminated as an indispensable part of a remedial process of desegregation;
3. what are the limits, if any, on the rearrangement of school districts and attendance zones, as a remedial measure; and
4. what are the limits, if any, on the use of transportation facilities to correct state-enforced racial school segregation.

## RACIAL BALANCES OR RACIAL QUOTAS

The constant theme and thrust of every holding from *Brown I* to date is that state-enforced separation of races in public schools is discrimination that violates the Equal Protection Clause. The remedy commanded was to dismantle dual school systems.

We are concerned in these cases with the elimination of the discrimination inherent in the dual school systems, not with myriad factors of human existence which can cause discrimination in a multitude of ways on racial, religious, or ethnic grounds. The target of the cases from *Brown I* to the present was the dual school system. The elimination of racial discrimination in public schools is a large task and one that should not be retarded by efforts to achieve broader purposes lying beyond the jurisdiction of school authorities. One vehicle can carry only a limited amount of baggage. It would not serve the important objective of *Brown I* to seek to use school desegregation cases for purposes beyond their scope, although desegregation of schools ultimately will have impact on other forms of discrimination. We do not reach in this case the question whether a showing that school segregation is a consequence of other types of state action, without any discriminatory action by the school authorities, is a constitutional violation requiring remedial action by a school desegregation decree. This case does not present that question and we therefore do not decide it.

Our objective in dealing with the issues presented by these cases is to see that school authorities exclude no pupil of a racial minority from any school, directly or indirectly, on account of race; it does not and cannot embrace all the problems of racial prejudice, even when those problems contribute to disproportionate racial concentrations in some schools.

In this case it is urged that the District Court has imposed a racial balance requirement of 71%–29% on individual schools. The fact that no such objective was actually achieved—and would appear to be impossible—tends to blunt that claim, yet in the opinion and order of the District Court of December 1, 1969, we find that court directing:

> that efforts should be made to reach a 71–29 ratio in the various schools so that there will be no basis for contending that one school is racially different from the others . . . , that no school [should] be operated with an all-black or predominantly black student body, [and] that pupils of all grades [should] be assigned in such a way that as nearly as practicable the various schools at various grade levels have about the same proportion of black and white students.

The District Judge went on to acknowledge that variation "from that norm may be unavoidable." This contains intimations that the "norm" is a fixed mathematical racial balance reflecting the pupil constituency of the system. If we were to read the holding of the District Court to require, as a matter of substantive constitutional right, any particular degree of racial balance or mixing, that approach would be disapproved and we would be obliged to reverse. The constitutional command to desegregate schools does not mean that every school in every community must always reflect the racial composition of the school system as a whole.

As the voluminous record in this case shows, the predicate for the District Court's use of the 71%–29% ratio was twofold: first, its express finding, approved by the Court of Appeals and not challenged here, that a dual school system had been maintained by the school authorities at least until 1969; second, its finding, also approved by the Court of Appeals, that the school board had totally defaulted in its acknowledged duty to come forward with an acceptable plan of its own, notwithstanding the patient efforts of the District Judge who, on at least three ocasions, urged the board to submit plans. As the statement of facts shows, these findings are abundantly supported by the record. It was because of this total failure of the school board that the District Court was obliged to turn to other qualified sources, and Dr. Finger was designated to assist the District Court to do what the board should have done.

We see therefore that the use made of mathematical ratios was no more than a starting point in the process of shaping a remedy, rather than an inflexible requirement. From that starting point the District Court proceeded to frame a decree that was within its discretionary powers, an equitable remedy for the particular circumstances.[1] As we said in *Green*, a school authority's remedial plan or a district court's remedial decree is to be judged by its effectiveness. Awareness of the racial composition of the whole school system is likely to be a useful starting point in shaping a remedy to correct past constitutional violations. In sum, the very limited use made of mathematical ratios was within the equitable remedial discretion of the District Court.

## ONE-RACE SCHOOLS

The record in this case reveals the familiar phenomenon that in metropolitan areas minority groups are often found concentrated in one part of the city. In some circumstances certain schools may remain all or largely of one race until new schools can be provided or neighborhood patterns change. Schools all or predominately of one race in a district of mixed population will require close scrutiny to determine that school assignments are not part of state-enforced segregation.

In light of the above, it should be clear that the existence of some small number of one-race, or virtually one-race, schools within a district is not in and of itself the mark of a system which still practices segregation by law. The district judge or school authorities should make every effort to achieve the greatest possible degree of actual desegregation and will thus necessarily be concerned with the elimination of one-race schools. No *per se* rule can adequately embrace all the difficulties of reconciling the competing interests involved; but in a system with a history of segregation the need for remedial criteria of sufficient specificity to assure a school authority's compliance with its constitutional duty warrants a presumption against schools that are substantially disproportionate in their racial composition. Where the school authority's proposed plan for conversion from a dual to a unitary system contemplates the continued existence of some schools that are all or predominately of one race, they have the burden of showing that such school assignments are genuinely nondiscriminatory. The court should scrutinize such schools, and the burden upon the school authorities will be to satisfy the court that their racial composition is not the result of present or past discriminatory action on their part.

An optional majority-to-minority transfer provision has long been recognized as a useful part of every desegregation plan. Provision for optional transfer of those in the majority racial group of a particular school to other schools where they will be in the minority is an indispensable remedy for those students willing to transfer to other schools in order to lessen the impact on them of the state-imposed stigma of segregation. In order to be effective, such a transfer arrangement must grant the transferring student free transportation and space must be made available in the school to which he desires to move.

## REMEDIAL ALTERING OF ATTENDANCE ZONES

The maps submitted in these cases graphically demonstrate that one of the principal tools employed by school planners and by courts to break up the dual school system has been a frank—and sometimes drastic—gerrymandering of school districts and attendance zones. An additional step was pairing, "clustering," or "grouping" of schools with attendance assignments made deliberately to accomplish the transfer of Negro students out of formerly segregated Negro schools and transfer of white students to formerly all-Negro schools. More often than not, these zones are neither compact [2] nor contiguous; indeed they may be on opposite ends of the city. As an interim corrective measure, this cannot be said to be beyond the broad remedial powers of a court.

Absent a constitutional violation there would be no basis for judicially ordering assignment of students on a racial basis. All things being equal, with no history of discrimination, it might well be desirable to assign pupils to schools nearest their homes. But all things are not equal in a system that has been deliberately constructed and maintained to enforce racial segregation. The remedy for such segregation may be administratively awkward, inconvenient and even bizarre in some situations and may impose burdens on some; but all awkwardness and inconvenience cannot be avoided in the interim period when remedial adjustments are being made to eliminate the dual school systems.

No fixed or even substantially fixed guidelines can be established as to how far a court can go, but it must be recognized that there are limits. The objective is to dismantle the dual school system. "Racially neutral" assignment plans proposed by school authorities to a district court may be inadequate; such plans may fail to counteract the continuing effects of past school segregation resulting from discriminatory location of school sites or distortion of school size in order to achieve or maintain an artificial racial separation. When school authorities present a district court with a "loaded game board," affirmative action in the form of remedial altering of attendance zones is proper to achieve truly non-discriminatory assignments. In short, an assignment plan is not acceptable simply because it appears to be neutral.

In this area, we must of necessity rely to a large extent, as this Court has for more than 16 years, on the informed judgment of the district courts in the first instance and on courts of appeals.

We hold that the pairing and grouping of non-contiguous school zones is a permissible tool and such action is to be considered in light of the objectives sought. . . . Maps do not tell the whole story since non-contiguous school zones may be more accessible to each other in terms of the critical travel time, because of traffic patterns and good highways, than schools geographically closer together. Conditions in different localities will vary so widely that no rigid rules can be laid down to govern all situations.

## TRANSPORTATION OF STUDENTS

The scope of permissible transportation of students as an implement of a remedial decree has never been defined by this Court and by the very nature of the problem it cannot be defined with precision. No rigid guidelines as to student transportation can be

given for application to the infinite variety of problems presented in thousands of situations. Bus transportation has been an
integral part of the public education system for years, and was
perhaps the single most important factor in the transition from
the one-room schoolhouse to the consolidated school. Eighteen
million of the nation's public school children, approximately
39%, were transported to their schools by bus in 1969–1970 in
all parts of the country.

The importance of bus transportation as a normal and accepted
tool of educational policy is readily discernible in this and the
companion case.[3] The Charlotte school authorities did not purport
to assign students on the basis of geographically drawn zones
until 1965 and then they allowed almost unlimited transfer privi-
leges. The District Court's conclusion that assignment of children
to the school nearest their home serving their grade would not
produce an effective dismantling of the dual system is supported
by the record.

Thus the remedial techniques used in the District Court's order
were within that court's power to provide equitable relief; implementation of the decree is well within the capacity of the school
authority.

The decree provided that the buses used to implement the plan
would operate on direct routes. Students would be picked up at
schools near their homes and transported to the schools they
were to attend. The trips for elementary school pupils average
about seven miles and the District Court found that they would
take "not over 35 minutes at the most."[4] This system compares
favorably with the transportation plan previously operated in
Charlotte under which each day 23,600 students on all grade
levels were transported an average of 15 miles one way for an
average trip requiring over an hour. In these circumstances, we
find no basis for holding that the local school authorities may not
be required to employ bus transportation as one tool of school
desegregation. Desegregation plans cannot be limited to the
walk-in school.

An objection to transportation of students may have validity
when the time or distance of travel is so great as to risk either
the health of the children or significantly impinge on the educational process. . . . It hardly needs stating that the limits on time
of travel will vary with many factors, but probably with none
more than the age of the students. The reconciliation of competing

values in a desegregation case is, of course, a difficult task with many sensitive facets but fundamentally no more so than remedial measures courts of equity have traditionally employed.

## VI

The Court of Appeals, searching for a term to define the equitable remedial power of the district courts, used the term "reasonableness." In *Green, supra,* this Court used the term "feasible" and by implication, "workable," "effective," and "realistic" in the mandate to develop "a plan that promises realistically to work, and . . . to work *now."* On the facts of this case, we are unable to conclude that the order of the District Court is not reasonable, feasible and workable. However, in seeking to define the scope of remedial power or the limits on remedial power of courts in an area as sensitive as we deal with here, words are poor instruments to convey the sense of basic fairness inherent in equity. Substance, not semantics, must govern, and we have sought to suggest the nature of limitations without frustrating the appropriate scope of equity.

At some point, these school authorities and others like them should have achieved full compliance with this Court's decision in *Brown I.* The systems will then be "unitary" in the sense required by our decisions in *Green* and *Alexander.*

It does not follow that the communities served by such systems will remain demographically stable, for in a growing, mobile society, few will do so. Neither school authorities nor district courts are constitutionally required to make year-by-year adjustments of the racial composition of student bodies once the affirmative duty to desegregate has been accomplished and racial discrimination through official action is eliminated from the system. This does not mean that federal courts are without power to deal with future problems; but in the absence of a showing that either the school authorities or some other agency of the State has deliberately attempted to fix or alter demographic patterns to affect the racial composition of the schools, further intervention by a district court should not be necessary.

For the reasons herein set forth, the judgment of the Court of Appeals is affirmed as to those parts in which it affirmed the judgment of the District Court. The order of the District Court dated August 7, 1970, is also affirmed.

## REFERENCES

1. In his August 3, 1970, memorandum holding that the District Court plan was "reasonable" under the standard laid down by the Fourth Circuit on appeal, the District Court explained the approach taken as follows: "This court has not ruled, and does not rule that 'racial balance' is required under the Constitution; nor that all black schools in all cities are unlawful; nor that all school boards must bus children or violate the Constitution; *nor that the particular order entered in this case would be correct in other circumstances not before this court.*"

2. We said in *Green, supra,* at 439: "The obligation of the district courts, as it always has been, is to assess the effectiveness of a proposed plan in achieving desegregation. There is no universal answer to complex problems of desegregation; there is obviously no one plan that will do the job in every case. The matter must be assessed in light of the circumstances present and the options available in each instance."

3. During 1967–1968, for example, the Mobile board used 207 buses to transport 22,094 students daily for an average round trip of 31 miles. During 1966–1967, 7,116 students in the metropolitan area were bused daily. In Charlotte-Mecklenburg, the system as a whole, without regard to desegregation plans, planned to bus approximately 23,000 students this year, for an average daily round trip of 15 miles. More elementary school children than high school children were to be bused, and four- and five-year-olds travel the longest routes in the system.

4. The District Court found that the school system would have to employ 138 more buses than it had previously operated. But 105 of those buses were already available and the others could easily be obtained. Additionally, it should be noted that North Carolina requires provision of transportation for all students who are assigned to schools more than one and one-half miles from their homes.

*Was the Supreme Court prepared to apply the remedies and logic of Swann to the North? In Keyes v. Denver School District No. 1 the Court answered yes. It also ruled that de jure segregation in a "meaningful portion of a school system" contaminated the whole system and could only be treated with a plan that reached all the schools in that system.*

# Keyes v. Denver
# School District No. 1

## (JUNE 21, 1973)

Mr. Justice Brennan delivered the opinion of the Court.

This school desegregation case concerns the Denver, Colorado, school system. That system has never been operated under a constitutional or statutory provision that mandated or permitted racial segregation in public education.[1] Rather, the gravamen of this action, brought in June 1969 in the District Court for the District of Colorado by parents of Denver school children, is that respondent School Board alone, by use of various techniques such as the manipulation of student attendance zones, school site selection and a neighborhood school policy, created or maintained racially or ethnically (or both racially and ethnically) segregated schools throughout the school district, entitling petitioners to a decree directing desegregation of the entire school district.

The boundaries of the school district are co-terminus with the boundaries of the City and County of Denver. There were in 1969 119 schools with 96,580 pupils in the school system. In early 1969, the respondent School Board adopted three resolutions . . . designed to desegregate the schools in the Park Hill area in the northeast portion of the city. Following an election which produced a Board majority opposed to the resolutions, the resolutions were rescinded and replaced with a voluntary student transfer program. Petitioners then filed this action, requesting an injunction against the rescission of the resolutions and an order directing that the respondent School Board desegregate and afford equal educational opportunity "for the School district as a whole." The District Court found that by the construction of a new, relatively small elementary school, Barrett, in the middle of the Negro community west of Park Hill, by the gerrymandering of student attendance zones, by the use of so-called "optional zones," and by the excessive use of mobile classroom units, among other things, the respondent School Board had engaged over almost a decade after 1960 in an unconstitutional policy of deliberate racial segregation with respect to the Park Hill schools. The court therefore ordered the Board to desegregate those schools through the implementation of the three rescinded resolutions.

Segregation in Denver schools is not limited, however, to the schools in the Park Hill area, and not satisfied with their success in obtaining relief for Park Hill, petitioners pressed their prayer that the District Court order desegregation of all segregated schools in the city of Denver, particularly the heavily segregated schools in the core city area. But that court concluded that its finding of a purposeful and systematic program of racial segregation affecting thousands of students in the Park Hill area did not, in itself, impose on the School Board an affirmative duty to eliminate segregation throughout the school district. Instead, the court fractionated the district and held that petitioners must make a fresh showing of de jure segregation in each area of the city for which they seek relief. Moreover, the District Court held that its finding of intentional segregation in Park Hill was not in any sense material to the question of segregative intent in other areas of the city. Under this restrictive approach, the District Court concluded that petitioners' evidence of intentionally discriminatory School Board action in areas of the district other than Park Hill was insufficient to "dictate the conclusion that this is de jure segregation which calls for an all-out effort to desegregate. It is more like de facto segregation, with respect to which the rule is that the court cannot order desegregation in order to provide a better balance."

Nevertheless, the District Court went on to hold that the proofs established that the segregated core city schools were educationally inferior to the predominantly "white" or "Anglo" schools in other parts of the district—that is "separate facilities . . . unequal in the quality of education provided." Thus, the court held that, under the doctrine of *Plessy v. Ferguson* (1896), respondent School Board constitutionally "must at a minimum . . . offer an equal educational opportunity," and, therefore, although all-out desegregation "could not be decreed, . . . the only feasible and constitutionally acceptable program—the only program which furnishes anything approaching substantial equality—is a system of desegregation and integration which provides compensatory education in an integrated environment." The District Court then formulated a varied remedial plan to that end which was incorporated in the Final Decree.

Respondent School Board appealed, and petitioners cross-appealed, to the Court of Appeals for the Tenth Circuit. That court sustained the District Court's finding that the Board engaged in an unconstitutional policy of deliberate racial segregation with respect to the Park Hill schools and affirmed the Final Decree in that respect. As to the core city schools, however, the Court of Appeals reversed the legal determination of the District Court that those schools were maintained in violation of the Fourteenth Amendment because of the unequal educational opportunity afforded, and therefore set aside so much of the Final Decree as required desegregation and educational improvement programs for those schools. In reaching that result, the Court of Appeals also disregarded respondent School Board's deliberate racial segregation policy respecting the Park Hill schools and accepted the District Court's finding that petitioners had not proved that respondent had a like policy addressed specifically to the core city schools.

We granted petitioners' petition for certiorari to review the Court of Appeals' judgment insofar as it reversed that part of the District Court's Final Decree as pertained to the core city schools. The judgment of the Court of Appeals in that respect is modified to vacate instead of reverse the Final Decree. The respondent School Board has cross-petitioned for certiorari to review the judgment of the Court of Appeals insofar as it affirmed that part of the District Court's Final Decree as pertained to the Park Hill schools. The cross-petition is denied.

# I

Before turning to the primary question we decide today, a word must be said about the District Court's method of defining a "segregated" school. Denver is a tri-ethnic, as distinguished from a bi-racial, community. The overall racial and ethnic composition of the Denver public schools is 66% Anglo, 14% Negro and 20% Hispano.[2] The District Court, in assessing the question of *de jure* segregation in the core city schools, preliminarily resolved that Negroes and Hispanos should not be placed in the same category to establish the segregated character of a school. Later, in determining the schools that were likely to produce an inferior educational opportunity, the court concluded that a school would be considered inferior only if it had "a concentration of either Negro or Hispano students in the general area of 70 to 75 percent." We intimate no opinion whether the District Court's 70% to 75% requirement was correct. The District Court used those figures to signify educationally inferior schools, and there is no suggestion in the record that those same figures were or would be used to define a "segregated" school in the *de jure* context. What is or is not a segregated school will necessarily depend on the facts of each particular case. In addition to the racial and ethnic composition of a school's student body, other factors such as the racial and ethnic composition of faculty and staff and the community and administration attitudes toward the school must be taken into consideration. The District Court has recognized these specific factors as elements of the definition of a "segregated" school, and we may therefore infer that the court will consider them again on remand.

We conclude, however, that the District Court erred in separating Negroes and Hispanos for purposes of defining a "segregated" school. We have held that Hispanos constitute an identifiable class for purposes of the Fourteenth Amendment. . . . Indeed the District Court recognized this in classifying predominantly Hispano schools as "segregated" schools in their own right. But there is also much evidence that in the Southwest Hispanos and Negroes have a great many things in common. The United States Commission on Civil Rights has recently published two Reports on Hispano education in the Southwest. Focusing on students in the States of Arizona, California, Colorado, New Mexico, and Texas, the Commission concluded that Hispanos suffer from the same educational inequities as Negroes and American Indians. In fact, the District Court itself recognized that "One of the things which the Hispano has in common with the Negro is economic and cultural deprivation and discrimination." This is agreement that, though of different origins, Negroes and Hispanos in Denver suffer identical discrimination in treatment when compared with the treatment afforded Anglo students. In that circumstance, we think petitioners are entitled to have schools with a combined predominance of Negroes and Hispanos included in the category of "segregated" schools.

## II

In our view, the only other question that requires our decision at this time is that subsumed in Question 2 of the Questions Presented by petitioners, namely, whether the District Court and the Court of Appeals applied an incorrect legal standard in addressing Petitioners' contention that respondent School Board engaged in an unconstitutional policy of deliberate segregation in the core city schools. Our conclusion is that those courts did not apply the correct standard in addressing that contention.

Petitioners apparently concede for the purposes of this case that in the case of a school system like Denver's, where no statutory dual system has ever existed, plaintiffs must prove not only that segregated schooling exists but also that it was brought about or maintained by intentional state action. Petitioners proved that for almost a decade after 1960 respondent School Board had engaged in an unconstitutional policy of deliberate racial segregation in the Park Hill schools. Indeed, the District Court found that "[b]etween 1960 and 1969 the Board's policies with respect to those northeast Denver schools show an undeviating purpose to isolate Negro students" in segregated schools "while preserving the Anglo character of [other] schools." This finding did not relate to an insubstantial or trivial fragment of the school system. On the contrary, respondent School Board was found guilty of following a deliberate segregation policy at schools attended, in 1969, by 37.69% of Denver's total Negro school population, including one-fourth of the Negro elementary pupils, over two-thirds of the Negro junior high pupils, and over two-fifths of the Negro high school pupils. In addition, there was uncontroverted evidence that teachers and staff had for years been assigned on a minority teacher-to-minority school basis throughout the school system. Respondent argues, however, that a finding of state-imposed segregation as to a substantial portion of the school system can be viewed in isolation from the rest of the district, and that even if state-imposed segregation does exist in a substantial part of the Denver school system, it does not follow that the District Court could predicate on that fact a finding that the entire school system is a dual system. We do not agree. We have never suggested that plaintiffs in school desegregation cases must bear the burden of proving the elements of de jure segregation as to each and every school or each and every student within the school system. Rather, we have held that where plaintiffs prove that a current condition of segregated schooling exists within a school district where a dual system was compelled or authorized by statute at the time of our decision in Brown v. Board of Education (Brown I), the State automatically assumes an affirmative duty "to effectuate a transition to a racially nondiscriminatory school system," Brown v. Board of Education (Brown II), see also Green v. County School Board, that is, to eliminate from the public schools within their school system "all vestiges of state-imposed segregation." Swann v. Charlotte-Mecklenburg Board of Education.

This is not a case, however, where a statutory dual system has ever existed. Nevertheless, where plaintiffs prove that the school authorities have carried out a systematic program of segregation affecting a substantial portion of the students, schools, teachers and facilities within the school system, it is only common sense to conclude that there exists a predicate for a finding of the existence of a dual school system. Several considerations support this conclusion. First, it is obvious that a practice of concentrating Negroes in certain schools by structuring attendance zones or designating "feeder" schools on the basis of race has the reciprocal effect of keeping other nearby schools predominantly white. Similarly, the practice of building a school—such as the Barrett Elementary School in this case—to a certain size and in a certain location, "with conscious knowledge that it would be a segregated school," has a substantial reciprocal effect on the racial composition of other nearby schools. So also, the use of mobile classrooms, the drafting of student transfer policies, the transportation of students, and the assignment of faculty and staff, on racially identifiable bases, have the clear effect of earmarking schools according to their racial composition, and this, in turn, together with the elements of student assignment and school construction, may have a profound reciprocal effect on the racial composition of residential neighborhoods within a metropolitan area, thereby causing further racial concentration within the schools. We recognized this in *Swann* when we said:

> They [school authorities] must decide questions of location and capacity in light of population growth, finances, land values, site availability, through an almost endless list of factors to be considered. The result of this will be a decision which, when combined with one technique or another of student assignment, will determine the racial composition of the student body in each school in the system. Over the long run, the consequences of the choices will be far reaching. People gravitate toward school facilities, just as schools are located in response to the needs of people. The location of schools may thus influence the patterns of residential development of a metropolitan area and have important impact on composition of inner-city neighborhoods.
>
> In the past, choices in this respect have been used as a potent weapon for creating or maintaining a state-segregated school system. In addition to the classic pattern of building schools specifically intended for Negro or white students, school authorities have sometimes, since *Brown,* closed schools which appeared likely to become racially mixed through changes in neighborhood residential patterns. This was sometimes accompanied by building new schools in the areas of white suburban expansion farthest from Negro population centers in order to maintain the separation of the races with a minimum departure from the formal principles of "neighborhood zoning." Such a policy does more than simply influence the short-run composition of the student body of a new school. It may well promote segregated residential patterns which, when combined with "neighborhood zoning," further lock the school system into the mold of separation of races. Upon a proper showing a district court may consider this in fashioning a remedy.

In short, common sense dictates the conclusion that racially inspired school board actions have an impact beyond the particular schools that are the subjects of those actions. This is not to say, of course, that there can never be a case in which the geographical structure of or the natural boundaries within a school district may have the effect of dividing the district into separate, identifiable and unrelated units. Such a determination is essentially a question of fact to be resolved by the trial court in the first instance, but such cases must be rare. In the absence of such a determination, proof of state-imposed segregation in a substantial portion of the district will suffice to support a finding by the trial court of the existence of a dual system. Of course, where that finding is made, as in cases involving statutory dual systems, the school authorities have an affirmative duty "to effectuate a transition to a racially nondiscriminatory school system." (*Brown II.*)

On remand, therefore, the District Court should decide in the first instance whether respondent School Board's deliberate racial segregation policy with respect to the Park Hill schools constitutes the entire Denver school system a dual school system. We observe that on the record now before us there is indication that Denver is not a school district which might be divided into separate, identifiable and unrelated units. The District Court stated, in its summary of findings as to the Park Hill schools, that there was "a high degree of interrelationship among these schools, so that any action by the Board affecting the racial composition of one would almost certainly have an effect on the others." And there was cogent evidence that the ultimate effect of the Board's actions in Park Hill was not limited to that area: the three 1969 resolutions designed to desegregate the Park Hill schools changed the attendance patterns of at least 29 schools attended by almost one-third of the pupils in the Denver school system. This suggests that the official segregation in Park Hill affected the racial composition of schools throughout the district.

On the other hand, although the District Court did not state this or indeed any reason why the Park Hill finding was disregarded when attention was turned to the core city schools—beyond saying that the Park Hill and core city areas were in its view "different"—the areas, although adjacent to each other, are separated by Colorado Boulevard, a six-lane highway. From the record, it is difficult to assess the actual significance of Colorado Boulevard to the Denver school system. The Boulevard runs the length of the school district, but at least two elementary schools, Teller and Steck, have attendance zones which cross the Boulevard. Moreover, the District Court, although referring to the Boulevard as "a natural dividing line," did not feel constrained to limit its consideration of *de jure* segregation in the Park Hill area to those schools east of the Boulevard. The court found that by building Barrett Elementary School west of the Boulevard and by establishing Colorado Boulevard as the eastern boundary of the Barrett attendance zone, the Board was able to maintain for a number of years the Anglo character of the Park Hill schools. This suggests that Colorado Boulevard is not to be regarded as the type of barrier that of itself could confine the impact of the Board's actions to an identifiable area of the school district, perhaps because a major highway is generally not such an effective buffer between adjoining areas. But this is a factual question for resolution by the District Court on remand. In any event, inquiry whether the District Court and the Court of Appeals applied the correct legal standards in addressing petitioners' contention of deliberate segregation in the core city schools is not at an end even if it be true that Park Hill may be separated from the rest of the Denver school district as a separate, identifiable and unrelated unit.

## III

The District Court proceeded on the premise that the finding as to the Park Hill schools was irrelevant to the consideration of the rest of the district, and began its examination of the core city schools by requiring that petitioners prove all of the essential elements of *de jure* segregation—that is, stated simply, a current condition of segregation resulting from intentional state action directed specifically to the core city schools. The segregated character of the core city schools could not be and is not denied. Petitioners' proof showed that at the time of trial 22 of the schools in the core city area were less than 30% in Anglo enrollment and 11 of the schools were less than 10% Anglo. Petitioners also introduced substantial evidence demonstrating the existence of a disproportionate racial and ethnic composition of faculty and staff at these schools.

On the question of segregative intent, petitioners presented evidence tending to show that the Board, through its actions over a period of years, intentionally created and maintained the segregated character of the core city schools. Respondents countered this evidence by arguing that the segregation in these schools is the result of a racially neutral "neighborhood school policy" and that the acts of which petitioners complain are explicable within the bounds of that policy. Accepting the School Board's explanation, the District Court and the Court of Appeals agreed that a finding of *de jure* segregation as to the core city schools was not permissible since petitioners had failed to prove "(1) a racially discriminatory purpose and (2) a causal relationship between the acts complained of and the racial imbalance admittedly existing in those schools." This assessment of petitioners' proof was clearly incorrect.

Although petitioners had already proved the existence of intentional school segregation in the Park Hill schools, this crucial finding was totally ignored when attention turned to the core city schools. Plainly, a finding of intentional segregation as to a portion of a school system is not devoid of probative value in assessing the school authorities' intent with respect to other parts of the same school system. On the contrary, where, as here, the case involves one school board, a finding of intentional segregation on its part in one portion of a school system is highly relevant to the issue of the board's intent with respect to other segregated schools in the system. This is merely an application of the well-settled evidentiary principle that "the prior doing of other similar acts, whether clearly a part of a scheme or not, is useful as reducing the possibility that the act in question was done with innocent intent." . . .

Applying these principles in the special context of school desegregation cases, we hold that a finding of intentionally segregative school board actions in a meaningful portion of a school system, as in this case, creates a presumption that other segregated schooling within the system is not adventitious. It establishes, in other words, a prima facie case of unlawful segregative design on the part of school authorities, and shifts to those authorities the burden of proving that other segregated schools within the system are not also the result of intentionally segregative actions. This is true even if it is determined that different areas of the school district should be viewed independently of each other because, even in that situation, there is high probability that where school authorities have effectuated an intentionally segregative policy in a meaningful portion of the school system, similar impermissible considerations have motivated their actions in other areas of the system. We emphasize that the differentiating factor between *de jure* segregation and so-called *de facto* segregation to which we referred in *Swann* is *purpose* or *intent* to segregate. Where school authorities have been found to have practiced purposeful segregation in part of a school system, they may be expected to oppose system-wide desegregation, as did the respondents in this case, on the ground that their purposefully segregative actions were isolated and individual events, thus leaving plaintiffs with the burden of proving otherwise. But at that point where an intentionally segregative policy is practiced in a meaningful or significant segment of a school system, as in this case, the school authorities can not be heard to argue that plaintiffs have proved only "isolated and individual" unlawful segregative actions. In that circumstance, it is both fair and reasonable to require that the school authorities bear the burden of showing that their actions as to other segregated schools within the system were not also motivated by segregative intent.

This burden-shifting principle is not new or novel. There are no hard and fast standards governing the allocation of the burden of proof in every situation. The issue, rather, "is merely a question of policy and fairness based on experience in the different situations." In the context of racial segregation in public education, the courts, including this Court, have recognized a variety of situations in which "fairness" and "policy" require state authorities to bear the burden of explaining actions or conditions which appear to be racially motivated. Thus, in *Swann,* we observed that in a system with a "history of segregation," "where it is possible to identify a 'white school' or a 'Negro school' simply by reference to the racial composition of teachers and staff, the quality of school buildings and equipment, or the organization of sport activities, a *prima facie* case of violation of substantive constitutional rights under the Equal Protection Clause is shown." Again, in a school system with a history of segregation, the discharge of a disproportionately large number of Negro teachers incident to desegregation "thrust[s] upon the School Board the burden of justifying its conduct by clear and convincing evidence." . . . Indeed, to say that a system has a "history of segregation" is merely to say that a pattern of intentional segregation has been established in the past. Thus, be it a statutory dual system or an allegedly unitary system where a meaningful portion of the system is found to be intentionally segregated, the existence of subsequent or other segregated schooling within the same system justifies a rule imposing on the school authorities the burden of proving that this segregated schooling is not also the result of intentionally segregative acts.

In discharging that burden, it is not enough, of course, that the school authorities rely upon some allegedly logical, racially neutral explanation for their actions. Their burden is to adduce proof sufficient to support a finding that segregative intent was not among the factors that motivated their actions. The courts below attributed much significance to the fact that many of the Board's actions in the core city area antedated our decision in *Brown*. We reject any suggestion that remoteness in time has any relevance to the issue of intent. If the actions of school authorities were to any degree motivated by segregative intent and the segregation resulting from those actions continues to exist, the fact of remoteness in time certainly does not make those actions any less "intentional."

This is not to say, however, that the prima facie case may not be met by evidence supporting a finding that a lesser degree of segregated schooling in the core city area would not have resulted even if the Board had not acted as it did. In *Swann*, we suggested that at some point in time the relationship between past segregative acts and present segregation may become so attenuated as to be incapable of supporting a finding of *de jure* segregation warranting judicial intervention. . . . We made it clear, however, that a connection between past segregative acts and present segregation may be present even when not apparent and that close examination is required before concluding that the connection does not exist. Intentional school segregation in the past may have been a factor in creating a natural environment for the growth of further segregation. Thus, if respondent School Board cannot disprove segregative intent, it can rebut the prima facie case only by showing that its past segregative acts did not create or contribute to the current segregated condition of the core city schools.

The respondent School Board invoked at trial its "neighborhood school policy" as explaining racial and ethnic concentrations within the core city schools, arguing that since the core city area population had long been Negro and Hispano, the concentrations were necessarily the result of residential patterns and not of purposefully segregative policies. We have no occasion to consider in this case whether a "neighborhood school policy" of itself will justify racial or ethnic concentrations in the absence of a finding that school authorities have committed acts constituting *de jure* segregation. It is enough that we hold that the mere assertion of such a policy is not dispositive where, as in this case, the school authorities have been found to have practiced *de jure* segregation in a meaningful portion of the school system by techniques that indicate that the "neighborhood school" concept has not been maintained free of manipulation. Our observations in *Swann* are particularly instructive on this score:

> Absent a constitutional violation there would be no basis for judicially ordering assignment of students on a racial basis. All things being equal, with no history of discrimination, it might well be desirable to assign pupils to schools nearest their homes. But all things are not equal in a system that has been deliberately constructed and maintained to enforce racial segregation. . . . "Racially neutral" assignment plans proposed by school authorities to a district court may be inadequate; such plans may fail to counteract the continuing effects of past school segregation resulting from discriminatory location of school sites or distortion of school size in order to achieve or maintain an artificial racial separation. When school authorities present a district court with a "loaded game board," affirmative action in the form of remedial altering of attendance zones is proper to achieve truly nondiscriminatory assignments. In short, an assignment plan is not acceptable simply because it appears to be neutral.

Thus, respondent School Board having been found to have practiced deliberate racial segregation in schools attended by over one-third of the Negro school population, that crucial finding establishes a prima facie case of intentional segregation in the core city schools. In such case, respondent's neighborhood school policy is not to be determinative "simply because it appears to be neutral."

## IV

In summary, the District Court on remand, *first,* will afford respondent School Board the opportunity to prove its contention that the Park Hill area is a separate, identifiable and unrelated section of the school district that should be treated as isolated from the rest of the district. If respondent School Board fails to prove that contention, the District Court, *second,* will determine whether respondent School Board's conduct over almost a decade after 1960 in carrying out a policy of deliberate racial segregation in the Park Hill schools constitutes the entire school system a dual school system. If the District Court determines that the Denver school system is a dual school system, respondent School

Board has the affirmative duty to desegregate the entire system "root and branch" *(Green v. County School Board).* If the District Court determines, however, that the Denver school system is not a dual school system by reason of the Board's actions in Park Hill, the court, *third,* will afford respondent School Board the opportunity to rebut petitioners' prima facie case of intentional segregation in the core city schools raised by the finding of intentional segregation in the Park Hill schools. There, the Board's burden is to show that its policies and practices with respect to school site location, school size, school renovations and additions, student attendance zones, student assignment and transfer options, mobile classroom units, transportation of students, assignment of faculty and staff, etc., considered together and premised on the Board's so-called "neighborhood school" concept, either were not taken in effectuation of a policy to create or maintain segregation in the core city schools, or, if unsuccessful in that effort, were not factors in causing the existing condition of segregation in these schools. Considerations of "fairness" and "policy" demand no less in light of the Board's intentionally segregative actions. If respondent Board fails to rebut petitioners' prima facie case, the District Court must, as in the case of Park Hill, decree all-out desegregation of the core city schools.

The judgment of the Court of Appeals is modified to vacate instead of reverse the parts of the Final Decree that concern the core city schools, and the case is remanded to the District Court for further proceedings consistent with this opinion.

## REFERENCES

1. To the contrary, Art. IX, § 8, of the Colorado Constitution expressly prohibits "any classification of pupils . . . on account of race or color." As early as 1927, the Colorado Supreme Court held that a Denver practice of excluding black students from school programs at Manual High School and Morey Junior High School violated state law.

2. The parties have used the terms "Anglo," "Negro," and "Hispano" throughout the record. We shall therefore use those terms.

"Hispano" is the term used by the Colorado Department of Education to refer to a person of Spanish, Mexican, or Cuban heritage.

*In Milliken v. Bradley the Supreme Court finally put a limit on the transportation remedies it had sanctioned in Swann and the contamination theory it had developed in Keyes. It ruled that the de jure segregation it found within the city of Detroit could not be remedied with a metropolitan busing plan even though it held the state was in part responsible for the segregation. For the North, it was the equivalent of saying that most white suburbs with their own school systems would be immune from busing.*

# Milliken v. Bradley

(JULY 25, 1974)

Mr. Chief Justice Burger delivered the opinion of the Court.

We granted certiorari in these consolidated cases to determine whether a federal court may impose a multidistrict, areawide remedy to a single district de jure segregation problem absent any finding that the other included school districts have failed to operate unitary school systems within their districts, absent any claim or finding that the boundary lines of any affected school district were established with the purpose of fostering racial segregation in public schools, absent any finding that the included districts committed acts which effected segregation within the other districts, and absent a meaningful opportunity for the included neighboring school districts to present evidence or be heard on the propriety of a multidistrict remedy or on the question of constitutional violations by those neighboring districts.

## I

The action was commenced in August of 1970 by the respondents, the Detroit Branch of the National Association for the Advancement of Colored People and individual parents and students, on behalf of a class later defined by order of the United States District Court, ED Michigan, dated February 16, 1971, to include "all school children of the City of Detroit and all Detroit resident parents who have children of school age." The named defendants in the District Court included the Governor of Michigan, the Attorney General, the State Board of Education, the State Superintendent of Public Instruction, and the Board of Education of the city of Detroit, its members and its former superintendent of schools. The State of Michigan as such is not a party to this litigation and references to the State must be read as references to the public officials, State and local, through whom the State is alleged to have acted. In their complaint respondents attacked the constitutionality of a statute of the State of Michigan known as Act 48 of the 1970 Legislature on the ground that it put the State of Michigan in the position of unconstitutionally interfering with the execution and operation of a voluntary plan of partial high school desegregation, known as the April 7, 1970 Plan, which had been adopted by the Detroit Board of Education to be effective beginning with the fall 1970 semester. The complaint also alleged that the Detroit Public School System was and is segregated on the basis of race as a result of the official policies and actions of the defendants and their predecessors in office, and called for the implementation of a plan that would eliminate "the racial identity of every school in the [Detroit] system and . . . maintain now and hereafter a unitary non-racial school system."

Initially the matter was tried on respondents' motion for preliminary injunction to restrain the enforcement of Act 48 so as to permit the April 7 Plan to be implemented. On that issue, the District Court ruled that respondents were not entitled to a preliminary injunction since at that stage there was no proof that Detroit had a dual segregated school system. On appeal, the Court of Appeals found that the "implementation of the April 7 Plan was [unconstitutionally] thwarted by state action in the form of the Act of the Legislature of Michigan," . . . and that such action could not be interposed to delay, obstruct, or nullify steps lawfully taken for the purpose of protecting rights guaranteed by the Fourteenth Amendment. The case was remanded to the District Court for an expedited trial on the merits.

On remand the respondents moved for immediate implementation of the April 7 Plan in order to remedy the deprivation of the claimed constitutional rights. In response the School Board suggested two other plans, along with the April 7 Plan, and urged that top priority be assigned to the so-called "Magnet Plan" which was "designed to attract children to a school because of its superior curriculum." The District Court approved the Board's Magnet Plan, and respondents again appealed to the Court of Appeals moving for summary reversal. The Court of Appeals refused to pass on the merits of the Magnet Plan and ruled that the District Court had not abused its discretion in refusing to adopt the April 7 Plan without an evidentiary hearing. The case was again remanded with instructions to proceed immediately to a trial on the merits of respondents' substantive allegations concerning the Detroit School System.

The trial of the issue of segregation in the Detroit school system began on April 6, 1971, and continued through July 22, 1971, consuming some 41 trial days. On September 27, 1971, the District Court issued its findings and conclusions on the issue of segregation finding that "Government actions and inaction at all levels, federal, state and local, have combined, with those of private organizations, such as loaning institutions and real estate associations and brokerage firms, to establish and to maintain the pattern of residential segregation throughout the Detroit metropolitan area." While still addressing a Detroit-only violation, the District Court reasoned:

> While it would be unfair to charge the present defendants with what other governmental officers or agencies have done, it can be said that the actions or the failure to act by the responsible school authorities, both city and state, were linked to that of these other governmental units. When we speak of governmental action we should not view the different agencies as a collection of unrelated units. Perhaps the most that can be said is that all of them, including the school authorities, are, in part, responsible for the segregated condition which exists. And we note that just as there is an interaction between residential patterns and the racial composition of the schools, so there is a corresponding effect on the residential pattern by the racial composition of the schools.

The District Court found that the Detroit Board of Education created and maintained optional attendance zones [1] within Detroit neighborhoods undergoing racial transition and between high school attendance areas of opposite predominant racial compositions. These zones, the court found, had the "natural, probable, foreseeable and actual effect" of allowing White pupils to escape identifiably Negro schools. Similarly, the District Court found that Detroit school attendance zones had been drawn along north-south boundary lines despite the Detroit Board's awareness that drawing boundary lines in an east-west direction would result in significantly greater desegregation. Again, the District Court concluded, the natural and actual effect of these acts was the creation and perpetuation of school segregation within Detroit.

The District Court found that in the operation of its school transportation program, which was designed to relieve overcrowding, the Detroit Board had admittedly bused Negro Detroit pupils to predominantly Negro schools which were beyond or away from closer White schools with available space.[2] This practice was found to have continued in recent years despite the Detroit Board's avowed policy, adopted in 1967, of utilizing transportation to increase desegregation:

> With one exception (necessitated by the burning of a white school), defendant Board has never bused white children to predominantly black schools. The Board has not bused white pupils to black schools despite the enormous amount of space available in inner-city schools. There were 22,961 vacant seats in schools 90% or more black.

With respect to the Detroit Board of Education's practices in school construction, the District Court found that Detroit school construction generally tended to have segregative effect with the great majority of schools being built in either overwhelmingly all Negro or all White neighborhoods so that the new schools opened as predominantly one race schools. Thus, of the 14 schools which opened for use in 1970–1971, 11 opened over 90% Negro and one opened less than 10% Negro.

The District Court also found that the State of Michigan had committed several constitutional violations with respect to the exercise of its general responsibility for, and supervision of, public education.[3] The State, for example, was found to have failed, until the 1971 Session of the Michigan Legislature, to provide authorization or funds for the transportation of pupils within Detroit regardless of their poverty or distance from the school to which they were assigned; during this same period the State provided many neighboring, mostly White, suburban districts the full range of state supported transportation.

The District Court found that the State, through Act 48, acted to "impede, delay and minimize racial integration in Detroit schools." The first sentence of § 12 of Act 48 was designed to delay the April 7, 1970, desegregation plan originally adopted by the Detroit Board. The remainder of § 12 sought to prescribe for each school in the eight districts criterion of "free choice" and "neighborhood schools," which, the District Court found, "had as their purpose and effect the maintenance of segregation."

The District Court also held that the acts of the Detroit Board of Education, as a subordinate entity of the State, were attributable to the State of Michigan thus creating a vicarious liability on the part of the State. Under Michigan law, Mich. Stat. Ann. § 15, 1961, for example, school building construction plans had to be approved by the State Board of Education, and prior to 1962, the State Board had specific statutory authority to supervise school site selection. The proofs concerning the effect of Detroit's school construction program were, therefore, found to be largely applicable to show State responsibility for the segregative results.

Turning to the question of an appropriate remedy for these several constitutional violations, the District Court deferred a pending motion by intervening parent defendants to join as additional parties defendant some 85 school districts in the three counties surrounding Detroit on the ground that effective relief could not be achieved without their presence. The District Court concluded that this motion to intervene was "premature," since it "has to do with relief" and no reasonably specific desegregation plan was before the court. Accordingly, the District Court proceeded to order the Detroit Board of Education to submit desegregation plans limited to the segregation problems found to be existing within the city of Detroit. At the same time, however, the state defendants were directed to submit desegregation plans encompassing the three-county metropolitan area despite the fact that the school districts of these three counties were not parties to the action and despite the fact that there had been no claim that these outlying counties, encompassing some 85 separate school districts, had committed constitutional violations.[4] An effort to appeal these orders to the Court of Appeals was dismissed on the ground that the orders were not appealable.

The sequence of the ensuing actions and orders of the District Court are significant factors and will therefore be catalogued in some detail.

Following the District Court's abrupt announcement that it planned to consider the implementation of a multidistrict, metropolitan area remedy to the segregation problems identified within the city of Detroit, the District Court was again requested to grant the outlying school districts intervention as of right on the ground that the District Court's new request for multidistrict plans "may, as a practical matter, impair or impede [the intervenor's] ability to protect" the welfare of their students. The District Court took the motions to intervene under advisement pending submission of the requested desegregation plans by Detroit and the state officials. On March 7, 1972, the District Court notified all parties and the petitioner school districts seeking intervention, that March 14, 1972, was the deadline for submission of recommendations for conditions of intervention and the date of the commencement of hearings on Detroit-only desegregation plans. On the second day of the scheduled hearings, March 15, 1972, the District Court granted the motions of the intervenor school districts subject, *inter alia*, to the following conditions:

> 1. No intervenor will be permitted to assert any claim or defense previously adjudicated by the court.
> 2. No intervenor shall reopen any question or issue which has previously been decided by the court.
>
> .  .  .  .  .  .
>
> 7. New intervenors are granted intervention for two principal purposes: (a) To advise the court, by brief, of the legal propriety or impropriety of considering a metropolitan plan; (b) To review any plan or plans for the desegregation of the so-called larger Detroit Metropolitan area, and submitting objections, modifications or alternatives to it or them, and in accordance with the requirements of the United States Constitution and the prior orders of this court.

Upon granting the motion to intervene, on March 15, 1972, the District Court advised the petitioning intervenors that the court had previously set March 22, 1972, as the date for the filing of briefs on the legal propriety of a "metropolitan" plan of desegregation and, accordingly, that the intervening school districts would have one week to muster their legal arguments on the issue. Thereafter, and following the completion of hearings on the Detroit-only desegregation plans, the District Court issued the four rulings that were the principal issues in the Court of Appeals.

(a) On March 24, 1972, two days after the intervenors' briefs were due, the District Court issued its ruling on the question of whether it could "consider relief in the form of a metropolitan plan, encompassing not only the city of Detroit, but the larger Detroit metropolitan area." It rejected the state defendants' arguments that no state action caused the segregation of the Detroit schools, and the intervening suburban districts' contention that inter-district relief was inappropriate unless the suburban districts had themselves committed violations. The court concluded:

> [I]t is proper for the court to consider metropolitan plans directed toward the desegregation of the Detroit public schools as an alternative to the present intra-city desegregation plans before it and, in the event that the court finds such intra-city plans inadequate to desegregate such schools, the court is of the opinion that it is required to consider a metropolitan remedy for desegregation.

(b) On March 28, 1972, the District Court issued its findings and conclusions on the three "Detroit-only" plans submitted by the city Board and the respondents. It found that the best of the three plans "would make the Detroit system more identifiably Black . . . thereby increasing the flights of Whites from the city and the system." From this the court concluded that the plan "would not accomplish desegregation within the corporate geographical limits of the city." Accordingly, the District Court held that "it must look beyond the limits of the Detroit school district for a solution to the problem," and that "[s]chool district lines are simply matters of political convenience and may not be used to deny constitutional rights."

(c) During the period from March 28, 1972, to April 14, 1972, the District Court conducted hearings on a metropolitan plan. Counsel for the petitioning intervenors was allowed to participate in these hearings, but he was ordered to confine his argument to "the size and expanse of the metropolitan plan" without addressing the intervenors' opposition to such a remedy or the claim that a finding of a constitutional violation by the intervenor districts was an essential predicate to any remedy involv-

ing them. Thereafter, on June 14, 1972, the District Court issued
its ruling on the "desegregation area" and related findings and
conclusions. The court acknowledged at the outset that it had
"taken no proofs with respect to the establishment of the boundaries of the 86 public school districts in the counties [in the Detroit area], nor on the issue of whether, with the exclusion of
the city of Detroit school district, such school districts have committed acts of de jure segregation." Nevertheless, the court designated 53 of the 85 suburban school districts plus Detroit as the
"desegregation area" and appointed a panel to prepare and submit "an effective desegregation plan" for the Detroit schools that
would encompass the entire desegregation area. The plan was to
be based on 15 clusters, each containing part of the Detroit
system and two or more suburban districts, and was to "achieve
the greatest degree of actual desegregation to the end that, upon
implementation, no school, grade or classroom [would be] substantially disproportionate to the overall pupil racial composition."

(d) On July 11, 1972, and in accordance with a recommendation
by the court-appointed desegregation panel, the District Court
ordered the Detroit Board of Education to purchase or lease "at
least" 295 school buses for the purpose of providing transportation under an interim plan to be developed for the 1972–1973
school year. The costs of this acquisition were to be borne by the
state defendants.

On June 12, 1973, a divided Court of Appeals, sitting en banc,
affirmed in part, vacated in part and remanded for further proceedings. The Court of Appeals held, first, that the record supported the District Court's findings and conclusions on the constitutional violations committed by the Detroit Board, and by the
state defendants.[5] It stated that the acts of racial discrimination
shown in the record are "causally related to the substantial
amount of segregation found in the Detroit school system," and
that "the District Court was, therefore, authorized and required
to take effective measures to desegregate the Detroit Public
School System."

The Court of Appeals also agreed with the District Court that
"any less comprehensive a solution than a metropolitan area
plan would result in an all black school system immediately surrounded by practically all white suburban school systems, with
an overwhelming white majority population in the total metropolitan area." The court went on to state that it could "not see

how such segregation can be any less harmful to the minority students than if the same result were accomplished within one school district."

Accordingly, the Court of Appeals concluded that "the only feasible desegregation plan involves the crossing of the boundary lines between the Detroit School District and adjacent or nearby school districts for the limited purpose of providing an effective desegregation plan." It reasoned that such a plan would be appropriate because of the State's violations, and could be implemented because of the State's authority to control local school districts. Without further elaboration, and without any discussion of the claims that no constitutional violation by the outlying districts had been shown and that no evidence on that point had been allowed, the Court of Appeals held:

> The State has committed de jure acts of segregation and . . . the State controls the instrumentalities whose action is necessary to remedy the harmful effects of the State acts.

An inter-district remedy was thus held to be "within the equity powers of the District Court."

The Court of Appeals expressed no views on the propriety of the District Court's composition of the metropolitan "desegregation area." It held that all suburban school districts that might be affected by any metropolitanwide remedy should, under Rule 19, Fed. Rule Civ. Proc., be made parties to the case on remand and be given an opportunity to be heard with respect to the scope and implementation of such a remedy. Under the terms of the remand, however, the District Court was "not required" to receive further evidence on the issue of segregation in the Detroit schools or on the propriety of a Detroit-only remedy, or on the question of whether the affected districts had committed any violation of the constitutional rights of Detroit pupils or others. Finally, the Court of Appeals vacated the District Court's order directing the acquisition of school buses, subject to the right of the District Court to consider reimposing the order "at the appropriate time."

## II

Ever since *Brown v. Board of Education,* judicial consideration of school desegregation cases has begun with the standard that:

> In the field of public education the doctrine of 'separate but equal' has no place. Separate educational facilities are inherently unequal.

This has been reaffirmed time and again as the meaning of the Constitution and the controlling rule of law.

The target of the *Brown* holding was clear and forthright: the elimination of state mandated or deliberately maintained dual school systems with certain schools for Negro pupils and others for White pupils. This duality and racial segregation was held to violate the Constitution in the cases subsequent to 1954, including particularly *Green v. County School Board of New Kent County*, 391 U.S. 430 (1968); *Raney v. Board of Education*, 391 U.S. 443 (1968); *Monroe v. Board of Commissioners*, 391 U.S. 450 (1968); *Swann v. Charlotte-Mecklenburg Board of Education*, 402 U.S. 1 (1971); *Wright v. Council of City of Emporia*, 407 U.S. 451 (1972); *United States v. Scotland Neck Board of Education*, 407 U.S. 484.

The *Swann* case, of course, dealt

> with the problem of defining in more precise terms than heretofore the scope of the duty of school authorities and district courts in implementing *Brown I* and the mandate to eliminate dual systems and establish unitary systems at once."

In *Brown v. Board of Education*, (*Brown II*), the Court's first encounter with the problem of remedies in school desegregation cases, the Court noted that:

> In fashioning and effectuating the decrees the courts will be guided by equitable principles. Traditionally, equity has been characterized by a practical flexibility in shaping its remedies and by a facility for adjusting and reconciling public and private needs.

In further refining the remedial process, *Swann* held, the task is to correct, by a balancing of the individual and collective interests, "the condition that offends the Constitution." A federal remedial power may be exercised "only on the basis of a constitutional violation" and, "[a]s with any equity case, the nature of the violation determines the scope of the remedy."

Proceeding from these basic principles, we first note that in the District Court the complainants sought a remedy aimed at the *condition* alleged to offend the Constitution—the segregation within the Detroit City school district. The court acted on this theory of the case and in its initial ruling on the "Desegregation Area" stated:

The task before this court, therefore, is now, and . . . has always
been, how to desegregate the Detroit public schools.

Thereafter, however, the District Court abruptly rejected the
proposed Detroit-only plans on the ground that "while it would
provide a racial mix more in keeping with the Black-White proportions of the student population, [it] would accentuate the
racial identifiability of the [Detroit] district as a Black school
system, and would not accomplish desegregation." "The racial
composition of the student body is such," said the court, "that
the plan's implementation would clearly make the entire Detroit
public school system racially identifiable" (Pet. App., at 54a),
"leav[ing] many of its schools 75 to 90 percent Black." Consequently, the court reasoned, it was imperative to "look beyond
the limits of the Detroit school district for a solution to the problem of segregation in the Detroit schools . . ." since "school district lines are simply matters of political convenience and may
not be used to deny constitutional rights." Accordingly, the District Court proceeded to redefine the relevant area to include
areas of predominantly White pupil population in order to ensure
that "upon implementation, no school, grade or classroom [would
be] substantially disproportionate to the overall racial composition" of the entire metropolitan area.

While specifically acknowledging that the District Court's findings of a condition of segregation were limited to Detroit, the
Court of Appeals approved the use of a metropolitan remedy
largely on the grounds that it is:

> impossible to declare 'clearly erroneous' the District Judge's con-
> clusion that any Detroit only segregation plan will lead directly to
> a single segregated Detroit school district overwhelmingly black in
> all of its schools, surrounded by a ring of suburbs and suburban
> school districts overwhelmingly white in composition in a state in
> which the racial composition is 87 percent white and 13 percent
> black.

Viewing the record as a whole, it seems clear that the District
Court and the Court of Appeals shifted the primary focus from a
Detroit remedy to the metropolitan area only because of their
conclusion that total desegregation of Detroit would not produce
the racial balance which they perceived as desirable. Both courts
proceeded on an assumption that the Detroit schools could not

be truly desegregated—in their view of what constituted desegregation—unless the racial composition of the student body of each school substantially reflected the racial composition of the population of the metropolitan area as a whole. The metropolitan area was then defined as Detroit plus 53 of the outlying school districts. That this was the approach the District Court expressly and frankly employed is shown by the order which expressed the court's view of the constitutional standard:

> Within the limitations of reasonable travel time and distance factors, pupil reassignments shall be effected within the clusters described in Exhibit P.M. 12 so as to achieve the greatest degree of actual desegregation to the end that, upon implementation, *no school, grade or classroom* [will be] substantially disproportionate to the overall pupil racial composition.

In *Swann*, which arose in the context of a single independent school district, the Court held:

> If we were to read the holding of the District Court to require as a matter of substantive constitutional right, any particular degree of racial balance or mixing, that approach would be disapproved and we would be obliged to reverse.

The clear import of this language from *Swann* is that desegregation, in the sense of dismantling a dual school system, does not require any particular racial balance in each "school, grade or classroom." [6]

Here the District Court's approach to what constituted "actual desegregation" raises the fundamental question, not presented in *Swann*, as to the circumstances in which a federal court may order desegregation relief that embraces more than a single school district. The court's analytical starting point was its conclusion that school district lines are no more than arbitrary lines on a map "drawn for political convenience." Boundary lines may be bridged where there has been a constitutional violation calling for inter-district relief, but, the notion that school district lines may be casually ignored or treated as a mere administrative convenience is contrary to the history of public education in our country. No single tradition in public education is more deeply rooted than local control over the operation of schools; local autonomy has long been thought essential both to the maintenance of community concern and support for public schools and to quality of the educational process. . . . Thus, in *San Antonio School District v. Rodriguez*, we observed that local control over the educational process affords citizens an opportunity to participate in decision-making, permits the structuring of school programs to fit local needs, and encourages "experimentation, innovation and a healthy competition for educational excellence."

The Michigan educational structure involved in this case, in common with most States, provides for a large measure of local control and a review of the scope and character of these local powers indicates the extent to which the inter-district remedy approved by the two courts could disrupt and alter the structure of public education in Michigan. The metropolitan remedy would require, in effect, consolidation of 54 independent school districts historically administered as separate units into a vast new super school district. Entirely apart from the logistical and other serious problems attending large-scale transportation of students, the consolidation would give rise to an array of other problems in financing and operating this new school system. Some of the more obvious questions would be: What would be the status and authority of the present popularly elected school boards? Would the children of Detroit be within the jurisdiction and operating control of a school board elected by the parents and residents of other districts? What board or boards would levy taxes for school operations in these 54 districts constituting the consolidated metropolitan area? What provisions could be made for assuring substantial equality in tax levies among the 54 districts, if this were deemed requisite? What provisions would be made for financing? Would the validity of long-term bonds be jeopardized unless approved by all of the component districts as well as the State? What body would determine that portion of the curricula now left to the discretion of local school boards? Who would establish attendance zones, purchase school equipment, locate and construct new schools, and indeed attend to all the myriad day-to-day decisions that are necessary to school operations affecting potentially more than three quarters of a million pupils?

It may be suggested that all of these vital operational problems are yet to be resolved by the District Court, and that this is the purpose of the Court of Appeals' proposed remand. But it is obvious from the scope of the inter-district remedy itself that absent a complete restructuring of the laws of Michigan relating to school districts the District Court will become first, a *de facto* "legislative authority" to resolve these complex questions, and then the "school superintendent" for the entire area. This is a task which few, if any, judges are qualified to perform and one which would deprive the people of control of schools through their elected representatives.

Of course, no state law is above the Constitution. School district lines and the present laws with respect to local control, are not sacrosanct and if they conflict with the Fourteenth Amendment federal courts have a duty to prescribe appropriate remedies. . . . But our prior holdings have been confined to violations and remedies within a single school district. We therefore turn to address, for the first time, the validity of a remedy mandating cross-district or inter-district consolidation to remedy a condition of segregation found to exist in only one district.

The controlling principle consistently expounded in our holdings is that the scope of the remedy is determined by the nature and extent of the constitutional violation. Before the boundaries of separate and autonomous school districts may be set aside by consolidating the separate units for remedial purposes or by imposing a cross-district remedy, it must first be shown that there has been a constitutional violation within one district that produces a significant segregative effect in another district. Specifically it must be shown that racially discriminatory acts of the state or local school districts, or of a single school district have been a substantial cause of inter-district segregation. Thus an inter-district remedy might be in order where the racially discriminatory acts of one or more school districts caused racial segregation in an adjacent district, or where district lines have been deliberately drawn on the basis of race. In such circumstances an inter-district remedy would be appropriate to eliminate the inter-district segregation directly caused by the constitutional violation. Conversely, without an inter-district violation and inter-district effect, there is no constitutional wrong calling for an inter-district remedy.

The record before us, voluminous as it is, contains evidence of *de jure* segregated conditions only in the Detroit schools; indeed, that was the theory on which the litigation was initially based and on which the District Court took evidence. With no showing of significant violation by the 53 outlying school districts and no evidence of any inter-district violation or effect, the court went beyond the original theory of the case as framed by the pleadings and mandated a metropolitan area remedy. To approve the remedy ordered by the court would impose on the outlying districts, not shown to have committed any constitutional violation, a wholly impermissible remedy based on a standard not hinted at in *Brown I* and *II* or any holding of this Court.

In dissent Mr. Justice White and Mr. Justice Marshall undertake to demonstrate that agencies having statewide authority participated in maintaining the dual school system found to exist in Detroit. They are apparently of the view that once such participation is shown, the District Court should have a relatively free hand to reconstruct school districts outside of Detroit in fashioning relief. Our assumption, *arguendo*, that state agencies did participate in the maintenance of the Detroit system, should make it clear that it is not on this point that we part company. The difference between us arises instead from established doctrine laid down by our cases. *Brown, supra, Green, supra, Swann, supra, Scotland Neck, supra,* and *Emporia, supra,* each addressed the issue of constitutional wrong in terms of an established geographic and administrative school system populated by both Negro and White children. In such a context, terms such as "unitary" and "dual" systems, and "racially identifiable schools," have meaning, and the necessary federal authority to remedy the constitutional wrong is firmly established. But the remedy is necessarily designed, as all remedies are, to restore the victims of discriminatory conduct to the position they would have occupied in the absence of such conduct. Disparate treatment of White and Negro students occurred within the Detroit school system, and not elsewhere, and on this record the remedy must be limited to that system.

The constitutional right of the Negro respondents residing in Detroit is to attend a unitary school system in that district. Unless petitioners drew the district lines in a discriminatory fashion, or arranged for White students residing in the Detroit district to attend schools in Oakland and Macomb Counties, they were under no constitutional duty to make provisions for Negro students to do so. The view of the dissenters, that the existence of a dual system *in Detroit* can be made the basis for a decree requiring cross-district transportation of pupils cannot be supported on the grounds that it represents merely the devising of a suitably flexible remedy for the violation of rights already established by our prior decisions. It can be supported only by drastic expansion of the constitutional right itself, an expansion without any support in either constitutional principle or precedent.[7]

**III**

We recognize that the six-volume record presently under consideration contains language and some specific incidental findings thought by the District Court to afford a basis for interdistrict relief. However, these comparatively isolated findings and brief comments concern only one possible inter-district violation and are found in the context of a proceeding that, as the District Court conceded, included no proofs of segregation practiced by any of the 85 suburban school districts surrounding Detroit. The Court of Appeals, for example, relied on five factors which, it held, amounted to unconstitutional state action with respect to the violations found in the Detroit system:

(1) It held the State derivatively responsible for the Detroit Board's violations on the theory that actions of Detroit as a political subdivision of the State were attributable to the State. Accepting, *arguendo*, the correctness of this finding of State responsibility for the segregated conditions within the city of Detroit, it does not follow that an inter-district remedy is constitutionally justified or required. With a single exception, discussed later, there has been no showing that either the State or any of the 85 outlying districts engaged in activity that had a cross-district effect. The boundaries of the Detroit School District, which are coterminous with the boundaries of the city of Detroit, were established over a century ago by neutral legislation when the city was incorporated; there is no evidence in the record, nor is there any suggestion by the respondents, that either the original boundaries of the Detroit School District, or any other school district in Michigan, were established for the purpose of creating, maintaining or perpetuating segregation of races. There is no claim and there is no evidence hinting that petitioners and their predecessors, or the 40-odd other school districts in the tricounty area—but outside the District Court's "desegregation area"—have ever maintained or operated anything but unitary school systems. Unitary school systems have been required for more than a century by the Michigan Con-

stitution as implemented by state law. Where the schools of only one district have been affected, there is no constitutional power in the courts to decree relief balancing the racial composition of that district's schools with those of the surrounding districts.

(2) There was evidence introduced at trial that, during the late 1950's, Carver School District, a predominantly Negro suburban district, contracted to have Negro high school students sent to a predominantly Negro school in Detroit. At the time, Carver was an independent school district that had no high school because, according to the trial evidence, "Carver District . . . did not have a place for adequate high school facilities." Accordingly, arrangements were made with Northern High School in the abutting Detroit School District so that the Carver high school students could obtain a secondary school education. In 1960 the Oak Park School District, a predominantly White suburban district, annexed the predominantly Negro Carver School District, through the initiative of local officials. There is, of course, no claim that the 1960 annexation had segregatory purpose or result or that Oak Park now maintains a dual system.

According to the Court of Appeals, the arrangement during the late 1950's which allowed Carver students to be educated within the Detroit District was dependent upon the "tacit or express" approval of the State Board of Education and was the result of the refusal of the White suburban districts to accept the Carver students. Although there is nothing in the record supporting the Court of Appeal's supposition that suburban White schools refused to accept the Carver students, it appears that this situation, whether with or without the State's consent, may have had a segregatory effect on the school populations of the two districts involved. However, since "the nature of the violation determines the scope of the remedy," this isolated instance affecting two of the school districts would not justify the broad metropolitan-wide remedy contemplated by the District Court and approved by the Court of Appeals, particularly since it embraced potentially 52 districts having no responsibility for the arrangement and involved 503,000 pupils in addition to Detroit's 276,000 students.

(3) The Court of Appeals cited the enactment of state legislation (Act 48) which had the effect of rescinding Detroit's voluntary desegregation plan (the April 7 Plan). That plan, however, affected only 12 of 21 Detroit high schools and had no causal

connection with the distribution of pupils by race between Detroit and the other school districts within the tri-county area.

(4) The court relied on the State's authority to supervise school site selection and to approve building construction as a basis for holding the State responsible for the segregative results of the school construction program in Detroit. Specifically, the Court of Appeals asserted that during the period between 1949 and 1962 the State Board of Education exercised general authority as overseer of site acquisitions by local boards for new school construction, and suggested that this State approved school construction "fostered segregation throughout the Detroit Metropolitan area." This brief comment, however, is not supported by the evidence taken at trial since that evidence was specifically limited to proof that school site acquisition and school construction within the city of Detroit produced de jure segregation within the city itself. Thus, there was no evidence suggesting that the State's activities with respect to either school construction or site acquisition within Detroit affected the racial composition of the school population outside Detroit or, conversely, that the State's school construction and site acquisition activities within the outlying districts affected the racial composition of the schools within Detroit.

(5) The Court of Appeals also relied upon the District Court's finding that:

> This and other financial limitations, such as those on bonding and the working of the state aid formula whereby suburban districts were able to make far larger per pupil expenditures despite less tax effect, have created and perpetuated systematic educational inequalities.

However, neither the Court of Appeals nor the District Court offered any indication in the record or in their opinions as to how, if at all, the availability of state financed aid for some Michigan students outside Detroit but not within Detroit, might have affected the racial character of any of the State's school districts. Furthermore, as the respondents recognize, the application of our recent ruling in San Antonio Independent School District v. Rodriguez, to this state education financing system is questionable, and this issue was not addressed by either the Court of Appeals or the District Court. This, again, underscores the crucial fact that the theory upon which the case proceeded related solely to the establishment of Detroit city violations as a basis for desegregating Detroit schools and that, at the time of trial, neither the parties nor the trial judge were concerned with a foundation for inter-district relief.

## IV

Petitioners have urged that they were denied due process by the manner in which the District Court limited their participation after intervention was allowed thus precluding adequate opportunity to present evidence that they had committed no acts having a segregative effect in Detroit. In light of our holding that absent an inter-district violation there is no basis for an inter-district remedy, we need not reach these claims. It is clear, however, that the District Court, with the approval of the Court of Appeals, has provided an inter-district remedy in the face of a record which shows no constitutional violations that would call for equitable relief except within the city of Detroit. In these circumstances there was no occasion for the parties to address, or for the District Court to consider whether there were racially discriminatory acts for which any of the 53 outlying districts were responsible and which had direct and significant segregative effect on schools of more than one district.

We conclude that the relief ordered by the District Court and affirmed by the Court of Appeals was based upon an erroneous standard and was unsupported by record evidence that acts of the outlying districts affected the discrimination found to exist in the schools of Detroit. Accordingly, the judgment of the Court of Appeals is reversed and the case is remanded for further proceedings consistent with this opinion leading to prompt formulation of a decree directed to eliminating the segregation found to exist in Detroit city schools, a remedy which has been delayed since 1970.

## REFERENCES

1. Optional zones, sometimes referred to as dual zones or dual overlapping zones, provide pupils living within certain areas a choice of attendance at one of two high schools.
2. The Court of Appeals found record evidence that in at least one

instance during the period between 1957–1958, Detroit served a suburban school district by contracting with it to educate its Negro high school students by transporting them away from nearby suburban White high schools, and past Detroit high schools which were predominantly White, to all or predominantly Negro Detroit schools.

3. School districts in the State of Michigan are instrumentalities of the State and subordinate to its State Board of Education and legislature. The Constitution of the State of Michigan, Art. VIII, § 2, provides in relevant part:

"The legislature shall maintain and support a system of free public elementary and secondary schools as defined by law."

Similarly, the Michigan Supreme Court has stated that "The school district is a state agency. Moreover, it is of legislative creation. . . ." *Attorney General v. Loweey,* 131 Mich. 639, 644, 92 N. W. 289, 290 (1902).

4. In its formal opinion, subsequently announced, the District Court candidly recognized that:

"It should be noted that the court has taken no proofs with respect to the establishment of the boundaries of the 86 public school districts in the counties of Wayne, Oakland and Macomb, nor on the issue of whether, with the exclusion of the city of Detroit school district, such school districts have committed acts of *de jure* segregation."

5. With respect to the State's violations, the Court of Appeals held: (1) that, since the city Board is an instrumentality of the State and subordinate to the State Board, the segregative actions of the Detroit Board "are the actions of an agency of the State" (484 F. 2d, at 238); (2) that the state legislation rescinding Detroit's voluntary desegregation plan contributed to increasing segregation in the Detroit schools (*Id.*); (3) that under state law prior to 1962 the state Board had authority over school construction plans and must therefore be held responsible "for the segregative results" (*Id.*); (4) that the "State statutory scheme of support of transportation for school children directly discriminated against Detroit" (484 F. 2d, at 240) by not providing transportation funds to Detroit on the same basis as funds were provided to suburban districts (484 F. 2d, at 238); and (5) that the transportation of Negro students from one suburban district to a Negro school in Detroit must have had the "approval, tacit or express, of the State Board of Education."

6. Disparity in the racial composition of pupils within a single district may well constitute a "signal" to a district court at the outset, leading to inquiry into the causes accounting for a pronounced racial identifiability of schools within one school system. In *Swann,* for example, we were dealing with a large but single, independent school system and a unanimous Court noted: "Where the proposed plan for conversion from a dual to a unitary system contemplates the continued existence of some schools that are all or predominantly of one race [the school authority has] the burden of showing that such school assignments are genuinely

nondiscriminatory." However, the use of significant racial imbalance in schools within an autonomous school district as a signal which operates simply to shift the burden of proof, is a very different matter from equating racial imbalance with a constitutional violation calling for a remedy. . . .

7. The suggestion in the dissent of Mr. Justice Marshall that schools which have a majority of Negro students are not "desegregated," whatever the racial makeup of the school district's population and however neutrally the district lines have been drawn and administered, finds no support in our prior cases. In *Green v. County School Board of New Kent County*, 391 U.S. 403 (1968), for example, this Court approved a desegregation plan which would have resulted in each of the schools within the district having a racial composition of 57% Negro and 43% White. In *Wright v. Council of the City of Emporia*, 407 U.S. 451 (1972), the optimal desegregation plan would have resulted in the schools being 66% Negro and 34% White, substantially the same percentages as could be obtained under one of the plans involved in this case. . . .

# The Social
# Scientists and
# "White Flight"

*James S. Coleman, Professor of Sociology at the University of Chicago and principal author of* Equal Educational Opportunity, *a 1966 government report most often cited as evidence for the beneficial effects of school desegregation, argues that busing and other wide-scale school desegregation remedies are likely to increase segregation by bringing about a further exodus of white children from central-city schools.*

# Racial Segregation in the Schools: New Research with New Policy Implications

## JAMES S. COLEMAN

Early school desegregation policies, whether they were carried out by school administrations on their own initiative or as the result of federal intervention or court order, consisted of elimination of dual school systems in the South. The intent was to eliminate *de jure* segregation. Throughout the sixties and into the seventies, some school systems have attempted to reduce (or in some cases eliminate) their *de facto* school segregation, primarily segregation resulting from residential patterns.

It has now become a policy of the Department of Health, Education, and Welfare to induce school systems which have at one time maintained dual systems to eliminate school segregation due to residential segregation as well as that due to past school board actions; that is, to eliminate all or most segregation in their schools.

Reprinted with permission of the editors of *Phi Delta Kappan*, 57, no. 2 (October, 1975).

Most recently, the courts have established precedent affecting
school administrations found guilty of actions that increase racial
segregation (the most common being gerrymandering of school
attendance zones); the remedy imposed by the courts has been
to require elimination of all racial segregation in the schools, requiring all schools to have nearly the same racial composition.
Boston is the most conspicuous example of such a ruling. The
effect has been to declare all segregation in such systems *de jure*
and to require its elimination, which in the larger cities requires
compulsory busing of children to a school other than their neighborhood school.

It is proper and necessary, when segregation arises from segregating actions of school administrations, to require administrations to undo the effects of those actions, for the actions constitute a denial of equal protection guaranteed by the Fourteenth
Amendment. But it is neither proper nor necessary to require the
elimination of school segregation that arises from individual actions (principally via residential segregation) without asking what
the policy accomplishes.[1] In fact, since elimination of all racial segregation within school systems—through compulsory busing when necessary—seems on the way to becoming national
policy, it is especially important to ask what the policy accomplishes.

I have recently carried out with two colleagues research which
examines a portion of this question. The research is published
elsewhere,[2] but I will give an overview of the results here. The
research is limited to examining three points: trends (from 1968
to 1973) in segregation within school systems; trends in segregation among or between school systems which arises through black
and white children living in localities served by different school
systems; and, finally, the possible effect of school desegregation
within central-city systems in leading to an increase in segregation
between systems through bringing about an exodus of white children from central-city schools. The research does not examine
achievement levels; it does not examine interracial attitudes; it
does not examine what goes on in the schools when they are integrated. But it does examine racial composition of central-city
schools and how that has been affected by integration of the
city's schools in those cities where extensive school desegregation
has taken place. The importance of this examination, of course,
lies in the fact that desegregating a city's school system accom-

plishes little if the school system is or becomes nearly all black, with whites in the suburbs.

I will summarize the research results and examine their implications for desegregation policies.

## TRENDS IN WITHIN-SYSTEM SEGREGATION

In different regions of the country, there were very different trends in segregation within school districts during the 1968–73 period. In the South (and particularly the Southeast), there was very extensive desegregation, much of it coming in 1970 when, under pressure from the courts, nearly all systems that were still functioning as dual systems integrated. Before this occurred, the South was aberrant in the profile of segregation it showed: The large-city systems were no more segregated than those in most Northern regions; but while in the North there was a sharp reduction in segregation with reduction in size of the school district, in the South segregation was high even in the smaller districts. The principal effect of the desegregation that occurred between 1968 and 1972 was to change the profile of Southern segregation so that it was similar to that of the North: high segregation in large cities, little in smaller school districts. However, even in the large Southern districts there had been some desegregation, bringing levels lower than comparable-sized districts in the North. By 1972, segregation in the South was the lowest of any region in the country.

Meanwhile, there was almost no change in segregation in the North. Declines in most regions were very slight; there was even a slight increase in the Middle Atlantic states.

The fact that segregation in the larger cities of the South was not reduced during this period as much as in smaller cities suggests the differing nature of segregation in large cities, and the differing means that may be necessary to reduce it. School segregation in large cities coincides principally with residential segregation, but this is less true of smaller cities, towns, and rural areas. Redrawing school attendance lines can and often does reduce segregation sharply in smaller cities. In large cities, with large racially homogeneous residential areas, often including a black ghetto area, extensive reduction of segregation requires the controversial policy of busing. The school segregation that remained in this country in 1972 was largely that which coincided with residential segregation. By the standards of 1954, *de jure* segregation had been largely eliminated, along with much segregation (principally in the South) which coincided with residence.

## TRENDS IN BETWEEN-SYSTEM SEGREGATION

In the meantime, however, another kind of racial segregation in the schools was increasing in every region of the country and in nearly every large metropolitan area: segregation that results from blacks living in one school district and whites in another. This type is even more profound than residential segregation within the same school district, for it ordinarily means residential separation of greater distances.

Among the country's large cities, only the Washington, D.C., metropolitan area showed a (slight) reduction in between-district segregation between 1968 and 1972. This reduction arose because the city schools were already almost entirely black, so that any increase of blacks in the suburbs meant a reduction of segregation between Washington and the surrounding counties. Everywhere else the racial disparity between city and suburbs was increasing, primarily through the exodus of whites from city schools. In some metropolitan areas, such as Detroit, Atlanta, San Francisco, New Orleans, St. Louis, and Indianapolis, the segregation between city and suburbs is already as large, or nearly as large, as the segregation among schools within the central-city district.

Among the regions, the South, with a combination of reduced within-district segregation and increased between-district segregation, came by 1972 to have greater segregation between districts than within. Thus, although in 1968 most of the segregation in the South was segregation within districts, by 1972 a large portion of segregation was that between districts. The Southern situation was becoming comparable to that of the North, where between-district segregation has always been great.

This increase in between-district segregation, as I have said, results principally from the movement of whites to districts with fewer blacks. Its increase is not checked by any policies of desegregation of central-city districts; yet it is clear that segregation of the future in metropolitan areas of the U.S. will be of this sort: central-city schools nearly all black, suburban schools largely white. This question can be asked, however: Has desegregation of central-city schools, when and where it has occurred, accelerated this process of segregation between city and suburbs? This is the third aspect of the research we have carried out, and the one that has generated the most controversy in the media.

## WHITE FLIGHT

First of all, there is a continuous loss of white students from central-city schools. The loss is greater as 1) the size of the city is greater; 2) the central-city school district has a higher proportion of black students; and 3) the racial disparity between city and suburbs is great, with a high segregation between districts—blacks in the central-city district and whites in the suburban ones.

Thus the loss of white children from the central-city school system has been especially great in large cities that have a large black population and are surrounded by predominantly white suburbs.

Beyond this, has there been any increase in loss of white children when cities have undergone substantial desegregation? This question was examined for two sets of central-city school districts: the 21 largest and the next 46 in size. It was examined by taking as a dependent variable in a regression analysis the proportionate change in white students in the district since the preceding year; the independent variables were the three factors mentioned above, plus the change from the preceding year in the degree of segregation in the central-city schools.

The findings (which stood the test of much more extensive analyses) were that the loss of whites did increase when there was a reduction of segregation. The effect was substantial for the group of large cities, but much smaller for the smaller cities. This is an average effect, and the effect for different cities differs considerably from the average. (For example, according to our estimates for some of those cities which had a substantial decrease in segregation over this period, it was largest in Atlanta and Memphis, less large in San Francisco and Indianapolis, and absent in Tampa.) The effect was intensified when the desegregating city had a high proportion of blacks and when there was a high disparity in racial composition between suburbs and city (i.e., a high segregation between districts). As indicated above, the effect was much smaller for the smaller cities.

Insofar as we could determine (though the evidence is not extensive enough to allow strong statements on this question), the accelerated loss of whites appears to be a one-time effect, occurring in the year of desegregation but without a continuing accelerated loss in subsequent years.

The magnitude of the long-term impact of this one-time loss can be seen by asking, for a hypothetical city with certain characteristics, what would be its racial composition 10 years hence in the presence and absence of substantial desegregation. We attempted this, for a city 50 percent black in the year of desegregation, with a high degree of segregation between city and suburbs, and with a reduction of about half in the segregation of the central-city district. We assumed no change in the size of the black student population, with the only change being movement of whites from city to suburbs. *Without* desegregation, in 10 years the black proportion in the central city is 65 percent, according to one estimate, and 67 percent according to another. (The two estimates are based on regression analyses of different complexity.) *With* desegregation, the proportion is 75 percent, according to one estimate, and 70 percent according to another. Thus, in the long run (that is, 10 years), substantial desegregation does, on the average, hasten the shift of the city to being predominantly black; but the impact is not enormous, simply because it is (as best we can tell), a one-time acceleration which does not continue in subsequent years.[3] The principal impact, for a city with the indicated characteristics undergoing the indicated amount of desegregation, results from the general loss of whites, rather than the increment to that loss when desegregation occurs. This would be even more the case for smaller cities, where the effect of desegregation on loss of whites is smaller.

Nevertheless, when the problem is viewed in terms of the continuing trends toward segregation between districts, desegregation in some large cities is certainly not solving the problem of segregation. Ironically, "desegregation" may be increasing segregation. That is, eliminating central-city segregation does not help if it increases greatly the segregation between districts through accelerated white loss.

## POLICY IMPLICATIONS

There are two opposing kinds of policy implications that can be drawn from these results. The results are clear that, quite apart from central-city desegregation but abetted by it, the emerging form of school segregation is one in which blacks and whites live in different school districts—most often, blacks in the central city, whites in suburbs.

From one point of view, these results provide a strong argument for metropolitanwide school desegregation through the courts. Since the emerging form of segregation is across district boundaries, then clearly the actions to address this must be actions that reduce segregation across district lines. This approach would take the emerging residential segregation as given—black cities and white suburbs—and would attempt to overcome its effects on school segregation by metropolitanwide school desegregation, i.e., through busing children to bring about racial balance over the metropolitan area.

From a second and different point of view, these results raise the question of just how far in the quest for racial integration of schools it is wise to go. It is certainly necessary to insure equal protection under the Fourteenth Amendment, and this means that courts should require school administrations to undo the effects of segregating actions they have taken. But once equal protection is assured, then school desegregation must be justified in terms of its consequences. The achievement benefits of integrated schools appeared substantial when I studied them in the middle 1960s. But subsequent studies of achievement in actual systems that have desegregated, some with a more rigorous methodology than we were able to use in 1966, have found smaller effects, and in some cases none at all.[4] I believe the achievement benefits do exist; but they are not so substantial that in themselves they demand school desegregation, whatever the other consequences. And particularly when desegregation occurs through bringing together for the school day students from several different neighborhoods, it is questionable whether the same achievement benefits arise.

According to this second point of view, the appropriate means of reducing school segregation that results from residential segregation is to reduce the residential segregation itself, or, if there is substantial community support for eliminating school segregation through busing, to bus in the face of residential segregation. But this means a slower process of reducing school segregation, and it means that the schools will never be racially balanced. It means there will always be some segregation between blacks and whites in schools, just as there is some segregation between Jews and Gentiles, Poles and Italians—between every pair of ethnic groups.

According to this second point of view, the focus in school desegregation should be on doing whatever possible to slow the exodus of whites from central cities and to facilitate the movement of blacks to the suburbs. The aim should be to reduce residential segregation, because it is this segregation which is particularly difficult to overcome, since it requires policies like busing which engender great resistance.

The policy implication, according to this second point of view, is for the courts to limit themselves to remedies which undo the segregating actions of school administrations, but also to undo state actions which have increased residential segregation, and for local communities to address the questions of just how much segregation they wish to eliminate from their schools and how they will do so.

There is another, broader issue. It concerns the rights of individuals. It is an issue made exceedingly difficult by the growth of large metropolitan areas.

When this country consisted principally of rural areas, small towns, and medium-sized cities, each family had the right (except in the dual systems of the South) to choose a school for its children by choosing its residence. This is a right that was unquestioned until recently, and a right that is still held and exercised by those who have the economic resources to move where they want. But in this earlier period the heterogeneity of the local community meant that the exercise of this right to choose a school through choice of residence did not lead to homogeneous schools. Children from differing social classes and backgrounds attended the same school.

Today, however, when transportation has made possible the separation of residence from workplace in metropolitan areas, exercise of this same right leads to schools that are homogeneous in social class or in race. The policy of busing reverses this, through elimination of one's right to choose his child's school through choice of residence. But the right is one that many Americans will not part with easily. Those with the most resources will continue to exercise the right in one way or another.[5] And those most concerned about their children's education will be most avid to exercise the right.[6]

What appears to be necessary is not elimination of this right, through citywide or metropolitan busing, nor a continuation of its full-scale exercise, as in the days when it did not lead to school segregation, but an effort to see how the exercise of the right can be made less segregating in its effects.

One approach would be to substitute for this right another which is even more extensive but which would reduce rather than increase segregation. This would be a right of each child in a metropolitan area to attend any school in that area, so long as the school to which he chose to go had no higher proportion of his race than his neighborhood school.[7] This is the right to attend one's own neighborhood school; but it adds the right to choose a school unconstrained by residence. This right would be most important both to blacks and to the economically disadvantaged. For it is first of all blacks, and second the economically disadvantaged of all races, whose residential location has been most constrained.[8]

The granting of such a right (which would of necessity be done at the state level, since no school district can give its children the right to attend school in another) would not, of course, eliminate all segregation due to residence. To some persons, those who see complete elimination of school segregation as the only ultimate goal, this solution is not satisfactory. But to others, for whom school integration is only a means to an end and not an end in itself, the elimination of all segregation is not the sole criterion for adoption of a policy. What this policy would do instead of requiring a child to attend a particular school—his neighborhood school, as in traditional attendance patterns, or an arbitrary school across town, as with desegregation through busing—would be to give each child the right to attend any school he wished, unconstrained by residence. The only constraint would be the school's racial composition.

This proposed right is merely an illustration of the general point: that a traditional right, exercised in large metropolitan areas, produces highly segregated patterns. But the elimination of this right without providing another equally satisfactory right will be intensely—and properly—resisted.

Thus, although from one point of view the research results I have outlined constitute a strong argument in favor of eliminating segregation at the metropolitan level, from another they suggest a reassessment of the means and goals of school desegregation. They also lead one to seek ways in which social goals can be realized, not through reduction of individual rights but through their expansion.[9]


## REFERENCES

1. Another issue is, What is the proper agency to decide what should be done about this form of segregation? The courts, through the precedent already described, have become this agency, and, by use of the precedent, they have chosen to eliminate residentially based school segregation. But some legal opinion holds that this goes quite beyond equal protection under the Fourteenth Amendment. I agree.

2. James S. Coleman, Sara D. Kelly, and John Moore, *Trends in School Segregation, 1968–1973* (Washington, D.C.: Urban Institute, 1975).

3. On the other hand, according to our estimates, full-scale (rather than half, as in the above estimates) desegregation in a city like Detroit, which is 75 percent black with large predominantly white suburbs, would lead to an almost all-black city system almost immediately. According to our estimates, the contact of blacks with whites in the city's schools would be *less* after one year than if no desegregation had taken place. I should caution, however, that cities vary in their reactions to desegregation, and prediction for a given city from the equation that characterizes all is likely to be wrong. What is important in our results is not predictions for particular cities, but that the extent of desegregation and the characteristics of the city and metropolitan area are estimated to have strong effects on the acceleration of white loss when desegregation occurs.

4. See Nancy St. John, *School Desegregation* (New York: John Wiley, 1975).

5. A study of school desegregation in Florida finds that rejection of the public school system after desegregation, through use of private schools, is unrelated to racial attitudes but is highly related to economic status, the most affluent turning to private schools four times as often as the less affluent. See Everett Cataldo et al., "Desegregation and White Flight," *Integrateducation,* January, 1955, pp. 3–5.

6. It is not primarily the racial prejudice of federal government officials that leads them to choose to live in Montgomery County, Maryland, rather than in Washington or elsewhere; for many of them it is their avid concern for the quality of their children's schools. Few federal officials would themselves be willing to give up this right if the schools to which their children were sent experienced a high crime rate or low overall achievement. They would instead move even farther out or resort to private schools.

7. One additional limitation would be necessary here: a capacity limitation for each school, so that no school would be required to go on split shifts or double shifts because of its popularity. A policy of this sort would necessitate, of course, state transfer of funds to follow the child across school district lines. This would not be simple to accomplish, but it is within the state's power.

8. A very similar right is the central provision of a bill introduced in the last Congress by Representative Richardson Preyer under the title, "The National Educational Opportunities Act." I understand that it will soon be reintroduced.

9. The fact that blacks along with whites see compulsory busing as a reduction of rights is shown by results of a 1974 Gallup Poll published in the *Phi Delta Kappan* for September, 1974. A national sample was asked, "Do you favor busing of school children for the purpose of racial integration, or should busing for this purpose be prohibited through a constitutional amendment?" Fifteen percent of whites and 40 percent of blacks favored the use of busing; but 75 percent of whites and 47 percent of blacks favored a constitutional prohibition of busing.

*Thomas Pettigrew, Professor of Social Psychology and Sociology at Harvard, and Robert Green, Dean of the College of Urban Development and Professor of Educational Psychology at Michigan State University, examine James S. Coleman's research and public statements on the relationship between school desegregation and white school enrollment. They find his research provides no basis for the conclusion that busing and urban school desegregation efforts lead to massive "white flight."*

# School Desegregation in Large Cities: A Critique of the Coleman "White Flight" Thesis

THOMAS F. PETTIGREW AND ROBERT L. GREEN

"A SCHOLAR WHO INSPIRED IT SAYS BUSING BACKFIRED," declared the June 7, 1975, headline in the *National Observer*. "COURT ORDERED INTEGRATION RAPPED BY SOCIOLOGIST WHO STARTED IT ALL," read a June 1, 1975, headline of the Lansing, Michigan, *State Journal*.

These and equally misleading headlines appearing in most of the nation's major newspapers were attempting to describe a series of press interviews held by James Coleman, professor of sociology at the University of Chicago. Coleman is best known as the chief author of the highly publicized study *Equality of Educational Opportunity*, published in 1966 and popularly called "the

Reprinted with permission from *Harvard Educational Review* 46, No. 1 (February 1976). Copyright © 1976 by President and Fellows of Harvard College.

Coleman Report."[1] He is not, nor has he ever claimed to be, the "scholar who inspired . . . busing" or the "sociologist who started it all." The man who might more truly be said to have started it all, four decades ago in *Missouri ex rel. Gaines v. Canada*,[2] is the late Charles Hamilton Houston, then chief counsel of the National Association for the Advancement of Colored People (NAACP); the United States Supreme Court handed down its historic public-school–desegregation ruling in 1954, a dozen years before the appearance of the Coleman Report.

Nevertheless, Professor Coleman is a highly regarded sociologist whose work and opinions are influential and deserve careful review. But this review is necessarily complicated. The events we discuss began in April 1975 and extended through December. Coleman's research has included three completely different analyses, put forward at various times; his results have been described in five different versions of a paper and thirty-nine pages of errata. Over the months, Coleman has repeatedly granted mass-media interviews; authored several articles in popular magazines; made an hour-long television appearance in Boston; submitted three affidavits in Boston's school-desegregation case; testified before the United States Senate's Judiciary Committee; and addressed a national conference in Louisville, Kentucky, on alternatives to busing.

We are not discussing, then, a single research study and the policy interpretations to be drawn from its findings. Rather, we are reviewing an unprecedented campaign by a sociologist to influence public policy. Consequently, it is important to review exactly what Coleman has said about busing and desegregation, what his research has found, and how his opinions and research results lend themselves to contrasting policy interpretations.

Given the complexity of this episode, the reader will find the chronological guide in table 1 useful in following our discussion. Since we shall analyze Coleman's research and policy recommendations, it may also help the reader to know in advance our major critical points.

(a) *There are serious methodological and conceptual problems in Coleman's work on so-called "white flight."* In particular, we challenge his principal conclusion: court-ordered, urban school desegregation is self-defeating because it *causes* massive white movement out of the public schools. Throughout our paper we shall refer to many problems in this research.

TABLE 1: *Chronological Guide*

| Date | Event | Referred to in Text as: |
|------|-------|------------------------|
| April 2 | Coleman delivers initial paper to the American Educational Research Association, citing the findings from an analysis of the extended effect of urban school desegregation, 1968–1970, on decline in white enrollment, 1970–1973. | Paper I<br><br>Analysis I |
| May–June | Coleman grants numerous media interviews. | |
| June 12 | Coleman submits his first affidavit to the federal court on behalf of the anti-busing Boston Home and School Association | Affidavit I |
| June 13 | The NAACP holds a press conference in New York City to reply to Coleman. | |
| June 24 | Kenneth Clark and seven other social scientists hold a press conference in New York City to reply to Coleman. | |
| July 3 | Meyer Weinberg presents "A Critique of Coleman" to the National Education Association. | |
| July 11 | The *New York Times* questions Coleman's Analysis I after discovering that none of the nineteen cities in question had had any court-ordered school desegregation during 1968 to 1970. | |
| July 14 | Coleman participates in an hour-long, question-and-answer, commercial program on Boston's WNAC-TV. | |
| July 27 | Coleman publishes an article in *Newsday* that refers to a new analysis and proposes an "entitlement" plan for limited metropolitan desegregation. | |
| July 28 | Coleman issues a second paper. Analysis I is dropped, but a radically new analysis investigates the concurrent effect of school desegregation on the loss of white students for each year, 1968–1973. This paper provides analytic details to the social-science community for the first time. | Paper II<br><br>Analysis II |
| August 4 | A group of experts at The Urban Institute makes a private review of Coleman's Analysis II. | |
| August 15 | Coleman issues a third paper with extensive revisions | Paper III |
| August 15 | A "Symposium on School Desegregation and White Flight" is held at the Brookings Institution. This second review of Coleman's research is open to the mass media and features a discussion of Reynolds Farley's research. | |
| August 27 | Coleman submits his second affidavit for the Boston Home and School Association to the federal court. | Affidavit II |
| August–September | Coleman continues to grant numerous media interviews. | |
| August 30 | The Urban Institute publishes the "final" version of Coleman's paper | Paper IV |

TABLE 1 — continued

| Date | Event | Referred to in Text as: |
|---|---|---|
| | Along with Analysis II, this paper introduces a new analysis that consists of a set of "white flight" projections for segregated and desegregated urban school systems. | Analysis III |
| September 3 | Christine Rossell presents research findings that contradict Coleman's in a paper delivered to the American Political Science Association. | |
| September 22 | Coleman submits his third affidavit for the Boston Home and School Association to the federal court. | Affidavit III |
| October | Coleman publishes another popular article, in the *Phi Delta Kappan*, and agrees to be a defense witness in the crucial federal court case involving metropolitan school desegregation in Wilmington, Delaware. | |
| October 22 | The Urban Institute issues a thirty-nine-page insert of errata for Paper IV. | Paper V |
| October 28 | Coleman testifies before the United States Senate's Judiciary Committee hearings on proposed anti-busing amendments to the Constitution. | |
| December 5 | Coleman speaks at a conference in Louisville, Kentucky, on alternatives to busing. | |
| December 8 | Coleman presents another version of his paper to the United States Commission on Civil Rights in which he admits that it "is not clear . . . whether desegregation itself induces an increased movement of Whites from the desegregated district." | Paper VI |

First, Coleman's research is conducted in a demographic vacuum. It ignores the fact that separation of the races between suburbs and central cities has been under way throughout this century and was a *fait accompli* well before court-ordered busing even began. Second, Coleman's projections of future "white flight" in northern cities are dubious on three grounds: the projections are based largely on data from desegregated southern cities; extreme conditions are posited to estimate average "effects" from misspecified models; and the projections assume stability in demographic factors. Third, Coleman's research involves purely aggregate data at the district level only; but interpretations about individual actions and "white flight" require either individual data or at least school-level data. Not one white parent was asked by Coleman if his or her child was removed from the public schools because of school desegregation, nor were any data by schools utilized. Thus the findings, even if they were valid on other grounds, would be open to a variety of interpretations.

We will explore two such interpretations. For one thing, parents who intend to leave the city for other reasons might hasten their move when school desegregation begins; thus, the accelerated decline in white enrollment in the first year of desegregation would be compensated by fewer white departures in later years. For another, some of what Coleman defines as "desegregation" very likely represents the temporary mixing of black and white children in schools located in areas undergoing residential shifts from white to black. In these instances, it may be that "white flight" leads to temporary school desegregation rather than that school desegregation leads to "white flight," as Coleman assumes.

Another objection to Coleman's investigation is that his findings depend heavily upon the cities he chose to study. "White flight" occurs in the very "largest" urban school districts, he suggests, and only slightly, if at all, in smaller urban districts. But a close examination of his data reveals that much of the "white flight" effect, even for the "largest" districts, is contributed by just two atypical cities in the deep South—Atlanta and Memphis. Moreover, Coleman inexplicably omitted from his sample a number of the truly largest urban school districts, such as Miami, Jacksonville, and Nashville. We shall demonstrate how including data from these omitted cities reduces the alleged effect of school desegregation upon the decline in white enrollment.

Not surprisingly, Coleman's "white flight" findings are not supported by other studies using similar data and a variety of methods. After describing these conflicting studies, we shall present our own analysis, which uses Coleman's data but yields very different results. We shall then try to resolve the apparent conflict.

(b) *There is only a tenuous connection between Coleman's research findings and his political opposition to school busing for racial desegregation.* Contrary to the impression conveyed by the mass media, Coleman's research has not been on busing, court orders for desegregation, student achievement, classroom disruptions, or the behavior of poor black children. We believe his opposition to court-ordered busing for school desegregation derives less from his research than from two beliefs which he has expressed publicly: changes in relationships between the races should flow from the will of the community and not from the federal courts; and only a small part of racial segregation in

schools is a result of state action—most of it is caused by individual actions beyond the appropriate reach of the law. We
shall critically consider these two beliefs.

(c) *The whole episode raises serious questions about the relationship between social science and the mass media.* First, the
news media tended to confuse Coleman's research with his political preferences. All too often his views were presented as if
they were results from a "second Coleman Report." Complicating
the matter further, Coleman and The Urban Institute, under
whose aegis the study was done, failed to provide the social-
science community with any analytic or methodological details
until four months after the initial paper was delivered. We shall
emphasize the lack of fit between social science and the mass
media, for it has led, in the Coleman episode and other instances,
to a disservice to the American public and to the two institutions
themselves.

## COLEMAN'S FIRST PAPER

The episode began on April 2, 1975, with Coleman's delivery of
"Recent Trends in School Integration" (hereafter referred to as
Paper I) at the American Educational Research Association's
annual meeting.[3] Copies of the paper were labeled "Draft for
discussion purposes only. Not to be quoted or cited." Although
the paper provided little analysis, it was restrained in tone and
content in contrast to what was to follow in Coleman's interviews with reporters.

The first paper's argument can be summarized in four points:

1. Intra-district public-school desegregation increased markedly
   from 1968 to 1972, primarily in the South. Simultaneously,
   intra-district desegregation declined slightly in the New England and Middle Atlantic states. During this period, desegregation trends were negatively related to district size; school
   segregation was most intense in large northern districts.
2. These trends, Coleman argued, were products of two often
   conflicting processes: the collective, formal process that can be
   shaped directly by government agencies; and the individual,
   informal process by which families remove their children from
   the public schools. Coleman called this latter process "white
   flight" and suggested that its rate may be accelerated by
   rapid school desegregation.[4]

3. Coleman calculated the effect on "white flight," as measured by the decline in white enrollment from 1970 to 1973, of three variables: the natural logarithm of district size, the district's 1970 proportion black of total enrollment, and the increase in school desegregation in the district from 1968 to 1970. Although he did not provide the regression equations, his results for the nineteen "largest" central-city districts showed that both the proportion black of total enrollment and the pace of desegregation were positively related to the net number of white children leaving the public schools. For the next fifty largest central-city districts, however, the results were sharply different: net losses of white pupils were related positively to the district's size and to the proportion black of total enrollment but *not* to desegregation.[5]
4. Coleman derived two major conclusions from these findings. First, "insofar as one intended consequence of integration is an increase in achievement of black children, the intent is largely defeated." [6] Second,

the courts are probably the worst instrument of social policy. Yet this does not answer the central questions, for the other agencies of government, which can initiate policies that excite fewer of the fears that ultimately defeat the policy, have often failed to initiate them. It is clear that if school desegregation policies are not to further separate blacks and whites in American society, far greater coordinated efforts on the part of different branches and levels of government are necessary than have taken place until now.[7]

## THE MEDIA INTERVIEWS BEGIN

While at first the mass media gave Paper I only moderate coverage and comment, Coleman later granted numerous interviews to reporters. At this point the furor began. In contrast to the caution of the initial paper, Coleman now offered blunt and far-ranging opposition to federal court orders that required extensive urban school desegregation. To Muriel Cohen of the *Boston Globe* he argued that "a whole generation of young legal talent thinks it can transform the society by winning court cases. That's enormously subversive of the whole political process in the United States." [8]

Coleman continued his attack in an interview with Bryce Nelson of the *Los Angeles Times:* "When the imposition of school integration occurs, and doesn't flow out of the will of the community, then the response on the part of the whites, if they have the income to leave, is to leave." The courts should recognize, he said, that the "much greater commitment" to school integration during the 1960s has diminished, and that such integration is no longer "the first national priority." [9]

For the *New York Times*, Coleman broadened his attack to include social-class as well as racial considerations, although class was not a variable in his study. Reporter Paul Delaney quoted him as saying:

> If integration had been limited to racial integration, then the fear of incidents would have been much less, and the experience with integration would have been much more positive. There has never been a case of lower-class ethnic integration in the schools, because schools historically were ethnically segregated by ethnic neighborhoods. [10]

Perhaps the most influential interview appeared in the *National Observer*. [11] After summarizing his research results, Coleman called the courts "the worst of all possible instruments for carrying out a very sensitive activity like integrating schools." Moreover, he said "the courts were wrong to consider the [Coleman] report in any way." He did not mention his own use of his earlier study when he served as an expert witness in desegregation cases in Washington, D.C., and Denver. Coleman also claimed that the courts are wrong when they attempt to eliminate all the racial segregation in a school system. "I think the courts constitutionally should limit their actions to undoing the effects of official discrimination. But the very large proportion of school segregation by race and by social class is due to individual action, and I think courts overstep their bounds when they try to counterbalance those individual actions." [12]

Beyond rendering these legal judgments, Coleman also speculated on the social-psychological difficulties of big-city schools. Desegregation seemed to cause "white flight" in only the largest central-city districts, he argued, because "there's a much greater feeling of inability to have any impact on the schools, a feeling that schools cannot maintain order and . . . protect the child." Much of this feeling, he believed, stems from the failure of big-city schools "to control lower class black children." [13]

When asked if metropolitan desegregation were not the answer to the problem he was raising, Coleman said he did not think so for two reasons. First, metropolitan districts would necessarily be even larger, and the problematic districts were already too large. Second, middle-class families would just move farther from the city.

Finally, when pressed for concrete policy recommendations, Coleman answered:

> I think there has to be an incentive either in Government money and assistance or in attractive programs. . . . More generally, school desegregation is not the only way to promote social integration. Nor is it, I believe, the best way. For example, activities that encourage racial intermarriage could be much more effective in creating stable forces for social integration.[14]

He did not specify what these "activities" might be.

These initial interviews met three of the mass media's major criteria as to what constitutes big news. They appeared to represent (1) a "surprising" reversal of position (2) by a publicly known authority (3) in a direction that fitted snugly with the prevailing national mood of retrenchment. Almost at once, newspapers throughout the country ran "Coleman" stories, and conservative editorialists had a field day. Rarely, if ever, had a sociologist's opinions been so sought after by the media. Earlier reluctant to deal with the media, Coleman granted dozens of separate interviews, many of them by telephone. In late June, *Newsweek* even sent two reporters to talk with Coleman at his remote vacation home in West Virginia.[15]

On June 12, while still vacationing, Coleman consented to give an affidavit to a lawyer for the anti-busing Boston Home and School Association. After outlining his research results, he concluded the affidavit by asserting that "when court-ordered remedies have gone beyond [the redress of specific state acts of segregation], they have exacerbated the very racial isolation they have attempted to overcome."[16] Coleman was apparently unaware of the fact that the court-imposed desegregation plan in Boston sought only to redress the consequences of the school committee's unconstitutional acts to promote segregation.[17] The appeals court later ruled that the affidavit was irrelevant.

In July, Coleman flew to troubled Boston and participated in an hour-long, commercially sponsored, question-and-answer television program on WNAC-TV. Entitled "Another Look at Busing," the program presented a large number of reporters firing often barbed queries at the sociologist. Coleman began by admitting that his "very appearance may be mischievous" in Boston, since the court ruling had already been handed down. Yet he continued to attack the federal courts for moving against segregation that he saw as caused by "individual action"; he described the important desegregation decision of the Supreme Court, *Swann v. Charlotte-Mecklenburg Board of Education*,[18] as the "wrong precedent"; and he stated flatly that the federal courts should not impose metropolitan desegregation. Coleman also accused his social-science critics of suffering from "motivated blindness," and, when pressed for a policy recommendation, said only, "I don't have a solution."

Coleman's sensitivity to his social-science critics may have been related to the fact that, during June, two press conferences had been held in New York City to rebut many of his contentions. The authors of this article, together with Roy Wilkins and Nathaniel Jones, executive director and chief legal counsel, respectively, of the NAACP, held the first press conference on June 13. Jones summed up a dominant reaction of black Americans to Coleman's unrelenting attack upon the federal judiciary:

> Less than a decade ago, white people were telling black people to get out of the streets, stop public protesting, and go use our constitutional safeguards through the courts. Now that we have followed that advice successfully in American cities, Coleman tells us to stop using the courts for they are an inappropriate source for remedies. Can black people seriously be expected to listen to him?[19]

In another press conference eleven days later, Kenneth Clark and seven other social scientists also countered many of Coleman's assertions. These initial criticisms received inside-page coverage in the *New York Times*[20] and were not widely reported in other newspapers and media. That a few "liberal social scientists" should "assail" the "new Coleman study" was not considered particularly newsworthy.

These first critiques of Coleman's position centered on three points. First, they stressed the complexity of the so-called "white flight" phenomenon and suggested the importance of variables that Coleman's work had not considered. Second, they questioned the scientific ethics of communicating opinions in the form of research results before any analysis was available for review by the social-science community. Third, they emphasized that even if Coleman's dire predictions of massive losses of white students were accurate, the appropriate policy response would be extensive metropolitan desegregation rather than the abandonment of constitutional protections.

Another early response to Coleman's research came on July 3 at the annual convention of the National Education Association. Meyer Weinberg, the editor of *Integrated Education*, presented a paper which faulted Coleman's total neglect of relevant research and reviewed five earlier studies of "white flight" that had presented diverse findings.[21]

All of these early critiques noted that little or no court-ordered school desegregation had occurred in the nation's largest central-city districts between 1968 and 1970, the period that Coleman had used in his research. Robert Reinhold of the *New York Times* checked this point for himself by calling each of the twenty districts in question. His story, headlined "COLEMAN CONCEDES VIEWS EXCEEDED NEW RACIAL DATA," appeared on the front page of the *Times*:

> The crux of his argument is that integration in the first two years, 1968–1970, led directly to a substantial exodus of white families in the following three years, 1970–1973, over and above the normal movement to the suburbs  However, a thorough check of all 20 cities—in which key officials were questioned by telephone—could find no court-ordered busing, rezoning or any other kind of coerced integration in any of the cities during the 1967–1970 period. Court suits were pending in many, but desegregation was limited to a few modest open enrollment plans, used mostly by blacks. If there was "massive and rapid" desegregation, as Dr. Coleman said, it could not have been due to court-imposed remedies.[22]

In response to these facts Coleman conceded, according to Reinhold, "that his public comments went beyond the scientific data he had gathered." "In answer to questions," wrote Reinhold, "he said that his study did not deal with busing, and that his arguments applied to trends in only two or three southern cities.

Nonetheless, he maintained that the 'over-all implications' of his remarks were still valid. . . ." [23] Later, Coleman asserted that he had been misquoted.[24]

## THE NEW ANALYSIS AND PAPER II

As the questioning of his initial analysis grew more widespread, Coleman and his colleagues at The Urban Institute undertook a second, more sophisticated, and sharply different analysis. The first public mention of the second analysis appeared in an article by Coleman in *Newsday*.[25] The article, which repeated the familiar argument that the courts should not correct *de facto* segregation, made little use of the new findings. Rather, Coleman placed a new emphasis on policy recommendations. Besides again suggesting interracial marriage, Coleman stressed a range of voluntary programs from specialized interracial schools and remedial programs in all-black schools to integrated summer camps. More significantly, for the first time he advocated a minimal metropolitan plan in which every central-city child would be entitled by the state to attend any public school in the metropolitan area, so long as racial segregation was not thereby increased. Suburban schools would be required to allot up to 20 percent of their enrollment capacity to out-of-district children.

The complete new analysis appeared in a sixty-seven-page document dated July 28, 1975, and entitled "Trends in School Segregation, 1968–73." [26] This second paper was distributed to a small group of social scientists invited to attend a one-day discussion with Coleman at The Urban Institute on August 4. This paper opened with a brief history of school-desegregation efforts and closed with a description of desegregation attempts in Wyandanch, New York. Both of these sections were largely irrelevant to the research; both came in for intense criticism at The Urban Institute meeting; and both were eliminated from later drafts and need not be discussed further. Again no mention was made of earlier research.

The new analysis attempted to ascertain the average effect of desegregation upon the loss of white students during each of the five school years from 1968 to 1973. In other words, unlike the initial analysis which looked at white-student loss from 1970 to 1973 *after* desegregation between 1968 and 1970, the new analysis examined the yearly relationship between concurrent changes in desegregation and white enrollment. Thus, reductions in segregation in 1968–1969 were related to white-student losses in 1968–1969, and so on for each of the five years in each of sixty-nine central cities. Each city/year combination was treated as a separate observation in the regression analysis and, consequently, no trends over time could be ascertained from this analysis. Once again the sample was split in two, roughly on the basis of system size (a somewhat arbitrary procedure which, as we shall later demonstrate, strengthens the "white flight" effect).

The corrected results, which were not made available until October, are provided in table 2. The table presents the regression coefficients together with their standard errors in parentheses and the variance accounted for by the predictors. Notice that for six of the thirty-two coefficients for which standard errors are computed the standard errors are *larger* than the coefficients and that many of the variables contribute little to the prediction. The two equation 1's use only three variables to predict white-student loss: the annual change in public-school desegregation ($\Delta R$); the proportion of student enrollment that was black (Prop. black); and the natural logarithm of the total number of students (ln $N$). These three variables together explain about 29 percent of the variance in white-enrollment change for the largest cities and about 26 percent of the variance for the medium-sized cities.

The second set of equations does not substantially improve the prediction. Adding two more predictors—the degree of inter-district school segregation in the Standard Metropolitan Statistical Area ($R$ SMSA), and an interaction term to allow for differential effects of desegregation in the South ($\Delta R \times$ SOUTH)—explains about 36 percent and 35 percent of the variance of annual white-enrollment changes in large and medium-sized cities, respectively.

A more interesting and dramatic increase in predictive power for the largest cities occurs in equation 3. Here three more variables have been added: a dummy (dichotomous) variable for the South (SOUTH) and interaction terms to allow the effect of desegregation to vary with inter-district metropolitan segregation ($\Delta R \times R$ SMSA) and with the proportion of students who are black ($\Delta R \times$ Prop. black). These eight variables explain 60 percent of the variance for large cities but only 40 percent for smaller cities. But note that this improvement derives largely from the

TABLE 2: *Coleman's Basic Regression Coefficients for Analyses of Decline in White Enrollment in Central City Schools*

|  | "Largest" 21 | Next 46 |
|---|---|---|
| **Equation 1** | | |
| $\Delta R$ (desegregation) | .279 (.062) | .056 (.026) |
| Prop. black students | -.133 (.028) | -.090 (.010) |
| In $N$ (system size) | .000 (.008) | -.042 (.010) |
| Constant | .013 | .452 |
| $R^2$ | .29 | .26 |
| Number of observations | (105) | (226) |

Including inter-district segregation in SMSA, and interaction term for desegregation with South:

| **Equation 2** | | |
|---|---|---|
| $\Delta R$ (desegregation) | .199 (.156) | -.148 (.137) |
| Prop. black students | -.044 (.039) | -.035 (.016) |
| In $N$ (system size) | .066 (.008) | -.041 (.010) |
| $R$ SMSA | -.165 (.050) | -.110 (.021) |
| $\Delta R \times$ SOUTH | .143 (.170) | .242 (.137) |
| Constant | -.059 | .438 |
| $R^2$ | .36 | .35 |

Including interactions of desegregation with proportion black and inter-district segregation, and also including South as a dummy variable:

| **Equation 3** | | |
|---|---|---|
| $\Delta R$ (desegregation) | -.459 (.184) | -.349 (.151) |
| Prop. black students | .051 (.037) | -.026 (.019) |
| In $N$ (system size) | .003 (.006) | -.039 (.009) |
| $R$ SMSA | -.210 (.044) | -.102 (.025) |
| $\Delta R \times$ SOUTH | .148 (.198) | .244 (.145) |
| $\Delta R \times$ Prop. black | 1.770 (.307) | .511 (.215) |
| $\Delta R \times R$ SMSA | .561 (.494) | .894 (.314) |
| SOUTH | -.006 (.010) | -.002 (.006) |
| Constant | -.039 | .414 |
| $R^2$ | .60 | .40 |

Source:   James S. Coleman, Sara D. Kelly, and John A. Moore, "Insert for Trends in School Segregation, 1968–73," The Urban Institute, Washington, D.C., Oct. 1975, textual revision for p. 59.

interaction between annual desegregation changes in a school system *and* the system's proportion black of total enrollment.

This interaction suggests that so-called "white flight" is a function less of desegregation *per se* than of the conditional relationship between desegregation and the proportion black of school enrollment. Although this crucial finding of the second Coleman analysis has not yet received public attention, we believe that its policy implications—to the extent that any policy implications can be safely drawn from this work—are potentially important and contrast sharply with those now publicly identified with this research. In short, we feel this finding offers further support for metropolitan approaches to school desegregation.

Rather than consider the implications of equation 3, Coleman next chose to use the regression results to project average annual rates of loss of white students after desegregation. To do this, he posited a set of extreme conditions—a system with 50 percent of its enrollment black and a one-year reduction of 0.2 in the segregation index. These conditions were atypical, since in 1970 the median black enrollment in his 69 cities was only 28 percent and in only 20 of his 342 city/year observations was there a segregation reduction of 0.2 or more. Indeed, only 4 of his 342 observations actually met both of these conditions.[27]

Under these unrealistic assumptions, Coleman's equation 1 models predict that desegregation would result in a loss of white students 5.5 percent greater than expected on the basis of the other predictor variables in the large cities and 1.8 percent greater in the medium-sized cities. The equation 2 models show the projected effect of major desegregation to be far greater in the South than in the North. For the largest urban systems, the model predicts that desegregation would lead to an additional white-enrollment loss of 6.8 percent in the South and 3.9 percent in the North; for the medium-sized systems, the comparable figure for the South is 2.6 percent and for the North, 0.2 percent.

Still using equation 2, Coleman turned to inter-district segregation and demonstrated that the difference in proportion black of all students between central-city schools and schools in surrounding suburbs is positively related to the annual loss of central-city white students, even in the absence of intra-district desegregation. This finding, too, presents a powerful argument for those interested in furthering metropolitan, interracial education.

Coleman used the equation 3 models to illustrate the critical interaction between desegregation and the proportion of the school district's enrollment which is black. Under the extreme condition of a 0.2 reduction in the segregation index, the projected decline in white enrollment in the largest central-city districts varies by a factor of two to four as the proportion black of total enrollment varies from 25 percent to 75 percent.

Coleman next attempted to determine if the loss of white enrollment he attributed to desegregation continues beyond the first year of the process. Though his results on this point were inconsistent, he concluded that the presumed effect of desegregation is concentrated in the first year. Then, in partial answer to his critics who had stressed additional variables related to so-called "white flight," Coleman tried to control for factors unique to each city by introducing into the regression equations a dummy variable for each city. This procedure only slightly reduces the equation 1 effect of desegregation on changes in white enrollment in the large-city schools. It does not, however, remove the need for more independent variables. Joseph Wisenbaker of Michigan State University has noted that, when using dummy (dichotomous) variables to control for inter-city differences unrelated to school attendance, one must assume that all such differences remained constant over the five-year period—a stringent and probably unjustifiable assumption.[28]

Finally, Coleman carried out what he reported as a full analysis of covariance that considered not only the rate of desegregation and dummy variables for each city but also the possibility that the effect of desegregation could vary from city to city. Again assuming a large one-year reduction of 0.2 in the school-segregation index, he projected figures for white-enrollment decline in excess of what would have occurred without desegregation. Of those eight cities which had actually experienced substantial desegregation, two showed predicted *gains* in white enrollment; four others showed only modest predicted losses in white enrollment. The only cities for which "massive" loss was predicted were Memphis and Atlanta. The average estimated loss for the eight cities was only 5.2 percent, and without Memphis and Atlanta, the average was only 1.5 percent.[29] Again we see what a crucial role just two atypical southern cities played in Coleman's *public* argument against court-ordered urban school desegregation throughout the United States. His own conclusion is less specific: "They show that the estimated white loss does vary considerably from city to city, and that the average loss rate specified earlier obscures very different loss rates in different cities."[30] Unfortunately, Coleman has consistently failed to make this point forcefully in his court affidavits and his many public interviews.

## THE URBAN INSTITUTE MEETING

The Urban Institute called a meeting at its offices in Washington, D.C., on August 4 to review in detail this second draft.[31] Coleman, his co-author Sara Kelly, and the president of the Institute, William Gorham, chaired the one-day session. Those in attendance included three economists, four sociologists, two demographers, one lawyer, and one social psychologist. The session was brisk, hard-working, direct, and friendly. The review panel's criticisms of the second paper centered on three issues: the study's political context, its demographic context, and its methodology.

Coleman opened the meeting by asking participants to limit their comments to the research paper under discussion and to refrain from discussing the opinions he had expressed publicly. Many participants rejected this request on the grounds that Coleman's opinions had been advanced in the mass media as if they derived directly from his research and that both the study's design and its interpretation were heavily influenced by its author's opinions.

Panelists agreed that the research dealt with few of the subjects about which Coleman had expressed opinions in his interviews. The research was *not* about student achievement, classroom disruptions, or the behavior of poor black children; it was not about busing or court orders. Strictly speaking, it was not even about "white flight," a prejudicial label that implies a phenomenon prompted solely by desegregation. Rather, it concerned the relationship between school desegregation—achieved by any means—and changes in white-student enrollment in urban public-school systems.

The group advanced many policy interpretations that contrasted with Coleman's. In particular, many felt that Coleman's results seemed to speak for metropolitan approaches to desegregation. At base, Coleman's interpretations reflected a firm political belief that since only a relatively small part of segregation has been caused by "state action" in the Fourteenth Amendment sense, only a small part of it should be dealt with by the courts.

Even the study's design had political overtones. If one were to set out to formulate a complex causal model to predict changes in white-student enrollment, one would ask broad questions, utilize a variety of predictor variables, and place the problem in its full demographic context. Coleman instead chose to test the narrow question of whether the racial desegregation of urban schools leads to a loss of white students. In doing so, he virtually ignored the broader demographic context of the problem. Any study that considers only the period from 1968 to 1973, without noting the fifty-year trend towards concentration of whites in the suburbs and Blacks in the central cities, is bound to be myopic and misleading.

As it stood, the study paid little attention to the possibility that central cities might have annexed white suburbs; it confounded race with social class; it ignored differences in residential segregation patterns among cities; and it did not control for differential birth rates by race.[32] Moreover, Coleman's projections erroneously assumed stability in demographic variables. For example, net black migration from the South to northern cities is now trickling to its end, and this will retard the increase of black enrollments in central-city schools. And in some metropolitan areas, blacks are beginning to move into the suburbs in substantial numbers.

Moreover, torn from their demographic context, the effects of desegregation are difficult to assess from only district-wide aggregate data. Coleman interpreted any unusual decline in white enrollment in a year of desegregation as "white flight"—white families with school-age children fleeing from interracial schools to private or suburban schools. But not one white family was actually asked about its motivations for staying or leaving, nor were data available from individual schools. Coleman here committed a classic ecological fallacy, inferring individual motives from broad-gauged aggregate data.[33] Since Coleman based his policy arguments on assertions about individual actions, this defect seriously weakens his case.

These issues and the great inter-city variation in Coleman's data led the panel to recommend that case studies be undertaken. Norman Chachkin of the Lawyers Committee for Civil Rights under Law offered an example which underscored the utility of such case studies and the danger of the ecological fallacy. Prior to 1972, the average annual decline in white enrollment in the Harrisburg, Pennsylvania, public schools had been below 3 percent. But during the 1972–1973 school year, when widespread desegregation took place, the decline was approximately 10 percent. In 1973–1974, the decline returned to 2.9 percent. An analyst using Coleman's approach would have assumed that the increased decline was caused by desegregation. But a case study would have revealed that a serious flood in June 1972 had caused many white families to leave Harrisburg.

Panel members further questioned the research on a number of methodological grounds. First, they criticized Coleman's choice of independent variables, noting that many had large standard errors and explained little variance. They went on to suggest a wide range of alternative variables, such as those Gregg Jackson of the United States Commission on Civil Rights had already demonstrated to be significant.[34] Employing Coleman's original research design and data, Jackson found four independent variables—population density, the 1960–1970 change in black population, median white income, and current per-pupil expenditures—each of which, in combination with the proportion black of student enrollment and school-system size, predicted decline in white enrollment *better* than did reduction of school segregation.

The panel also noted that the dependent variable, change in white enrollment, indicates the *net* effect of gains and losses and was not decomposed into its constituent parts. And many questioned the wisdom of using average effect estimates to predict future decline in white enrollment. Moreover, it is incorrect to interpret the positive correlation between desegregation and decline in white enrollment as necessarily indicating that the former causes the latter: decline in white enrollment often precedes desegregation, as it did in Detroit, Birmingham, Atlanta, and Memphis.

Perhaps the most serious issue raised by the review panel was the difference between Coleman's key results and the findings of previous research on the topic. For instance, Jane Mercer and Terrence Scout had earlier investigated twenty-three desegregating school districts in California and sixty-seven districts there which had not desegregated.[35] They found no significant differences between the two groups in direction or rate of change in the proportions of student enrollment that were black or Chicano.

Furthermore, Reynolds Farley, using the same national data source as Coleman, failed to uncover a significant relationship between school desegregation and decline in white enrollment in southern or northern cities.[36] We will later discuss at greater length Farley's research and two other important studies which fail to replicate Coleman's critical result.

Review of Coleman's work by social scientists and lawyers continued through August. On August 15, 1975, the Center for National Policy Review of the Catholic University Law School and the Center for Civil Rights of Notre Dame University co-sponsored a "Symposium on School Desegregation and White Flight" at the Brookings Institution in Washington, D.C. Unlike the meeting at The Urban Institute, this one-day session was open to the press. It featured a presentation by Coleman, a panel discussion by three civil-rights lawyers on the legal significance of the controversy, and four papers by social scientists.

Coleman produced yet another draft of his paper (Paper III) for the occasion.[37] Paper III remained essentially the same as the earlier versions. Although the new version was longer, included references to a few previous studies, contained two additional appendices, and thanked members of the earlier review panel, it reflected little response to the panel's many criticisms.[38] The final paragraph avoided the loaded term "white flight" and interpreted the results somewhat more cautiously:

> All this leads to general conclusions consistent with those from earlier sections of this examination: that the emerging problem with regard to school desegregation is the problem of segregation between central city and suburbs; and in addition, that current means by which schools are being desegregated are intensifying that problem, rather than reducing it. The emerging problem of school segregation in large cities is a problem of metropolitan area residential segregation, black central cities, and white suburbs, brought about by a loss of whites from the central cities. This loss is intensified by extensive school desegregation in those central cities, but in cities with high proportion of blacks and predominantly white suburbs, it proceeds at a relatively rapid rate with or without desegregation.[39]

Most specialists would agree with the basic thrust of this conclusion. At issue is whether court-ordered desegregation within central cities significantly hastens the development of two separate Americas—black central cities and white suburbs. This formulation of the issue is far different from the simple "busing backfires" argument that Coleman's numerous press interviews led the nation to focus upon.

TABLE 3: *Coleman's Prediction of Proportion Black in Years after Desegregation*

|                              | 0  | 1   | 2   | 3   | 4   | 5   | 6   | 7   | 8   | 9   | 10  |
|------------------------------|----|-----|-----|-----|-----|-----|-----|-----|-----|-----|-----|
| *Equation 1*                 |    |     |     |     |     |     |     |     |     |     |     |
| With desegregation (.4)      | .5 | .54 | .56 | .58 | .60 | .61 | .63 | .65 | .67 | .69 | .70 |
| Without desegregation        | .5 | .51 | .53 | .55 | .56 | .58 | .60 | .61 | .63 | .65 | .67 |
| *Equation 3*                 |    |     |     |     |     |     |     |     |     |     |     |
| With desegregation (.4)      | .5 | .58 | .60 | .62 | .63 | .65 | .67 | .69 | .71 | .73 | .75 |
| Without desegregation        | .5 | .51 | .52 | .54 | .55 | .56 | .58 | .59 | .61 | .63 | .65 |

Source:   James S. Coleman, Sara D. Kelly, and John A. Moore, *Trends in School Segregation, 1968–73*, (Washington, D.C.: The Urban Institute, Aug. 1975), p. 74.

In his third paper, Coleman added one additional analysis that demonstrates—even under extreme conditions—how trivial are the policy implications of his results. Even positing conditions so rare that they never occurred in his 342 observations—an enormous district (169,000 students) [40] with 50 percent black student enrollment and a huge one-year reduction of 0.4 in the segregation index—the model predicts minimal effects of desegregation on a school system's racial proportions (table 3).[41] On the basis of equation 1 (see table 2), the projected percentage black of total enrollment in cities with desegregated schools would exceed that in cities with no desegregation by only 3 percentage points in the first year and the same 3 percentage points in the tenth year. The next projections, using equation 3 (see table 2), are based on data from northern cities only and posit several further assumptions: suburbs are entirely white and equal in population to the central city; all white-student losses in the central city appear as gains in the suburbs; and there is no movement of Blacks to the suburbs. Although the omission of southern cities addresses one major criticism of the research, the latter two conditions are unrealistic and inflate the projected effect of within-city desegregation. Even under these assumptions, the equation 3 projections reveal a difference between desegregated and segregated cities of only 7 percentage points in the first year and a total of 10 by the tenth year after desegregation.

Since Coleman's own successive analyses revealed smaller and smaller effects, it is hardly surprising that other investigators at the symposium reported results that belie the much-heralded

warning that desegregation prompts "white flight." For example, Michael Giles of Florida Atlantic University reported on his
detailed desegregation research in seven Florida school districts.[42]
Since these districts were all county-wide, residential relocation
was impractical and transfer to private schools offered the only
mechanism of "white flight." Giles found that avoidance of desegregation among Whites was *unrelated* to racial prejudice or to
"busing," was greatest among upper-status families, and was
least among families whose children attended schools with less
than 30 percent black enrollment.

Luther Munford presented his study of thirty Mississippi
school districts that had been desegregated between 1968 and
1970. He demonstrated that, for his sample, "white flight" was
explained by the "black/white ratio in the population as a whole
rather than just the ratio in the schools." [43]

A third paper, by Gary Orfield, a political scientist at Brookings, provided the symposium with a political analysis of "white
flight research." "Too often," he warned, "selective, half-digested
reports of preliminary research findings are disseminated by the
media and become weapons in the intense political and legal
battle being fought in major cities." [44] Emphasizing the difficulty
of sorting out the forces that accelerate suburbanization, he
stated: "It is impossible now to demonstrate that school integration, in itself, causes substantial white flight." [45] His conclusion echoed a consensus among race-relations specialists: "There
is no evidence that stopping school desegregation would stabi-
lize central city racial patterns. If those patterns are to be significantly modified, positive, coordinated, and often metropolitan-
wide desegregation efforts will probably be required." [46]

Reynolds Farley delivered the fourth paper at the symposium.[47] As noted earlier, this paper presented evidence that from
1967 to 1972 there was no statistically significant relationship
between racial desegregation and decline in white enrollment in
large or medium-sized urban districts in the North or South (see
figure 1). Though this material, unlike Coleman's, had been in
print since January 1975, the news media first mentioned it in a
story about the Brookings symposium in the Sunday *New York
Times* of August 17, 1975.[48] But Farley's results were not publicized beyond the major newspapers.

Farley's research differed from Coleman's in five ways. First,
Farley used a larger sample of cities, fifty in the South and

FIGURE 1: *Percentage Change in White Enrollment Plotted Against Change in School Segregation, 1967 to 1972, Twenty Largest Cities or Districts in Each Region*

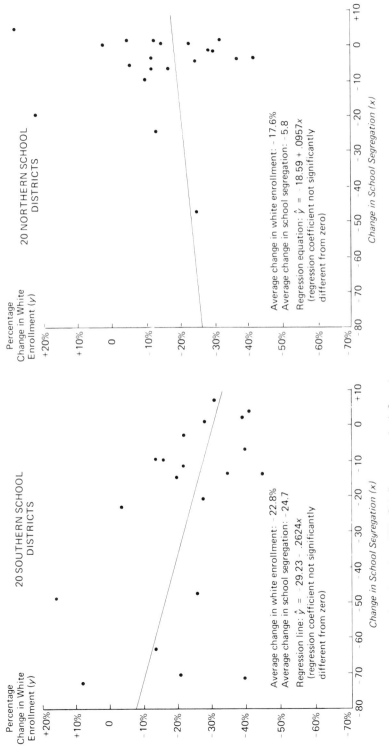

Source   Reynolds Farley, "School Integration and White Flight," paper presented at the Symposium on School Desegregation and White Flight, Brookings Institution, Washington, D.C., 15 Aug. 1975, Figure 2.

seventy-five in the North. Rather than limit his sample, he considered all cities with a 1970 population of one hundred thousand or more and at least 3 percent black enrollment in their public schools. He also ran analyses using only the twenty largest cities of each region, as shown in figure 1. Second, Farley investigated the 1967 to 1972 period rather than the period 1968 to 1973. Third, rather than examine annual changes in the variables, Farley analyzed changes across the entire five-year span. Fourth, Farley employed only elementary-school data, while Coleman used data from all grades. (This difference should have been unimportant, since Coleman showed that the relationship he discerned appeared to exist about equally across the grades.) Finally, Farley used a different index of school segregation. Both his and Coleman's indices measure whether black and white students attend the same schools, and both are independent of the school districts' racial compositions. It has been shown, for a sample of 2,400 school districts, that the two indices are correlated at 0.88.[49]

Unable to show any systematic relationship between white loss and school desegregation for either his extensive urban sample or his subsamples of the largest cities, Farley concluded:

> To be sure, when the public schools are desegregated or when they become predominantly black, some white parents—perhaps many —hasten their move away from the central city. However, whites are moving out of central cities for many other reasons. We have shown that cities whose schools were integrated between 1967 and 1972 did not lose white students at a higher rate than cities whose schools remained segregated.[50]

Why should two studies with comparable data reach opposite conclusions? Coleman suggested that Farley failed to control fully for the proportion of students who were black. Farley did find that this variable was significantly related to the decline in white enrollment in the fifty southern cities but not in the seventy-five northern cities. Yet Farley also demonstrated that cities in both regions in which the 1967 black percentage of all pupils was high and schools were desegregated did not lose unusually high proportions of white enrollment.

Farley offered two other possible explanations for the difference in results. He suggested that the one-year effect Coleman found might represent only a hastening of migration by some whites who were about to leave anyway and that, over a five-year span, this "hastening" effect disappears. Farley also noted

> . . . the great weight he [Coleman] placed upon observations for a
> few cities, particularly Atlanta and Memphis. Most of his data
> describe the 1968 to 1972 span but for several cities he analyzed
> 1973 segregation data. In both Atlanta and Memphis integration
> orders went into effect between 1972 and 1973. Whites have been
> migrating out of Atlanta's central city at least since 1960 and white
> public school enrollment dropped sharply prior to school integra-
> tion. Undoubtedly the white out-migration continued between
> 1972 and 1973. Exclusively white freedom schools sprang up in
> southern cities in reaction to public school integration. However,
> these are often short-lived as parents appreciate the tremendous
> costs of establishing private school systems. Many Memphis
> parents enrolled their children in private schools in 1973 but it is
> probable that enrollment in such institutions will decline. In my
> view, it is inappropriate to draw overarching conclusions about
> school integration causing white flight from data for a few cities.[51]

White-enrollment figures in the Memphis public schools in the fall of 1975 bore out Farley's prediction that private-school attendance would decline.[52]

## COLEMAN'S FOURTH PAPER, THIRD ANALYSIS

Two weeks after the Brookings symposium, Coleman produced a fourth version of his paper. Among other things, Paper IV included a third analysis which appeared to show enormous differences in "white flight" between central cities with desegregating schools and those with segregated schools.

By attempting to demonstrate that school desegregation does indeed accelerate "white flight," Analysis III responded to critics who had charged that Coleman's earlier analyses merely measured a long-term decline in white enrollment that was unrelated to school desegregation. In published form, the new analysis was described as "a rough test" and took up less than a page of discussion.[53] However, Coleman emphasized Analysis III in public statements after August 1975. He described it in an interview in the New York Times Magazine [54] and offered it as evidence in his second affidavit in the Boston desegregation case.

In Analysis III, Coleman used several subsets of what he called the "largest" central-city school districts (twenty-one districts in

all) and predicted losses of white students for the years 1969–
1973 from data for a single year, 1968–1969. Next, he grouped
the districts into two sets: those that had a reduction of 0.1 or
more on his school-desegregation index during 1968 to 1973 (ten
districts) and those that did not (eleven districts). The predicted
loss of white students from the eleven still-segregated systems
(18 percent) was approximately what one would expect had
desegregation not occurred (15 percent), but the desegregating
systems had an average loss of about two and one half times
that expected (26 percent instead of 10 percent). Inexplicably, in
his public statements Coleman referred to a different version of
this analysis based on the original subset of nineteen districts
that omitted Denver and San Francisco. Using this sample, he
found an average decline in white enrollment almost four times
that expected (26 percent instead of 7 percent).

There are many serious problems with this much-publicized
"rough test." First, the use of a single year as the base upon
which to compute expectancies is a dubious practice at best.
Second, the sample is small and unrepresentative: three of the
ten desegregating districts, all in the deep South, provide most
of the effect. When Memphis, Atlanta, and New Orleans are removed from the analysis, the remaining seven desegregating districts exhibit only an 18 percent decline instead of an expected
11 percent.

The third problem is the absence of controls for variables other
than school desegregation that might be related to decline in
white enrollment. Cities are divided into two categories (districts
with more than 0.1 reduction in school segregation and those with
less), with no control for other differences between them. Specifically, the lower expected rate of decline in the desegregating
districts is in large part an artifact of regional differences. All
eleven of the segregated urban districts are in the North, and six
of the ten desegregating districts are in the South. Region in turn
is a surrogate for such variables as suburbanization, in which the
South lags a generation or more behind other regions. For the six
southern desegregating systems (Atlanta, Dallas, Houston, New
Orleans, Memphis, and Tampa), the average decline in white
enrollment during the years from 1969 to 1973 was 29.5 percent
compared with an expected decline of 7.5 percent. For the four
northern desegregating systems (Denver, Indianapolis, St. Louis,
and San Francisco), there was an average white loss during 1969

to 1973 of 21 percent compared with a predicted 15 percent. Yet Coleman generalized his basically southern results to Boston and other northern cities.

Despite Coleman's claim that this new analysis is "more stringent" because the 1968–1969 baseline projections cause each city to act as its own control, one cannot assume, as Coleman seems to, that all relevant variables in a given city will remain stable over a five-year period. For example, major highway construction or annexation of suburbs can cause great variability in student-attendance figures from year to year. A more detailed analysis of year-by-year data, which became available in early September, was to highlight further the inadequacies of Coleman's approach.

## CHRISTINE ROSSELL'S ANALYSIS

Christine Rossell, a political scientist at Boston University, presented another analysis at the annual meeting of the American Political Science Association.[55] Her paper provided further evidence that conflicted both with Coleman's opinions about the political consequences of desegregation and with his findings about "white flight."

Rossell first considered the effects of public-school desegregation upon community politics. Her analysis of detailed time-series data on seventy urban school districts in the North from 1963 to 1973 revealed that school desegregation increased both voter turnout and dissent voting. Districts with highly educated voters most sharply displayed the increased turnout effect; low-education districts, the increased dissent effect. And while the increase in dissent voting was temporary and rarely halted the desegregation process, the increased turnout for school-board elections appeared to be stable over time. Rossell concluded from these results that "there is the possibility that in many [especially high-education] communities, school desegregation has more socially integrative characteristics than disintegrative with regard to voting behavior." [56]

Rossell next directed her analyses to the question of "white flight." She supplemented the HEW school-desegregation data used by Coleman and Farley with pre-1967 and case-history data, which she collected directly from each district. All told, Rossell assembled data on eighty-six northern and western districts. Twenty-six had undergone no desegregation, while sixty had experienced varying degrees of desegregation; but of the latter, only eleven were actually under court orders. This prodigious effort yielded an analysis of trends in pre- and post-desegregation white enrollment by district.

Pasadena and Pontiac, the two cities with the greatest proportion of school reassignments, showed significant white-enrollment decline over the first three and two years, respectively. But in Rossell's sample of sixty cities, these two were striking exceptions. In no other case was the implementation of a court-ordered plan followed by a significant increase in the decline of the white proportion of total enrollment. Schools in South Bend, Indiana, for example, actually became significantly more white following a plan for minimal desegregation.[57]

Table 4 summarizes Rossell's data using five categories of districts: those with *Court Ordered* desegregation, those that reassigned over 20 percent of their pupils for desegregation (*High Desegregation*), those that reassigned between 5 percent and 20 percent (*Medium Desegregation*), those that reassigned less than 5 percent (*Low Desegregation*), and finally a *Control Group* of districts that reassigned no children whatsoever for desegregation. The two right-hand columns in table 4 give the slopes of the pre- and post-desegregation trends in white enrollment. The "significance level" column indicates that there are no statistically significant differences either between the full pre-desegregation

TABLE 4: *Change in Percentage White for Four Desegregation Groups and a Control Group*

| Group | \-4 Years | \-3 Years | \-2 Years | \-1 Year | 0 Years | 1 Year | 2 Years | 3 Years | Signif. Level | Pre- Slope | Post- Slope |
|---|---|---|---|---|---|---|---|---|---|---|---|
| | | | | **Change in % White** | | | | | | | |
| Court Ordered | −1.1 | −1.8 | −2.2 | −1.0 | −1.8 | −2.1 | −1.4 | | N.S. | .0 | .2 |
| High Desegregation (> 20%) | −1.5 | −1.8 | −1.8 | −1.2 | −2.4 | −1.8 | − .8 | | N.S. | .1 | .8 |
| Medium Desegregation (5–20%) | −1.1 | − .7 | − .9 | − .9 | −1.0 | −1.0 | −1.0 | | N.S. | .0 | .1 |
| Low Desegregation (< 5%) | −1.8 | −1.8 | −1.4 | −1.5 | −1.6 | −1.6 | −1.5 | −1.7 | N.S. | .1 | −.1 |
| Control Group (0%) | | −1.5 | −1.5 | −1.9 | −2.2 | −1.8 | −1.3 | −1.2 | N.S. | −.5 | .3 |

Source:　Christine H. Rossell, "The Political and Social Impact of School Desegregation Policy: A Preliminary Report," paper presented at the Annual Meeting of the American Political Science Association, San Francisco, Calif., 3 Sept. 1975; Table 10.

trend and the trend for the first year of desegregation or between the pre- and post-desegregation trends. Notice that there are no significant differences in the rate of decline in the proportion white between pre- and post-desegregation years for any of the four categories of desegregating districts. Furthermore, to whatever extent decline in the proportion white of total enrollment represents "white flight," there was not significantly more "white flight" in districts with court-ordered desegregation than in those without it, in districts with extensive desegregation than in those with minimal desegregation, or in districts with desegregation than in districts without it. Especially noteworthy is the absence of a significant change in white-enrollment trends in districts which had court-ordered desegregation. Recall that Coleman had repeatedly attacked the federal judiciary and had alleged that their far-reaching desegregation orders resulted in "white flight" —without ever employing data on court orders like those used by Rossell.

Thus, in her extensive sample of northern urban districts, Rossell, like Farley, found no relationship between desegregation and "white flight." Why did Rossell and Coleman reach such different conclusions? Let us consider differences in their approaches and data.

Although both investigators based their work on the HEW data for 1968 to 1972, Rossell also included HEW's 1967 data (which Coleman ignored) and as much pre-1967 information as she could gather from individual districts. Rossell, then, could discern comparatively accurate and reliable pre-desegregation racial-enrollment trends. Coleman, as we noted earlier, based the trend calculations in his third analysis on the single base year of 1968–1969.

The two researchers also employed different samples of cities. Rossell limited her study to urban school districts in the North and West. Coleman did report a "white flight" effect for desegregation in large northern cities, but it was smaller than that reported in such southern cities as Atlanta and Memphis. Such an effect did not exist among the largest cities in Rossell's sample. As table 5 indicates, large northern cities with populations of over five hundred thousand showed no greater desegregation effect than did smaller northern cities.

The most fundamental differences between the Rossell and Coleman studies were their operational definitions of the two

TABLE 5: *Change in Percentage White for Three Desegregation Groups and a Control Group by City Size*

| Group | -4 Years | -3 Years | -2 Years | -1 Year | 0 Years | 1 Year | 2 Years | 3 Years | Signif. Level | Pre- Slope | Post- Slope |
|---|---|---|---|---|---|---|---|---|---|---|---|
| *Large Cities* (> 500,000) | | | | | | | | | | | |
| High Desg. | -1.3 | .7 | -2.8 | - .4 | -2.3 | -2.3 | -1.4 | | N.S. | .1 | .5 |
| Med. Desg. | -4.0 | -1.0 | -1.1 | - .9 | -1.1 | -1.1 | | | a | a | a |
| Low Desg. | | -1.5 | -1.7 | -3.6 | - .8 | - .9 | - .4 | | N.S. | -1.1 | .2 |
| Control | -2.1 | -1.3 | -1.3 | -1.9 | -1.7 | -1.6 | | | a | .1 | a |
| *Medium Cities* (100,000-500,000) | | | | | | | | | | | |
| High Desg. | -1.3 | -1.6 | - .3 | -1.3 | -2.0 | -1.8 | -2.2 | - .8 | N.S. | .1 | .3 |
| Med. Desg. | - .8 | -1.3 | - .6 | -1.2 | -1.2 | -2.1 | -1.1 | -1.1 | N.S. | - .1 | .1 |
| Low Desg. | -1.3 | -2.5 | -1.8 | -1.3 | -1.3 | -1.6 | -1.4 | -1.3 | N.S. | .1 | .0 |
| Control | | -1.0 | -2.0 | -2.1 | -2.4 | -1.8 | -1.3 | -1.3 | N.S. | - .6 | .4 |
| *Small Cities* (< 100,000) | | | | | | | | | | | |
| High Desg. | -2.2 | -3.3 | -4.8 | -1.8 | -3.6 | -1.2 | -1.1 | | N.S. | - .0 | 1.3 |
| Med. Desg. | - .2 | - .7 | -1.2 | - .2 | - .9 | - .3 | - .9 | | N.S. | - .1 | .0 |
| Low Desg. | | | - .6 | - .5 | - .7 | -1.5 | -1.5 | | a | a | a |
| Control | | | | | -2.2 | -1.9 | -1.6 | -1.2 | a | a | a |

aUnable to compute.

Source: Same as for Table 4.

key concepts—"white flight" and "desegregation." Coleman defined "white flight" as the percentage decline in the *absolute* number of white students in a district. But changes in the numbers of white *and* black students are significantly and positively associated across urban school districts, and black enrollments in some central-city systems are beginning to decline. Consequently, Rossell defined "white flight" as the percentage decline in the *proportion* white of total enrollment, a definition that considered both black and white students.

These contrasting definitions can produce widely varying estimates of "white flight." Consider the critical case of San Francisco. Coleman showed a 1971–1972 loss of 22.4 percent (7,534 out of 33,601) of the city's white public-school pupils following San Francisco's major desegregation effort in 1971; in contrast, Rossell showed that the white proportion declined by only 5.1

percent. The difference is explained by the decline of black enrollment during these years. As Gary Orfield observed, "from September 1972 to September 1974, San Francisco's black enrollment declined by a ninth and its Latino enrollment by a twelfth." [58] In short, these two rival definitions of "white flight" will converge for cities where the number of black students is relatively stable and will diverge for cities with a rapidly changing number of black students.

Coleman and Rossell also differed in their operational definition of "desegregation." Coleman, as we have seen, regarded any reduction in his system-wide index of school racial segregation as evidence of desegregation, whether it resulted from governmental action, court orders, or demographic change. Rossell, on the other hand, measured desegregation in terms of governmental action, by the percentage of students reassigned to schools in order to further racial desegregation. She also distinguished between desegregation that was court-ordered and that which was not.

Coleman's operational definition of desegregation introduces a potentially major artifact into his analysis. As the review panel at The Urban Institute noted, much of the decline in his segregation index for particular cities may have resulted not from desegregation efforts but from neighborhood transition. Some cases of what Coleman labeled "white flight" caused by school desegregation were actually temporary instances of school desegregation caused by black movement into formerly white neighborhoods.

Rossell makes the point cogently:

> Although Coleman has claimed in television appearances and to journalists that he is conducting research on school desegregation policy, he is doing nothing of the sort. Indeed, there is no evidence he knows what school desegregation policy has been implemented in the school districts he is studying. . . . By simply measuring the changes in school segregation (which is much easier than tracking down the data on school segregation policy), Coleman cannot distinguish between ecological succession in neighborhood school attendance zones and an actual identifiable governmental policy resulting in the same thing—integration. In the case of ecological succession in school attendance zones, the integration will be temporary and the eventual re-segregation will look like white flight resulting from school 'desegregation.' This confusion of two differ-

ent phenomena means that his model is invalid for the case of governmental or court-ordered school desegregation policy.[59]

We have, then, three studies that have used basically the same HEW data base to investigate the same problem. Farley and Rossell report no relationship between school desegregation and "white flight"; Coleman reports a significant relationship. A number of factors have been cited as possible explanations for these differences. It is significant, however, that although Farley and Rossell differed in the scope of their samples, the years they studied, the research designs they employed, and their definitions of "white flight" and desegregation, both concluded, in contrast to Coleman, that school desegregation was related only weakly, if at all, to decline in white enrollment in urban schools.

## YET ANOTHER ANALYSIS

We offer yet another analysis in an attempt to clarify this puzzle. We maintain that many of Coleman's results may stem from his choice of particular subsets of "largest" urban school systems.

Recall that in his first paper Coleman did not list the urban districts in his sample. Only four months and hundreds of headlines later was the list of the twenty "largest" urban school districts revealed: New York City, Los Angeles, Chicago, Philadelphia, Detroit, Houston, Baltimore, Dallas, Cleveland, Memphis, Milwaukee, San Diego, Columbus, Tampa, St. Louis, New Orleans, Indianapolis, Boston, Washington, D.C., and Atlanta. Washington was cited in this list, although it had been dropped during Analysis I due to its lack of white students.[60] This left only nineteen in the crucial subset of "largest" urban districts.

But these are *not* the nineteen largest urban school districts in the United States. Omitted and never mentioned in any of the four versions of Coleman's paper are Miami-Dade, Jacksonville-Duval, and Fort Lauderdale-Broward, all county-wide urban systems in Florida. Yet Tampa-Hillsborough, also a Florida metropolitan school district, was included, although it is smaller than the three omitted districts. Miami and Jacksonville, like Tampa, experienced widespread court-ordered school desegregation without a significant decline in white enrollment, while Fort Lauderdale's white enrollment *increased* by 39.2 percent from 1968 to 1972 during an extensive school-desegregation program.

Thus, Coleman's unexplained exclusion of these three huge districts may have contributed to his findings.

The problem of sample selection is yet more complicated. At times Coleman seemed to invoke criteria other than school-district size to designate his subset of "largest" urban school districts. For example, in his second analysis he included Denver and San Francisco, raising the number of cases to twenty-one, because they "were two of the few northern cities to undergo extensive desegregation during the period 1968–73. . . ." He excluded Albuquerque because it "is not among the first fifty [cities] in population," [1] even though its school system is larger than that of San Francisco. No mention is made, however, of Nashville, which has a larger school system than San Francisco and ranks thirtieth in city population.

Nor did Coleman provide a rationale for cutting off his sample of "largest" urban school districts after San Francisco. This decision is particularly perplexing since it excluded Charlotte-Mecklenburg, North Carolina, the next largest urban school system and the district involved in the critical *Swann* decision. Under court order, this metropolitan school district experienced a larger drop in segregation, as measured by Coleman's segregation index, than any in his big-city sample save Tampa.

A less arbitrary procedure would have been to use Farley's method of choosing all urban school districts which enrolled a certain number of students in a given year. Employing Coleman's own rankings by 1972 enrollment, a sample of all urban school districts with more than seventy-five thousand students would have included not only Miami, Jacksonville, Fort Lauderdale, Denver, Nashville, Albuquerque, and San Francisco but also Charlotte, Newark, Cincinnati, and Seattle. All these cities except Albuquerque, Fort Lauderdale, and Charlotte are among the nation's fifty largest.

Our analysis uses both Coleman's sample and the one outlined above to show how Coleman's findings are influenced by his selection of urban school districts and his year-by-year procedure. We shall use Coleman's time period (1968 to 1973); his definitions of "white flight" and "desegregation"; his data as provided in Appendix 3 of the fourth version of his paper; [2] and his two principal control variables—the proportion of students who are black and the natural logarithm of the total size of each school system. However, in order to take into account factors like the "hastening effect" and residential transition, we shall use Farley's method of analyzing changes in the variables across the span of 1968 to 1973 rather than Coleman's year-by-year procedure.

Figure 2 presents our basic data and indicates the relationship between the amount of desegregation from 1968 to 1973 and the percentage change in white enrollment over these same years. If there were a strong positive relationship between desegrega-

FIGURE 2: *Scatter Diagram of Desegregation and White-Enrollment Losses, 1968-73*

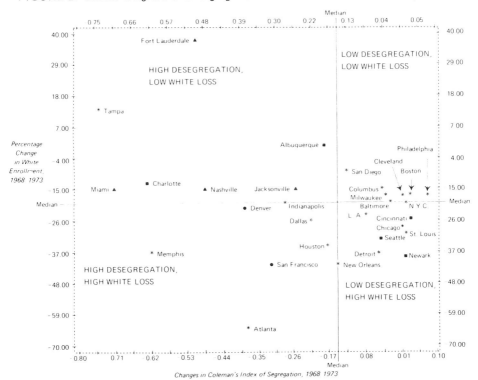

LEGEND
* Coleman's original sample of 19 urban school districts
● Cases which were added in Coleman's second analysis
▲ Cases which should have been included in sample of "largest" urban school districts
■ Cases which would be included if a standard cutoff of 75,000 district enrollment in 1972 were used

tion and "white flight," we would expect the data points representing the thirty urban school districts to fall predominantly in the high-desegregation/high-loss and the low-desegregation/low-loss quadrants (lower-left to upper-right diagonal).

But figure 2 does not reveal this much-heralded relationship. Only a few of the thirty districts lie in the two predicted quadrants ($r = -0.30$). This replicates Farley's earlier results for the districts shown in figure 1. Now notice the importance for Coleman's argument of the two extreme points in the lower-left quadrant. Not surprisingly, these points represent Memphis and Atlanta; figure 2 shows how unusual they are among the nation's

FIGURE 3: *Scatter Diagram of Proportion of Black Students in 1968 and White-Enrollment Losses, 1968-1973*

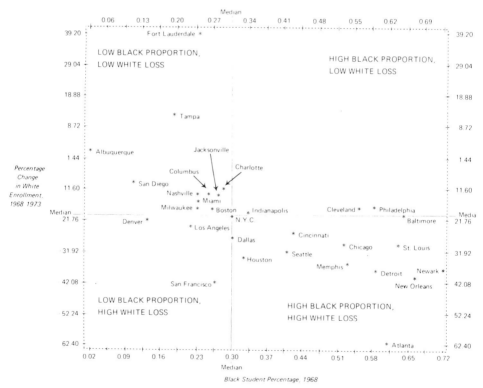

*Black Student Percentage, 1968*

thirty largest urban school systems. Finally, Denver and San Francisco, the two districts Coleman added as an afterthought in his second analysis, are also in the high-desegregation and high-loss quadrant.

Six of the nine districts that should have been included in the big-district sample are located in the high-desegregation/low-loss quadrant, including all four of the districts larger than San Francisco. The remainder—Cincinnati, Newark, and Seattle—are located in the low-desegregation/high-loss quadrant. In short, *the two additions Coleman made to his subset of big districts for his second analysis contributed to the positive association between white loss and degree of desegregation; the nine he left out would have severely reduced the association.*

Figure 3 describes the same thirty urban school districts but relates the 1968 proportion black of total enrollment to declines in white enrollment from 1968 to 1973. Note the strong association that now emerges: those districts that had relatively high proportions of black students in 1968 tended to experience the largest decline in proportions white of total enrollment over the next five years ($r = -0.57$). As Coleman has stated, though, such a strong predictor must be controlled to allow a fair test of the effect of desegregation.

Table 6 provides the relevant coefficients for the various subsets of large urban school districts. As figure 3 suggested, the Pearson correlation coefficients in table 6 show that the key variable associated with declines in white enrollment from 1968 to 1973 is the 1968 proportion black of total enrollment. In all five sets of districts, the first-order (column A), multiple (column D), and partial correlation coefficients (column E) are virtually identical. Neither degree of school-desegregation nor school-system size is strongly related to the percentage decline in white enrollment over this five-year span. Controlling for proportion black and system size using desegregation as the independent variable (column F) does decrease the negative relationship between desegregation and decline in white enrollment, but the coefficients (columns B and F) remain trivial. Moreover, small but interesting changes in the five partial coefficients for desegregation (column F) among the various subsets of districts further suggest that Coleman's choice of cases tainted his results. Indeed, the final two coefficients (column F, rows 4 and 5) show

TABLE 6: *Prediction of Decline in White Enrollment (1968-1973) for Various Subsets of Large School Districts*

| | First-order correlations of decline in white enrollment with: | | | | Partial correlations of decline in white enrollment with: | |
|---|---|---|---|---|---|---|
| | A. Prop. black, 1968 | B. Desegregation, 1968–1973 | C. Natural log system size, 1972 | D. Three-variable multiple correlation | E. Prop. black (size and desegregation held constant) | F. Desegregation (size and prop. black held constant) |
| 1. Original 19 districts | .610 | −.062 | .003 | .612 | .610 | .059 |
| 2. Original districts plus Denver and San Francisco | .522 | −.026 | −.048 | .535 | .531 | .087 |
| 3. 27 districts whose cities rank in 50 largest | .577 | −.174 | −.081 | .583 | .556 | .023 |
| 4. 21 districts of (2) plus Miami, Jacksonville, Nashville, and Fort Lauderdale | .516 | −.256 | .034 | .525 | .470 | −.108 |
| 5. Full 30 districts | .574 | −.298 | .020 | .584 | .523 | −.123 |

Data Sources:  For the original nineteen "largest" school districts plus those of Denver, San Francisco, Albuquerque, Newark, Charlotte, Cincinnati, and Seattle, the data for these analyses are taken from James S. Coleman, Sara D. Kelly, and John A. Moore, *"Trends in School Segregation, 1968–73.* The Urban Institute (Washington, D.C.: Aug. 1975), Appendix 3. For the four cities omitted from Coleman's analyses and Appendix 3 (Miami, Fort Lauderdale, Jacksonville, and Nashville), enrollment data are from the same HEW source utilized by Coleman; and the desegregation estimates are taken from Farley's index for elementary desegregation, 1967–1972, which for other districts closely approximates Coleman's index for all grade levels, 1968–1973.

modest *negative* relationships between desegregation and decline in white enrollment, although they do not approach statistical significance.

The plot thickens as we push our analysis beyond Coleman's, which was largely confined to white Americans even though the policy issue even more crucially involves black Americans. Using the same format as table 6, table 7 repeats the analysis for the percentage *gains* in *black* student enrollment.

We should clarify one potentially confusing difference between tables 6 and 7. In table 6, following Coleman, we were using *declines* in white enrollment; now in table 7 we are looking

TABLE 7: *Prediction of Black Enrollment Gains (1968-1973) for Various Subsets of Large School Districts*

|  | First-order correlations with: | | | Partial correlations with: | | |
| --- | --- | --- | --- | --- | --- | --- |
|  | A. Prop. black, 1968 | B. Desegregation, 1968-1973 | C. Natural log system size, 1972 | D. Three-variable multiple correlation | E. Prop. black (size and desegregation held constant) | F. Desegregation (size and prop. black held constant) |
| 1. Original 19 districts | −.583 | .247 | .000 | .605 | −.565 | .198 |
| 2. Original districts plus Denver and San Francisco | −.490 | .193 | .056 | .515 | −.467 | .145 |
| 3. 27 districts whose cities rank in 50 largest | −.486 | .256 | .162 | .527 | −.428 | .145 |
| 4. 21 Districts of (2) plus Miami, Jacksonville, Nashville, and Fort Lauderdale | −.491 | .237 | .060 | .517 | −.451 | .132 |
| 5. Full 30 districts | −.505 | .283 | .126 | .550 | −.455 | .175 |

Data Sources: Same as for Table 6.

at *gains* in black enrollment. These two dependent variables are negatively correlated for all thirty cities $(r = -0.34)$. In other words, white and black enrollments across these large urban districts were positively associated, tending to rise or fall together during this five-year period.

The fact that both white and black enrollments decline in districts with high proportions of black students suggests that this variable acts as a surrogate for other factors. Thus, large cities with a high proportion of Blacks often have highly unfavorable tax bases, old housing stocks, declining employment, and other financial problems.

Of greater interest is the contrasting operation of the desegregation variable in the two tables. In table 6, we have noted virtually no effect of desegregation upon white losses, although there was some slight variation according to which subset of big-city systems we used. Yet in table 7, across all five subsets of districts, desegregation has a modest but consistent *positive* association with black-enrollment gains column B). Part of this relationship is indirectly due to the fact that cities with low proportions of Blacks have had more desegregation; thus, the coefficients are substantially reduced when we control for proportion black and system size (column F).

These analyses of white and black student enrollments lead to a conclusion that is in stark contrast to Coleman's. When viewed in a five-year perspective, *desegregation had no discernible effect on the general trend of decline in white enrollment in the nation's truly largest urban school districts.* It is particularly important for policy makers to observe that districts which are metropolitan in scope (Miami, Fort Lauderdale, Jacksonville, Tampa, Nashville, and Charlotte) seem especially resistant to the phenomenon (figure 2). Given that these districts are in the South, this resistance is especially noteworthy. Our analyses suggest further that desegregation *may* help enlarge black enrollments, perhaps by providing hope to black communities that public education for their children will improve. Our larger point is simply that a rounded scientific and policy perspective on interracial processes requires careful attention to black as well as white Americans.

## A PROPOSED RESOLUTION

Since all four of these "white flight" studies employ essentially the same HEW data base, there should be an underlying resolution of the discrepant findings. We believe that there is such a resolution, and that it consists of the following six generalizations that one or more of the four studies support and none contradicts.

*There has been an enormous, long-term trend of whites leaving the central cities for the suburbs and Blacks coming into the largest central cities.* This trend began in many areas after World War I, gained momentum throughout the nation after World War II, and represents a "triumph of national housing policy."[63] Consistently during this period, federal programs such as urban renewal, public housing, Model Cities, discriminatory mortgage programs of the Veterans Administration and the Federal Housing Administration, and even federal highway construction have furthered the separation of the races between city and suburb. This separation antedated school desegregation by decades. This trend toward residential segregation has been so massive that school desegregation could have at most a relatively small impact. Inflation, energy shortages, the decline in black out-migration from the South, and the movement of Blacks to the suburbs could slow the trend in the future.

*The studies indicate that desegregation has little or no effect on "white flight" in small and medium-sized cities.* The few cases in which desegregation was accompanied by substantial decline in white enrollment often involved special factors unrelated to desegregation.

*The studies also indicate that desegregation has little or no effect on "white flight" in metropolitan school districts.* Figure 2 shows that the six southern metropolitan school districts in our sample of the thirty largest districts—Miami, Jacksonville, Tampa, Nashville, Charlotte, and Fort Lauderdale—experienced a high degree of desegregation and, correspondingly, a low decline in white enrollment.

*Court-ordered desegregation has had no greater effect on "white flight" than equivalent non-court-ordered desegregation.* Rossell's data on this point are summarized in table 4.

*The decline of both white and black enrollment in large urban school systems is related to the proportion of the system's enrollment which is black.* This generalization must be qualified in two ways. First, this is not true for all cities. But in general, as revealed in tables 6 and 7, the relationship holds for both races. Second, the fact that both white and black enrollments varied in the same way with proportion black suggests that, in addition to racial factors, this variable is a surrogate for a range of variables—such as receding tax bases, old housing, and high unemployment rates—which characterize districts with relatively high percentages of Blacks.

*Extensive school desegregation in the largest nonmetropolitan school districts, particularly in the South, may hasten "white flight" in the first year of the process, but at least part of this effect may disappear in later years.* Coleman showed only a one-year effect, part of which probably reflected neighborhood transition. Rossell also showed this effect in the first year for rapidly desegregating urban districts in the North. But she showed, too, that by the second and third years these same districts have an average rate of decline in white enrollment below both their own predesegregation rate and the rates of other districts (tables 4 and 5). It seems, then, that, with the onset of school desegregation, some white families may well hasten their already formed plans to move to the suburbs, especially if there is prosegregationist political leadership as in Memphis and Boston. But a longer period of observation suggests that this first-year loss is often a short-term phenomenon and may be followed by a loss in later years which is lower than normal.

## THE INTERVIEWS CONTINUE

The media continued to devote attention to Coleman's views throughout August and September. Walter Goodman published an interview in the *New York Times Magazine* entitled "Integration, Yes: Busing, No." Coleman repeated his now-familiar arguments and discussed his entitlement idea that central-city children be allowed to attend any school in their metropolitan area. Intermeshed with comments on his research were renewed attacks upon housing: "What's wrong with compulsory busing is that it's a restriction of rights. We should be expanding people's rights, not restricting them." [64]

In this interview, Coleman introduced two new pieces of data, both questionable, to support his argument. He stated flatly that "surveys indicate that a majority of blacks as well as whites oppose busing." [65] This assertion conflicts with the results of numerous national surveys. A November 1974 Gallup survey, for example, established that 75 percent of "non-white" respondents in a national sample favored "busing school children to achieve better racial balance in schools." [66] Coleman also chose this interview as the forum in which to present for the first time a large-district analysis which, he argued, indicated that school desegregation causes "white flight":

> Eleven cities out of the first 19 experienced little or no desegregation at all between 1968 and 1973. Based on the white loss that occurred in these 11 cities in 1968–69, they would have been expected to lose 15 percent of white students between 1969 and 1973; their actual loss was 18 percent, only slightly greater than expected. Eight cities experienced some desegregation; some of those experienced large desegregation, others not so large. Those eight cities, based on their losses in 1968–69, before desegregation occurred, would have been expected to lose only 7 percent of white students between 1969 and 1973; they actually lost 26 percent, nearly four times what would have been expected. [67]

This misleading statement actually refers to the *third* analysis, which had not yet been made public. This analysis, as we have seen, was to appear in modified form in the fourth version of Coleman's ever-changing study.[68] The casual Sunday *Times* reader might have concluded that even mild desegregation causes a fourfold increase in "white flight," instead of the more modest increase projected by Coleman's own earlier one-year models positing extreme conditions. Moreover, the *Times* reader had no way of knowing that "the first nineteen" cities were arbitrarily selected; that just three southern cities—Atlanta, Memphis, and New Orleans—provided virtually all of the "effect"; or that Tampa, the district with the most desegregation, was the only district of the nineteen to post a *gain* in white student enrollment from 1969 to 1973.

Many leading newspapers now began to run stories critical of Coleman's research and questioning the validity of his often-quoted opinions. John Mathews, a *Washington Star* staff writer, provided a detailed description of Coleman's study under the banner "IS COURT-ORDERED DESEGREGATION SELF-DE-FEATING?" [69] Unlike early stories, Mathews's article cited at length Reynolds Farley's research and took pains to describe the many cities in which large-scale school desegregation had occurred without massive "white flight." William Grant, education writer for the *Detroit Free Press,* contrasted Coleman's cautious style in academic settings with his free-wheeling manner in media interviews.[70] Grant quoted Coleman as saying: "Crime in the cities is clearly correlated with the proportion [of] blacks. It's not something people like to talk about, but . . . whether [whites] leave because of the fear of crime or whether because of the fear of blacks . . . I think it still adds up to the same thing." Coleman's argument, then, seems to be that the range of urban problems that might lead whites to leave are themselves created by black citizens. This blaming-the-victim argument can, of course, be seriously challenged. In an extensive article that considered both Coleman's position and that of his critics, Steve Twomey, education writer for the *Philadelphia Inquirer,* stressed Coleman's novel metropolitan entitlement strategy and quoted his description of his critics as "a lot of . . . people who would rather pursue a common path and attempt to ignore the fact that this [de-segregation] may be having unintended and undesired conse-quences." [71]

Coleman continued to make unfortunate *ad hominem* attacks on his critics in his second intervention in the Boston school-desegregation case. On August 27, 1975, he provided the anti-busing Boston Home and School Association with a second affidavit, much of which was a reply to criticisms of his work.[72] Coleman repeated the argument he had made in his *New York Times Magazine* interview, which implied that school desegregation multiplies "white flight" by a factor of four. This, he contended, ". . . should leave little doubt in any but the most fixed mind that substantial desegregation in a large city produces substantial increases in the rate of loss of whites from the city's schools."[73] Coleman predicted that "full-scale desegregation in Boston, occurring this fall, will have substantial effects in bringing about an additional loss of whites," and closed his affidavit with a blast at the present authors:

> I cannot conclude without mentioning what seems to me an unfortunate phenomenon in social science. On certain questions, there appears to be a kind of conspiracy of silence, and then a rush to the attack when anyone dares to break the silence. I have the impression that if Professors Green and Pettigrew saw the fires in the sky during the riots of 1967, they would have attributed them to an extraordinary display of the Northern Lights. I believe that it does no one any good in the long run for us to blind ourselves to reality, because it is reality, not our fond hopes about it, which measures the effectiveness of government actions.[74]

Affidavits, unlike depositions, are not subject to cross-examination. But Coleman's second affidavit was answered two weeks later in an affidavit submitted by Norman Chachkin, the one lawyer who had participated in the review panel at The Urban Institute.[75] In addition to raising again some of the panel's methodological concerns, Chachkin made two points. First, Coleman had indicated in the panel discussion that his views on the proper role of the courts in school desegregation were personal and not based on the results of his study. Second, Coleman had also stated both in the discussion and in writing that his study was not intended for use in judicial proceedings. Chachkin quoted from the final printed version of Coleman's paper:

> It is useful also to point out that data such as these which show the indirect and unintended consequences of school desegregation actions may be relevant for certain desegregation actions, but not

for others. They are relevant for an executive or legislative body which is attempting in its action to achieve a desirable social consequence. They are not relevant for a court decision which is acting to insure equal protection under the 14th Amendment.[78]

Coleman's public pronouncements continued unabated into the fall. He wrote another article reiterating his views in the October 1975 issue of *Phi Delta Kappan*. He now conceded that his findings could well be interpreted as affording "a strong argument in favor of eliminating segregation at the metropolitan level. . . ." [77] But he flatly rejected this possibility.

On September 22, 1975, Coleman rendered his third affidavit for the Boston Home and School Association. This time he replied to Christine Rossell's conflicting research, which the plaintiffs had submitted to the court.[78] In his July television appearance in Boston, his three affidavits, and his repeated interviews with Boston reporters, Coleman had given particular attention to that tense city even though the federal school-desegregation order had been handed down long before. Yet, except for admitting that his television appearance "may be mischievous," Coleman never publicly discussed the possibility that his warnings that Boston would experience a massive white exodus might act as a self-fulfilling prophecy.

Later in the fall, Coleman shifted his attention to Louisville, Kentucky, the nation's other desegregation trouble spot. On October 28, testifying along with Louisville and Kentucky officials before the Senate Judiciary Committee in Washington, he briefly reviewed his Analysis II and maintained that "policies of school desegregation which go beyond the elimination of de jure segregation . . . are counterproductive in our large cities. . . ." [79] He did not specify which, if any, federal court decisions had ever gone "beyond the elimination of de jure segregation." (We know of none.) Interestingly enough, Coleman opposed the proposed antibusing amendments to the Constitution as improper. "This, I recognize, is not a very satisfactory position," he concluded, "because it leaves me with only the hope that the courts will themselves see the incorrectness of the precedent that has evolved; but it is the only position I find myself able to take." [80]

On December 5, Coleman delivered the major address at a national conference on busing alternatives held in Louisville. He repeated his anti-busing arguments and his "white flight" conclusions. In yet another telephone interview, he had told Berl Schwartz of the *Louisville Times* (October 8, 1975) that the conference could serve to "give legitimacy to anti-busing sentiments." [81]

Yet three days after the conference, at a special session of the United States Commission on Civil Rights in Wsahington, D.C., Coleman suddenly withdrew his firm conclusion about "white flight": "What is not clear is whether desegregation itself induces an increased movement of whites from the desegregated district," [82] Coleman told the Commission—thousands of headlines and eight months after he had initiated his campaign.

## COLEMAN'S OPPOSITION TO COURT-ORDERED SCHOOL DESEGREGATION

We have seen how limited Coleman's research results are, and how tenuous is their connection to his publicly expressed political views against court-ordered school desegregation. A review of his dozens of statements in articles, in affidavits, on television, and to interviewers suggests that his opposition to such judicial decisions as that in the *Swann* case derives, at root, less from his research than from two related and publicly expressed beliefs:

1. Change in racial relations should flow not from the federal courts, but from the will of the community. It is critical that whites accept such change, for whites ultimately have the power to defeat it.
2. Only a small part of segregation is *de jure*, that is, a result of state action. Most segregation, especially school segregation, is *de facto*, the result of individual actions, and thus beyond the appropriate reach of the law. Under the Fourteenth Amendment, federal courts are obliged to end all *de jure* segregation in public education; but they are wrong when they attempt to undo *de facto* school segregation as well, for in so doing they abridge individual rights.

Let us consider each of these beliefs in more detail.

### The Will of the Community

Coleman's argument is remarkably similar to the position of the nineteenth-century Social Darwinists. "Stateways cannot change folkways" was their dogma, and this reasoning is embedded in the 1896 Supreme Court decision in *Plessy v. Ferguson*[83] which affirmed the legitimacy of "separate-but-equal" public facilities.

But the past generation has experienced change in racial relations that William Graham Sumner and his followers could not have foreseen. In 1954, the segment of white America most hostile to the reduction of discrimination against black people resided in the rural South. Yet in desegregating public facilities, the polls, and even schools, the rural South has made at least as much progress as any other part of the nation. To be sure, serious racial problems remain in the rural South, but the progress there is genuine and profound.

Most of this progress obviously did not flow from "the will of the community" but was imposed largely by government intervention—not the least of which was from the federal judiciary. How could this forward leap in the individual rights of the most oppressed portion of black America have taken place against the will of powerful white communities? Coleman himself, in his brilliant *Resources for Social Change: Race in the United States*, supplies part of the answer.[84] Blacks, even in the rural South, had personal and collective resources which could be converted into power and social change. Access to litigation was and is one of these resources, although Coleman rightly notes its limitations if unaccompanied by other assets.[85]

Another part of the answer to how such sweeping change has been possible in the rural South lies in the power of a *fait accompli*. Indeed, opinion surveys record that the most startling shifts in racial attitudes and behavior among white Americans occurred *after* racial desegregation had been achieved, often under court order.[86]

This is not to argue that mobilized white opposition cannot thwart progress in racial relations. Educational desegregation, like any other program, can be made to fail if national, state, or local leaders, such as those in Boston's school system, dedicate their efforts to making it fail. "White flight" at the onset of desegregation may even be induced, we suspect, by the dire predictions of such leaders. A principal objection to Coleman's position, then, is that, by implication, it takes the success of racist opposition to desegregation as reason for the United States to forsake its still unattained goal of racial justice.

### De Facto Segregation and Individual Rights

Coleman's second underlying belief is remarkable for two reasons. It assumes that most racial segregation, especially in schools, is de facto and therefore should not fall under the "state action" provisions of the Fourteenth Amendment. It further assumes that this segregation is de facto because of "individual actions"—whites and Blacks freely making residential choices, unfettered by such structural limitations as government-sanctioned discrimination in housing and employment. We believe that both of these assumptions are wrong.

In the few available historical studies of the origins of school segregation within northern cities, virtually all segregation has been found to be de jure in origin. Racial discrimination and segregation do not just happen in America; they are planned and provided for, sometimes years in advance, by government agencies—school boards, city councils, state legislatures, and often federal bureaus as well.[87] The briefs of plaintiffs in Boston, Detroit, San Francisco, and other cities literally bulge with detailed evidence for these contentions. Such compelling evidence helps explain why conservative, strict-constructionist, federal district-court judges have repeatedly found system-wide de jure school segregation throughout the North. In so doing, they have not, as Coleman implies, abused judicial power; their decisions have been based on an overwhelming mass of evidence,[88] with which Coleman has apparently not acquainted himself.

Coleman emphasizes that the growing trend of school segregation between central city and suburb is caused mainly by individual actions and therefore should not be addressed by the courts with metropolitan remedies. Coming from a sociologist, this argument is perplexing, for it seems to deny institutional structure and to assume that society is composed simply of the sum of its freely acting individual members. It disregards a history of residential discrimination and of state action to bring about a pattern of black cities with white suburbs. The social-science research literature documents beyond dispute the federal government's involvement, since the passage of the first national housing act in 1935,[89] in creating this pattern. Inter-district segregation did not "just happen" any more than did intra-district segregation.

When Coleman argues that metropolitan remedies and extensive busing for desegregation are wrong because they limit individual rights, he is speaking largely of white rights and, in effect, of a white right to discriminate. Recall his entitlement plan, whereby each black child in the central city would have the right to attend any school in the metropolitan area up to a fixed percentage in each school. Notice how this proposed remedy, which constitutes his principal suggestion in 1975 for extending black rights, places the full burden of desegregation on the black child.

In short, Coleman would limit the federal courts in urban cases exclusively to intra-district remedies that would involve little or no busing or mixing of social classes. This is another point where his recommendations and his research findings diverge, for his data on the separation of the races between cities and suburbs show clearly that observing these limitations would effectively mean no racial desegregation of the public schools of large urban districts. Unless he is opposed to racial desegregation as a goal— and he has insisted in many interviews that this is not the case— we cannot reconcile his political position with his own data on urban school-desegregation trends.

In the last analysis, our major policy disagreement with Coleman involves the issue of metropolitan desegregation. His data and our own on the relationship between "white flight" and desegregation in six metropolitan districts indicate that metropolitan approaches are essential if desegregation is to be attained. Such remedies for segregation do not necessitate one huge school district. They can result in more districts than now exist, for they are meant only to disallow urban boundaries which function as racial "Berlin walls." In many areas, metropolitan approaches could minimize transportation as well as deter "white flight," and they could avoid placing the major burden of desegregation on working-class children, as in Boston. Inter-district arrangements would allow most schools to draw students from a wider geographical area and thus achieve a stable proportion of Blacks and Whites. In sum, metropolitan approaches to school desegregation could eliminate the constraints of present political boundaries.

We are not blind to demographic changes by race, although we believe that "black containment" is a more accurate descriptive term than "white flight." We do not believe that Coleman has convincingly proven that school desegregation *causes* "white flight," as he himself candidly admitted in his Civil Rights Commission paper. But we are aware—indeed, as race-relations specialists, we have for fifteen years been aware—that large central cities have long been becoming ever blacker and suburban rings ever whiter. We agree with Coleman completely that this is one of the most basic and threatening realities of modern race relations in America. We further agree that public policies brought this reality about—not court-ordered school desegregation in the 1970's but federal housing policies from the 1930's on. And under present housing policies these trends will continue with or without school desegregation.

Given this situation, what do we do about urban school desegregation? We agree that the present situation of court-ordered school desegregation confined within large central-city districts is not ideal. Coleman suggests that we should abandon such court orders and try interracial marriage and voluntary methods that have already failed. We believe that rather than abandoning the racial integration of public education, we should fashion our remedies to fit the problem. Since urban desegregation must overcome metropolitan-wide obstacles, it must be planned on a metropolitan-wide basis. This is why for over a decade we have sought support for metropolitan approaches to school desegregation.

## SOCIAL SCIENCE AND PUBLIC POLICY

This article has not been easy to write. The information necessary to evaluate Coleman's much-publicized research has been consistently difficult to obtain. Throughout the furor created by Coleman's statements, there has been confusion about where his limited research ends and his sweeping opposition to court-ordered desegregation begins. When critics questioned his views, they repeatedly suffered ad hominem abuse. Some critics have hurled such abuse at Coleman. We regret all such ad hominem remarks deeply. They make good copy for the mass media, perhaps, but they cheapen the debate, lower the public's respect for social science, and divert public attention from real issues. Indeed, the whole episode goes beyond racial issues or attacks on personalities, to raise painful ethical questions about the relationship between social science and public policy.[90]

From April until August of 1975, the social-science community did not receive the analysis upon which Coleman's widely publicized statements were reportedly based. The details of the first analysis were never released; the second draft of the paper presented the details of an entirely new analysis with a radically different research design. All told, over an eight-month period, Coleman presented five editions of his paper (plus a thirty-nine-page erratum edition) containing three contrasting analyses of his data. Although Coleman's research was constantly changing, his expressed views remained substantially the same. Telephone calls to The Urban Institute in June requesting methodological detail were summarily rejected on the grounds that the analysis was "still in progress," yet there had already been two months of national publicity about policy recommendations said to flow from this still-in-progress research. Coleman's only statement about this serious problem appeared late in August in his second affidavit against the plaintiffs in the Boston desegregation case:

> First, many of the complaints in the Pettigrew-Green paper, the Weinberg paper, and the *New York Times* article are complaints about the absence of methodological detail in a paper presented orally to a lay audience. For example, in that presentation, I had no chance to state which 19 cities in the analysis as the largest central city school districts [*sic*]. Boston is one of these cities. . . . It is unfortunate that the full report was not available earlier to those commentators, and I am to blame for that.[91]

What made the four-month delay even more "unfortunate" was the consistent confusion between Coleman's personal opinions and his research findings. Most of the hundreds of articles and editorials about the episode presented Coleman's views as if they were the results of a new and massive study of urban desegregation. For example, the cover caption to his article in the October 1975 *Phi Delta Kappan* read: "HAS FORCED BUSING FAILED? JAMES COLEMAN OFFERS NEW INSIGHTS FROM RECENT RESEARCH." "New insights from [his] recent research" could not have concerned the success or failure of busing, of course, for the research did not even include a measure of busing.

Social scientists, like other citizens, have a right to express their political views on any subject without the support of research results. Problems arise, it seems to us, when a social scientist misrepresents or allows misrepresentation of personal opinions as results of extensive scientific investigation. If the social scientist in question is highly respected and popularly known, and if he or she chooses to engage in a mass-media campaign to influence public policy, these problems are exacerbated.[92]

Coleman's statements and personal attacks upon his critics suggest that he is certain his views are correct. His data, he told the Boston federal court, "should leave little doubt in any but the most fixed mind that substantial desegregation in a large city produces substantial increases in the rate of loss of whites from the city's schools. . . ."[93] Those who dare disagree with him must suffer from "motivated blindness"; must be part of "a kind of conspiracy of silence"; must mistake race-riot fires for "an extraordinary display of the Northern Lights"; must be "people who would rather pursue a common path and attempt to ignore the fact that this [desegregation] may be having unintended and undesired consequences." Such summary dismissal of criticism is likely to cause a scientist to ignore the accumulation of contrasting evidence on the same issue that other competent and honest scientists have uncovered.

We firmly believe that social science can and should influence public-policy issues on which it can responsibly bring research and theory to bear. Perhaps specialized groups of social scientists, checked in part by peer review, could best perform this task. Individual social scientists could also carry out this function responsibly by basing their views on published and widely available material and by presenting them in situations, such as courtrooms and legislative committee hearings, where they are subject to formal cross-examination or at least to informed questioning. Mass-media campaigns are a hazardous way to introduce social science into public-policy debates. The Coleman episode of 1975 is the most extensive example of such a campaign in sociology, but it is by no means the first nor, we fear, the last.

Communicating material from the social sciences via the media is complicated by limitations in both institutions. Few social scientists other than economists have experience in dealing with the media. Until recently, sociologists, psychologists, and political scientists have seldom been taken seriously in matters of public importance. To be candid, academicians are often flattered by sudden attention from the media and offer bold views which contrast markedly with the cautious presentations they make to their colleagues. And professional associations offer little guidance.

Within the news media, social science has yet to be elevated to the status of a regular, specialized "beat." One television network and a few newspapers and magazines now have economics reporters, but the term "science writers" still refers largely to specialists in the physical sciences. All too often, non-specialists fit their stories into "human-interest" format that emphasizes *ad hominem* charges and countercharges among the participants in a controversy, while ignoring the central issues.

The Russell Sage Foundation, Philip Meyer of the Knight Newspapers,[94] and a few other individuals and organizations have directed attention in recent years to this dangerous incongruity between the news media and the social-science profession. Unless structural changes are made in both institutions and each learns to take the other more seriously, the nation will continue to witness examples of extremely inadequate reporting of social-science findings relevant to public policy. In time, the public might understandably conclude that social scientists have nothing to contribute to policy debates except their own highly politicized opinions.

## REFERENCES

1. James S. Coleman, Ernest Q. Campbell, Carol J. Hobson, James McPartland, Alexander M. Mood, Frederic D. Weinfeld, and Robert L. York, *Equality of Educational Opportunity* (Washington, D.C.: GPO, 1966).

2. 305 U.S. 337 (1938).

3. James S. Coleman, Sara D. Kelly, and John A. Moore, "Recent Trends in School Integration," paper presented at the Annual Meeting of the American Educational Research Association, Washington, D.C., 2 April 1975. Hereafter referred to as Paper I.

4. There are two main forms of what is commonly called "white flight" from the schools: (1) white students being withdrawn from public schools undergoing desegregation and being enrolled in private or religious schools; and (2) white students being withdrawn from public schools as they and their families move from cities undergoing school desegregation to cities or suburbs not undergoing school desegregation. In both cases, "white flight" implies that the withdrawal is caused by school desegregation. The distinction is important because the two forms of educational "white flight" from the schools have very different relations to residential "white flight."

In Coleman's definition of "white flight" from the schools, it is not entirely clear whether he means the first form of the process, the second, or both. Nevertheless, his operational definition—percentage change in the absolute number of white students enrolled in public schools—includes both forms. Although it is important to distinguish between the two forms of educational "white flight," particularly when drawing inferences (as Coleman does) regarding residential segregation, throughout the remainder of this paper and in the literature reviewed operational definitions of educational "white flight" include both forms of the process.

5. This first version of Coleman's paper did not list the cities that constituted his two categories of central cities. Four months later, this vital information was provided in Coleman's second paper. Only then was it known that both the exclusion of some of the nation's largest urban school districts (e.g., Miami-Dade, Fort Lauderdale-Broward) and the placement of the dividing line between the two categories were arbitrary. These decisions, as we shall subsequently review in detail, acted to enhance the association between school desegregation and the loss of white pupils. For this first paper, the nineteen "largest" central-city districts were New York, Los Angeles, Chicago, Philadelphia, Detroit, Houston, Baltimore, Dallas, Cleveland, Memphis, Milwaukee, San Diego, Columbus, Tampa-Hillsborough, St. Louis, New Orleans, Indianapolis, Boston, and Atlanta. The next largest, medium-sized urban districts, as categorized by Coleman, were Denver, Albuquerque, San Francisco, Charlotte-Mecklenburg, Newark, Cincinnati, Seattle, San Antonio, Tulsa, Pittsburgh, Portland (Oregon), Baton Rouge, Mobile, Oakland, Kansas City (Missouri), Buffalo, Long Beach, Omaha, Tucson, El Paso, Toledo, Minneapolis, Oklahoma City, Birmingham, Wichita, Greenville (South Carolina), Austin, Fresno, Akron, Shreveport, Dayton, Garden Grove (California), Louisville, Sacramento, Norfolk, St. Paul, Winston-Salem–Forsythe, Corpus Christi, Gary, Richmond (Virginia), Rochester, Fort Wayne, Des Moines, Rockford (Illinois), Jersey City, Anaheim, San Jose, Montgomery, and Colorado Springs. Richmond was later dropped from the analysis because of its extensive annexation of white suburbs, although other cities (e.g., Dallas, Denver, Houston, and Memphis) with similar annexation during these five years were retained in later analyses. Tucson was dropped in an October set of corrections due to reporting difficulties. Moreover, for the completely different analysis of the second, third, and fourth versions of the paper, Denver and San Francisco were shifted over to the "largest" district category—a shift which, as we shall later demonstrate, also acted to heighten the critical correlation between desegregation and white loss.

6. Coleman et al., Paper I, p. 18.

7. Ibid., p. 22.

8. "Desegregation's Architect Unhappy with Overall Results," *Boston Globe,* 18 May 1975, p. 8, cols. 1–8, and p. 9, cols. 5–7.

9. "Courts Scored as Going Too Far in School Integration," *Los Angeles Times,* 29 May 1975, Part I, p. 10, cols. 1–4, and p. 11, cols. 1–4.

10. "Long-Time Desegregation Proponent Attacks Busing as Harmful," *New York Times,* 7 June 1975, p. 25, cols. 4–8.

11. Mark R. Arnold, "A Scholar Who Inspired It Says Busing Backfired," *National Observer,* 7 June 1975, p. 1, cols. 1–2, and p. 18, cols. 1–6.

12. Ibid., p. 18.

13. Ibid., p. 18.

14. Ibid., p. 18.

15. Merrill Sheils and Diane Camper, "Second Thoughts," *Newsweek,* 23 June 1975, p. 56.

16. Affidavit of James S. Coleman, Morgan v. Kerrigan, United States Court of Appeals for the First Circuit, C.A. No. 72-911-G, 12 June 1975, pp. 3–4. Hereafter referred to as Affidavit I.

17. Roger I. Abrams, "Not One Judge's Opinion: Morgan v. Hennigan and the Boston Schools," *Harvard Educational Review,* 45 (1975), 5–16.

18. 402 U.S. 1 (1971).

19. Comment made at a press conference held in New York City, 13 June 1975.

20. Barbara Campbell, "Five-Year Study on Busing Scored: Finding That It Causes White Exodus Disputed," *New York Times,* 14 June 1975, p. 12, cols. 1–2; and Iver Peterson, "Clark Group Assails New Coleman Study," *New York Times,* 25 June 1975, p. 49, cols. 1–3.

21. "A Critique of Coleman," paper presented at the Annual Meeting of the National Education Association, Los Angeles, Calif., 3 July 1975.

22. Robert Reinhold, "Coleman Concedes Views Exceeded New Racial Data," *New York Times,* 11 July 1975, p. 1, cols. 3–4, and p. 7, cols. 1–2.

23. Ibid., p. 7.

24. Reply Affidavit of James S. Coleman, Morgan v. Kerrigan, 28 Aug. 1975. Hereafter referred to as Affidavit II.

25. James S. Coleman, "Another Look at Integration," *Newsday,* 27 July 1975, Ideas Sec., p. 1.

26. James S. Coleman, Sara D. Kelly, and John A. Moore, "Trends in School Segregation, 1968–73," unpublished paper, The Urban Institute, Washington, D.C., 28 July 1975. Hereafter referred to as Paper II. Notice the shift in the title from "School Integration" in the first paper to "School Segregation" in this and all later versions.

27. Coleman et al., Paper II, p. 51. The four times these rare circumstances occurred were in Memphis (1972–1973), Birmingham (1969–1970), and Richmond (1960–1970, 1970–1971); only the first two cities were employed in Coleman's second analysis.

28. "A Critique of 'Trends in School Segregation, 1968–73,' " unpub-

lished paper, College of Urban Development, Michigan State Univ., Lansing, Mich., Nov. 1975.

29. James S. Coleman, Sara D. Kelly, and John A. Moore, "Insert for Trends in School Segregation, 1968–73," unpublished paper, The Urban Institute, Washington, D.C., Oct. 1975. Hereafter referred to as Paper V. Coleman stressed that his figures probably *underestimated* "white flight" in the cities listed because a number of them had annexed white areas during the years he studied. But he failed to mention in any of the various discussions of this table the fact that the extreme conditions posited for his calculations undoubtedly *overestimated* "white flight."

30. Coleman et al., Paper II, p. 62.

31. A partial, edited transcript of this meeting is available from The Urban Institute, 2100 M Street, N.W., Washington, D.C. 20037. References made to the meeting's discussion are taken from this transcript.

32. The total number of white students fell during this period, in part because of a rapid decline in the white birth rate in the 1960's; the decrease in white migration *into* the central city; the changing white age structure; and the rise of non-educational urban problems that drove both white and black families out of the city.

33. For a discussion of ecological fallacy, see Hanan C. Selvin, "Durkheim's *Suicide* and Problems of Empirical Research"; W. S. Robinson, "Ecological Correlations and the Behavior of Individuals"; and Herbert Menzel, "Comment on Robinson's 'Ecological Correlations and the Behavior of Individuals'"; all in *Sociology: Progress of a Decade,* ed. Seymour M. Lipset and Neil J. Smelser (Englewood Cliffs, N.J.: Prentice-Hall, 1961).

34. Gregg Jackson, "Recent Trends Critique: III. Reanalyses of Coleman's Data and Additional Data," unpublished paper, United States Commission on Civil Rights, Washington, D.C., July 1975. Jackson found each of these four variables predicted changes in white-student enrollment better than did degree of school desegregation.

35. Jane R. Mercer and Terrence M. Scout, "The Relationship between School Desegregation and Changes in the Racial Composition of California School Districts, 1963–73," unpublished paper, Sociology Department, Univ. of Calif., Riverside, 1974.

36. "Racial Integration in the Public Schools, 1967 to 1972: Assessing the Effects of Governmental Policies," *Sociological Focus,* 8 (1975), 3–26; and "School Integration and White Flight," paper presented at the Symposium on School Desegregation and White Flight, Brookings Institution, Washington, D.C., 15 Aug. 1975.

37. James S. Coleman, Sara D. Kelly, and John A. Moore, "Trends in School Segregation, 1968–73," unpublished paper, The Urban Institute, Washington, D.C., 15 Aug. 1975. Hereafter referred to as Paper III.

38. For example, four citations of other research on "white flight"

which had been provided Coleman at the August 4 meeting were now mentioned briefly in footnotes. Coleman et al., Paper III, pp. 46, 50.

39. Ibid., pp. 68–69. This conclusion was retained in the fourth version, Paper IV, pp. 79–80.

40. There are only seven school districts in the nation that are this large or larger. The figure is an average of the sizes of the particular twenty-one urban districts Coleman chose as the "largest." But an average is a poor measure of central tendency for a highly skewed, small distribution, where New York alone has over a million students. The median figure for Coleman's twenty-one urban districts in 1972 is 128,000 (Milwaukee). James S. Coleman, Sara D. Kelly, and John A. Moore, *Trends in School Segregation, 1968–73* (Washington, D.C.: The Urban Institute, Aug. 1975), p. 5. Hereafter referred to as Paper IV.

41. The only situation that even approaches these conditions is Memphis in 1972–1973; but in 1972 it had a total of 139,000 students, not 169,000.

42. Michael W. Giles, Everett F. Cataldo, and Douglas S. Gatlin, "Desegregation and the Private School Alternative," paper presented at the Symposium on School Desegregation and White Flight, Brookings Institution, Washington, D.C., 15 Aug. 1975; also Everett F. Cataldo, Michael W. Giles, Douglas S. Gatlin, and Deborah Athos, "Desegregation and White Flight," *Integrated Education*, 13 (1975), 3–5.

43. Luther Munford, "Schools that Quit 'Tipping' in Mississippi," paper presented at the Symposium on School Desegregation and White Flight, Brookings Institution, Washington, D.C., 15 Aug. 1975, p. 7. Also Munford, "White Flight from Desegregation in Mississippi," *Integrated Education*, 11 (1973), 12–26.

44. "White Flight Research: Its Importance, Perplexities, and Possible Policy Implications," paper presented at the Symposium on School Desegregation and White Flight, Brookings Institution, Washington, D.C., 15 Aug. 1975, p. 1.

45. Orfield, p. 2.

46. Ibid., p. 21.

47. Farley, "School Integration and White Flight."

48. Edward R. Fiske, "Integration Role on Cities Assayed," *New York Times*, 17 Aug. 1975, p. 19, col. 1.

49. Barbara Zolotch, "An Investigation of Alternative Measures of School Desegregation," *Institute for Research on Poverty Discussion Papers*, Univ. of Wisconsin, Madison, 1974.

50. Farley, "School Integration and White Flight," p. 10.

51. Ibid., pp. 6, 9.

52. Task Force on Education of the L.Q.C. Lamar Society, "Public Schools in Memphis: Struggling but with Head Well Above Water," *Southern Journal*, 4 (1975), 3–4.

53. Coleman et al., Paper IV, pp. 70–71.

54. Walter Goodman, "Integration, Yes: Busing, No," *New York Times Magazine,* 24 Aug. 1975, pp. 10–11, 42, 46, 48.

55. "The Political and Social Impact of School Desegregation Policy: A Preliminary Report," paper presented at the Annual Meeting of the American Political Science Association, San Francisco, Calif., 3 Sept. 1975. See also Rossell, "School Desegregation and White Flight," *Political Science Quarterly,* 90 (1975–1976), 675–95.

56. Rossell, "Political and Social Impact," abstract.

57. Ibid., table 10.

58. Orfield, p. 10.

59. Rossell, "Political and Social Impact," p. 55.

60. We do not question the decision to drop Washington, D.C., because of its tiny percentage of white pupils, but we wonder why a comparable cutoff was not employed for districts with tiny percentages of black students. Thus, Coleman analyzed Garden Grove, Anaheim, and San Jose, all in California, though each had less than 2 percent black school enrollments. This is apparently another example of Coleman's exclusive concentration on white Americans.

61. Coleman et al., Paper IV, p. 56, n. 22. Coleman has since stated that he included San Francisco and Denver at our suggestion. He is mistaken. We suggested only that he rerun his analysis without Atlanta and Memphis so as to gauge the critical importance of these cities to his results. To the best of our knowledge, this suggestion has not been followed.

62. Ibid., pp. 99–121. We utilized the data for all school levels combined. Later Coleman discovered that major errors had been made in his analyses of elementary-school enrollments (Paper V), but these errors do not affect our present results. For the four cities omitted from Coleman's analyses and Appendix 3 (Miami, Fort Lauderdale, Jacksonville, and Nashville), enrollment data are from the HEW source utilized by Coleman; their desegregation estimates are taken from Farley's index for elementary desegregation, 1967–1972, which for other districts closely approximates Coleman's index for all grade levels, 1968–1973.

63. Orfield, pp. 18–20.

64. Goodman, p. 48.

65. Ibid., p. 48.

66. *Gallup Opinion Index Report 113* (Princeton, N.J.: The American Institute of Public Opinion, Nov. 1974).

67. Goodman, p. 11.

68. Coleman et al., Paper IV, pp. 69–70.

69. "Is Court-Ordered Desegregation Self-Defeating?" *Washington Star,* 4 Sept. 1975, Sec. A, p. 1, cols. 1–6, and p. 10, cols. 3–8.

70. "Sociologist's Busing Switch Based on Questionable Data," *Detroit Free Press,* 19 Aug. 1975, Sec. A, p. 3, cols. 6–8, and p. 16, cols. 1–8.

71. "Busing Advocate Changes Course," *Philadelphia Inquirer,* 31 Aug. 1975, Sec. 1, p. 1, cols. 1–4, and p. 2, cols. 1–4.

72. Coleman, Affidavit II.

73. Ibid., p. 5.

74. Ibid., pp. 5–6.

75. Affidavit of Norman J. Chachkin, Morgan v. Kerrigan, 9 Sept. 1975.

76. Coleman, Paper IV, p. 5.

77. "Racial Segregation in the Schools: New Research with New Policy Implications," *Phi Delta Kappan,* 57 (1975), 75–78.

78. Reply Affidavit of James S. Coleman, Morgan v. Kerrigan, 22 Sept. 1975. Hereafter referred to as Affidavit III. Coleman noted some of the differences between Rossell's study and his own that we have discussed previously; he particularly stressed her different operational definition of "desegregation." He also overestimated the loss of white students from Boston's public schools during desegregation, because apparently he was unaware that the Boston School Committee had included Spanish-speaking pupils in the "white" total for 1973–1974 but excluded them in 1974–1975. This shifting designation of Latino children over recent years has also occurred in Florida and California and has probably caused Coleman's estimate of "white flight" in these areas to be inflated.

79. James S. Coleman, "Testimony of James S. Coleman before the Senate Judiciary Committee," Washington, D.C., 28 Oct. 1975.

80. Coleman, "Testimony," p. 4.

81. Berl Schwartz, "Conference Being Set Up on Alternatives to Busing," *Louisville Times,* 8 Oct. 1975, Sec. B, p. 1, cols. 1–3.

82. Coleman, "School Desegregation and Loss of Whites from Large Central-City School Districts," paper presented to the United States Commission on Civil Rights, 8 Dec. 1975, Washington, D.C., p. 7. Hereafter referred to as Paper VI.

83. 163 U.S. 537 (1896).

84. *Resources for Social Change: Race in the United States* (New York: Wiley, 1971).

85. Coleman, *Resources,* pp. 54–60.

86. Gallup polls for May 1963, May 1966, July 1969, March 1970, and October 1973. The American Institute of Public Opinion, Princeton, N.J. Additional evidence that demonstrates the growth of pro-desegregation attitudes among white Southerners after desegregation is provided by Herbert H. Hyman and Paul B. Sheatsley, "Attitudes toward Desegregation," *Scientific American,* 211 (1964), 16–23.

87. For evidence on the widespread patterns of blatant de jure segregation and discrimination in the northern states even before the Civil War, see Leon F. Litwack, *North of Slavery* (Chicago: Univ. of Chicago Press, 1961). For historical evidence on education, see David B. Tyack, *The One Best System: A History of American Education* (Cambridge, Mass.: Harvard Univ. Press, 1974), pp. 109–25, 217–29, 279–85.

88. Abrams.

89. See Thomas F. Pettigrew, ed., *Racial Discrimination in the United States* (New York: Harper & Row, 1975).

90. See, for example, Thomas F. Pettigrew, "Sociological Consulting in Race Relations," *American Sociologist,* 6 (supplementary issue) (1971), 44–47.

91. Coleman, Affidavit II, p. 1.

92. Coleman has expressed surprise that two social scientists who have often expressed their views could criticize him for expressing his views. This misses our point completely. It is the persistent confusion of political opinions with new research findings in an intense media campaign which concerns us—not the exercise of Coleman's right to express his views.

93. Coleman, Affidavit II, p. 5–6.

94. Philip Meyer, *Precision Journalism: A Reporter's Introduction to Social Science Methods* (Bloomington, Ind.: Indiana Univ. Press, 1973). The Russell Sage Foundation sponsors a joint program in social science and journalism and periodically publishes papers from its studies.

*In his response to the Pettigrew-Green critique of his work, James S. Coleman defends his research on "white flight" and goes on to argue that central-city desegregation efforts such as busing are "disastrous for the long-term integration of our society."*

# Response to Professors Pettigrew and Green

JAMES S. COLEMAN

Pettigrew and Green, in a paper that appeared in the February 1976 issue of *Harvard Educational Review,* "School Desegregation in Large Cities: A Critique of the Coleman 'White Flight' Thesis," carried out a detailed critique of my recent statements and writing on school desegregation and disputed the results of my research, which showed an accelerated loss of whites when school desegregation occurred in large central cities. Their paper is only the latest in an enormous barrage of material designed to counter statements I have made and to undermine the results of my recent research. This barrage ranges from press conferences (two last June, others since) and symposia with the press in attendance, to papers in academic and semiacademic journals. One might ask why all the frantic activity, and I will ask that later. But first I would like to reply to points raised in the Pettigrew-Green paper.

The most important question is the substantive question: does desegregation in large central cities accelerate the loss of whites from those cities, or not? My colleagues and I find that it does,

Reprinted with permission from *Harvard Educational Review,* 46, No. 2 (May 1976). Copyright © 1976 by President and Fellows of Harvard College.

while some others, including Reynolds Farley, Christine Rossell, and, in their own analysis, Pettigrew and Green, do not. There are two basic reasons for the difference, along with some special reasons in the case of Rossell. One is that the three studies which find no effect confound metropolitan-area or county-wide desegregation with central-city desegregation. The other is that we examined losses in the year of desegregation itself, while Farley and Pettigrew-Green consider losses over a five-year period (although about half of the desegregation took place in the latter part of that period).

The confounding of central-city and metropolitan desegregation arises because Pettigrew-Green and Farley include in their analysis of large cities a number of cities not classified as central-city school districts by the U.S. Office of Education. This can be seen in Pettigrew-Green's figure 2, which relates loss of whites to desegregation. In the upper left quadrant (high desegregation, low white loss) fall Fort Lauderdale, Tampa, Miami, Charlotte-Mecklenburg, Nashville, Jacksonville, and Albuquerque. *All* of these school districts are county-wide districts, covering all or nearly all the metropolitan area. Only three are classified by the U.S. Office of Education as central-city districts (and most are in the "sun belt" that is currently experiencing a population boom). In addition, most have a small proportion of Blacks. It is not surprising that these metropolitan areas do not experience the same loss of whites when desegregation occurs as do central-city districts with large black populations in the large older cities.[1] Thus, the analyses include a mixture of low desegregation-induced losses in metropolitan-wide districts in growing urban areas with high desegregation-induced losses in central-city districts. This is compounded by the fact that there has been more desegregation in these metropolitan-wide low-proportion-black districts than in larger cities with already declining populations.

By separating these factors out, we showed in our analysis (equation 3 referred to by Pettigrew-Green) that one would expect negligible losses of whites where the proportion black in the district is low and where there are no predominantly white suburbs. I do not fault Farley for not taking the latter into account, for when his analysis was carried out, it was not apparent that the availability of predominantly white suburban school districts in the metropolitan area was such an important factor in the acceleration of white loss when desegregation occurs. Pettigrew and Green, however, have no excuse, for their analysis was carried out in full cognizance of our findings on this point. By adding these metropolitan-wide districts, they have only restated results that we obtained; but they give the appearance of refuting those results.

Second, both Farley and Pettigrew-Green use the five-year losses, from 1967 to 1972 in Farley's case and from 1968 to 1973 in Pettigrew-Green's case. What happened is this: about half the desegregation occurred in the latter half of this period (whichever period is taken), so the use of five-year losses combines about equal quantities of pre-desegregation losses and post-desegregation losses. Thus for the desegregating cities, the pre- and post-desegregation losses are completely confounded by this procedure.

One might still say, however, that the post-desegregation losses, though diluted by this procedure, should nevertheless lead to enlarged five-year losses, even though the five years included on the average only about two and a half years of desegregation. The losses are enlarged by desegregation, but the reason this does not show up as larger losses than non-desegregating districts in Farley's and Pettigrew-Green's five-year method is that, on the average, desegregating districts had lower pre-desegregation losses than did non-desegregating districts. Non-desegregating districts were, on the whole, larger, older, more in the North, with a higher proportion black, and with more white suburbs than desegregating districts. They had recent histories of greater population decline. For example, projecting the pre-desegregation losses of 1968–69 forward for the four additional years to 1973 would predict for the ten desegregating cities of the twenty-two large cities I studied a loss of 10 percent of the whites by 1973. Projecting forward the 1968–69 losses for the twelve non-desegregating cities would predict a loss of 17 percent of the whites. Again, Farley had no reason to suspect this, and cannot be faulted for not taking it into account; but again, Pettigrew and Green have no excuse for obscuring this fact; they were fully aware of it when they carried out their analysis.

It is, then, principally for these two reasons that the analyses of Farley and Pettigrew-Green give results different from ours. Rossell's analysis was of a different sort altogether. For her measure of desegregation, she uses the proportion of children reassigned by the district. This, however, does not measure the actual change in segregation. For example, she classifies Baltimore as having engaged in "medium desegregation" from 1970 to 1971 on the basis of "pupil reassignment." But Baltimore showed exactly the *same* degree of segregation in 1971 as in 1970: a value of .70 on the index of segregation in both years. Secondly, for her dependent variable, she did not measure the loss of whites but the change in the proportion white in the system. As Pettigrew and Green note, this may be affected by changes in numbers of Blacks or other population groups, not only by changes in numbers of whites. To exemplify how white loss is obscured in Rossell's analysis, she concluded in the case of Boston that the general trend in loss of whites was not much affected in 1974 by desegregation.[2] But the figures tell a very different story: the average loss of whites for the six years before 1974 was 3.7 percent per year; in 1974, when partial desegregation occurred, it was 16.2 percent.[3] When a method can obscure such a change as this, then the method obviously has serious shortcomings.

There is a further issue about the particular cities used in the analysis. Apart from the implications by Pettigrew and Green that our selection of cities was a motivated one (a matter to which I will return), there is the substantive question of how strongly the results were influenced by the particular set of cities used. It is clear that for the simpler analyses, such as our equation 1 referred to by Pettigrew-Green, their own analysis, and those of Farley and Rossell, the particular cities would make a difference. However, in our analysis that took into account the availability of predominantly white suburban districts (equation 3), it is equally clear that the particular set of cities does not have a strong effect.[4] Even inclusion of Pettigrew-Green's non-central-city districts covering all or nearly all the metropolitan area would hardly have affected that result, for the result is very similar for two distinct sets of central cities: the largest twenty-one, and the next forty-six in size. These results, reproduced as table 1, indicate that the effects we found are not greatly distorted, as Pettigrew and Green argue, by Atlanta and Memphis, for Atlanta and Memphis are among the largest twenty-one, and not the next forty-six. The table shows the expected percentage of whites lost in the year of desegregation (partial desegregation consisting of a reduction of .2 in the index of segregation) based on the desegregation experience of 1968–73. The losses vary in

TABLE 1: *School Desegregation and the Loss of White Students, 1970-1973*

| Between-district Segregation | Largest 21*<br>Proportion Black | | | Next 46<br>Proportion Black | | |
|---|---|---|---|---|---|---|
| | .25 | .50 | .75 | .25 | .50 | .75 |
| .0 | 2% | 10% | 17% | 3% | 6% | 9% |
| .2 | 9 | 16 | 24 | 8 | 11 | 15 |
| .4 | 15 | 23 | 30 | 14 | 17 | 20 |

*Of the twenty-two cities referred to earlier, Washington is excluded because it is 97 percent black.

each column according to the proportion black in the district; and they vary in each row according to the availability of predominantly white suburban districts. The latter is measured by the "between-district segregation," which if high represents a high disparity between the racial composition of the city schools and those in the surrounding districts. The figures for the two groups of cities are very similar, except for larger losses in the larger cities. The entry in the top line and left-hand column for each group shows the expected losses in metropolitan-area districts of the sort that Pettigrew and Green added to the sample: the expected losses are 2 percent and 3 percent—very small, as those metropolitan districts actually showed. But it is in the central-city districts with large proportions black and predominantly white suburban districts (the bottom row and third column) where the losses are very great when desegregation occurs—in both sets of cities.

There is one modification of our results that I would now make, but this is a modification that shows somewhat worse consequences of large central-city desegregation than we had found until now. It is important to discover whether it is true, as our data tentatively showed, that the desegregation-induced losses occur only in the year of desegregation, or continue beyond. For if they continue, the long-term consequences of school desegregation are much more dismal for maintaining cities with a racially mixed population than if the losses are confined to the first year. To obtain more evidence on this, I obtained enrollment data by race for 1974 and 1975 from the eight cities among the largest twenty-one that had carried out desegregation of .1 or more in a single year between 1968 and 1973, and for Boston, which carried out such desegregation in 1974. In general, the accelerated losses continue, not as high as in the year of desegre-

TABLE 2

|  | Before Desegregation: | | Year of Deseg- regation | After Desegregation: | | | |
| --- | --- | --- | --- | --- | --- | --- | --- |
|  | 2 Years | 1 Year |  | 1 Year | 2 Years | 3 Years | 4 Years |
| Average % loss | 4.1% | 4.8% | 12.4% | 7.0% | 6.7% | 10.1% | 8.1% |
| Number of cities | 7 | 9 | 9 | 9 | 8 | 5 | 5 |

Note: If Memphis and Atlanta are excluded, as Pettigrew and Green would prefer (because their deseg-regation losses are large), the numbers are all smaller, but the same tendency exists: pre-desegregation, 3.7%, 3.1%; year of desegregation, 8.6%; post-desegregation, 5.2%, 5.6%, 6.1%, 5.2%.

gation, but higher than before desegregation. In one city, Memphis, which experienced the greatest desegregation loss (35 percent of the whites) in 1973, the 1975 figures showed no loss over 1974, apparently because the returns from private schools balanced the other losses. But in most cities, the results were otherwise. This can be seen from the average losses of white students in the two years before desegregation, the year of desegregation, and the four years after, for these nine cities (see table 2). (The data are not as good as one would wish, because data for two years before and four years after desegregation are not available in all cases. Also, some districts annexed suburbs when desegregation occurred, thus understating the losses in the year of desegregation.)

This effect can also be seen by looking at individual cities. In Dallas, the rate of white loss rose from about 2 percent to 9 percent when partial desegregation involving compulsory busing occurred in 1971, and it has stayed there since; in San Francisco, the average rate of loss for the two years before partial desegregation was 6.9 percent, while the average rate after was 11.7 percent per year; in Houston, the rate before partial desegregation was 5.1 percent, and for the six years after has averaged 7.6 percent per year; in Atlanta, the rate in the year before partial desegregation was 7.5 percent, while the rate in the six years after has averaged 19.1 percent per year; in Indianapolis, the average rate for the four years before partial desegregation was 4.8 percent and the average rate in the three years after was 7.4 percent; in Denver, the average for three years before partial desegregation was 1.1 percent per year, and for six years after was 6.4 percent. The conclusion that one must draw from these statistics for individual cities is, I believe, that current desegregation policies are having serious long-term demographic effects.

For example, if we consider a city that is 60 percent white and project forward for ten years the average of the two pre-desegregation losses from table 2 (4.1 and 4.8), then assuming the black student population remains constant, the white student population would be 49 percent of the total in ten years. If, however, we assume desegregation occurs and take the desegregation loss, the four post-desegregation losses, the white student population would be only 38 percent of the total. And this is not for an extraordinary city, but only for the average of these nine, which includes few of the oldest and largest American cities most susceptible to loss of whites. As table 1 shows, the expected loss even in the first year is considerably higher than the average shown in table 2 when the city already has a high proportion black and predominantly white suburban districts outside it. Thus, school desegregation can be predicted to erode the population mix most strongly in those cities that are already least able to maintain a racially mixed population—cities like Detroit, Cleveland, Baltimore, Philadelphia, Chicago, St. Louis. It is in several of these cities, incidentally, that current desegregation suits and HEW administrative actions are being most strongly pursued. The prediction, considering these post-desegregation data, would be for a much greater long-term effect for such cities than shown in our table of projections which Pettigrew-Green include as their table 3. That is, the ten-year effect of strong desegregation for those cities would be expected to be considerably more than the 10 percent difference in proportion black that we showed in that table, because the effect apparently does not stop after the first year in most cities, as we assumed there.

I should add a sentence or two about the charade that Pettigrew and Green go through in examining changes in the black student population in large cities. That it is an empty gesture in the direction of "equity" is evident when one sees that they examine the wrong question. What is important for the integration of our large metropolitan areas is the maintenance of whites in the central city and the movement of Blacks into the suburbs. Thus, what is important to examine is what's happening to the white student population in the central city and what's happening to the black student population *outside* the city, in the suburbs. In their rush to equity, Pettigrew and Green forget that the problem that has been plaguing Blacks for years, and one of the sources of the increasing segregation in our major cities, has been their exclusion from the suburbs and their enclosure in the city itself.

Pettigrew and Green go beyond an attempt to show that current desegregation plans do not produce white flight; they make a broad attack on various of my actions. They imply that our selection of cities was motivated by the expected results. It was, of course, not so. Pettigrew has known at least since August 4 that the criterion for selection was the largest twenty school districts classified by the U.S. Office of Education as central-city districts; and it was his complaint on that date that this sample contained too little Northern desegregation experience to allow generalization beyond the South that led me to add Denver and San Francisco—two of the next three districts in size, both of which were Northern and had undergone some desegregation. They complain that the data were not available; but the only written request for data from any investigator, made on July 15, was fulfilled on July 21.

Beyond this is the broad issue of my public statements, and the reaction they have produced, including the public statements of those who have declared themselves my opponents. By no means have I sought out the media, much less engaged in a mass-media campaign. On the contrary, I remained largely unavailable to reporters, even unreachable by telephone throughout the summer. It was my self-declared opponents, including Pettigrew and Green, who engaged in an extensive campaign, of which the recent paper is a part. They have been aided in this by some nondeclared opponents in the media.

I have, however, written extensively on these matters, I have given testimony before Congress, and I have given affidavits in a court case; Pettigrew and Green have done likewise. I have done so because I believe that the integration actions currently imposed by the courts—most prominently and most recently, compulsory racial balance in large cities—go far beyond eradication of de jure segregation, and thus must be judged not on constitutional grounds but in terms of their consequences. And my research results convince me that these consequences in large central-city school districts are disastrous for the long-term integration of our society, by exacerbating the black-city white-suburb racial separation.

Pettigrew and Green apparently feel otherwise. They are free to express their opinions, and they certainly have done so in a variety of ways. I do not question their right to do so, indeed their obligation to speak out on policy they believe has important consequences. But they have not confined themselves to that. Instead, they have attempted from the outset to throw doubt on our research results and destroy the legitimacy of my opposition to current large-city desegregation actions. I believe the force of this reaction stems from their recognition that when opposition to desegregating actions gains legitimacy, there is no longer a simple division between "the good guys" favoring any and all desegregating actions and "the bad guys" opposing all desegregation, and then the policies must be judged instead on their merits.

There is, I think, a common belief among those deeply committed to the current policies of compulsory racial balance that social-science research should be wholly in the service of those policies. Several actions follow from this belief. One is to attempt to suppress, counteract, or throw doubt on any research that leads to questioning of these policies.[5] Another is to use favorable research results (even when the research is poorly done) in a very fast and loose way, with no thought of ever being challenged. And the advocates seldom have been challenged, even when the excesses have been great. Eleanor Wolf, for example, shows this strikingly for the Detroit school desegregation case.[6]

I would like now to put professional matters aside, and refocus attention on the substantive issues at hand. Now, when the black population in central cities is stabilizing due to reduced rural-urban migration and reduced birth rates, and when many older cities have major inner-city rebuilding plans, is a time which brings an opportunity to create of our large cities stably integrated urban centers. For some cities, this is a last opportunity, because stabilization can occur only if there is a sufficiently racially-mixed population base in the cities. Affirmative integration policies in schools (for that is what the current court remedies have become, despite the protest that it is only de jure segregation that is being eliminated) should be directed to strengthening and stabilizing that racial mix—not toward destroying it, as many existing desegregation plans are doing.[7]

Because social-science research in this area has been largely in the service of the advocates of compulsory racial balance and their policies, the advocates have enjoyed a comfortable monopoly of legitimacy. Opponents could be labeled segregationists or racists, and guilt by association was a convenient and often-used tool. And now when the remedy can be legitimately questioned on the basis of its consequences, the advocates protest. What is serious and shocking to me is not that the questioning of compulsory racial balance in schools has now become legitimate, but that it has *only* now become legitimate—that social-science research has only recently broken the monopoly of legitimacy so that the policy can be examined on its merits.

If there is to be a lasting consequence of the turmoil that has surrounded my research and writing on this issue over recent months, I trust that it will be a mechanism for breaking such monopolies, such limitation on inquiry and expression, so that destructive policies can no longer be exempt from questioning.

## REFERENCES

1. In their analysis Pettigrew and Green added eight cities to my twenty-two largest central-city districts. Five were county-wide or metro-politan-wide districts which desegregated; three (Cincinnati, Seattle, and Newark) were cities that did not. All five of the desegregating districts had been *gaining* white student population before desegregation; all three of the non-desegregating districts had been losing. It is interesting to note, though Pettigrew and Green fail to do so, that even in these metropolitan districts that had been gaining whites, four of the five experienced a loss of white students in the years they desegregated.

2. Christine H. Rossell, "School Desegregation and White Flight," *Political Science Quarterly,* 90, Winter 1975–76, 675–95. See footnote 24.

3. Pettigrew and Green incorrectly state in footnote 78 that Spanish-speaking pupils in Boston were classified as "white" in 1973 and separated out in 1974. This is not so; in my data from HEW and the Boston School Committee, the Spanish-surnamed pupils are for all years considered separately. They constitute 5.4 percent of the total in 1972, 6.5 percent in 1973, 8.0 percent in 1974, and 8.4 percent in 1975. Thus the white loss is as I have stated it: 16.2 percent in 1974 (with a projected 7.9 percent loss in the spring of 1975, which grew to 18.9 percent by December 31, 1975, after Phase II of Boston's desegregation plan was implemented). I pointed this out to Green in December, yet their error persists.

4. Similarly, in our analysis of covariance in which each city was a covariate, the particular set of cities has only a small effect.

5. Pettigrew has shown such a disposition earlier; the role in which he

has cast himself in this case is not a new one for him. In 1972, he engaged in a similar attack on David Armor, who had carried out research that threw into question the beneficial achievements and attitudinal consequences of desegregation that I and others had found earlier. See David Armor, "The Evidence on Busing," The Public Interest, Summer 1972; and Thomas Pettigrew et al., "Busing: A Review of 'The Evidence,' " and David Armor, "The Double Double Standard: A Reply," The Public Interest, Winter 1973.

6. Eleanor Wolf, "Social Science and the Courts: The Detroit School Case," The Public Interest, Winter 1976.

7. I have described such a policy elsewhere; see "Racial Segregation in the Schools," Phi Delta Kappan, October 1975.

*In their reply to James S. Coleman, Professors Pettigrew and Green renew their criticism of his research and then explore the public role he has acquired through the attention focused on his work by the mass media.*

# A Reply to Professor Coleman

## THOMAS F. PETTIGREW AND ROBERT L. GREEN

Professor Coleman's response to our recent article about his attacks upon court-ordered school desegregation serves to sharpen further our conflicting views about both research and racial justice. Indeed, his retort illustrates again many of our central points, not only in what it states and the way it states it but even more by what it omits.

Coleman addresses only two of our many concerns about his research: his selected subset of the "largest" urban school districts, and the inability of other investigators to detect a *causal* relationship between "white flight" and school desegregation. He claims that he selected the nineteen largest central-city school systems as listed by the United States Office of Education. And he added Denver and San Francisco to his later analyses to meet our complaint on August 4 that his "sample contained too little Northern desegregation experience to allow generalization beyond the South. . . ."

But this explanation is insufficient. Unfortunately, Coleman does not here or elsewhere provide a citation as to where and when the U.S. Office of Education published such a list of "central city districts." Neither does he tell us how the office happened to concoct such a strange list nor why he employed it. Any

Reprinted with permission from *Harvard Educational Review*, 46 No. 2 (May 1976). Copyright © by President and Fellows of Harvard College.

listing of "largest" districts that includes one metropolitan district in Florida (Tampa—despite what Coleman now says about such districts in the "sun belt") but excludes three other districts all of which are larger (Miami, Jacksonville, and Fort Lauderdale) is odd, to say the least. Moreover, none of the officials at the Office of Education and the National Institute of Education contacted about this matter is aware of any such list as Coleman describes. To be sure, the office has had a number of listings over recent years of twenty "large cities," but those provided us all include Phoenix and San Antonio (not in Coleman's sample) and exclude Tampa and Atlanta (included in Coleman's sample, the latter of crucial importance to his argument).[1] Moreover, Denver and San Francisco (two more crucial cases) were added by Coleman in July and included in the second version of his paper issued in late July; hence, any discussions we had with him on August 4 could not possibly have influenced the inclusion of these two additional cities. Nor does this explanation account for the arbitrary line drawn after San Francisco that excluded negative cases for his contentions (e.g., Newark, Seattle, and Cincinnati).

Other investigators (such as Professor Reynolds Farley[2] of the University of Michigan and ourselves) have failed to uncover "white flight" caused by school desegregation, in Coleman's opinion because we employed the wrong set of cities and the wrong method. A robust effect worthy of having sweeping national policies based upon it should be readily detected by a range of competent methods applied by various investigators on essentially the same data. But Coleman apparently believes that only his special sample of cities and his method can detect what he is confident is the complete truth of the matter. Actually, the reader may recall that our analysis failed to support his thesis even when we did use his particular subset of "largest" urban districts.

So the analyses over time utilized by Farley and ourselves became the crux of the matter. This method compares the number of white students in a school district at a time prior to much big-city desegregation (1967 or 1968) with the number in the district five years later. Coleman condemns this method on the grounds that post-desegregation losses are obscured, in two related ways, by the use of data from the late 1960s: any pre-desegregation white student increases, or lower-than-average pre-desegregation white losses relative to segregated districts.

TABLE 1: *School Desegregation and the Loss of White Students, 1970-1973*

| | N | *Partial Correlation Holding Constant 1970 Black Student Proportion and Natural Log of 1970 District Student Size* | P |
|---|---|---|---|
| Original Coleman sample of 19 cities including Atlanta and Memphis | 19 | +.300 | .13 |
| Original 19 cities including Atlanta and Memphis plus Denver and San Francisco | 21 | +.288 | .12 |
| Original 19 cities minus Atlanta and Memphis | 17 | −.276 | .16 |
| Original 19 cities plus Denver and San Francisco and minus Atlanta and Memphis | 19 | −.174 | .26 |

Save for metropolitan districts and Memphis (through annexation), however, none of the urban districts had pre-desegregation
increases in white pupil enrollment. Yet his contention about the
possible effects of below-average losses in 1968 and 1969 prior
to most desegregation is a good point worth testing. So we redid
our analyses for just 1970–1973, omitting the 1968–1969 years in
question. The relevant findings are shown in table 1.

Following Coleman's equation 1, table 1 provides, for four subsets of cities, the partial correlations between school desegregation and the decline of white enrollments while holding constant
the 1970 figures for the school districts' proportion of black students and total enrollments. Keep in mind that table 1 employs
Coleman's data, his index of desegregation, his samples of cities,
and his recommended three critical years of 1970 to 1973. Yet
none of these relationships even approaches statistical significance—much less policy significance. Just as revealing is the
change in signs between those subsets of cities that include Atlanta and Memphis and those that do not. Once these two Deep
South cities are removed from the analysis, not even weak support is provided for Coleman's argument. These results answer
Coleman's objection to the over-time method of analysis, and
then emphasize again the crucial importance of just two atypical
cities for his sweeping arguments.

Why, then, does the over time method used by Farley and ourselves not show the same magnitude of effect as Coleman's analysis? We advanced two possibilities in our paper, neither of which Coleman mentions in his response. The over-time method substantially avoids two artifacts capitalized upon by Coleman's method of looking for white enrollment changes in the same year as the desegregation. Analyzing the problem over time lessens the "hastening up" effect caused by parents who, planning to move in any event, simply left the central city one or more years earlier than they would have without desegregation. It also avoids the "neighborhood transition" effect where schools in a residential area that is racially changing boast temporarily a greater degree of racial mixture. Here "white flight" actually causes the temporary school desegregation, but Coleman's analysis interprets it in the reverse causal sequence.

Similarly, Coleman rejects Rossell's conflicting research findings on the grounds that he likes his index of school desegregation better than the policy-oriented one she used. Actually, Rossell's measure of the student proportion which was reassigned to school for desegregation correlates highly across a wide range of urban districts (+.68) with Farley's dissimilarity measure of segregation, which in turn is essentially the same as Coleman's own measure (+.88).[3] There will be cases, of course, where the Rossell and Coleman measures diverge; the most appropriate measure to use depends on the research focus. Coleman cites Baltimore, which had a busing program in one area of the city, whose desegregation effects were obscured at the district level by growing segregation in other areas. But he might also have cited San Diego, where his index revealed considerable school desegregation (largely from residential change), though the district had only one small busing effort.[4] One might have thought that his policy interests in busing and court orders would have led Coleman to favor an index such as Rossell's. But, in any event, both indices have value; and Rossell's disconfirmation of Coleman's "white flight" results in all but a few cities remains unanswered.

Coleman now readily, if belatedly, concedes that metropolitan districts are less likely to suffer significant white student losses when they desegregate. This fact, he assures us, is consistent with his earlier analysis. Metropolitan districts lack the two key characteristics which lead to large losses of white pupils "when desegregation occurs"—high proportions of black students in the system and predominantly white suburbs. But actually his own analyses reveal that these two factors relate to the loss of whites *whether or not there is desegregation.* Are these not additional arguments for metropolitan approaches to public school desegregation?

Much as he abandoned without further mention his initial analysis of April 1975 labeled Analysis I in our paper), Coleman appears to be abandoning his arguments based on his three-variable equation 1 in preference for his five-variable equation 3 (Analysis II in our table 2).[5] Equation 3 uncovers interesting interactions between school desegregation and the black pupil proportion as well as between desegregation and the intra-district school segregation across central cities and their suburbs. Coleman now stresses the desegregation interaction with white suburbs, though its standard error (.494) approaches the magnitude of its coefficient (.561). Nonetheless, we welcome this shift, for we pointed out in our paper the potential importance of these findings "to the extent that any policy implications can be safely drawn from this work." Though equation 3 is also mis-specified and devoid of demographic context, it does alert us to two potentially critical mediators of any possible loss of white students traceable to school desegregation. And both of these mediators—the black pupil proportion and predominantly white suburbs—are significantly modified by metropolitan approaches to school desegregation.

The value of equation 3 relates, too, to a more generic point. It is not realistic to anticipate large first-order effects, positive or negative, from national programs that actually consist of literally hundreds or even thousands of different sub-programs at the local level. Does Headstart "work"? Does desegregation "work"? Such sweeping questions for such variegated programs are virtually meaningless and involve what has been called "the total effect fallacy." Likewise, Coleman finds great variability among his cities for his presumed "white flight" effect, though he has not emphasized that fact. Thus, more precise and answerable evaluation questions for national programs are: Where does the program "work"? Where does it not "work"? And what are the differences between these types of programs? Only Coleman's equation 3 and its two interactions, imperfect as they are, get at this needed specification of effects.

In addition, Coleman now presents in his table 2 new, if crude, data to argue his case. These data may be useful for political polemic, but they are of no scientific interest for two reasons. First, no control data for comparable segregated districts over these same years are provided. Second, as Coleman admits, "the data are not as good as one would wish," for the subset of cities changes across the critical later years.[6] Moreover, Coleman can hardly be demanding a realignment of national policy on the basis of five cases.

Unfortunately, Coleman does not address an array of other problems that have been raised about his research. To appreciate how much he has chosen to ignore, the reader should read our article in the last issue of this journal. Briefly stated here, Coleman has not responded to such matters as:

1. His research on essentially a demographic problem has been conducted in a demographic vacuum, and he has omitted variables that other investigators have shown to predict the loss of white students better than school desegregation[7] (indeed, his new tables 1 and 2 repeat these difficulties).
2. His future projections are inflated by unrealistic assumptions (this practice, too, is repeated in his table 1).
3. An ecological fallacy is involved in his assertions of individual motivation ("white flight") from gross district-wide data.

Our basic point, however, is that the racial desegregation of schools has not been proven to *cause* so-called "white flight" in any rigorous sense. Recall that Coleman has conceded this point in a paper delivered to the U.S. Commission on Civil Rights last December, but not mentioned in his response: *"What is not yet clear is whether desegregation itself induces an increased movement of Whites from the desegregated district"*[8] (italics added).

Turning to policy issues, we disagree with Coleman's assertion that "the most important question is the substantive question: does desegregation in large central cities accelerate the loss of whites from those cities, or not?" First, our paper demonstrated that, even if his research could be accepted at face value, Coleman's findings argue strongly for metropolitan approaches to public school desegregation. Especially is this true now that he is emphasizing the interactions of equation 3. Second, it was demonstrated that there is at best "only a tenuous connection between Coleman's research findings and his political opposition to school busing for racial desegregation." Thus, "the whole episode raises serious questions about the relationship between social science and the mass media" as it involves public policy. Consider each of these points now in the light of Coleman's present response, for the "most important question" concerns the policy implications that have been drawn by Coleman and others from his research.

1. *Metropolitan Desegregation vs. No Desegregation.* Rather than responding to our article's policy contentions, Coleman reacts sharply to his perception of self-styled " 'good guys' " who "in the rush to equity" favor "any and all desegregating actions. . . ." For the record, we have not and do not favor "any and all desegregating actions"; we have testified as expert witnesses in desegregation cases for southern school districts as well as for black plaintiffs; and we have opposed the rigid application of "racial balance" percentages.[9] Nor have we forgotten "the problem" of housing discrimination "that has been plaguing blacks for years"; indeed, we discussed it at length in our article and pointed out how Coleman had omitted it from his formulations. But more distressing is Coleman's failure to explain in his response why he so stoutly rejects current metropolitan efforts to achieve school desegregation even when his own research results clearly (as he concedes elsewhere) [10] point to that form of remedy. We can only repeat the policy statement of our article which Coleman virtually ignored:

> We are not blind to demographic changes by race, although we believe that "black containment" is a more accurate descriptive term than "white flight." . . . [A]s race-relations specialists, we have for fifteen years been aware that large central cities have long been becoming ever blacker and suburban rings ever whiter. We agree with Coleman completely that this is one of the most basic and threatening realities of modern race relations in America. We further agree that public policies brought this reality about—not court-ordered school desegregation in the 1970's but federal housing policies from the 1930's on. And under present housing policies these trends will continue with or without school desegregation. Given this situation, what do we do about urban school desegregation? We agree that the present situation of court-ordered school desegregation confined within large central-city districts is not ideal. Coleman suggests that we should abandon such court orders and try interracial marriage and voluntary methods that have already failed. We believe that rather than abandoning the racial integration of public education, we should fashion our remedies to

fit the problem. Since urban desegregation must overcome metropolitan-wide obstacles, it must be planned on a metropolitan-wide
basis. This is why for over a decade we have sought support for
metropolitan approaches to school desegregation. (pp. 49–50)

2. *Research Results and Political Beliefs.* Our article maintained that Coleman's opposition to such "destructive policies"
as court-ordered school desegregation flowed less from his research than from two firmly held political beliefs: that change in
race relations should come not from courts but from "the will of
the community"; and that the courts are wrong when they reach
beyond the small amount of de jure segregation that exists and
attempt to eliminate de facto segregation. In his response, Coleman appears to accept this analysis. Rather than modifying these
beliefs, he restates the second one even more trenchantly:

I believe that the integration actions currently imposed by the
courts—most prominently and most recently compulsory racial balance in large cities—go far beyond eradication of de jure segregation, and thus must be judged not on constitutional grounds but in
terms of their consequences. And my research results convince me
that these consequences in large central-city school districts are
disastrous for the long-term integration of our society, by exacerbating the black-city white-suburb racial separation.

Notice first that Coleman provides no citations to those cases
where courts have gone beyond the requirements of the Fourteenth Amendment, though our article asked specifically for this
information. We know of no such cases, nor do the constitutional
law experts we have questioned on the point.[11] Remedies have
been fit carefully to the demonstrated constitutional violations.
If Coleman is to construct his arguments upon this basic belief,
he must come forward with the evidence of which legal scholars
are as yet unaware.

Notice, too, that Coleman's revealing statement indicates his
readiness to dispose of the relevant "constitutional grounds"
in favor of judging the "consequences" as he views them. Courts,
of course, do attempt to foresee the consequences of their rulings; but they must, and the society should, judge the consequences within the framework of the Constitution. We believe
that this is precisely what the federal courts have in fact been
doing. We agree with Coleman that social scientists can aid this

process by providing competent and responsible testimony concerning the consequences of various options open to the courts; but we are not as willing as he to remove constitutional considerations from the school desegregation process. Finally, Coleman's statement reiterates the mistaken notion that his research investigated the consequences of court orders against de facto school segregation. Our article took pains to demonstrate that his research actually studied school desegregation resulting from any source and not just court action. Indeed, Rossell's data on court-ordered desegregation showed no differences on enrollments from other desegregation of comparable magnitude (table 4, p. 30).

3. *Social Science, the Mass Media, and Public Policy.* Coleman also pays scant attention in his reply to our discussion of the problems involved with the mass media of communication serving as a principal mediator of social science influence upon public policy. He does tell us that one written request for his data from a federal agency was honored three-and-a-half months after he made his initial "white flight" speech. But he does not deny the fact that earlier requests for information about his research by individual social scientists were rejected by The Urban Institute.

Coleman also objects to our characterization of his activities last year as a "mass media campaign" on the grounds that he had "remained largely unavailable to reporters, even unreachable by telephone throughout the summer." Whatever you wish to call it, many dozens of media interviews were granted and together with television appearances and popular writings constitute unprecedented media coverage of a sociologist and his policy opinions. Even without a telephone last summer, for example, he granted interviews to, among others, *Newsweek, The New York Times, The New York Times Magazine, The Washington Star, The Detroit Free Press,* and *The Philadelphia Inquirer* as well as an hour-long question-and-answer commercial television broadcast with over twenty-five reporters on Boston's WNAC-TV in July.[12] But our critical point was not Coleman's First Amendment right to engage in intensive media exposure, but rather the persistent media confusion, which he failed to correct, between his research and his political views. There is also the risk of the self-fulfilling prophecy entailed in such massive national coverage. Coleman cites 1975 data from Boston, for instance, without mention of his own possible role as a major figure in that embattled city's controversies.[13]

Another point that Coleman illustrates but does not respond to concerns the unfortunate use of harsh and often *ad hominem* remarks. Our analyses are a "charade"; and our article was immediately described to the media as "scurrilous." [14] Any questioning of his work is an attempt to maintain a "monopoly of legitimacy," "to suppress, counteract, or throw doubt on any research that leads to questioning of these [desegregation] policies." Here he ignores our published work that contains "negative" findings for school desegregation as well as our critiques of research with "positive" findings. He infers that our ideas are governed only by our politics, while his are those of an objective social scientist. If such behavior becomes the norm of policy debates within social science, will civil and fruitful discourse be possible?

Coleman's efforts may well have served, as he intended, to legitimate "opposition to desegregating activities" in Boston, Louisville, and elsewhere. But his extraordinary activities toward this single-minded end, we fear, have also hurt the legitimacy of social-science influence upon public policy in general.[15]

## REFERENCES

1. For example, Betty J. Foster, *Statistics of Public Elementary and Secondary Day Schools, Fall 1971* (Washington, D.C.: G.P.O., 1972), pp. 10, 24; Betty J. Foster, *Statistics of Public Elementary and Secondary Day Schools, Fall 1972* (Washington, D.C.: G.P.O., 1973), pp. 20–21; and W. Vance Grant, *Digest of Educational Statistics, 1974* (Washington, D.C.: G.P.O., 1975), p. 36. We are not suggesting, as Coleman asserts, that his selection of large urban school districts was "a motivated one"; had it been, Tampa (a very negative case for his argument) would surely have been excluded. Our points are simply that: (1) there have been many listings of large central-city districts issued in recent years by the U.S. Office of Education; (2) whatever listing he employed is not so definitive as to be readily locatable today without a citation; and (3) the prior rationale for his utilization of such atypical listing is not obvious and should have been initially explained.

2. "Racial Integration in the Public Schools, 1967 to 1972: Assessing the Effects of Governmental Policies," *Sociological Focus*, 8 (1975), 3–26; and "Is Coleman Right?" *Social Policy*, 6 (Jan.–Feb. 1976), 14–23.

3. Christine H. Rossell and Robert L. Crain, "Evaluating School De-

segregation Plans Statistically," unpublished paper, Center for Metropolitan Planning and Research, Johns Hopkins Univ., Baltimore, Maryland, Nov. 1973, p. 39; and Barbara Zolotch, "An Investigation of Alternative Measures of School Desegregation," *Institute for Research on Poverty Discussion Papers,* Univ. of Wisconsin, Madison, 1974.

4. Rossell, private communication.

5. For example, equation 3 is the basis of table 1 in his response. But, as we noted in our paper, the projections of this table are made questionable by the inflating assumption of an enormous .2 one-year drop in his desegregation index. This condition happened in only 6 percent of his 342 city/year observations.

6. Inexplicably, Coleman states that "some districts annexed suburbs when desegregation occurred, thus understating the losses in the year of desegregation" without also mentioning that the largest annexation occurred in Memphis *before* desegregation, thus understating the losses prior to desegregation. Also note in table 2 that the removal of the two critical cities of Memphis and Atlanta alone reduces the reported post-desegregation white student losses by about a third.

7. For example, Gregg Jackson, "Reanalysis of Coleman's 'Recent Trends in School Integration,' " *Educational Researcher,* 4 (Nov. 1975), 21–25.

8. James S. Coleman, "School Desegregation and Loss of Whites from Large Central-City School Districts," paper presented to the United States Commission on Civil Rights, 8 Dec. 1975, Washington, D.C., p. 7.

9. Throughout his reply, Coleman prefers the term "compulsory racial balance" to "school desegregation." The former is, of course, a politically loaded phrase that does an injustice both to our position and to that of the federal courts. No federal court to our knowledge is requiring a large city to meet narrow "racial balance" limits. The city often cited in this regard, Charlotte, North Carolina, operated last year with school percentages ranging roughly from 16 percent up to at least 40 percent. Rational discussion of social issues requires the use of less polemical and more accurate conceptualization.

10. Coleman admitted that his findings could well be interpreted as affording "a strong argument in favor of eliminating segregation at the metropolitan level . . ." but he rejected the possibility. James S. Coleman, "Racial Segregation in the Schools: New Research with New Policy Implications," *Phi Delta Kappan,* 57 (1975), 75–78.

11. For the Boston case, which Coleman seems to regard as an example of his belief, see Roger I. Abrams, "Not One Judge's Opinion: *Morgan v. Hennigan* and the Boston Schools," *Harvard Educational Review,* 45 (1975), 5–16. More recently, the appellate court, in supporting the rulings of Judge Arthur Garrity of Boston's federal district court, specifically held that Garrity's remedies had confined themselves to the demonstrated constitutional violations.

12. Merrill Sheils and Diane Camper, "Second Thoughts," *Newsweek,* 23 June 1975, p. 56; Robert Reinhold, "Coleman Concedes Views Exceeded New Racial Data," *New York Times,* 11 July 1975, p. 1, cols. 3–4, and p. 7, cols. 1–2; Walter Goodman, "Integration, Yes; Busing, No," *New York Times Magazine,* 24 Aug. 1975, pp. 10–11, 42, 46, 48; John Mathews, "Is Court-Ordered Desegregation Self-Defeating?" *Washington Star,* 4 Sept. 1975, Sec. A, p. 1, cols. 1–6, and p. 10, cols. 3–8; William Grant, "Sociologist's Busing Switch Based on Questionable Data," *Detroit Free Press,* 19 Aug. 1975, Sec. A, p. 3, cols. 6–8, and p. 16, cols. 1–8; Steve Twomey, "Busing Advocate Changes Course," *Philadelphia Inquirer,* 31 Aug. 1975, Sec. 1, p. 1, cols. 1–4, and p. 2, cols. 1–4.

13. Coleman alleges only one factual error in our article regarding footnote 78 and the inflation of Boston's 1974 reported loss of white students due to an incorrect categorization of the Spanish-surnamed. If Coleman would check again the Boston data from the U.S. Department of Health, Education and Welfare, however, he would note that the footnote is correct and that the reported loss in 1974 was not 16.2 percent as he states but 14.4 percent (and how much of this is actually truancy and the unreliable record keeping of a resistant and inefficient school system, we may never know). This is a small correction for Boston. But Farley (personal communication) points out that the growing ethnic consciousness among Latinos in the United States together with changing school practices in designating "minorities" can inflate sharply and erroneously the estimates of "white loss" in such cities as Houston, Dallas, Denver, San Diego, and San Francisco—all of which Coleman relies on.

14. "Coleman Raps Critics of 'White Flight' Theory," *Boston Herald American,* 16 March 1976, p. 12, cols. 5–6.

15. Our fears are already being substantiated: see, for example, Noel Epstein, "The Scholar as Confuser: Or, Why the Busing Issue Is not about White Flight," *Washington Post,* 15 Feb. 1976.

In this challenge to James Coleman's "white flight" thesis Christine Rossell, Assistant Professor of Political Science at Boston University, argues that what is important to remember is that "after the first year school systems with extensive desegregation have less than normal white enrollment decline in post-implementation years" and that "all desegregation plans show a substantial increase in the proportion white in the average black child's school."

# School Desegregation and White Flight

## CHRISTINE H. ROSSELL

White flight from cities has been a much discussed phenomenon in the last decade. Despite widespread speculation over which policies aggravate this trend and which slow it down, there has been little systematic research as to its causes and consequences. Nevertheless, administrators and politicians often claim that school desegregation, perhaps one of the most controversial policies of the last decade, is counterproductive because it accelerates white flight. The most recent proponent of this theory is James Coleman, best known for *Equal Educational Opportunity*, often called the "Coleman Report." [1] He has stated that "The extremely strong reactions of individual whites in moving their children out of large districts engaged in massive and rapid desegregation suggests that in the long run the policies that have been pursued will defeat the purpose of increasing overall contact

Reprinted with permission from *Political Science Quarterly*, 90 (Winter 1975–76).

among races in schools." [2] The mass media has tended to dis-
seminate statements such as these with little attempt to ascertain their accuracy, despite the mounting criticism within academic circles of Coleman's methods and findings.

The data in this article show that school desegregation has little
or no effect on white flight. Even in the two high desegregation
school districts that had significant white flight, it is minimal
(about a 3 percentage point increase over the previous trend)
and temporary. By the third year after desegregation, white
flight stabilizes to a rate lower than the predesegregation period
in these districts. For all "high desegregation" school districts the
rate of decline is lower by the third year after desegregation than
any year prior to desegregation. Furthermore, if a school district
does have any negligible white flight it typically comes before the
opening of school in the first year of the major plan, and rarely
after that. Desegregation under court order does not increase
white flight, nor does massive desegregation in large school districts. In short, this study contradicts Coleman's recent assertions
regarding the deleterious effect of school desegregation on white
flight, and demonstrates the fundamental error in his measurement of that phenomenon.

## METHODOLOGY AND PRIOR RESEARCH

In conducting public policy research, it is important that one's
methodology be appropriate to the phenomenon being studied.
While on the face of it, a longitudinal design seems the most
appropriate method of determining the impact of a policy, certain
kinds of longitudinal designs can be extremely misleading. For
example, just looking at the white enrollment before and after
school desegregation—a technique often used by newspapers,
local school officials, and desegregation opponents—obscures the
fact that while there may be a loss of whites incurred after
school desegregation, it is usually no greater than losses incurred in previous years. Thus, this type of design does not uncover patterns of white out-migration that developed long before the school issue was litigated. Longer longitudinal designs
of the type used by Coleman can be misleading if there is no
attempt to fix the point of school desegregation policy implementation, and changes in school racial mixtures are simply compared
to changes in percentage white enrollment. This technique, while

seemingly more sophisticated than a before and after design, also errs in confusing the covariation of two secular demographic trends (white flight from cities and ghetto expansion into white school attendance zones) with a causal relationship between white flight and governmentally or court-imposed desegregation policy.

Probably the most appropriate methodology for analyzing public policy impact is a time series quasi-experimental design. None of the previous analysts of school desegregation and white flight has used this design. This may be due to unfamiliarity with it, or to an unwillingness or inability to spend the necessary time and money collecting data over time. The particular quasi-experimental design used here is the interrupted multiple times series quasi-experiment with a nonequivalent control group, developed by Campbell and Stanley.[3] It is characterized by (1) periodic measurement on some variable (e.g., percentage white enrollment) obtained at equally spaced points in time; (2) the "introduction" of a quasi-experimental variable (e.g., school desegregation) somewhere into the series; and (3) a control group, which has not received the quasi-experimental variable against which the experimental groups can be compared. In this article, then, the effect of school desegregation on white flight will be analyzed as a time series quasi-experiment. (A more detailed explanation of the methodology is presented in Appendix 1.)

The small amount of academic research on school desegregation and white flight has, with the exception of Coleman's work, tended to show no relationship between the two phenomena. Clotfelter found no statistically significant relationship between school desegregation and white flight when a number of demographic and economic variables were controlled for, although his measures of school desegregation is a dichotomous variable not easily generalizable, and his longitudinal analysis only involves two points in time. Reynolds Farley, using a measure of school integration similar to Coleman's in that it does not measure actual policy, but using more sophisticated statistical controls, found integration has no discernible effect, on the average, on the rate of white flight.[4]

A research design prepared by the Rand Corporation for the U.S. Commission on Civil Rights analyzes the change in the percentage white students in the Washington, D.C., public schools

over a twenty-three-year period. The analysis shows school desegregation (open enrollment after the 1954 Supreme Court decision) to have had a minimal effect in increasing the flight of
whites to the suburbs. However, since open enrollment typically
involves very few students, it is difficult to generalize from this
finding to that of mandatory busing.[5]

One of the most promising studies of school desegregation and
white flight is summarized in a recent issue of *Integrated Education*. The study was conducted in eight desegregated school
districts in Florida in 1973. Only 3.6 percent of the parents interviewed rejected school desegregation by withdrawing their children from their assigned schools. The authors conclude that if a
low annual rate of aggregate white flight is a prime criterion for
evaluating progress, then school desegregation in these districts
should be rated at least a qualified success.[6] The findings of most
studies then, despite differing methodologies, is that the effect
of school desegregation on white flight is negligible when compared to other factors that cause relocation of whites.

## CONDUCT OF THE STUDY

### Sample and Data Collection

In this analysis aggregate data are used to describe a sample of
eighty-six northern cities and their school districts. This represents
the northern sample of a larger study of both northern and southern school districts (yet to be analyzed) and is biased in favor of
medium and large cities/school districts.[7]

### Defining School Desegregation

Most research, including Coleman's, defines "school desegregation" as any situation where there happens to be a significant
number of black and white children in the same school at the
same point in time.[8] The problem with this definition is that it
obscures the reason for the integrated situation. For a good many
schools in the United States, integration is, thus, unstable and
temporary. Actual governmental or court implemented school
desegregation, on the other hand, is not the result of ghetto expansion into an attendance zone (also called "ecological succession") and is, not surprisingly, characterized by different patterns.

This study attempts to overcome the limitations of measures of school desegregation commonly used in the past, by defining "school desegregation" as the reassignment of black or white students by a local governmental body or court for the purposes of school integration.[9] Data were collected by means of a mail questionnaire that listed the biracial schools (defined as a minimum of 10 percent black and 10 percent white)[10] in a district and asked administrators to indicate the reason for their biracialness and the approximate date of any action taken to adjust racial balance.[11] The measures of school desegregation policy were computed as follows: the number of black and white students in a school in the year in which an action was taken was subtracted from the number in the same school during the preceding year. The difference was attributed to administrative action if it increased racial integration. The number of black and white students reassigned in this way in each school was totaled for the school district. This was then standardized by converting the raw number of blacks and whites reassigned into the percentage of the total school district black population that was reassigned and the percentage of the total school district white population "reverse integrated" (sent to predominantly black or formerly black schools). These figures (percentage blacks and percentage whites reassigned) were added together to comprise an index measuring school desegregation for each year from 1963–1964 through 1972–1973.[12]

Further policy classification was unnecessary because the percentage of black and white students reassigned proved to be highly related to the type of action. Mandatory busing results in the highest percentage of students reassigned, while voluntary busing never amounts to more than a small percentage of students reassigned.[13] Furthermore, a straightforward quantitative measure avoids the problems of semantics encountered with inflammatory policy issues.

The effect of school desegregation on white flight is measured by the percentage white enrolled in public schools for as many years before and after the major school desegregation plan as data are available, with 1972–1973 being the last year of the study. Data of percentage white were obtained from HEW statistics from fall 1967 to fall 1972. For periods earlier than that, data were collected by writing to each school district in the sample.

## FINDINGS

The change in percentage white students in each of the eighty-six northern school districts before and after their major desegregation plan is presented in Appendix 2.[14] The index of the percentage of black students reassigned added to the percentage of white students reassigned in the largest desegregation action is presented in column 1. The change in the percentage white in each year before the major desegregation plan is given in columns 3 through 9. The change in the percentage in each year beginning with the major plan is presented in columns 11 through 18. School desegregation actions taken in addition to the major action are indicated by asterisks next to the change in the percentage white for that school year. For example, Pasadena's major desegregation plan reassigned 98.48 percent of the black and white students in 1970. The opening of school in the first year of the plan saw an increase in the average annual decline in percentage white of about 2 percentage points. In the fall of 1972, as indicated by the asterisk in column 13, Pasadena implemented more school desegregation. By this time, however, the decline in the percentage white is close to the trend exhibited prior to the major desegregation plan. The additional action brought their total desegregation, presented in column 22, up to 100.8.[15]

The first figure in column 17 is the result of the single-Mood test, while the second figure is the result of the double-Mood test, both explained in Appendix 1. (When N.S.—not significant—is reported, it means that the change in percentage white after desegregation is probably no greater than fluctuations that occurred before desegregation.) The figures reported for Pasadena indicate that a decline of 4.2 in 1970 (column 11) is large enough to be the result of school desegregation, rather than simply being random fluctuation. The second figure indicates that the change in percentage white when the whole postdesegregation period is examined is again large enough to be the result of school desegregation.

Column 20 shows the average change in percentage white from year to year in the predesegregation period, and column 21 shows the average change in percentage white from year to year in the postdesegregation period. While in general there is greater white flight after desegregation than before, it stabilizes by the third year after school desegregation (column 13) to a rate similar to that of the predesegregation period.

Pontiac, the second school district shown in Appendix 2, also has a significant increase in white flight after their major school desegregation plan. However, the decline stabilizes by the second year so that the rate is lower than any year before the desegregation. Both Pontiac and Pasadena desegregation plans were court ordered, but as we shall see, of the eleven court-ordered school districts, they are the only two that had a significant increase in white flight.

The remarkable characteristic of these data is that, of the top ten school districts that implemented a high degree of school desegregation, only two showed any significant increase in white flight. Furthermore, there is some indication that other factors probably contributed to white flight in Pasadena.[16] Further research on Pontiac may turn up additional factors here as well. These ten "high desegregation" school districts include one of the few school districts in the entire sample to ever have an increase in their percentage white. By the third and fourth year after their 1968 desegregation plan, the percentage white in the Berkeley school district actually increased by .2 percent and .9 percent respectively.

The next group of school districts, those implementing an intermediate degree of school desegregation, have not a single case of any school district exhibiting significant white flight after their major desegregation plan. In the third group of school districts, those that reassigned less than 5 percent of their black and white students in their major plan, one had less decline than would have been expected from the previous trend (South Bend, Indiana), and three others had a significant increase in white flight. However, the three exhibiting white flight implemented so little desegregation that the relationship to school desegregation should be treated with suspicion. As indicated in Appendix 1, the control group (those implementing no school desegregation) was assigned a "treatment point" of 1968. In other words, changes in percentage white before 1968 are compared to changes after 1968. This point comes after the 1968 summer riots and is also when a good number of school districts desegregated. In this way, it was hoped that possible secular trends could be isolated. Unfortunately, the control group suffers from poor record keeping (in some cases because it was illegal to keep such data). However, of those school districts that had pre-1967 data, two show a significant increase in white flight after the summer of 1968. Other school districts show a large increase from the previous year, but without the pre-1967 data it is impossible to tell if this is a change in the trend. At the very least, it is useful to compare these data to those of the desegregating school districts.

In order to summarize the data, the school districts are divided into five groups: court ordered; high desegregation (greater than 20 percent); medium desegregation (5–20 percent); low desegregation (less than 5 percent); and the control group. The average for each group for four years before and four years after their major plan is presented in Table 1 and represented graphically in Figure 1. As Table 1 indicates, none of the various desegregating groups shows any significant white flight, although the highest desegregation group shows a negligible increase of about 1 percentage point from the previous trend.[17] The important phenomenon here is that any loss of whites occurs *before* school opens in the first year of the plan. After that, white flight stabilizes to a rate slightly better than the predesegregation period. Therefore, white flight, if it occurs at all, occurs not from the problems experienced during the first year of desegregation, but from the fear of problems. In other words, if whites leave, it is typically not because they participated in the plan and did not like it, but because they refused to participate at all. Apparently, whites who did participate in the first year of the plan did not leave after that. This has enormous policy implications because it means administrators should concentrate their efforts on eliminating fear and controversy *before* the plan is implemented.

The findings of this study thus support the proposition that school desegregation does not cause significant white flight, and tend to disprove Coleman's thesis. Furthermore, although Coleman has maintained that "in an area such as school desegregation . . . the courts are probably the worst instrument of social policy,"[18] Figure 1 and Table 1 show no significant increase in white flight in northern school districts that desegregated under court order.

Table 2 shows the change in percentage white before and after school desegregation, controlling for degree of desegregation and city size. Within each desegregating group and the control group, the larger cities show no greater white flight than the medium and small cities, and none is significant. Although Coleman has

FIGURE 1

*Change in Percentage White for Four Desegregation Groups
and a Control Group (0 Desegregation)*

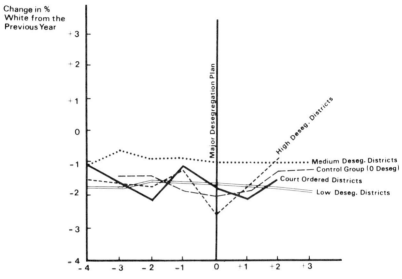

School Years Before and After Desegregation

maintained that the greatest white flight is in "large districts engaged in massive and rapid desegregation,"[19] the two large school districts, San Francisco and Denver, that engaged in such massive and rapid desegregation show no significant white flight. Nor do most of the other large school districts that implemented lesser degrees of school desegregation (Seattle; Milwaukee; Kansas City, Mo.; Indianapolis; Baltimore; Philadelphia; Los Angeles; and Chicago). Thus the data of the present study contradict almost every claim Coleman has made regarding school desegregation and white flight.[20]

## IMPLICATIONS

It appears that, although Coleman has claimed in television appearances and newspaper interviews that he is conducting research on school desegregation policy, this is not precisely what he is doing. Indeed, there is no evidence that he knows what

TABLE 1: Change in Percentage White for Four Desegregation Groups and a Control Group

| Group | Change in % White | | | | | | | | Signif. Level | Average Pre-series | Average Post-series |
|---|---|---|---|---|---|---|---|---|---|---|---|
| | −4 Years | −3 Years | −2 Years | −1 Years | 0 Years | 1 Years | 2 Years | 3 Years | | | |
| Court ordered | −1.1 | −1.8 | −2.2 | −1.0 | −1.8 | −2.1 | −1.4 | | N.S. | −1.5 | −1.8 |
| High desegregation (> 20%) | −1.5 | −1.8 | −1.8 | −1.2 | −2.4 | −1.8 | −.8 | | N.S. | −1.5 | −1.7 |
| Medium desegregation (5–20%) | −1.1 | −.7 | −.9 | −.9 | −1.0 | −1.0 | −1.0 | | N.S. | −.9 | −1.0 |
| Low desegregation (< 5%) | −1.8 | −1.8 | −1.4 | −1.5 | −1.6 | −1.6 | −1.5 | −1.7 | N.S. | −1.6 | −1.6 |
| Control group (0) | | −1.5 | −1.5 | −1.9 | −2.2 | −1.8 | −1.3 | −1.2 | N.S. | −1.2 | −1.6 |

TABLE 2: Change in Percentage White for Four Desegregation Groups and a Control Group Controlling for City Size

| Group | −4 Years | −3 Years | −2 Years | −1 Years | 0 Years | 1 Years | 2 Years | 3 Years | Signif. Level | Average Pre-series | Average Post-series |
|---|---|---|---|---|---|---|---|---|---|---|---|
| *Large cities (> 500,000)* | | | | | | | | | | | |
| High desg. | −1.3 | −.7 | −2.8 | −.4 | −2.3 | −2.3 | −1.4 | | N.S. | −1.0 | −2.0 |
| Med. desg. | −4.0 | −1.0 | −1.1 | −.9 | −1.1 | −1.1 | | | a | −1.8 | −1.1 |
| Low desg. | | −1.5 | −1.7 | −3.6 | −.8 | −.9 | −.4 | | N.S. | −2.3 | −.7 |
| Control | −2.1 | −1.3 | −1.3 | −1.9 | −1.7 | −1.6 | | | N.S. | −1.6 | −1.7 |
| *Med. cities (100,000–500,000)* | | | | | | | | | | | |
| High desg. | −1.3 | −1.6 | −.3 | −1.3 | −2.0 | −1.8 | −2.2 | −.8 | N.S. | −1.1 | −1.7 |
| Med. desg. | −.8 | −1.3 | −.6 | −1.2 | −1.2 | −2.1 | −1.1 | −1.1 | N.S. | −1.0 | −1.4 |
| Low desg. | −1.3 | −2.5 | −1.8 | −1.3 | −1.3 | −1.6 | −1.4 | −1.3 | N.S. | −1.7 | −1.4 |
| Control | | −1.0 | −2.0 | −2.1 | −2.4 | −1.8 | −1.3 | −1.3 | N.S. | −1.7 | −1.7 |
| *Small cities (< 100,000)* | | | | | | | | | | | |
| High desg. | −2.2 | −3.3 | −4.8 | −1.8 | −3.6 | −1.2 | −1.1 | | N.S. | −3.0 | −1.9 |
| Med. desg. | −.2 | −.7 | −1.2 | −.2 | −.9 | −.3 | −.9 | | N.S. | −.6 | −.7 |
| Low desg. | | | −.6 | −.5 | −.7 | −1.5 | −1.5 | | a | −.6 | −1.2 |
| Control | | | | | −2.2 | −1.9 | −1.6 | −1.2 | a | a | −1.7 |

aUnable to compute.

school desegregation policy has been implemented in the school districts he is studying. A *New York Times* research study of Coleman's twenty cities—in which key officials in each were questioned by telephone—could find no court-ordered desegregation in any of the cities during the 1968–1970 period he studied, despite Coleman's assertion that such desegregation was causing massive white flight. Court suits were pending in many cities, but desegregation was limited to a few modest open-enrollment plans, used mainly by blacks. If there was "massive and rapid" desegregation as Coleman said, it could not have been due to court-ordered remedies.[21] Since there has been no massive and rapid desegregation in the South without a court order, there is not much evidence of any kind of rapid and massive desegregation in his sample. In fact, in the same *New York Times* article, Coleman conceded he was "quite wrong" to have called the change in segregation "massive." [22]

The fact is that Coleman is studying changes in school racial mixtures, not school desegregation policy, and while he briefly acknowledges the difference in his later paper, "Trends in School Segregation, 1968–73," he continues to draw conclusions and policy recommendations that use the term, "school desegregation." [23] The clearest indication that he does not understand the difference can be seen in Coleman's affidavit in *Morgan et al. v. Kerrigan et al.* Nos. 75–1184; 75–1194; 75–1197; 75–1212, filed in the U.S. Court of Appeals for the 1st Circuit (September 3, 1975) on behalf of the Boston Home and School Association, an antibusing group in Boston. In this affidavit, he predicts that full-scale desegregation will increase the number of whites leaving the city, and that the exodus will be caused by the citywide scope of the desegregation plan and its impact at the elementary school level.[24] However, his prediction is based on his prior research in which he only measures changes in racial mixtures through a statistical measure of the proportion of blacks and whites attending school with the opposite race, and therefore does not distinguish between ghetto expansion into a white attendance zone (ecological succession) and an actual governmental policy resulting in the same thing—integration. As mentioned earlier, in the case of ecological succession, the integration will be temporary and the eventual resegregation will look like white flight resulting from "school desegregation policy." This confusion of two different phenomena means that, in most cases, Coleman's prediction is invalid for governmental or court-ordered school desegregation policy.[25]

Furthermore, in a careful review of the issues and policy implications of white-flight research, Orfield points out that even if one were to accept both the validity of Coleman's method of analysis and the maximum force of his results, his study suggests only that the initiation of desegregation in a city with a 50 percent black enrollment will produce an additional loss of 5.5 percent of the white students. This "flight" is significantly less than the same school system can expect to lose for other reasons in a normal year. In short, it seems that Coleman himself has not followed his research to its logical conclusion—that at worst, his model predicts desegregation of a 50 percent black school system would bring the schools to their ultimate ghetto status only about a year sooner than otherwise projected.[26] Therefore, an even greater problem than the inappropriate methodology used by Coleman is his apparent unwillingness to accept the policy implications of his own research.

## CONCLUSIONS

This study has demonstrated that school desegregation causes little or no significant white flight, even when it is court ordered and implemented in large cities. Despite the popularity of the claim, researchers and analysts familiar with the white-flight phenomenon in cities should have been able to predict that the effect of school desegregation would be minimal compared to other, more important, forces such as increasing crime and public fears of violence, rapid movement of jobs to suburban facilities, much greater housing construction in the suburbs than in the cities, decline in the actual level of some central city services, major urban riots, and deteriorating city schools and declining achievement scores. These and other factors have contributed to the suburbanization of middle-class families who tend to be predominantly, although not exclusively, white.[27]

While almost all school districts (with the exception of Berkeley, California) are still experiencing white flight, it is quite encouraging that by the second and third year after desegregation, the school districts engaging in massive and rapid desegregation have a rate of white flight that is lower than their rate in the predesegregation period and lower than that of any other group, including those that did not implement any desegregation at all. This is a heartening phenomenon and may mean that school desegregation, and the educational innovation that typically accompanies it when it is city wide, could impede the increasing ghettoization of American cities. While a good number of researchers and citizens maintain that the only way to avoid the problem of white flight and accomplish stable integration is to integrate housing, the findings of this study suggest that the process could in fact be the reverse. As Orfield points out, it would be extremely difficult to implement stable housing integration involving a large number of blacks, without a framework of area-wide integrated schools.[28] Once blacks begin to move into a particular area, that area tends to become increasingly more black unless new white families move in to replace those who leave in the normal process of residential mobility. Under the existing laissez-faire system, however, there is absolutely no incentive for a white family to move into a neighborhood with a substantial number of black neighbors because, based on past experience, the neighborhood school will in all probability become predominantly black in the future. Even those who would accept integration will very seldom allow their child to be in an all-black school. Therefore, without a desegregation plan, the white family often does not perceive a choice between an integrated and an all-white school, but only between an all-white school and one that is almost certain to become virtually all black. The only way to break this cycle of expectations is to assure families that the schools will be integrated wherever they move in the city, and they will not become overwhelmingly black anywhere. This assurance, which can only be supported by a city-wide school desegregation plan, could stem the flight of whites to the suburbs in search of schools that will not become all black in the near future.

Serious recommendations about school desegregation policy should be based on an analysis of policy alternatives that might lessen the incentives for the departure of the middle class in all cities, and even provide some encouragement for their return. It is not enough to simply say white flight is not increased by school desegregation. We need to know how to stop flight altogether. Perhaps the most important step to be taken next in the research described here is to determine how Berkeley was able to increase its white percentage, and why Pasadena and Pontiac experienced a brief significant white flight after school desegregation and other school districts did not. In addition, it is necessary to understand the mechanisms operating in school desegregation that account for the fact that, if any white flight occurs, it typically occurs before school opens in the first year of the plan, and rarely after, and why there is a decline in the rate of white flight by the second and third year after the major plan is implemented. Closer study of the best and worst cases, and of the intricacies of the patterns observed, might well suggest procedures and policies that can help avoid any initial loss of enrollment, and perhaps stop the loss of whites altogether from central cities.[29]

## POSTSCRIPT: 1978

Despite all the critiques of Coleman's research, including my own, the most recent evidence (the survey referred to in footnote 29 completed and updated through Fall 1975) now indicates that he was partially correct in one area: school desegregation does significantly increase the decline in white public school enrollment in the year of implementation, *if* it includes the reassignment of white students to formerly black schools, averaging for school districts with citywide two way busing plans, a doubling of the normal loss in Northern school districts and a tripling of the normal loss in Southern school districts. But *after the first year* school systems with extensive desegregation have less than normal white enrollment decline in post implementation years. Coleman also found this, but rejected it as "improbable." Nevertheless, it is what has happened, and the net effect of this less-than-normal post implementation decline means that by the beginning of the fifth year many school districts have made up their implementation year loss, at least relative to those school districts that have not desegregated. It is only in school districts at or above 35 percent black that we still have a desegregation effect at the end of five years, and even in these school districts, the implementation year loss is cut in half.

Finally, all desegregation plans show a substantial increase in the proportion white in the average black child's school regardless of how much white flight is associated with implementation, and paradoxically this benefit is greatest in school districts at or above 35 percent black, although these are also the school districts with the greatest white enrollment losses.

## APPENDIX 1: METHODOLOGY

Because this study is comparative and school desegregation occurs at different times for different school districts, a modification had to be made in the interrupted multiple times series quasi-experimental design. The treatment point is usually a fixed point or year for all cases in quasi-experimental designs. Unfortunately for the neatness of the design, some school districts take two and occasionally three years to complete their desegregation plans. However, one action is usually much larger than any of the others and that was the point chosen for those taking multiple actions. Change is then analyzed for as many years before and after the major desegregation plan as data are available (ending in 1972–1973), although for some school districts this will mean the first point in the series is 1963 and for others it is 1967. However, most school districts desegregated in 1968, with the next largest groups desegregating in 1969 and 1970 respectively. For the control group—those that did not desegregate at all—1968 is used as the "treatment" point because it is the year in which the largest number of districts desegregated, and it is a year in which a good deal of disruption and change occurred in this country. Therefore, 1968 marks a turning point used to isolate possible short- or long-term systematic trends.

### Measuring Discontinuity: Tests of Significance

The question of whether the occurrence of an event under study had an effect on the variables being measured cannot be solved simply by visual inspection of plots of data. A test of significance must be applied to estimate whether or not an observed change exceeds the limits of what is expected on the basis of chance fluctuations.

Two tests of significance, the single-Mood and double-Mood tests, are used in the interrupted time series. Each of these tests is based on a calculation of the difference between expected and observed values of points or distributions (or expected and expected values in the case of the double-Mood test), where expected values are based on an extrapolation of the regression line. The two tests, plus an additional one, are described in Joyce Sween and Donald T. Campbell, "The Interrupted Time Series as Quasi-Experiment: Three Tests of Significance" (Evanston, Ill., 1965, mimeographed). (The computer program that utilizes these tests is distributed by the Northwestern University Computing Center as NUC 0049 Timex.)

The first test, the single-Mood test (Alexander Mood, *Introduction to the Theory of Statistics*, New York, 1950, pp. 297–298), is a t-test using a simple least-squares line-fitting technique where the slope of the line is used to "predict" the first value occurring after the quasi-experiment. The standard error is based on pretest variance only. The single-Mood test is appropriate for testing hypotheses regarding the immediate effect of an event.

The double-Mood test extends the logic of the single-Mood test to include both a prechange linear fit as well as a postchange linear fit (see Mood, *Introduction to the Theory of Statistics*, pp. 350–358; and Walker and J. Lev, *Statistical Inference*, New York, 1953, pp. 390–400). The comparison is between two predictions by these two estimates of a hypothetical value lying midway between the last prechange and the first postchange point. The standard error is based on the entire series variance.

An underlying assumption of these tests is that there is no auto-correlation (correlation of errors). Since it rarely happens that errors are uncorrelated in longitudinal studies, Sween and Campbell have determined through Montecarlo simulation the degree of adjustment necessary in the significance level at which one should reject the null hypothesis for various levels of auto-correlation (Sween and Campbell, "The Interrupted Time Series," pp. 11–17).

APPENDIX 2: CHANGE IN PERCENTAGE WHITE FROM THE PREVIOUS SCHOOL YEAR COMPUTED FOR EACH YEAR BEFORE AND AFTER SCHOOL DESEGREGATION

| | (1) % Students Re-assigned | (2) Court Ordered | (3) -7 Years | (4) -6 Years | (5) -5 Years | (6) -4 Years | (7) -3 Years | (8) -2 Years | (9) -1 Year | (10) Major Plan Date | (11) +0 Years | (12) +1 Year | (13) +2 Years | (14) +3 Years | (15) +4 Years | (16) +5 Years | (17) +6 Years | (18) +7 Years | (19) Signif. Level | (20) Average Pre-series | (21) Average Post-series | (22) Total Deseg. |
|---|---|---|---|---|---|---|---|---|---|---|---|---|---|---|---|---|---|---|---|---|---|---|
| Pasadena, Calif. | 98.48 | yes | | -2.7 | -1.5 | -1.9 | -2.1 | -2.0 | -2.4 | 1970 | -4.2 | -4.5 | -2.5* | | | | | | .01 .05 | -1.2 | -3.7 | 100.80 |
| Pontiac, Mich. | 83.47 | yes | | -1.3 | -1.0 | -3.0 | -3.1* | -1.7 | -2.4* | 1971 | -5.4 | -.4 | | | | | | | .02 .02 | -2.1 | -2.9 | 87.09 |
| Berkeley, Calif. | 57.72 | | | * | | -2.2* | -2.2 | .7 | -1.6 | 1968 | -2.2 | -.6 | -.8 | .2 | .9 | | | | N.S. | -.9 | -.3 | 66.32 |
| Wichita, Kans. | 44.36 | | | | -.8* | -.4 | -.4* | -1.0* | -1.0* | 1971 | -1.3 | -1.4 | | | | | | | N.S. | -.7 | -1.4 | 56.63 |
| San Francisco, Calif. | 42.49 | yes | | | -2.9 | -1.2 | 0 | -4.1 | -.2 | 1971 | -3.0 | -2.1* | | | | | | | N.S. | -1.7 | -2.6 | 46.58 |
| Ft. Wayne, Ind. | 34.60 | | | | -.4 | -.5 | -1.6 | .2 | -1.1 | 1971 | -.8 | -1.0 | | | | | | | N.S. | -.7 | -.9 | 34.00 |
| Waukegan, Ill. (el Schl's) | 31.72 | yes | | | | -1.3 | -3.5 | -7.8 | -1.1 | 1968 | -1.8 | -1.9 | -1.1 | -1.0 | -1.9 | | | | N.S. | -3.4 | -1.5 | 31.72 |
| Denver, Colo. | 24.64 | yes | | | | -1.3 | -1.4 | -1.5 | -.6 | 1969 | -1.5 | -2.4* | -1.0 | -2.0* | -1.7* | -1.0 | | | N.S. | -1.2 | -1.8 | 29.77 |
| Providence, R.I. | 24.10 | yes | | | | | | .7 | -.6* | 1967 | -1.5 | -2.0 | -1.4 | -.2* | -1.0 | -1.4 | -1.5 | | a | a | -.9 | 36.00 |
| Riverside, Calif. | 21.40 | | | | | | | .7 | 0 | 1966 | -1.5 | -1.2* | .9 | -2.2* | -1.0 | -1.4 | | | a | a | -1.1 | 38.20 |
| Las Vegas, Nev. | 19.24 | yes | | | -2.2 | .3 | -.6* | .7 | -.3* | 1972 | -.8 | | | | | | | | N.S. | -.1 | -.8 | 30.05 |
| Evansville, Ind. | 15.77 | yes | -.1* | | | -.1 | -.9 | -.6* | 1.2* | -.3* | 1972 | -.7 | | | | | | | | a | -.2 | -.7 | 29.57 |
| Muncie, Ind. | 15.10 | | | | | .3 | -.9 | -2.6 | 1.9 | -.3* | 1972 | -.3 | | | | | | | | a | -.8 | -.7 | 15.10 |
| Stamford, Conn. | 13.20 | | | | | -1.3* | -.8 | -1.8* | 1.8 | -1.1 | 1970 | -1.5 | -.9 | | | | | | | a | -1.1 | -1.3 | 21.42 |
| Niagara Falls, N.Y. | 11.76 | | | | -2.6 | | | -.4* | -.6 | 1970 | -1.3 | -.5 | -.7 | | | | | | N.S. | -1.7 | -.8 | 30.26 |
| Sacramento, Calif. | 11.10 | yes | | | | | | * | -1.3 | 1966 | -.2 | 1.2 | -.3* | -1.0 | -1.1 | -1.1 | -1.0 | | N.S. | -.5 | -.5 | 19.98 |
| Oklahoma City, Okla. | 10.82 | | | | | | | -2.2 | -1.1 | 1968 | -3.1 | -4.9 | -.2* | -.4 | -1.6 | | | | N.S. | -1.7 | -1.9 | 11.50 |
| Saginaw, Mich. | 9.60 | yes | | | -.1 | -1.8 | -.5 | -.6 | -2.3 | 1972 | -1.3 | | | | | | | | a | -1.5 | -2.2 | 9.60 |
| Grand Rapids, Mich. | 9.40 | | | | | -1.8 | | | -3.7* | 1965 | -3.1 | -1.9 | -.3 | -1.8 | -2.2* | -.8 | -1.1 | -1.2* | a | -1.6 | -2.0 | 10.16 |
| Springfield, Mass. | 9.10 | | | | | -4.0 | -1.0 | .9* | -.5 | 1968 | -1.3 | -1.9 | -2.7 | -2.2 | -2.0* | -.4 | | | N.S. | a | -1.6 | 23.05 |
| Ann Arbor, Mich. | 9.00 | | | | | -.4 | -4.8 | -1.1 | | 1965 | -.1 | -1.1 | -.9 | -2.3 | -.6 | -.8 | -1.1 | | a | -.5 | -.9 | 15.48 |
| Lexington, Ky. | 8.91 | | | | -1.5 | | -1.0 | -1.1 | -.9 | 1967 | -1.1 | -.2 | -.4* | -1.1* | -.3 | | | | a | -2.5 | -.2 | 9.66 |
| Baltimore, Md. | 7.92 | | | -6.2 | -.2 | -4.0 | -4.8 | -1.1 | -.6* | 1971 | -.5* | 0 | | | | | | | N.S. | -1.0 | -1.1 | 7.92 |
| Tulsa, Okla. | 7.83 | yes | | -.1 | | -.4 | 0 | -1.2 | -.9 | 1968 | -1.9* | -1.0* | -1.1* | -1.4* | | | | | N.S. | a | -1.2 | 14.36 |
| Peoria, Ill. | 7.83 | | -.6 | | | | | | -.9 | 1972 | -.9 | 2.0 | | | | | | | a | -.7 | .6 | 15.86 |
| Cambridge, Mass. | 7.30 | | | 0 | -.1 | -1.8 | 0 | -1.2 | -.9 | 1969 | -.9 | -1.4 | | | | | | | N.S. | -.7 | -1.5 | 7.30 |
| Lansing, Mich. | 7.18 | | | | | -.2 | -.6 | -1.1 | -2.2* | 1969 | -.7 | -1.8* | | -2.1* | | | | | N.S. | -1.0 | | 22.54 |

APPENDIX 2: CHANGE IN PERCENTAGE WHITE FROM THE PREVIOUS
SCHOOL YEAR COMPUTED FOR EACH YEAR BEFORE AND AFTER SCHOOL DESEGRATION (CONT.)

| | (1) | (2) | (3) | (4) | (5) | (6) | (7) | (8) | (9) | (10) | (11) | (12) | (13) | (14) | (15) | (16) | (17) | (18) | (19) | (20) | (21) | (22) |
|---|---|---|---|---|---|---|---|---|---|---|---|---|---|---|---|---|---|---|---|---|---|---|
| | % Students | Court | Change in % White Students | | | | | | | Major | Change in % White Students | | | | | | | | | Average | Average | Total |
| School District | Re-assigned | Ordered | -7 Years | -6 Years | -5 Years | -4 Years | -3 Years | -2 Years | -1 Year | Plan Date | +0 Years | +1 Year | +2 Years | +3 Years | +4 Years | +5 Years | +6 Years | +7 Years | Signif. Level | Pre-series | Post-series | Deseg. |
| Racine, Wisc. | 6.80 | | | | | | | -1.1* | -.4* | 1967 | -.5 | -.4 | -.7* | -.8 | -.1 | -.9 | | | N.S. | -.6 | -.6 | 12.30 |
| Tacoma, Wash. | 6.50 | | | | | | -.7 | -.7 | -.3 | 1968 | -1.4* | -.6* | -.9 | -.9* | -.1 | | | | N.S. | -.6 | -.8 | 9.44 |
| San Bernardino, Calif. | 5.10 | | | | | | -.9* | -.1 | -.7 | 1970 | -.8 | -1.3 | -.5 | | | | | | N.S. | -.6 | -.9 | 7.10 |
| Minneapolis, Minn. | 4.90 | | | -.6 | -.4 | | -1.0* | -1.3 | -1.0* | 1971 | -1.5 | -1.3 | | | -.1 | | | | N.S. | -1.0 | -1.4 | 11.16 |
| Waterbury, Conn. | 4.80 | | | | -.4 | -1.5 | | -2.4 | -1.3 | 1970 | -.9 | -1.7 | -.5 | | | | | | N.S. | -1.9 | -1.0 | 4.80 |
| Rochester, N.Y. | 4.30 | | | -2.4 | -2.5 | -1.6 | -3.0 | -2.8 | -2.4* | 1971 | -3.3 | -3.1 | | | | | | | N.S. | -2.4 | -3.2 | 5.16 |
| Seattle, Wash. | 4.14 | | -1.0 | -1.1* | -1.5 | -.6 | -.8* | -.9 | -1.6 | 1971 | -1.5 | -1.1 | | | | | | | N.S. | -1.1 | -1.3 | 10.25 |
| Dayton, Ohio | 3.20 | | | | | | | | -.6 | 1969 | -1.1 | -1.4* | -2.0 | -2.0 | | | | | a | -.6 | -1.6 | 3.96 |
| Buffalo, N.Y. | 3.20 | | | | | | | | | 1967 | -2.5 | 4.0* | -1.3* | -1.3* | -1.2 | -2.2 | | | a | a | -2.1 | 5.79 |
| Warren, Ohio | 2.80 | | | | | | | | -.5 | 1969 | -.7 | -.3 | -.5 | -.9 | | | | | a | -.5 | -.6 | 2.80 |
| St. Paul, Minn. | 2.57 | | | | | | | | | 1965 | | * | * | . | -1.0 | -.5 | .7 | .5 | a | a | -1.3 | 6.77 |
| South Bend, Ind. | 2.50 | | | | | | | -1.3 | -1.0 | 1970 | 0 | -1.2 | -.9 | -1.1 | | | | | N.S. .05 (less decline than expected) | -1.2 | -.5 | 3.80 |
| Rockford, Ill. | 2.40 | | | | | | | | .7 | 1969 | .9 | -1.3 | | | | | | | a | .7 | .7 | 2.40 |
| Flint, Mich. | 2.39 | | | | | | -3.5 | -1.5* | -2.0 | 1971 | -2.9 | -1.7* | | | | | | | N.S. | -2.3 | -2.3 | 3.69 |
| Syracuse, N.Y. | 2.20 | | | | | | -2.6 | -1.4 | -1.7* | 1967 | -1.9 | -1.8* | -1.7 | -2.0 | -1.7 | -2.0* | | | N.S. | -1.9 | -1.9 | 3.65 |
| Colorado Springs, Colo. | 2.10 | | | | | | | .4* | -.3 | 1971 | -.1 | -.2 | | | | | | | a | .1 | -.1 | 2.30 |
| Indianapolis, Ind. | 2.02 | yes | * | | | | -.2 | -1.4 | -1.7 | 1970 | -1.1 | -1.9* | -1.7* | | | | | | N.S. | -1.1 | -1.5 | 3.06 |
| New York, N.Y. | 1.76 | | | | -1.3 | -1.0 | -1.8 | -1.6 | -2.2 | 1964 | -2.6 | -2.9* | -2.0* | -3.0* | -2.9* | -3.3* | -2.3* | -1.4 | a .3.02,N.S. | -1.9 | -2.4 | 7.67 |
| Pittsburgh, Pa. | 1.44 | | | | | | | | -.5* | 1968 | -1.7 | -.5* | -.5 | -.4 | -.8 | -.8* | | | N.S. .02 | -.4 | -.8 | 3.18 |
| Toledo, Ohio | 1.20 | | | | | | | -.3 | -4.3 | 1969 | -.1 | .2 | -1.0* | -.2 | | | | | a | -4.3 | -.4 | 1.37 |
| Waterloo, Iowa | 1.91 | | | | | | | -.6* | -.4 | 1971 | -.5* | -.4 | | | | | | | a | -.5 | -.5 | 2.25 |
| Gary, Ind. | 1.30 | | | | | | | | | 1967 | -.6 | -2.2 | -1.6 | -1.3 | -2.4 | -1.5* | | | a | a | -1.8 | 1.64 |
| Milwaukee, Wisc. | 1.10 | | | | | | -2.4 | -.3 | -2.5 | 1972 | -1.9 | -2.2 | | | | | | | a | -1.4 | -1.9 | 2.02 |
| Louisville, Ky. | .83 | | | | | -.9 | -1.2 | -1.0 | -.5 | 1972 | -2.2 | | | | | | | | a | -1.9 | -2.2 | .83 |
| Des Moines, Iowa | .82 | | | | | | | * | 0* | 1969 | -.1 | -.4 | | -.6 | | | | | a | 0 | -.4 | 1.10 |
| Los Angeles, Calif. | .66 | | | | | | .2* | -1.5 | -1.8* | 1971 | -1.6 | -1.5 | | | | | | | a | -1.0 | -1.6 | 1.56 |
| E. St. Louis, Ill. | .29 | | | | | | | | | 1967 | | -3.7 | -2.5* | -4.2 | -4.3* | -4.4 | | | a | a | -3.8 | .73 |
| Kansas City, Mo. | .26 | | | | | -2.4 | | -2.7* | -1.6 | 1969 | -1.8 | -1.6 | -1.9 | -2.3* | -1.2* | | | | N.S. | -2.1 | -1.9 | .44 |
| Detroit, Mich. | .25 | | | | | -4.5 | -1.8 | -1.9 | -1.9 | 1967 | -1.3 | -1.9 | -2.8 | -2.0* | -.4 | | | | N.S. | -2.5 | -1.8 | .26 |
| San Diego, Calif. | .19 | | | | | | | -1.2 | -2.0 | 1967 | -5.6 | .1 | -.5 | -.2 | | -1.3 | | | N.S. .01 | -1.6 | -1.3 | .19 |
| Chicago, Ill. | .17 | | | | | | -1.4 | -1.4 | -4.9 | 1968 | -3.7 | -1.6* | -1.5* | -2.0 | -1.8* | | | | N.S. | -2.5 | -2.1 | .46 |
| Philadelphia, Pa. | .02 | | | | | | -1.4 | -.9 | -1.1 | 1972 | -.1 | -.4 | | | | | | | a | -1.8 | -.1 | .02 |
| Hartford, Conn. | .01 | | -2.0 | -3.0 | -1.0 | -3.3 | -3.8 | -3.7 | -2.5 | 1968 | -3.6 | -4.7 | -3.7 | -1.9 | -2.3 | | | | N.S. | -3.3 | -3.2 | .01 |

APPENDIX 2: CHANGE IN PERCENTAGE WHITE FROM THE PREVIOUS
SCHOOL YEAR COMPUTED FOR EACH YEAR BEFORE AND AFTER SCHOOL DESEGRATION (CONT.)

| School District | (1) % Students Re-assigned | (2) Court Ordered | (3) −7 Years | (4) −6 Years | (5) −5 Years | (6) −4 Years | (7) −3 Years | (8) −2 Years | (9) −1 Year | (10) Major Plan Date | (11) +0 Years | (12) +1 Year | (13) +2 Years | (14) +3 Years | (15) +4 Years | (16) +5 Years | (17) +6 Years | (18) +7 Years | (19) Signif. Level | (20) Pre-series Average | (21) Post-series Average | (22) Total Deseg. |
|---|---|---|---|---|---|---|---|---|---|---|---|---|---|---|---|---|---|---|---|---|---|---|
| **Control Group:** | | | | | | | | | | | | | | | | | | | | | | |
| Akron, Ohio | 0 | 0 | | | | | −1.0 | −1.0 | −1.0 | — | −1.0 | −.7 | −.9 | −.5 | −1.1 | | | | a | −1.0 | −.8 | 0 |
| Albany, N.Y. | 0 | 0 | | | | | | | −3.1 | — | −1.8 | −2.2 | −1.1 | −2.1 | −1.1 | | | | a | −3.1 | −1.7 | 0 |
| Albuquerque, N.M. | 0 | 0 | | | | | | | | — | | −1.3 | −.3 | −.5 | −.4 | | | | a | a | −.6 | 0 |
| Boston, Mass. | 0 | 0 | | | | | −1.4 | −.3 | −1.5 | — | −3.9 | −2.5 | −1.9 | −2.6 | −1.9 | | | | .05, .01 | −1.0 | −2.6 | 0 |
| Camden, N.J. | 0 | 0 | | | | | | | | — | −4.4 | −2.7 | −2.3 | −2.8 | −1.8 | | | | a | a | −2.8 | 0 |
| Charleston, W. Va. | 0 | 0 | | | | | | | | — | .1 | −.2 | 0 | .1 | | | | | a | a | −.0 | 0 |
| Cleveland, Ohio | 0 | 0 | | | | | | | | — | .2 | −1.2 | −1.0 | .1 | .3 | | | | a | a | −.4 | 0 |
| E. Orange, N.J. | 0 | 0 | | | | | | | | — | −4.7 | −3.9 | −3.2 | −3.4 | −2.6 | | | | a | a | −3.6 | 0 |
| Erie, Pa. | 0 | 0 | | | | | | | | — | −.3 | −.7 | −.6 | −.2 | −.9 | | | | a | a | −.5 | 0 |
| Hamilton, Ohio | 0 | 0 | | | | | | | | — | −.2 | −.2 | .3 | −.2 | −.2 | | | | a | a | −.1 | 0 |
| Jersey City, N.J. | 0 | 0 | | | | | | | | — | −3.9 | −2.1 | −2.9 | −1.0 | −2.0 | | | | a | a | −2.4 | 0 |
| Kansas City, Kans. | 0 | 0 | | | | | | | | — | −3.3 | −1.6 | −.9 | −2.0 | −1.7 | | | | a | a | −1.9 | 0 |
| Lima, Ohio | 0 | 0 | | | | | | | | — | −1.3 | −1.5 | −.5 | −1.4 | .6 | | | | a | a | −.8 | 0 |
| Omaha, Neb. | 0 | 0 | | | | | | | | — | −1.3 | −.6 | −.1 | −.5 | | | | | a | a | −.6 | 0 |
| Newark, N.J. | 0 | 0 | | | | | | | | — | −2.7 | −2.9 | −.9 | −2.0 | −.6 | | | | a | a | −.6 | 0 |
| Santa Monica, Calif. | 0 | 0 | | | | | | −3.0 | −2.2 | — | | | | | | | | | N.S. | −2.6 | −2.1 | 0 |
| Trenton, N.J. | 0 | 0 | | | | | | | | — | .1 | −.6 | −2.1 | −.6 | −.9 | | | | a | a | −.8 | 0 |
| Utica, N.Y. | 0 | 0 | | | | | | | | — | −4.1 | −2.2 | −1.9 | −1.8 | −.9 | | | | a | a | −2.2 | 0 |
| Washington, D.C. | 0 | 0 | | | −2.3 | −1.9 | −1.8 | −1.4 | −1.5 | — | −1.3 | −.6 | −.7 | −1.4 | −.5 | | | | N.S. | −1.8 | −.9 | 0 |
| Portland, Oreg. | 0 | 0 | | | | | −.6 | −.3 | −.2 | — | −2.1 | −.6 | −.5 | −.6 | −.4 | | | | .02, .01 | −.4 | −.8 | 0 |
| Passaic, N.J. | 0 | 0 | | | | | | | | — | −2.5 | −.9 | −.6 | −.9 | −1.1 | | | | a | a | −1.2 | 0 |
| Paterson, N.J. | 0 | 0 | | | | | | | | — | −7.8 | −2.6 | −3.7 | −3.4 | −2.4 | | | | a | a | −4.0 | 0 |
| Phoenix, Ariz. | 0 | 0 | | | | | | | | — | −3.8 | −3.1 | −3.9 | −2.3 | −1.5 | | | | a | a | −2.9 | 0 |
| Wilmington, Del. | 0 | 0 | | | | | | | | — | −1.4 | −1.1 | 0 | −1.2 | 0 | | | | N.S. | a | −.7 | 0 |
| Youngstown, Ohio | 0 | 0 | | | | | −3.0 | −2.3 | −3.4 | — | −3.9 | −7.1 | −3.9 | −1.3 | −1.8 | | | | a | −2.9 | −3.6 | 0 |
| Springfield, Ill. | 0 | 0 | | | | | | | | — | −.1 | −2.0 | −1.3 | .4 | −1.6 | | | | a | a | −1.1 | 0 |
| | | | | | | | | | | | −.5 | −1.1 | −.5 | −.4 | −1.0 | | | | a | a | −.7 | 0 |

*Additional desegregation implemented.
N.S. = not significant.
a = unable to compute.

APPENDIX 3: POSTON'S PHASE I AND PHASE II DESEGREGATION
(1974 AND 1975)

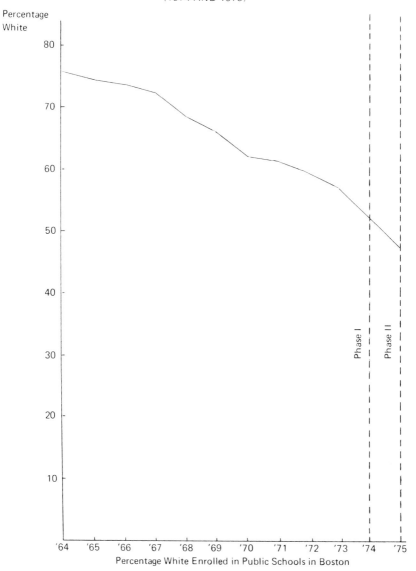

Percentage White Enrolled in Public Schools in Boston

# REFERENCES

1. The earlier work on which Coleman built his reputation is a massive study showing that school desegregation raises the achievement scores of black students: James S. Coleman et al., *Equality of Educational Opportunity* (Washington, D.C., 1966). The latest work in which he claims school desegregation increases white flight is James S. Coleman, Sara D. Kelly, and John Moore, "Recent Trends in School Integration," paper presented at the annual meeting of the American Educational Research Association, Washington, D.C., April 2, 1975; James S. Coleman, Sara D. Kelly, and John Moore, "Trends in School Segregation, 1968–73," Urban Institute Working Paper, August 1975.

2. Coleman, Kelly, and Moore, "Recent Trends in School Integration," pp. 21–22.

3. Donald T. Campbell and Julian Stanley, *Experimental and Quasi-Experimental Designs for Research* (Chicago, 1963), pp. 47–48.

4. Charles Clotfelter, "The Detroit Decision and White Flight," *Journal of Legal Studies*, forthcoming; Reynolds Farley, "School Integration and White Flight," paper presented at the Brookings Symposium on School Desegregation and White Flight, Washington, D.C., August 15, 1975.

5. Robert L. Crain et al., *Design for a National Longitudinal Study of School Desegregation,* Vol. II, *Research Design and Procedures* (Santa Monica, Calif., September 1974), p. 79.

6. Everett Cataldo, Michael Giles, Deborah Athos, and Douglas Gatlin, "Desegregation and White Flight," *Integrated Education* (January 1975), pp. 3–5. The compliance/rejection status of their respondents was determined from official school records. Compliers were defined as those parents who had a child attending public school in both 1971–1972 and 1972–1973. Rejecters were those who had a child in public school in 1971–1972, but transferred the child to private school in 1972–1973. The eight county school districts were Dade, Palm Beach, Duval, Leon, Jefferson, Escambia, Manatee, and Lee.

7. All but two of the eighty-six school districts in this study have the same name and virtually the same boundaries as the city. The decision to desegregate in every case involves interaction between the city and school officials and citizens of both legal entities. The result is that for most practical purposes the distinction between city and school district is almost nonexistent.

8. Coleman, et al., "Recent Trends in School Integration"; U.S. Commission on Civil Rights, *Racial Isolation in the Public Schools,* 2 vols. (Washington, D.C., 1967); Thomas Dye, "Urban School Segregation, A Comparative Analysis," *Urban Affairs Quarterly,* 4 (December 1968), 141–165, the last two using a measure of the percentage of black students

in predominantly black schools. Reynolds Farley and Alma F. Taeuber, "Racial Segregation in the Public Schools," *American Journal of Sociology*, 79 (January 1974), 888–890, and Farley, "School Integration and White Flight," both using an index of dissimilarity adapted from the Taeuber Index of residential segregation. Another recent study uses a measure of the change in the proportion of minority students attending "ethnically balanced" schools from 1966 to 1971: Eldon L. Wegner and Jane R. Mercer, "Dynamics of the Desegregation Process: Politics, Policies, and Community Characteristics as Factors in Change," in Frederick M. Wirt (ed.), *The Polity of the School* (Lexington, Mass., 1975), pp. 123–143.

9. Studies using other measures have been: Donald R. Matthews and James W. Prothro, "Stateways versus Folkways: Critical Factors in Southern Reactions to *Brown v. Board of Education*," in Gottfried Dietze (ed.), *Essays on the American Constitution* (Englewood Cliffs, N.J., 1964); James W. Prothro, "Stateways versus Folkways Revisited: An Error in Prediction," *Journal of Politics*, 34 (May 1972), 352–364; Robert L. Crain, Morton Inger, Gerald McWhorter, and James J. Vanecko, *The Politics of School Desegregation* (New York, 1969), all using a dichotomous variable: did desegregate—or did not desegregate. David J. Kirby, T. Robert Harris, and Robert L. Crain, *Political Strategies in Northern School Desegregation* (Lexington, Mass., 1973) used a qualitative measure of the characteristics of the desegregation plan.

10. Other minorities, such as Asian-Americans, Spanish surname, and Indian have been excluded from the computation of this measure because the concern of this study is with the political pressures and responses to the segregation of blacks from whites. Nonblack minorities simply do not exert the same kinds of pressures nor arouse the same fears as blacks. Indeed, even in many western school districts where their proportions are larger than in other regions, nonblack minorities have often sided with the white majority against desegregation. Therefore, desegregation plans have tended to be overwhelmingly focused on integrating blacks into white schools.

11. Racial composition data were obtained from the U.S. Department of Health, Education, and Welfare, *Directory of Public Elementary and Secondary Schools in Selected Districts, Fall 1970, Enrollment and Staff by Racial/Ethnic Groups* (Washington, D.C., 1971). There are also volumes for Fall 1967, Fall 1968, and unpublished data for the odd years since 1967. Data for desegregation claimed in earlier years was obtained from published records of the school districts themselves. A more detailed explanation of this measure can be found in Christine H. Rossell and Robert L. Crain, *Evaluating School Desegregation Plans Statistically* (Baltimore, Md., 1973), pp. 4–11; or Kirby, Harris, and Crain, "Measuring School Desegregation," *Political Strategies in Northern School Desegregation*, chap. 12.

12. The two measures were combined because they are highly correlated (.80) and there is so little reassignment of whites to black or formerly black schools.

13. The relationship between the percentage of a plan which is mandatory and the percentage of students reassigned is .94 for white students and .77 for black students using gamma.

14. Data on the actual percentage white in each school district for these years can be obtained by writing the author.

15. Since the index represents the percentage of black students reassigned to white schools, and the percentage of white students reassigned to black or formerly black schools, the index could go as high as 200 percent. However, reassigning 100 percent of each race is not efficient. The most efficient reassignment in a perfectly segregated system is 50 percent of each race which equals an index of 100. Because school districts also have political and social considerations, they tend to avoid reassigning whites to black or formerly black schools, and thus the index usually reflects the percentage of black students reassigned to white schools. Pasadena is one of the few school districts that reassigned a large proportion of white students to black or formerly black schools. Either they did more reassignment than was efficient, or there is some measurement error in the index.

16. Wirt points out that although Pasadena's white (Anglo) student population declined after school desegregation, two districts in the San Gabriel Valley (the hot, smoggy valley in which Pasadena is located) that did not desegregate lost even more whites than Pasadena. Frederick M. Wirt, "Understanding the Reality of Desegregation," (unpublished paper, Berkeley, Calif., June 21, 1972).

17. The school districts were also grouped according to their total desegregation, rather than their largest action. This made little difference in the trend for each group, although the highest desegregating group showed even less change in white flight, after school desegregation.

18. Coleman et al., "Recent Trends in School Integration," p. 21.

19. Ibid.

20. In the later paper, "Trends in School Segregation, 1968–73," Coleman acknowledges that the estimated loss in northern cities which have undergone desegregation is less than in the southern ones, but this did not stop him from filing another court affidavit on September 2, 1975, in Boston on behalf of antibusing groups, predicting that school desegregation will increase white flight in Boston. In general, while the second paper is much more reasonable in the conclusions it draws, Coleman's public statements have not reflected this.

21. Robert Reinhold, "Report of Failure of Busing Conceded by Author to Exceed Scientific Data," *The New York Times,* July 11, 1975.

22. Ibid.

23. Coleman et al., "Trends in School Integration, 1968–73."

24. In an analysis of Boston's Phase I and Phase II desegregation plans (fall 1974 and fall 1975) recently completed by the author and included in Appendix 3, the percentage white in Boston public schools declined by five percentage points after Phase I. This represents an increase of only 3 percentage points from the average rate of white flight prior to Phase I. Furthermore, even with many white students still boycotting, the rate of white flight has declined during Phase II to a rate lower than that experienced after Phase I.

25. Coleman also measures loss in white enrollment in a way that may tend to exaggerate white flight in some cities. He compares the raw figures on white enrollment in one year to the raw figures on white enrollment in the previous year and then claims white flight if the latter is lower than the former. Yet one can easily predict cases where due to job layoffs, factory closings, etc., both whites and blacks leave a city at a faster rate than before, but blacks leave at a higher rate. Although this would result in the percentage black decreasing and the percentage white increasing, Coleman would still call this white flight, even though it might more properly be called "black flight." In the final analysis, the most important variable for policy purposes is the percentage white, not the number white.

26. Gary Orfield, "White Flight Research: Its Importance, Perplexities, and Possible Policy Implication," Brookings Institution paper, September 1975.

27. Orfield points out that middle-class black families are also fleeing cities whenever they are allowed to buy suburban housing. Moreover, among black families who retain central city residence, there are substantial numbers who have fled to private schools. In Washington, D.C., for example, the suburbs experienced a 61 percent increase in black population in the first four years of the 1970s, and among the blacks who remained in the city, about 10,000 are using private schools. Ibid., pp. 8–9.

28. Ibid., pp. 15–18.

29. This is a revision of a paper, "The Political and Social Impact of School Desegregation," presented at the American Political Science Convention, September 1975. The APSA paper was a preliminary report of a study of the social and political impact of school desegregation in 113 northern and southern school districts from 1963–1973. The study analyzes the effect of school desegregation on voting patterns, racial composition of school boards, white flight, residential integration, community organizational participation, attendance, suspensions, expulsions, racial composition and integration of teaching staff, student organizations, and athletic teams. Steve Cohen adapted the quasi-experimental computer program to the IBM 360 at Boston University and completed all the computer runs.

*Diane Ravitch, Adjunct Assistant Professor of History and Education at Teachers College, Columbia University, and most recently author of* The Revisionists Revised: A Critique of the Radical Attack on the Schools, *reviews the busing-white flight controversy and concludes that, in the aftermath of the Supreme Court's 1974 decision in the Detroit case, new ways of improving urban schools must be found if resegregation between city and suburb is to be stopped.*

# The "White Flight" Controversy

## DIANE RAVITCH

In the spring of 1975, James Coleman released the "preliminary results" of a new study concluding that school desegregation contributed to "white flight" from big cities and was fostering resegregation of urban districts. On the basis of his findings, Coleman maintained that whites were leaving both large and middle-sized cities with high proportions of blacks, and specifically that whites in big cities were fleeing integration, while whites in middle-sized cities were "not moving any faster from rapidly integrating cities than from others." In short, according to Coleman, "the flight from integration appears to be principally a large-city phenomenon."

In the most controversial passage of his study, Coleman argued:

> The extremely strong reactions of individual whites in moving their children out of large districts engaged in massive and rapid desegregation suggest that in the long run the policies that have been

Reprinted with permission of *The Public Interest*, No. 51 (Spring, 1978). Copyright © 1978 by National Affairs, Inc.

pursued will defeat the purpose of increasing overall contact among races in schools. . . . Thus a major policy implication of this analysis is that in an area such as school desegregation, which has important consequences for individuals and in which individuals retain control of some actions that can in the end defeat the policy, the courts are probably the worst instrument of social policy.

Coleman's study provoked bitter attacks from proponents of activist desegregation policies, such as Roy Wilkins and Kenneth Clark, not only because his findings were inimical to their cause, but because his "defection" seemed especially traitorous. After all, he had been the principal author of the Equal Educational Opportunity Survey (known as the Coleman Report), which had been authorized by Congress as part of the Civil Rights Act of 1964 and had served, since its publication in 1966, as the chief evidence of the beneficial effects of school desegregation. Coleman had also taken an outspoken public role as a leading scholarly advocate of school desegregation.

Coleman presented his paper (co-authored by Sara Kelly and John Moore of the Urban Institute) at a meeting of the American Educational Research Association on April 2, 1975, but it was not reported in The New York Times until June 7, 1975. (Some of Coleman's adversaries later attacked him for carrying his views to the press, but the delay in reporting the story indicates that he did not initiate the media attention.) Then, on July 11, 1975, Robert Reinhold of The New York Times reported that the 20 central-city districts in Coleman's study had not undergone court-ordered busing, and Coleman admitted that his views "went somewhat beyond the data." He acknowledged that he had not studied the effects of busing, since the cities under scrutiny had not been subject to court order, and he conceded that he he had been "quite wrong" to have called the integration "massive" where it had occurred. But he nonetheless defended the overall implication of his work and continued to maintain that court-imposed desegregation exacerbated the rate of "white flight."

Mobilized by Coleman's well-publicized statements, scholars committed to desegregation lost no time in taking issue with his findings. On August 15, 1975, a "Symposium on School Desegregation and White Flight" was convened, funded by the National Institute of Education, co-sponsored by the Catholic University Center for National Policy Review and the Notre Dame Center for

Civil Rights, and hosted by the Brookings Institution. Though Coleman was a participant, the papers that emerged from the symposium consisted entirely of rebuttals of his position. Later, Gregg Jackson, of the United States Commission on Civil Rights, criticized both Coleman's data and his methodology in two articles, a technical version in *Educational Researcher* (November 1975) and a popular version in *Phi Delta Kappan* (December 1975). Coleman's claim that desegregation accelerated "white flight" was vigorously denounced by Robert Green, of Michigan State University, and Thomas Pettigrew, of Harvard University, first at a press conference called by the NAACP, and then in jointly written articles in *Phi Delta Kappan* (February 1976) and in *Harvard Educational Review* (February 1976). Green and Pettigrew charged that Coleman had been selective in his choice of school districts and that their own reanalysis of districts with more than 75,000 pupils revealed no correlation between the degree of desegregation and the rate of "white flight."

There were three major criticisms of Coleman's study: that his conclusions were invalid because he did not look at enough districts and because the districts he did examine had not undergone court-ordered desegregation; that "white flight" from central cities is a long-term phenomenon predating school desegregation; and that desegregation does not cause "white flight" since the same level of "white flight" can be observed in big cities whether or not they have enacted desegregation plans. The policy implication of these criticisms is that framers of desegregation plans need not be concerned about the impact of "white flight," because desegregation does not cause greater numbers of whites to leave than would have left anyway. Green and Pettigrew state this directly:

> While extensive school desegregation may hasten the white flight phenomenon, particularly in the largest nonmetropolitan districts in the South, the effect, if it obtains at all, may only be temporarily during the first year of desegregation, and then only for those families which have already made plans to move.

The counterargument against Coleman was strengthened during the summer of 1975 by another new study of the effects of desegregation on "white flight," written by Christine Rossell, an assistant professor of political science at Boston University. Her paper, presented to the American Political Science Association in September 1975 and published in *Political Science Quarterly* (Winter 1975), sought to establish definitively that school desegregation causes "little or no significant white flight, even when it is court ordered and implemented in large cities." Gary Orfield, editor of the papers from the August symposium on "white flight" (and also an author of one of the rebuttals to Coleman), called Rossell's study "particularly impressive," and Robert Green described it as "the most serious challenge to the Coleman position." And indeed, Rossell sought not only to refute Coleman's arguments but to prove that desegregation had little or no impact on "white flight," and that "white flight" was, at most, a temporary and minimal occurrence.

Rossell collected data from 86 school districts and grouped them by the degree to which students had been reassigned for purposes of school integration. She came to the conclusion that of the 10 districts with the highest degree of desegregation, only two (Pasadena and Pontiac) experienced any significant "white flight," but it was "minimal (about a 3-percent increase over the previous trend) and temporary." The whole group of cities with the highest amount of desegregation showed "a negligible increase of about 1 percent from the previous trend":

> The important phenomenon here is that any loss of whites occurs *before* school opens in the first year of the plan. After that, white flight stabilizes to a rate slightly better than the pre-desegregation period. Therefore, white flight, if it occurs at all, occurs not from the problems experienced during the first year of desegregation, but from the fear of problems. In other words, if whites leave, it is typically not because they participated in the plan and did not like it, but because they refused to participate at all.

Busing did not cause "white flight," she held, since she found "no significant increase in white flight in Northern school districts that desegregated under court order." Where Coleman had asserted that "white flight" was greatest in large districts undergoing rapid desegregation, Rossell disagreed:

> The two large school districts, San Francisco and Denver, that engaged in such massive and rapid desegregation show no significant white flight. Nor do most of the other large school districts that implemented lesser degrees of school desegregation (Seattle; Mil-

waukee; Kansas City, Mo.; Indianapolis; Baltimore; Philadelphia; Los Angeles; and Chicago). Thus the data of the present study contradict almost every claim Coleman has made regarding school desegregation and white flight.

Indeed, according to Rossell, mandatory city-wide school desegregation may be the best means to insure racial stability:

> While almost all school districts (with the exception of Berkeley, California) are still experiencing white flight, it is quite encouraging that by the second and third year after desegregation, the school districts engaging in massive and rapid desegregation have a rate of white flight that is lower than their rate in the predesegregation period and lower than that of any other group [of cities in the study], including those that did not implement any desegregation at all. This is a heartening phenomenon and may mean that school desegregation and the educational innovation that typically accompanies it when it is city wide, could impede the increasing ghettoization of American cities.

Thus, in Rossell's view, not only is school desegregation not a cause of "white flight," it may actually be the remedy for whatever minimal "white flight" occurs.

But if Rossell is right, how could a distinguished scholar like James Coleman have become so concerned about a relatively insignificant problem? Why had the media accepted the idea that "white flight" was of large proportions, when it was no more than one or two percent of white pupils each year? Conversely, how did Rossell come to the conclusion that "white flight" was minimal and of little or no significance?

To understand Rossell's optimistic conclusions, it is necessary to follow her method of calculating the rate of "white flight." She measured the effect of desegregation on "white flight" by observing changes in the percentage of white pupils enrolled in public schools before and after the major desegregation plan in each city, for as many years as data were available, with 1972–73 the final year of the study. If a district was 58-percent white one year, then dropped to 56-percent white and then to 53-percent white, Rossell would say that the district lost 2 percent the first year, 3 percent the second, and so on. For example, Table 1 presents five of the cities she analyzed, all in her "high desegregation"

TABLE 1: *Change in Percentage of White Students in "High Desegregation" Cities (Rossell's Calculations)*[1]

| | PERCENTAGE OF PUPILS REASSIGNED | YEARS BEFORE PLAN DATE | | | | | | | PLAN DATE | | YEARS AFTER PLAN DATE | | | |
|---|---|---|---|---|---|---|---|---|---|---|---|---|---|---|
| | | 7 | 6 | 5 | 4 | 3 | 2 | 1 | | | 1 | 2 | 3 | 4 |
| Pasadena[2] | 98.48% | 71.6% | 68.9% | 67.4% | 65.5% | 63.4% | 61.4% | 59.0% | 1970 | 54.8% | 50.3% | 47.8% | — | — |
| Pontiac[2] | 83.47 | 74.7 | 73.4 | 72.4 | 69.4 | 66.3 | 64.6 | 62.2 | 1971 | 56.8 | 56.4 | — | — | — |
| Berkeley | 57.72 | — | — | 54.0 | 51.8 | 49.6 | 50.3 | 48.7 | 1968 | 46.5 | 45.9 | 45.1 | 45.2% | 46.1% |
| San Francisco[2] | 42.49 | — | 45.3 | 42.4 | 41.2 | 41.2 | 37.1 | 36.9 | 1971 | 33.9 | 31.8 | — | — | — |
| Denver[2] | 24.64 | — | — | 70.4 | 69.1 | 67.7 | 66.2 | 65.6 | 1969 | 64.1 | 61.7 | 60.3 | 58.3 | — |

[1] Source: Paper presented by Rossell before the American Political Science Association (September 1975).
[2] Court-ordered desegregation.

TABLE 2: *Racial Change in Pasadena Public Schools**

| YEAR | TOTAL NUMBER OF PUPILS | WHITES | | MINORITIES | | WHITE LOSS | |
|---|---|---|---|---|---|---|---|
| | | NUMBER OF PUPILS | PERCENTAGE OF TOTAL | NUMBER OF PUPILS | PERCENTAGE OF TOTAL | NUMBER OF PUPILS | PERCENTAGE OF 1968 NUMBER |
| 1968 | 31,259 | 19,201 | 61.4% | 12,058 | 38.6% | — | — |
| 1972 | 26,225 | 12,523 | 47.8 | 13,702 | 52.2 | 6,678 | 34.8% |

*Source: Author's calculations.

group. Thus, Rossell represents the decline in percentage white in Pasadena before desegregation with the following figures: –2.7, –1.5, –1.9, –2.1, –2.0, –2.4. A desegregation plan was adopted in 1970 and in that year the figure representing white decline was –4.2; in the next two years, the figures were –4.5 and –2.5. In San Francisco, where a "massive and rapid" court-ordered busing plan was implemented in 1971, before desegregation the figures were –2.9, –1.2, 0, –4.1, –.2; after desegregation, they were –3.0 and –2.1. (Rossell obtained these figures by subtracting the percentage white in any given year from the percentage white in the previous year.) As noted earlier, Rossell argued that none of the cities in her study except Pasadena and Pontiac experienced any significant "white flight," and even in those two cities it was minimal and temporary. Indeed, since her method of comparing percentages yields such small figures to represent the declining proportions of white pupils each year, "white flight" appears to be s sorely overdramatized issue.

Unhappily, this is not the case. Rossell has selected a statistical method that will show small declines even in the face of large absolute movements. Consider, for example, a school district with 250,000 pupils, 200,000 whites (80 percent of the total) and 50,000 blacks (20 percent of the total). If 40,000 white pupils were to leave the district in a single year, it would then have 160,000 whites (76.2 percent of the total) and 50,000 blacks (23.8 percent of the total). Rossell would say that the change in the percentage white was –3.8, that is, a drop of 3.8 *percentage points.* But what *has actually happened is that 20 percent of the white pupils have left the district* (since 40,000 is 20 percent of 200,000). It is precisely Rossell's method of calculating "white flight" by subtracting percentages that leads her to her conclusions. In Pasadena, for example, Rossell's tables show a decline in percentage white from 61.4 percent in 1968 to 47.8 percent in 1972, a drop of 13.6 points. But the absolute numbers of whites in the Pasadena school system declined by 34.8 percent, while the absolute number of minorities rose slightly (see Table 2).

Since Rossell maintains that "white flight" rarely occurs after desegregation, it is worth noting that the Pasadena school district continued to lose white pupils: By 1976–77, its total enrollment was 25,718, and its white population had declined to 9,839, a loss of 48.8 percent of the number of whites enrolled in 1968 and of 21.4 percent of whites enrolled in 1972.

Rossell explains why she preferred to compare percentages rather than absolute numbers:

> Coleman . . . measures loss in white enrollment in a way that may tend to exaggerate white flight in some cities. He compares the raw figures on white enrollment in the previous year and then claims white flight if the latter is lower than the former. Yet one can easily predict cases where due to job layoffs, factory closings, etc., both whites and blacks leave a city at a faster rate than before, but blacks leave at a higher rate. Although this would result in the percentage black decreasing and the percentage white increasing, Coleman would still call this white flight, even though it might more properly be called "black flight." In the final analysis, the most important variable for policy purposes is the percentage white, not the number white.

However, this criticism applies not to anyone using absolute numbers, which clearly reveal any joint fluctuation of racial groups, but to the researcher using only percentages, which can mask substantial changes in enrollments. In other words, Rossell is criticizing her own technique. For example, when black enrollment is growing while white enrollment is fairly stable, as it was in Boston during the 1960s, the method of comparing percentages gives an impression of "white flight" where none exists.

The best way to avoid the choice between percentages and absolute numbers is to supply both. When both are presented for the four other districts used by Rossell (in Table 1), a very different picture emerges, as evident from Table 3. Only in Berkeley, a small atypical university town that initiated its own desegregation plan, not under court order, was the white pupil loss truly insignificant. San Francisco, which Rossell maintains had "no significant white flight," lost one third of its white pupils during the period of her study. Furthermore, subsequent events in San Francisco and Denver (the two large urban districts with massive court-ordered desegregation) do not sustain her hypothesis that "white flight" rarely occurs after the implementation of major desegregation plans. A court order was enacted in San Francisco in 1971; the number of white pupils in public schools there declined from 26,067 in 1972 to 14,958 in 1976, a loss of 42.6 percent of white enrollment in only four years. Nor did Denver, where a city-wide plan was imposed in 1974, maintain its white enrollment: Its 53,412 white pupils in 1972 declined to 36,539 in 1976,

TABLE 3: *Racial Change in "High Desegregation" Cities**

| City | Year | Total Number Of Pupils | Whites | | Minorities | | White Loss | |
|---|---|---|---|---|---|---|---|---|
| | | | Number Of Pupils | Percentage Of Total | Number Of Pupils | Percentage Of Total | Number Of Pupils | Percentage Of 1968 Number |
| Pontiac | 1968 | 23,832 | 15,789 | 66.3% | 8,043 | 33.7% | — | — |
| | 1972 | 21,141 | 11,929 | 56.4 | 9,212 | 43.6 | 3,860 | 24.4% |
| Berkeley | 1968 | 16,204 | 7,535 | 46.5 | 8,669 | 53.5 | — | — |
| | 1972 | 15,213 | 7,017 | 46.1 | 8,196 | 53.9 | 518 | 6.9 |
| San Francisco | 1968 | 94,154 | 38,824 | 41.2 | 55,330 | 58.8 | — | — |
| | 1972 | 81,970 | 26,067 | 31.8 | 55,903 | 68.2 | 12,757 | 32.9 |
| Denver | 1968 | 96,577 | 63,398 | 65.6 | 33,179 | 34.4 | — | — |
| | 1972 | 91,616 | 53,412 | 58.3 | 38,204 | 41.7 | 9,986 | 15.8 |

*Source: Author's calculations.

TABLE 4: *"Percentage White in Boston Public Schools, 1964-1975" (Rossell's Calculations)**

| 1964 | 1965 | 1966 | 1967 | 1968 | 1969 | 1970 | 1971 | 1972 | 1973 | 1974 | 1975 (Estimated) |
|---|---|---|---|---|---|---|---|---|---|---|---|
| 75.6 | 74.2 | 73.9 | 72.4 | 68.5 | 66.0 | 64.1 | 61.5 | 59.6 | 57.2 | 52.3 | 47.8 |

*Source: Press release by Rossell (December 1975).

TABLE 5: *Enrollment in the Boston Public Schools, 1964-1976*[*]

| Year | Total Number Of Pupils | Whites Number Of Pupils | Whites Percentage Of Total | Minorities Number Of Pupils | Minorities Percentage Of Total | White Loss Number Of Pupils | White Loss Percentage Of Number In Previous Year |
|------|------------------------|-------------------------|----------------------------|-----------------------------|--------------------------------|-----------------------------|--------------------------------------------------|
| 1964 | 91,800 | 69,400 | 75.6% | 22,400 | 24.4% | — | — |
| 1965 | 93,055 | 69,046 | 74.2 | 24,009 | 25.8 | 359 | 0.5% |
| 1966 | 92,127 | 68,082 | 73.9 | 24,045 | 26.1 | 964 | 1.4 |
| 1967 | 92,441 | 66,927 | 72.4 | 25,512 | 27.6 | 1,155 | 1.7 |
| 1968 | 94,174 | 64,509 | 68.5 | 29,665 | 31.5 | 2,418 | 3.6 |
| 1969 | 94,885 | 62,624 | 66.0 | 32,261 | 34.0 | 1,885 | 2.9 |
| 1970 | 96,696 | 61,982 | 64.1 | 34,714 | 35.9 | 642 | 1.0 |
| 1971 | 96,400 | 59,286 | 61.5 | 37,114 | 38.5 | 2,696 | 4.3 |
| 1972 | 96,239 | 57,358 | 59.6 | 38,881 | 40.4 | 1,928 | 3.3 |
| 1973 | 93,647 | 53,593 | 57.2 | 40,054 | 42.8 | 3,765 | 6.6 |
| 1974 | 85,826 | 44,937 | 52.4 | 40,889 | 47.6 | 8,656 | 16.2 |
| 1975 | 76,461 | 36,243 | 47.4 | 40,218 | 52.6 | 8,694 | 19.3 |
| 1976 | 76,889 | 34,561 | 45.0 | 42,328 | 55.0 | 1,682 | 4.6 |

[*]Source: Author's calculations.

a loss of nearly a third of the white pupils in four years. In September 1977, Denver's white pupils declined by another 3,000 to 47.0 percent of the Denver system, having dropped from a majority of 65.6 percent in 1968 and 58.3 percent in 1972. Any statistical method that declares these demographic shifts "insignificant" is, at the very least, not very useful.

The use of Rossell's statistical method in the case of Boston, that maelstrom of desegregation woes, is so at variance with common knowledge as to throw social science into disrepute. Rossell released the following statement to the press in December 1975:

> Much has been made of the claim that school desegregation in Boston (Phase I in the Fall of 1974 and Phase II in the Fall of 1975) has caused massive white flight. The accompanying graph and table indicate that the decline in the percentage white enrolled in the public schools is part of a trend that began at least as early as 1964 and probably earlier. While the implementation of school desegregation appears to have somewhat accelerated this trend, a projection of the former trends indicates that Boston would have been a majority non-white system, even if it had not desegregated, by the fall of 1976. Therefore, desegregation is only responsible for accelerating by one year, the trend toward a majority non-white school system.

This statement was accompanied by Table 4.

But consider the absolute figures, which are shown in Table 5. The absolute figures reveal that white enrollment dropped by 7,418 (10.7 percent) from 1964 until 1970, an average loss of 1.8 percent annually. However, the loss in white pupils from 1970 through 1976 was 27,421 (44 percent), four times the rate of the previous six years. "White flight" was significantly higher during the implementation of the desegregation plan, and there is simply no way of knowing whether those who left had already been planning to go. It is possible to argue that the 1974–1975 desegregation of Boston's public schools was necessary and correct regardless of the number of whites who left the system. But it is indefensible to argue, against the evidence, that the desegregation plan caused only a one year acceleration in the transition to a majority non-white school system.

We have inspected Rossell's case against Coleman in detail because it illustrates some of the issues involved in the debate. But the argument concerns more than the proper presentation of the data on declining white enrollments. Coleman also used econometric models to attempt to determine the extent to which desegregation as such was leading to declining white enrollments. These models could take into account the effect of whether a city was Southern or not, whether it had nearby high-percentage-white suburbs, and whether a trend independent of desegregation was reducing white enrollment (suburban movement or other factors). On these matters, the debate is too technical to summarize easily.

One of the issues was the proper measure of desegregation. Coleman argued that, independent of the specific causes (e.g., a court order) leading to it, an increase in the degree to which whites are exposed to blacks seemed, under certain circumstances, to reduce the number of whites. Ultimately, Coleman's model required some important qualifications. The increase in the amount of "white flight" that occurred with an increase in desegregation was particularly marked in larger cities, in cities with a large black school population, and in cities with adjacent school districts with a high proportion of white students. Coleman's conclusions, supported by mathematical models, also seem to conform to common sense and experience. His models have been modified, attacked, and retested, but the general conclusions still hold. After reanalyzing the data and taking into account various criticisms made of Coleman, Charles Clotfelter has concluded:

> The estimates in the current paper of the effect of desegregation—measured by hypothetical changes in exposure rates—support the view that desegregation has a strong overall effect on white enrollments in the largest school districts. Within these large districts, however, desegregation is a significant stimulus of white losses only in districts where blacks make up more than 7 percent of students. . . . For smaller districts, response to desegregation appears to be less intense. . . .

By attempting to deny the long-term significance of "white flight" and by refusing to acknowledge the impact of court-ordered busing on white pupil losses, Coleman's critics have confused and confounded the analysis of desegregation policy. Worse yet, the issue has been unfairly politicized by the charge that those who worry about the relationship between desegregation

TABLE 6: Racial Change in Urban Public Schools, 1968-1976[1]

| CITY[2] | YEAR | TOTAL NUMBER OF PUPILS | WHITES | | MINORITIES[3] | | WHITE LOSS | | TOTAL LOSS | |
|---|---|---|---|---|---|---|---|---|---|---|
| | | | NUMBER OF PUPILS | PERCENTAGE OF TOTAL | NUMBER OF PUPILS | PERCENTAGE OF TOTAL | NUMBER OF PUPILS | PERCENTAGE OF 1968 NUMBER | NUMBER OF PUPILS | PERCENTAGE OF 1968 NUMBER |
| New York City | 1968 | 1,063,787 | 467,365 | 43.9% | 596,422 | 56.1% | 139,300 | 29.8% | (+13,403) | (+1.3%) |
| | 1976 | 1,077,190 | 328,065 | 30.5 | 749,125 | 69.5 | | | | |
| Los Angeles | 1968 | 653,549 | 350,909 | 53.7 | 302,640 | 46.3 | 131,550 | 37.5 | 60,618 | 9.3 |
| | 1976 | 592,931 | 219,359 | 37.0 | 373,572 | 63.0 | | | | |
| Chicago | 1968 | 582,274 | 219,478 | 37.7 | 362,796 | 62.3 | 88,693 | 40.4 | 58,053 | 10.0 |
| | 1976 | 524,221 | 130,785 | 25.0 | 393,436 | 75.0 | | | | |
| Houston | 1968 | 246,098 | 131,099 | 53.3 | 114,999 | 46.7 | 59,305 | 45.2 | 36,073 | 14.7 |
| | 1976 | 210,025 | 71,794 | 34.2 | 138,231 | 65.8 | | | | |
| Detroit | 1968 | 296,097 | 116,250 | 39.3 | 179,847 | 60.7 | 71,636 | 61.6 | 56,883 | 19.2 |
| | 1976 | 239,214 | 44,614 | 18.7 | 194,600 | 81.3 | | | | |
| Philadelphia | 1968 | 282,617 | 109,512 | 38.7 | 173,105 | 61.3 | 27,502 | 25.1 | 24,675 | 8.7 |
| | 1976 | 257,942 | 82,010 | 31.8 | 175,932 | 68.2 | | | | |
| Miami | 1968 | 232,465 | 135,598 | 58.3 | 96,867 | 41.7 | 37,236 | 27.5 | (+7,529) | (+3.2) |
| | 1976 | 239,994 | 98,362 | 41.0 | 141,632 | 59.0 | | | | |
| Baltimore | 1968 | 192,171 | 66,997 | 34.9 | 125,174 | 65.1 | 28,005 | 41.8 | 32,050 | 16.7 |
| | 1976 | 160,121 | 38,992 | 24.4 | 121,129 | 75.6 | | | | |
| Dallas | 1968 | 159,924 | 97,888 | 61.2 | 62,036 | 38.8 | 44,880 | 45.8 | 20,844 | 13.0 |
| | 1976 | 139,080 | 53,008 | 38.1 | 86,072 | 61.9 | | | | |
| Cleveland | 1968 | 156,054 | 66,324 | 42.5 | 89,730 | 57.5 | 19,941 | 30.1 | 33,348 | 21.4 |
| | 1976 | 122,706 | 46,383 | 37.8 | 76,323 | 62.2 | | | | |
| Washington, D.C. | 1968 | 148,725 | 8,280 | 5.6 | 140,445 | 94.4 | 3,796 | 45.8 | 22,138 | 14.9 |
| | 1976 | 126,587 | 4,484 | 3.5 | 122,103 | 96.5 | | | | |
| Milwaukee | 1968 | 130,445 | 95,161 | 73.0 | 35,284 | 27.0 | 33,423 | 35.1 | 20,880 | 16.0 |
| | 1976 | 109,565 | 61,738 | 56.3 | 47,827 | 43.7 | | | | |
| Memphis | 1968 | 125,813 | 58,271 | 46.3 | 67,542 | 53.7 | 24,423 | 41.9 | 8,317 | 6.6 |
| | 1976 | 117,496 | 33,848 | 28.8 | 83,648 | 71.2 | | | | |
| Jacksonville | 1968 | 122,637 | 87,999 | 71.8 | 34,638 | 28.2 | 14,269 | 16.2 | 11,930 | 9.7 |
| | 1976 | 110,707 | 73,730 | 66.6 | 36,977 | 33.4 | | | | |

| City | Year | | | % | | % | | % | | % |
|---|---|---|---|---|---|---|---|---|---|---|
| St. Louis | 1968 | 115,582 | 42,174 | 36.5 | 73,408 | 63.5 | 18,964 | 45.0 | 34,090 | 29.5 |
|  | 1976 | 81,492 | 23,210 | 28.5 | 58,282 | 71.5 | | | | |
| New Orleans | 1968 | 110,783 | 34,673 | 31.3 | 76,110 | 68.7 | 16,740 | 48.3 | 17,419 | 15.7 |
|  | 1976 | 93,364 | 17,933 | 19.2 | 75,431 | 80.8 | | | | |
| Columbus, Ohio | 1968 | 110,699 | 81,655 | 73.8 | 29,044 | 26.2 | 16,998 | 20.8 | 14,327 | 12.9 |
|  | 1976 | 96,372 | 64,657 | 67.1 | 31,715 | 32.9 | | | | |
| Indianapolis | 1968 | 108,587 | 72,010 | 66.3 | 36,577 | 33.7 | 26,823 | 37.2 | 26,585 | 24.5 |
|  | 1976 | 82,002 | 45,187 | 55.1 | 36,815 | 44.9 | | | | |
| Atlanta | 1968 | 111,227 | 42,506 | 38.2 | 68,721 | 61.8 | 33,275 | 78.3 | 28,747 | 25.8 |
|  | 1976 | 82,480 | 9,231 | 11.2 | 73,199 | 88.8 | | | | |
| San Diego | 1968 | 128,414 | 98,163 | 76.1 | 30,751 | 23.9 | 18,010 | 18.3 | 7,491 | 5.8 |
|  | 1976 | 121,423 | 80,153 | 66.0 | 41,270 | 34.0 | | | | |
| Denver | 1968 | 96,577 | 63,398 | 65.6 | 33,179 | 34.4 | 26,859 | 42.4 | 21,340 | 22.1 |
|  | 1976 | 75,237 | 36,539 | 48.6 | 38,698 | 51.4 | | | | |
| Boston | 1968 | 94,174 | 64,500 | 68.5 | 29,674 | 31.5 | 29,939 | 46.4 | 17,285 | 18.4 |
|  | 1976 | 76,889 | 34,561 | 45.0 | 42,328 | 55.0 | | | | |
| San Francisco | 1968 | 94,154 | 38,824 | 41.2 | 55,330 | 58.8 | 23,866 | 61.5 | 28,899 | 30.7 |
|  | 1976 | 65,255 | 14,958 | 22.9 | 50,297 | 77.1 | | | | |
| Seattle | 1968 | 94,025 | 77,293 | 82.2 | 16,732 | 17.8 | 35,670 | 46.1 | 32,206 | 34.3 |
|  | 1976 | 61,819 | 41,623 | 67.3 | 20,196 | 32.7 | | | | |
| Nashville | 1968 | 93,720 | 71,039 | 75.8 | 22,681 | 24.2 | 16,517 | 23.3 | 15,722 | 16.8 |
|  | 1976 | 77,998 | 54,522 | 69.9 | 23,476 | 30.1 | | | | |
| Cincinnati | 1968 | 86,807 | 49,231 | 56.7 | 37,576 | 43.3 | 18,534 | 37.6 | 21,172 | 24.4 |
|  | 1976 | 65,635 | 30,697 | 46.8 | 34,938 | 53.2 | | | | |
| San Antonio | 1968 | 79,353 | 21,310 | 26.9 | 58,043 | 73.1 | 11,348 | 53.3 | 13,641 | 17.2 |
|  | 1976 | 65,712 | 9,962 | 15.1 | 55,750 | 84.9 | | | | |
| Pittsburgh | 1968 | 76,628 | 46,005 | 60.3 | 30,263 | 39.7 | 14,051 | 30.5 | 17,606 | 23.0 |
|  | 1976 | 59,022 | 31,954 | 54.1 | 27,068 | 45.9 | | | | |
| Kansas City | 1968 | 74,202 | 39,510 | 53.2 | 34,692 | 46.8 | 21,950 | 44.4 | 23,155 | 31.2 |
|  | 1976 | 51,047 | 17,560 | 34.4 | 33,487 | 65.6 | | | | |

[1] Source: Prepared by the author for a conference sponsored by the National Institute of Education and the Hudson Institute (September 15-16, 1977).

[2] Two big cities—Phoenix and San Jose—are not included because both have numerous districts not coextensive with the city's boundaries. Both are predominantly white.

[3] Includes blacks, Hispanics, Asians, and American Indians.

and "white flight" are subverting the civil rights organizations. In view of the rate of white exodus from the public schools of Boston, Denver, and San Francisco, as well as the projected declines in Los Angeles after the implementation of busing, it is impossible to contend that court-ordered racial assignment does not accelerate "white flight" in large cities. It is not a contradiction to recognize that cities where there has been no court-ordered busing have also experienced significant "white flight" (though in no city has the rate of "white flight" been as great as in a single year as it was in Boston in 1974 and again in 1975). No matter how many qualifications are attached to Coleman's methodology or research design, his central concern about the diminishing number of whites in urban schools remains valid.

This conclusion should not be misunderstood: Even if it were clearly proved that desegregation causes "white flight," it would still be imperative to eliminate unconstitutional racial discrimination. Certainly, no one—least of all, Coleman—would propose maintaining racially segregated schools as a way of inducing whites to remain in city schools. Coleman's question, raised not in defense of segregation but about the long-range utility of system-wide racial balance plans, was whether court-ordered busing makes desegregation harder to achieve by hastening the departure of whites from city schools. "White flight," in cities under court order and in cities not under court order, is a real problem; it will not be solved by denying its existence or seriousness.

Table 6 demonstrates the extent of racial change in the 29 biggest cities in the United States from 1968 to 1976. (This list is of *big-city school districts*, not districts that have been made large by court order for purposes of integration.) All have had desegregation controversies, but only a few have court-ordered racial balance plans. *Of the 29 biggest city school districts in the nation, only eight still have a white majority:* Milwaukee, Jacksonville, Columbus, Indianapolis, San Diego, Seattle, Nashville, and Pittsburgh. And three of these eight are fast approaching the 50-percent mark (Milwaukee, Indianapolis, and Pittsburgh). During this eight-year period, the following districts made the transition from majority white to majority non-white: Los Angeles, Houston, Miami, Dallas, Denver, Boston, Cincinnati, and Kansas City.

It seems unlikely that we will ever know with any degree of

certainty whether whites (and some middle-class blacks) are leaving the city because of concern about desegregation or crime or poor services or racial tensions or the quality of life or for some other reason or combination of reasons. But if it is impossible to measure the precise impact of school desegregation on "white flight," it is equally insupportable to claim that there is no effect whatever. Court-ordered busing may or may not be the primary stimulus of white withdrawal from city schools, but it is very likely a contributing factor—and, at least in Boston, an important contributing factor. Just as it is impossible to determine whether it is the direct cause, it is equally impossible to prove that it has no bearing at all on family decisions to remove children from urban schools.

Behind the controversy over Coleman's findings is a struggle over the future direction of policy. Coleman is urging a cautious and deliberate approach that takes into account the possibility of "white flight" and resegregation. His views, furthermore, support the idea that court remedies should be specific, rather than broad and system-wide.

Coleman's critics are committed to racial balancing of pupil populations as the best, most demonstrable assurance of full integration. The integration forces may not have won every court battle, but they have succeeded in popularizing the notion that every black school, regardless of the reason for its racial concentration, is a segregated school, the result of official discrimination rather than affinity or choice. In the aftermath of the Supreme Court's 1974 Detroit decision, which limited urban-suburban busing, integration advocates, in many instances, have had to confine their demands for busing to individual school districts. In our largest cities, this is not a solution likely to satisfy anyone for very long: "Success" in most big cities will mean a school system in which every school is predominantly non-white, and from which white pupils continue to leave every year. Unless "white flight" is stopped or reversed, racial balancing within cities will very likely produce the phenomenon of resegregation between city and suburb that Coleman has warned about.

The inadequacy of racial balancing within big-city school districts is likely to generate new pressures for metropolitan-area school integration. This is a proposal long favored by the United States Civil Rights Commission and civil rights groups, and it is

already in effect in several smaller cities and counties. How such
a proposal might be implemented in a city school district with a
quarter-million, a half-million, or a million pupils is uncertain, as
are the educational implications. What is predictable, however,
is the political reaction: To date, no metropolitan region has
voluntarily adopted a full city-suburban merger for school integration, and opposition can be anticipated from suburban districts
(whose residents include many who fled the city schools), state
legislatures (where urban interests are a minority), and Congress
(which regularly passes ineffective busing curbs). Nothing less
than a reversal of the Supreme Court's 1974 Detroit decision
could produce the enforcement mechanism to impose metropolitan-area integration on a large scale. For now, at least, that is not
in the offing.

But if racial balancing is of limited practicality because of the
diminishing number of white pupils in most big cities, and if
metropolitan cross-busing is of limited applicability because of
the Supreme Court's 1974 ruling, what then? Few urban districts
have had the capacity to look or plan beyond the latest political
or fiscal crisis, but clearly some fresh synthesis is needed to restore a sense of direction to urban education. Atlanta is one city
that offers hope of a new approach. Its schools are 90-percent
black, and its professional leadership is predominantly black. At
the instigation of the local NAACP (which defied the national
NAACP), a deal was struck in court to forego busing in exchange
for jobs and black control of the system. Now the system is intent on demonstrating that the schools can be made to work.

The Atlanta schools are stressing the kind of curriculum and
values that will enable black children (and white children) to
succeed in the mainstream of American life; this means an early
emphasis on basic skills, taught in an orderly atmosphere in
which achievement and hard work are rewarded. Atlanta has
decided to build a new high school, and remarkably, it will be a
selective, admission-by-academic-examination school, possibly
the first new such school anywhere in the country for many years.

Meanwhile, the American Civil Liberties Union is pressing a
court suit to compel the merger of the Atlanta school district and
the surrounding white suburban districts, in order to make blacks
a minority within a predominantly white metropolitan district; not
surprisingly, the Atlanta district has shown no interest in surren-
dering its independence. The theory of Atlanta's educational

leaders is that equal educational opportunity can be achieved through quality education. If they are right, and if they can create the kind of productive, effective schools that all parents want, their system could become a showplace for urban American schools and a magnet pulling back the children of those who fled the city during the past two decades. Andrew Young, while he was Atlanta's Congressman, predicted in a newspaper interview in 1975 that Atlanta's schools would ultimately prove to be better than the suburban schools, both because of their clear and purposeful educational approach and because of the city's considerable cultural resources, which no suburban shopping mall can match. Imagine that: "white flight" to the city, resulting not from coercion or condescension, but from an earnest search for good public schools.

# National
# and
# Local Politics

*Throughout the 1970s both the President and the Congress sought to limit school busing. In this essay Gary Orfield, Professor of Political Science at the University of Illinois and author of* Must We Bus?, *details the attack on busing that came out of Washington and shows what it accomplished.*

# The President, Congress, and Antibusing Politics

## GARY ORFIELD

When President Lyndon Johnson signed the Civil Rights Act of 1964, it seemed certain to begin a period of revolutionary change in American race relations, a change then supported by a broad spectrum of political forces and evoking virtually unanimous support from American blacks. The first southern President since before the Civil War signed the bill as supporters—including conservative Republicans—looked on. Soon he chose the bill's floor leader and one of the nation's most eloquent civil rights advocates, Hubert Humphrey, as his running mate. In the fall, against one of the bill's new prominent nonsouthern opponents, Barry Goldwater, the President won a landslide victory that produced the most progressive congressional majority in recent history. All of the six major civil rights organizations had strongly supported enactment of the law and there was a seemingly unanimous black commitment to enforcement. Southern opponents were defeated and demoralized. Seldom has a social movement achieved a more unambiguous triumph.

Reprinted with permission from *Must We Bus? Segregated Schools and National Policy.* Copyright © 1978 by the Brookings Institution, Washington, D.C.

The act brought about change in southern racial practices. Public accommodations were integrated. More black students went into desegregated schools in the first year of enforcement than had in the previous decade. The 1965 Voting Rights Act enfranchised blacks of the Deep South for the first time in the century. Changes that had seemed all but impossible took place rapidly and peacefully.

The underlying political consensus soon began to erode, however, particularly on the question of school segregation. By the early 1970s, white Americans had consolidated against urban school desegregation. Now, after more than a decade of political attacks on busing and annual battles over antibusing legislation, little of consequence has been accomplished. Congress has enacted few significant antibusing amendments and presidential promises of more decisive action against the courts have come to nothing.

Still, the political battles and public statements deserve attention because of their influence on the national discussion of integration. They have left the federal courts more isolated than ever. They have been used to justify the removal of executive branch agencies' power to enforce civil rights laws. Finally, the negative character of the antibusing movement has meant that there has been no serious examination for some time of the ways in which the power of government could be used to produce an integrated society in the cities.

The Goldwater campaign, the emergence of George Wallace as a national figure, and the Nixon campaign strategies injected racial polarization into national politics. Presidential candidates apparently decided that there was more to be gained by dwelling on whites' fear of racial change than by appealing for black votes. The shift of the southern white vote to the GOP in the 1960s seemed to vindicate the strategy. Nixon was elected president with almost no black votes. More and more Republicans in the House and some in the Senate followed a similar strategy. This break with the progressive element of the party's tradition brought to office officials whose effective constituencies were almost entirely white.

When the courts began to order desegregation through busing the prominence in American politics of racial change rapidly became apparent on Capitol Hill. Long-time civil rights supporters suddenly encountered polarized public feeling unprecedented in their careers. A number of congressmen from Michigan and Massachusetts and other trouble spots executed fast, 180-degree changes in voting. Major education bills and huge appropriations measures were often ignored as busing amendments took precedence. Presidents Nixon and Ford threatened to veto their programs if antibusing provisions were not tough enough.

The House, with its short terms and narrow constituencies, responded to the issue first and consistently approved presidential proposals to restrain the courts. The Senate—where many members are free of immediate election worries, where statewide constituencies encourage responsiveness to both black and white demands, and where, unlike in the House, the rural western states, which have very few minority children, are represented equally—consistently restrained the House and blocked presidential demands.

The story of antibusing legislation is rich in examples of how policy is affected by tactics. Committed civil rights supporters with positions of seniority have used conference committees, control of committee agendas, filibusters, muddled legislative language, and a variety of other strategems to frustrate antibusing majorities. Time after time the tactics the South used to preserve segregation have been used to defend desegregation requirements.

Both presidential and congressional politics reflected the decentralized nature of American society. The Wallace movement and the southern congressional attacks crested in the late 1960s and early 1970s, when the threat of change was imminent and the people were aroused. In 1972 the *Milliken* case in Detroit dominated Michigan politics. But by the time of the 1976 primaries, busing was a fact of life in many parts of the South and the issue was one of secondary importance. In many states it was academic since no cases were pending or there was almost no one to desegregate. Only in Boston was it dominant.

The long battles illustrated a feature of American politics that is too seldom described—the willingness of a surprising number of political leaders to go against strong public opinion on behalf of a principle they believe in or simply in defense of the law. During the most intense local polarization many members of Congress spent their political resources to prevent limitations on the courts. Most northern Democrats in the Senate and many in the House consistently voted against the national consensus. So did a number of Senate Republicans. The men and women who defied public opinion were a minority, but they prevented a collision between Congress and the Supreme Court.

## THE EROSION OF SUPPORT

The initial breakdown of the civil rights consensus can be ascribed to many causes. The changes soon reached beyond issues peculiar to the South. Deciding to act against vicious official racism in another region did not imply support for social transformation at home. Even when people agreed that something was wrong, they were divided on how much the *federal government* should do.

The divisiveness emerged rapidly during the process of enforcing the Civil Rights Act. When the Office of Education required southern school districts to begin token desegregation under "freedom of choice" plans in the fall of 1965, the adjustment was difficult but it was accepted. The next year, when federal civil rights officials realized that freedom of choice was not going to work, the Department of Health, Education, and Welfare escalated its requirements. The focus of enforcement changed from the surface equity of the process to the result—actual annual progress toward genuinely integrated schools. This went beyond what many courts were requiring at the time and was bitterly protested.

At the same time the civil rights movement was breaking up. In 1964 it had been completely integrationist. Within two years, some groups had turned to the issues of black power, cultural nationalism, and community building. Although these groups represented only a small fraction of the black population, they received a great deal of attention. Politically this meant that there was no unified black voice on civil rights issues. For the next several years some widely publicized black leaders attacked the premises of desegregation head on. Those who remained steadfast to the principles of 1954 and 1964 were belittled as traditionalists of declining importance. The movement was in disarray.[1]

The problems were magnified by the urban riots of 1965–68 and by the growing preoccupation of liberals with the Vietnam War. White Americans were shocked and terrified by the mass rioting and looting of blacks. The riots forced the public to focus on the immense racial problems of the cities, but hardly in a way designed to foster support for the changes necessary to produce desegregation.

The mood of Congress changed quickly. Even before a more conservative Congress was elected in 1966, the most liberal Congress in many years had unceremoniously killed a new civil rights bill. The House voted to limit federal school desegregation powers. It was the first of a long series of annual setbacks.

## Congressional Views of Segregation

The first signs of resistance to urban desegregation appeared in the congressional debate on the 1964 Civil Rights Act. Many members believed the South was a special case.

The House adopted amendments to one section of the bill forbidding the Justice Department to file litigation to force the busing of children for the purpose of racial balance.[2] In the Senate the fear of future busing actions was voiced by Senator Robert Byrd of West Virginia (who became the Democratic Senate leader in 1977). Under pressure from Byrd, the bill's floor manager, Hubert Humphrey, stated his belief that the fund-withholding sanction could not be applied to de facto segregation. He assured opponents that President Johnson would reject "racial balancing" requirements.[3]

The statements about desegregation rested on the then prevailing understanding of constitutional requirements. Humphrey said that de facto segregation had been omitted from the bill because the Supreme Court had recently let stand a lower court decision that the Gary, Indiana, schools had no obligation to abolish segregation.[4] The Supreme Court's refusal to hear the case was widely cited as proof that northern segregation was constitutional.[5]

The Civil Rights Act, however, emerged from Congress with its major enforcement provision intact. In one of the most sweeping and important sentences in federal statutory law, the act stated: "No person in the United States shall on the ground of race, color, or national origin, be excluded from participation in, be denied the benefits of, or be subjected to discrimination under any program or activity receiving federal financial assistance."[6] This language laid the groundwork for broad administrative power to define and enforce standards: as the Court fleshed out constitutional requirements, the responsibilities of the Department of Health, Education, and Welfare would expand.

When HEW began actively enforcing the law in 1965, the initial response was calm. Congressional opponents turned belligerent only when the agency made clear that it was actually aiming at transformation of the southern school systems. Southerners were shocked that HEW was prepared to take the almost unprecedented step of cutting off large amounts of federal grants-in-aid. Many agencies had the power to cut the flow of federal money under certain conditions, but they almost never did. Under President Johnson, HEW frequently did.

When enforcement began, southern members of Congress were still reeling from their first serious defeat on civil rights legislation in Congress in almost ninety years. For some time southern leaders had denounced desegregation orders as undemocratic usurpations by the courts. Now that Congress had ratified the policy of the courts, that rationale was gone. Only after HEW raised its requirements and southern opponents regrouped was there real resistance.[7]

## The Beginning of Northern Opposition

The first political confrontation to undermine congressional support took place outside the South, in Chicago. Neither Congress nor HEW had given much thought to the issue of northern and western segregation. It was clear, however, that both the Constitution and the 1964 Civil Rights Act prohibited intentional segregation in the North. How intent could be proved was unclear.

A 1965 civil rights complaint in Chicago not only alleged that there was a wide variety of segregationist practices but also claimed that the city intended to use the funds it would receive from the new Elementary and Secondary Education Act to reinforce segregation.[8] A confrontation between the city's black community and the local school system led to mass boycotts, hundreds of arrests, and a congressional hearing on the local situation.

Just a week after a small team of HEW staff members began to investigate Chicago, Commissioner of Education Francis Keppel deferred $32 million in new federal aid funds the city had been due to receive. The action came before the HEW staff had gathered any of the evidence necessary to sustain a fund cutoff and it put the administration in direct conflict with the most powerful Democratic political organization in the country. Commissioner Keppel had expected that the Chicago school officials would cooperate quietly to avoid publicizing the fact that their funds were being held up, but his action quickly became known.

The action drew attacks from the Chicago congressional delegation and from Senate GOP Leader Everett Dirksen of Illinois. Mayor Richard J. Daley threatened to end his delegation's support for all federal education legislation. Though HEW quickly retreated, the affair aroused the suspicion and hostility of a number of northern urban congressmen.

In 1966 the most liberal House since the depression voted against the HEW school desegregation program. In the same House that had passed the Voting Rights Act, the Elementary and Secondary Education Act (ESEA), Medicare, Model Cities, and many other social reforms, opposition to school desegregation was growing. This was the first sign of what was to become a long-term shift. Each year from 1966 to 1977 the House passed at least one amendment designed to restrain school integration.

HEW had magnified its political problems when it issued new guidelines requiring far more desegregation in the South. Southern congressmen claimed that the tougher requirements were illegal and that HEW was forcing arbitrary changes which disrupted local educational systems.[9] By August 9, 1966, things had changed enough for the House to pass an amendment sponsored by Representative Howard "Bo" Callaway, a very conservative Georgian, which forbade HEW to require "assignment of students to public schools in order to overcome racial imbalance." The amendment was intended to prohibit any desegregation action in the South beyond "free choice" plans, which usually left schools highly segregated, and it appealed to northerners disturbed by the Chicago incident and beginning to worry about busing.[10] An even more sweeping amendment, submitted by North Carolina Congressman Basil Whitener but always called the Whitten amendment because Mississippi Congressman Jamie Whitten has resubmitted it annually, directing HEW to allow the perpetuation of segregation in southern "free choice" systems failed by nine votes.[11]

As the 1966–67 school year approached, opponents in Congress grew increasingly active. Eighteen southern senators had appealed in May to their old comrade, President Johnson, for a relaxation in the policy, but he supported enforcement.[12] Southern members inundated the enforcement staff with requests and letters and denunciations.

September also saw the first attempt by a northern congressman to exploit the backlash. Republican Representative Paul Fino of New York City, formerly one of his party's strong civil rights supporters, attacked a draft policy proposal, prepared to find new answers to urban school problems. Fino assailed what he saw as a plan to force busing across school district lines into the suburbs, although this was immediately disavowed by the administration. When the high priority Model Cities bill came before the House, its sponsors initiated an amendment, which was approved by voice vote, forbidding administrators to require desegregation as a condition for receiving the funds.[13] This became part of the act.[14]

One of the few positive ideas of the period was quietly sidetracked in a Senate committee. Senator Edward Kennedy had proposed federal aid for northern and western school districts that voluntarily desegregated. This relatively noncontroversial proposal had enjoyed good prospects, but in September the liberal Senate Labor and Public Welfare Committee killed it. Even voluntary action in the North was not popular.

The southerners in the House concentrated their attack at first on obscure enforcement procedures little understood by civil rights supporters. Frontal attacks on desegregation would come later. First, they weakened HEW's power to hold up money for new federal aid programs in school districts where the department believed illegal segregation was taking place. The House passed an amendment to the ESEA by Representative L. H. Fountain of North Carolina forbidding the deferral procedure.[15]

However, this was the first of many occasions when liberal senior members of conference committees protected civil rights agencies. The general practice of relying on committee and subcommittee seniority in selecting conferees meant that the House members of the conference committee were a liberal group headed by Harlem Congressman Adam Clayton Powell, Jr., and that the Senate conferees too were led by strong supporters of civil rights. The 1966 conference committee eviscerated the Fountain amendment. Angry southerners were unable to persuade the House to risk defeat of the entire ESEA bill by attempting to force the Senate to reconsider in the final days of the session.[16]

Civil rights supporters had managed to preserve the basic structure of the 1964 Civil Rights Act in the first skirmishes, but these
battles would go on incessantly into the mid-seventies. Supporters were reduced to skillful use of the tools of minorities
attempting to frustrate majorities in Congress. The tactics that
had prevented congressional passage of civil rights legislation for
decades now forestalled its repeal.

## The Threat to Education Legislation

The 1967 Democratic opponents of civil rights enforcement by
HEW joined Republicans to attack both the structure of federal
aid to education and civil rights enforcement. The race issue
threatened to split northern and southern Democrats. The danger in the House was so grave that HEW tacitly approved some
of the less damaging civil rights amendments being drafted in
the House and reorganized the enforcement program.

Again the HEW program was protected, but only because its
enemies on the House floor were disorganized. Southerners,
most Republicans, and some northern Democrats had rallied behind proposals drafted by Representative Edith Green of Oregon
requiring that all HEW guidelines be based on particular parts of
the Civil Rights Act and that they be applied equally to all fifty
states. Southerners believed that the vague words of the statute
would make it hard to justify the specific requirements of the
guidelines. Since no one was going to launch a serious enforcement effort in the North, they thought, much less would be done
in the South in the future.

When the 1967 ESEA amendments reached the House floor,
however, Congresswoman Green confused everyone by accepting
an amendment that allowed HEW to rely on court decisions to
support standards. In the end the amendments were so unclear
that HEW could continue its existing program while the program's foes could take credit for votes against it. This was to
become a frequent pattern.

One thing showed the direction of the drift. The Fountain
amendment limiting the deferral of funds, fought so hard the
previous year, was enacted in the 1967 education bill. The administration accepted the weakening of the deferral power as
part of a bargain intended to gain southern votes for extending the life of the ESEA.

Southern senators threatened to filibuster against the bill, and Dirksen came within a hair's breadth of amending it to forbid the use of any federal money to bus students, even for voluntary integration. Dirksen's move was defeated only by the opposition of freshman GOP Senator Robert Griffin of Michigan.[17] This was ironic, since Griffin later became a leader of the antibusing drive when Detroit was threatened with desegregation.

To extricate the education bill from the Senate, HEW Secretary John W. Gardner finally offered another compromise. HEW promised to further limit deferral actions, persuading the Senate's southern caucus to end any threat of filibuster.[18]

Again the liberal conference committee threw out the House restrictions. House opponents were once more presented with a take-it-or-leave-it package, brought to the floor on the final hectic day of the 1967 session. HEW retained its powers.

The second year of congressional combat had left some marks on HEW's effort to enforce the Civil Rights Act. The most visible and committed spokesman for the effort, Commissioner of Education Harold Howe II, had lost his authority over the program. The enforcement staff was scattered in regional offices. The deferral power and enforcement credibility had been weakened.

### The 1968 Campaign

Although there was still very little city school desegregation in the nation, the fear of change grew after the Supreme Court's 1968 decision in *Green v. New Kent County,* which held that school systems segregated by official action must actually integrate, not merely offer blacks "free choice" to transfer for desegregation. In the courts civil rights lawyers were pressing the urban districts.

Both George Wallace and Richard Nixon emphasized desegregation in their campaigns. Wallace roused southern audiences with his passionate attack on HEW bureaucrats. His rapidly rising strength in the polls and his dominance in the Deep South suggested that he might gain enough votes to hold the balance of power in the electoral college.[19]

In his victorious campaign, Nixon attacked busing. He told the southern caucus at the GOP national convention that he believed judges were unqualified to make local school decisions. He promised a more conservative Supreme Court. He endorsed "freedom of choice." He said it was "dangerous" to use the threat of federal aid cutoffs to "force a local community to carry out what a Federal administrator or bureaucrat may think is best for that local community." [20] It was the first overt attack on civil rights enforcement by a successful presidential candidate in recent history.

During the election campaign Congress, through an amendment to a spending bill, came close to ending HEW's authority to desegregate southern schools by outlawing HEW's regulations. As the courts and HEW had begun to insist on the desegregation of southern city schools, southerners had been pointing out that similar segregation was ignored in the North and West. They succeeded in inserting into the 1968 HEW appropriations measure a directive that half of HEW's enforcement staff be used to investigate northern cases.[21] Appropriations bills in future years would frequently be the targets of congressional attacks on civil rights enforcement. This approach had two important tactical advantages: appropriations bills must be passed every year and they go to conservative conference committees.

### Nixon's Racial Politics

After President Nixon's inaugural, enforcement officials in the federal agencies found themselves under pressure from Capitol Hill and the White House to slow down. For the first time since 1954, both elected branches of government opposed the courts, attempting to delay change and hoping eventually to restrict judicial power to order desegregation. Pressure grew, first for a partial repeal of the Civil Rights Act and later for a showdown on the issue between the judiciary and the elected branches of government.

Nixon won election as the first president since Woodrow Wilson committed to slowing the momentum of racial change. After taking office he had to decide what to do about the existing drive to complete desegregation in the rural South and about desegregating urban areas. On both issues he decided to oppose desegregation.

As a result there was less and less disposition in Congress to fight efforts to narrow the Civil Rights Act. Once again Whitten submitted the amendment that would force HEW to accept "free choice" plans as being in full compliance with the Civil Rights

Act. The Johnson administration had fought the proposal, but this time the new attorney general, John Mitchell, told a meeting of GOP congressmen that he could see nothing wrong with the amendment. The House promptly passed it. Only Senate resistance and a belated HEW statement of opposition succeeded in defeating the measure.[22]

The Nixon administration politicized the enforcement process, and negotiations between local officials, HEW's civil rights staff, and congressional offices were transferred to Washington. The momentum and credibility of the federal drive for integration were greatly diminished.[23] Only the unanimous October 1969 Supreme Court decision, *Alexander v. Holmes*,[24] prevented a collapse of the southern desegregation effort. This, the first major decision of the Court under Chief Justice Warren Burger, a Nixon appointee, summarily rejected the administration's insistence on delay and ordered that plans be carried out at once.

The busing issue was growing. In his long-awaited March 1970 statement of school desegregation policy, President Nixon sharpened the White House attack on the courts. He denounced "extreme" court orders, which, he said, "have raised widespread fears that the nation might face a massive disruption of public education: that wholesale compulsory busing may be ordered and the neighborhood school virtually doomed." [25] In conformity with the President's policy, the Justice Department went into court in 1970 to fight a federal district court decision ordering desegregation of the Charlotte, North Carolina, school system, carrying its battle to the Supreme Court.

### The Senate

By early 1970 congressional civil rights supporters appeared to have been routed. A skillful drive, led by Senator John Stennis of Mississippi and supported by the White House, produced the first serious Senate defeat for school integration.

Stennis documented northern segregation in great detail and then challenged northern senators to require all cities to meet the standards that had been set for the South. His amendment to the ESEA of 1965 to apply the law *equally* "without regard to the origin or cause of such segregation" meant that, unless the administration was prepared to move out in front of the federal courts and require desegregation in the North, nothing could be done in the South. Since the President had consistently opposed the desegregation of northern cities, civil rights supporters believed he would use the Stennis amendment to equalize conditions by ending change in Dixie. Senate Democratic leaders and GOP leader Hugh Scott fought the amendment but could not defeat it so long as it enjoyed quiet White House backing.[26]

The Senate vote indicated that the nation's backward movement on desegregation had now reached major proportions. A Gallup poll published shortly after the Senate vote reported that nine people in ten were opposed to busing, even though most of the whites against busing said they were willing to send their children to half-black schools.[27]

Civil rights groups were deeply discouraged. The President was hostile to urban desegregation, his appointments were making the Supreme Court more conservative, the House had been hostile for years, and now the last bastion, the Senate, seemed to have fallen. If the Senate joined the White House and the House of Representatives in resisting, the pressure on the courts would be immense. It was a congressional election year—the year of Spiro Agnew's biting attacks on liberals of campus polarization on Cambodia, and of GOP efforts to mobilize the "silent majority"—and the administration used the busing issue in a strident campaign to put a new conservative majority on Capitol Hill.

The obituary for school integration turned out to be premature. When the House and Senate went to conference on the Stennis amendment, a strange thing happened. The bill emerged from conference not only without the Stennis provision, but with directions to HEW to formulate separate policies for de facto and de jure segregation and to apply each nationally.[28]

In February 1970 the Senate established the Select Committee on Equal Educational Opportunity, with Walter Mondale as chairman, to explore the complex issues. In its three years of existence, the Mondale committee investigated and attacked the Nixon administration's failure to enforce civil rights laws. It gave school officials and civil rights spokesmen an opportunity to rebut the administration's contention that desegregation was failing in communities across the country. The committee's work helped improve the Emergency School Aid (desegregation aid) legislation. More important, it provided some counterforce to the heavy weather that was pushing the Senate toward an attempt to override the courts.[29]

### Aid for Desegregation

One section of President Nixon's March 1970 school desegregation policy statement was well received by both civil rights supporters and school officials—his call for a large grant program to help desegregating school systems do the job better. Since the Supreme Court had made further delays in desegregating the rural South impossible, the President proposed to ease the transition with a two-year $1.5 billion emergency program.

The administration soon faced the necessity of translating the President's broadly stated promise, inserted in his desegregation statement at the last moment, into a specific legislative proposal. The resulting bill was built around helping districts that were facing "emergencies" created when the courts ordered sudden massive desegregation. When a local school district was directed to desegregate immediately, its major out-of-pocket expense was often the purchase of new buses. Local administrators, not wanting to disrupt educational plans on short notice, hoped to use federal funds for this purpose.

After HEW had drafted the bill, the President added a new-provision prohibiting use of the money for busing. This, in effect, dissociated the administration from busing, and it was strongly opposed by school officials and civil rights groups and provoked new battles in Congress. Congress rapidly approved interim 1970 appropriations of $75 million while committees worked on the legislation for the much larger program.

The pilot program produced serious administrative abuses. White House insistence on rapid action meant that there were no effective civil rights reviews and the money was simply sent out. Jackson, Mississippi, for instance, was granted $1.3 million four days *before* HEW received the city's official application.[30] It was discovered that much of the money had gone to districts continuing to segregate. In some places, the districts receiving the money were systematically firing black teachers and principals and segregating black children in classes in nominally "desegregated" buildings. The General Accounting Office, Congress' investigatory agency, reported that in many of the approved applications there was no pretense that the money would be spent for integration.[31]

The battle over the Emergency School Aid Act stretched into 1971 and 1972. In the end, Congress transformed an amorphous plan for a one-shot grant without strings to southern districts into a program with a more national orientation, strong administrative strings, and some incentives for desegregation. The desegregation requirements were so unambiguous that HEW continued enforcing them long afer it stopped enforcing the Civil Rights Act. The temporary two-year program was twice extended. On the other hand, President Nixon eventually had his way on the prohibition against using the money for busing. His opposition and that of President Ford to increased appropriations for the program were effective; the effort peaked in 1973 but was severely eroded by inflation during the next four years.

## POLITICS AND POLARIZATION

The politics of antibusing legislation began to change rapidly after the Supreme Court handed down its unanimous and surprisingly tough 1971 decision in the Charlotte case.[32] The busing remedy became available in the North too, once lawyers had proved *de jure* violations. That fall the issue was suddenly brought home to the white suburbanites of the country when a federal district judge in Michigan ordered the preparation of a desegregation plan for metropolitan Detroit.[33]

The votes on antibusing measures in the House in 1971–72 consolidated Republican sentiment against school desegregation and began to weaken northern Democratic support. In 1972, antibusing forces started out with a large, stable core of House votes and tended to pick up more votes as a growing number of northern Democrats joined their southern counterparts (see Table 1). Southerners had always said that the politics of the issue would change when the North was forced to desegregate. They were right. Some members of the Michigan, Colorado, Massachusetts, and Delaware congressional delegations suddenly reversed their position. In the House the antibusing fights that had been led by southerners were now taken over by Michigan members.

This produced odd coalitions. Often moderate and liberal members felt they had to vote for amendments sponsored by extremely conservative members whose lead they would follow on no other issue. A principal author of the House antibusing language, for example, was Representative John Ashbrook of Ohio, a leader of the most conservative Republicans. A number of

*Table 1: Changing Factional Alliances on House Antibusing Votes, 1968-72*

Percent

| Factional agreement | Whitten amendment[a] | 1972 ESEA amendments[b] | Nixon antibusing bill[c] |
|---|---|---|---|
| Republican–southern Democrat | 65.6 | 89.6 | 86.2 |
| Northern Democrat–southern Democrat | 20.4 | 48.9 | 46.0 |

Source: James Bolner and Robert Shanley, *Busing: The Political and Judicial Process* (Praeger, 19749, pp. 116, 118-19.
a. From 1968 to 1971 there were five roll call votes on the Whitten amendment.
b. In 1972 there were seven roll call votes on the ESEA amendments.
c. In 1972 there were nine votes on the Nixon bill, the most drastic effort to limit judicial power.

Democrats who had recently enjoyed almost perfect (by the standards of Americans for Democratic Action) voting records found themselves supporting Ashbrook. On the Senate side, antibusing authors included such improbable figures as Senator Jesse Helms of North Carolina, whose views made most of the older southern Democrats look liberal by comparison, and Senator Edward Gurney of Florida, who at the time was under indictment in a political scandal.

As the controversy intensified, political leaders faced an unusual situation. Opinion against busing was so strong that many congressmen with largely white constituencies could see no support for the policy the courts were attempting to implement. In middle class communities threatened by court orders, the public protested on an unprecedented scale. There was little organized support for the policy from the black community, and social scientists publicly stated that the policy did no good anyway. Politically, there was little to lose by opposing busing and there was the possibility of gaining an active new constituency.

The congressional mood in the 1971–76 period was reminiscent of that in southern state legislatures in the late 1950s. Although most legislators knew they lacked the authority to repeal Supreme Court decisions, public pressure was so intense that legislators often cast almost unanimous ballots for patently ridiculous positions. In the 1950s the Virginia legislature pronounced the 1954 Supreme Court decision null and void and gave the governor authority to shut down public schools if integration was threatened. On Capitol Hill in the 1970s members of Congress found themselves debating measures to cut off the gasoline for school buses, to permit resegregation of southern schools, and to tell the Supreme Court how to handle its school cases. Many of these measures had been proposed or strongly endorsed by the President and all passed the House. In the 1950s the southern legislators had attempted to forestall litigation by laws restricting the NAACP; in 1974 Congress restricted legal services lawyers. Though they could handle most legal problems of the poor, legal services lawyers could not represent clients who were attempting to end their children's unconstitutional segregation in a *de jure* segregated school system.

## The Constitutional Amendment

The most extreme response was a drive to amend the Constitution so that federal authority to require positive local action to desegregate urban schools would be ended. The favored vehicle was an amendment reading: "No public school student shall, because of his race, creed, or color, be assigned to or required to attend a particular school." This "affirmation of equal opportunity" would of course proscribe any desegregation plan that attempted to overcome *de jure* segregation by reassigning children. It would prohibit not only busing but also numerous other techniques of urban school desegregation. With existing urban housing patterns, it would mean almost nothing could be done.

The amendment drive peaked in early 1972, when President Nixon publicly stated that he might support a constitutional amendment unless Congress could end busing by legislation. This statement, however, was promptly attacked by both Republican and Democratic leaders of the Senate and even by Vice-President Agnew.[34] Gerald Ford, then House GOP Minority Leader, and Senator Henry Jackson, a Democrat, strongly endorsed amendments but theirs was a minority view.[35]

The amendment was introduced by thirty-one members of the House in early 1972, and supporters organized a discharge petition to force it out of the Judiciary Committee. After more than one-third of the House had signed the petition, the committee agreed to hold hearings. Some seventy members of the House either appeared before the committee or submitted statements on the amendment. The great majority favored it.[36] But the committee bottled it up after the President decided to first try legislation limiting court orders. The amendment process, he told a national television audience, has "a fatal flaw—it takes too long." [37]

An analysis of the voting records of the more than 150 members who signed the discharge petition showed that they had consistently been opponents of civil rights measures. From 1968 to 1971, in a series of crucial votes, they had been against actions to strengthen civil rights enforcement by more than 7–1. Although opponents of busing frequently said they favored integration so long as neighborhood schools were naturally integrated, the amendment's supporters had voted almost 5–1 against the 1968 fair housing law on its key test. Ten out of eleven also opposed strong enforcement against job discrimination.[38]

If legal authorities are correct in stating that a constitutional amendment is the only way to reverse judicial decisions requiring student transportation, opponents of busing are up against extraordinarily difficult political obstacles; among them, that in almost half of the states there are almost no minority students to bus and in a few states segregation has been virtually eliminated. Even if an amendment could be extracted from a hostile House Judiciary Committee, proponents would have to muster two-thirds margins in both House and Senate and overcome a probable Senate filibuster. They would then need ratification by three-fourths of the states. This would take years at best.

In a 1972 national poll a majority of the respondents supported legislation limiting desegregation but fewer than one-third favored a constitutional amendment (see Table 2). A 1976 poll for *Time*, however, reported a 51–39 percent majority for an amendment.[39] The House Democratic caucus in November 1975 voted 2–1 to table an amendment proposal although at the time there were protests and disruption in Boston and Louisville.[40]

Constitutional amendments can be enacted only when there is a broad national consensus on an issue. Strong minority opposition can easily block the drive for two-thirds majorities in both houses. Polls indicate that the proposed constitutional amendment to permit prayer in schools, for instance, is supported by a much

*Table 2: Public Support for Antibusing Legislation and*
*Constitutional Amendment*

Percent

| | Answer | | |
|---|---|---|---|
| *Question* | *Favor* | *Oppose* | *No opinion* |
| A law has been introduced in Congress to prohibit busing of children beyond the nearest schools even where the courts have found unlawful segregation. Do you feel it would be right or not right for Congress to pass such a law? | 57 | 29 | 14 |
| Would you favor or oppose a constitutional amendment which would make it lawful to keep schools segregated? | 30 | 53 | 17 |

Source: U.S. Commission on Civil Rights, "Public Knowledge and Busing Opposition" (March 13, 1973; processed), appendix, p. 2, reporting data collected by Opinion Research Corporation in November and December 1972 based on 2,006 interviews.

larger (77–17 percent) majority of the public yet has been blocked in Congress.[41]

Congress is hesitant to tamper with the Constitution or with the tradition of an independent judiciary. In the busing debates, arguments were often based on constitutional law and the separation of powers, not on substance. Many members of Congress are lawyers, as are all members of the Judiciary Committees, which must handle constitutional amendments. This is a substantial barrier to precipitate constitutional change and has surely influenced the politics of the issue. President Nixon never submitted an amendment, nor did President Ford, even after the idea was endorsed in the 1976 GOP platform. Antibusing leaders in the House continued to try to force a vote with a discharge petition in 1977 but failed to obtain enough signatures.

### The Midnight Amendments

Until 1971 the battles in Congress had been primarily over limiting HEW's power to enforce the 1964 Civil Rights Act. But in a late evening House debate on November 4, 1971, the Michigan delegation led the House toward a direct challenge to the authority of the federal courts. The fight was over a complex higher education bill that also carried the Nixon desegregation assistance program.

Without hesitation, the House adopted an amendment introduced by suburban Detroit Congressman William Broomfield which said that future court orders requiring transportation of students to achieve racial balance must not take effect until the school system concerned had had a chance to appeal the case to the Supreme Court. This directly opposed a decision by the Court, which had ruled unanimously in 1969 that desegregation orders must be carried out immediately, even though appeals were pending.[42] Although the amendment was obviously intended to delay the execution of a metropolitan Detroit desegregation plan, it was drafted so broadly that it would have blocked plans even where there were no unsettled legal issues. The amendment was adopted with little discussion, 235–125.

A second amendment devised by Representative John Ashbrook, which would come up time after time in the debates of the next several years, prohibited the use of federal grant money for busing students or teachers for desegregation. The amendment was a break with the tradition of giving local districts discretion in the use of school aid and would constitute a special hardship on some 2,000 districts already under desegregation plans requiring busing. Though it was strongly opposed by many school officials, it passed by a huge margin.

Next the House adopted Congresswoman Edith Green's amendment forbidding federal officials to encourage integration. The amendment stated that federal administrators must not "urge" or "persuade" local authorities to use their own state or local money for busing. Federal officials, sworn to uphold the Constitution, would be forbidden even to suggest that local governments comply with the clear requirements of the Constitution as interpreted by a unanimous Supreme Court. More ominous was the amendment's partial repeal of the 1964 Civil Rights Act. If the Green amendment became law, HEW would lose its power to cut off federal aid to school districts that defied federal court orders requiring busing.[43]

When the House finally passed the higher education bill with all these amendments included, much more attention and energy had been devoted to busing than to all the complex provisions of one of the most significant college aid measures in U.S. history.

## Election Year Showdown

The issue plagued the Senate in 1972, producing a close and ugly fight during the spring primary campaigns and a down-to-the-wire battle, complete with an unusual liberal filibuster, in the session's final days. A district court order for desegregation of the Richmond, Virginia, city and suburban school systems and George Wallace's triumphant victory in his one-issue Florida primary campaign made it impossible for Democrats to ignore the issue.[44] No civil rights question had divided the party so deeply for many years. President Nixon did his best to exploit the opposition's division and to strengthen his antibusing credentials by repeatedly demanding congressional action to stop busing.

During the spring battle the civil rights forces held their tiny majority by offering a "compromise" on the moratorium issue: Majority Leader Mike Mansfield and Minority Leader Hugh Scott jointly sponsored an amendment that would delay only the enforcement of metropolitan orders and only until 1973. While the amendment made little practical difference at the time, it was a significant change of principle. In the Senate, which had usually opposed even attempts to restrain HEW, the moderate leadership now felt it was necessary to endorse a compromise restraining the courts.

Although disheartening to civil rights groups, the Scott-Mansfield amendment was only another tactical retreat. It gave the conservatives rhetorical satisfaction while attempting to protect most of the authority of the judiciary.

Things really heated up at this stage. Before the House and Senate could work out their differences on the higher education bill, Wallace's victory in Florida and a nationally televised antibusing speech by the President two days later intensified the pressure on Congress. The administration demanded action by the conference committee supporting the House position and quickly prepared its own antibusing package, which would come to the floor later in the session.

The executive branch concentrated first on the conference committee, encouraging votes in the House instructing conferees to insist on antibusing language. The House instructed its conferees twice, each time by approximately 2–1.[45] Discouraged civil rights supporters prevented Senate adoption of the wide-ranging House amendments by a single vote.[46]

A compromise was eventually hammered out. The conferees accepted the sweeping language of the House's moratorium amendment in the hope that the courts would find the poorly drafted language either meaningless or unconstitutional. On the other hand, the amendment forbidding the spending of federal aid money for busing was rendered harmless.[47]

The compromise was attacked by liberals and conservatives in both houses, but it held and the higher education bill was enacted.[48] The President signed it but called the antibusing language "inadequate, misleading and entirely unsatisfactory" and the most "manifest congressional retreat from an urgent call for responsibility" of his entire administration.[49] The busing fight had completely overshadowed the educational sections of the bill.

The contest was far from over for the year. Unsatisfied, President Nixon pressed hard for the passage of an "Equal Educational Opportunities" bill he had presented in March. It not only attempted to delay court orders but also incorporated deep infringements of judicial autonomy. It prescribed the kind of desegregation plans courts could approve and the priority they must give to various remedies. It said that courts could neither order the transfer of any elementary school student further from his neighborhood than the next closest school or substantially increase the total busing in a school district. School boards would be authorized to reopen existing court orders that went beyond these standards, permitting the resegregation of many blacks who had been integrated in southern schools.[50]

Civil rights supporters were on the defensive again. The liberals on the House Education and Labor Committee dragged out committee action on the President's plan as long as possible, hoping to delay House action until near the end of the session.

The committee reported an amended version in August, which the House proceeded to make more rigid: the majority voted to prohibit the busing of secondary as well as elementary students beyond the next closest school.[51]

The administration's draft bill had been written to go to the limit of whatever authority Congress might have to restrain the judicial branch. Most constitutional authorities thought it went well beyond. More than 500 law professors signed a letter expressing their belief that the bill was unconstitutional. The administration could produce only one authority, Robert Bork of Yale Law School, to testify that the measure was probably contitutional.[52] Changes made on the House floor, however, had moved the measure so much further toward detailed congressional control of the courts that even some of the administration loyalists balked. Representative Albert Quie, GOP spokesman on education, for example, found that he could not support them.[53]

The administration bill finally came to the Senate floor in October 1972, about a month before the presidential election. Feeling certain of a Nixon landslide victory over George McGovern, most senators seemed ready to vote for almost any bill. Civil rights supporters decided that their only choice was to filibuster.

The filibuster began on October 6, and liberals proved in three successive votes that they had the strength to prevent cloture. Conservatives, who had used a filibuster earlier in the year to block a bill granting strong enforcement powers to the Equal Employment Opportunities Commission, found their favorite tool being used against them. Longtime enemies of the filibuster system joined in the delaying tactic only to hear their obstructionism denounced in southern accents. The filibuster held in spite of White House lobbying and a strong appeal from President Nixon.[54]

## Turning Off the Gas

Although the President promised to give the matter "highest priority" in 1973, antibusing legislation may well have been one of the many casualties of Watergate. It was not an election year and the Supreme Court removed some of the pressure when it failed to order metropolitan desegregation in Richmond. Congress did not attempt to enact major education legislation during the year. Only at the end of the year, when legislation dealing with the Arab oil embargo was being seriously considered, did busing again become significant. Congress voted against every proposed cutback in the use of gasoline—from recreational aviation to recreational travel—but busing was different.

Congressman John Dingell, a Democrat from the Detroit suburbs, offered an amendment denying gasoline "for the transportation of any public school student to a school farther than the public school closest to his home offering educational courses for the grade level and course of study of the student within the boundaries of the school attendance district wherein the student resides." [55]

Representative Jonathan Bingham of New York protested, saying that the House would "allow oil to be allocated . . . for all kinds of recreational and nonessential purposes but here is an educational purpose and we say no oil for this purpose." He pointed out that one effect of the amendment would be to prohibit voluntary desegregation efforts. The restriction would not apply to private schools, which would still be allocated gasoline to bus students as far as they wished. Only school systems attempting to enforce federal court orders would be denied.[56] Representative Bella Abzug of New York called it "scandalous demagoguery." In response to her claim that the amendment was "demagogic or racist," Speaker Carl Albert took the extraordinary step of striking her words from the Congressional Record.[57] It was the first time in a decade that this had been done.

Representative Charles Wiggins of California, a critic of busing, thought that Dingell had the wrong answer. "To me," he said, "this is much like the Congress denying to the Supreme Court energy and power, because we are unhappy with its decisions." [58]

Representative Dale Milford of Texas claimed that the amendment would win "public acceptance" for conservation. "The fuel saved will help to heat a few more homes. It will help to save a few more jobs and it will make literally millions of people happier." [59] The amendment was not really "anti-minority," said a Florida member, but "pro-American." [60]

Black congressmen denounced the tactic. Ronald Dellums, who came from Berkeley, where busing had stabilized racial patterns in a community for the better part of a decade, told the House of his "feeling of desperation, anguish, and cynicism." [61] Parren Mitchell of Maryland recalled his sadness when a young black student asked, "Why do they hate us so?" "Mr. Chairman," said Baltimore's first black congressman, "that question may well be raised on this floor today, and I do so raise it." [62]

The debate was largely wasted. Everyone knew that any antibusing amendment would pass. This one did, 221–192.[63]

The next day two Democratic congressmen from Texas attempted to modify the ban. Bob Eckhardt of Houston proposed that gas be allocated for transporting students when a local school board wished to do so. He did not want to cut off a program in his district where white families were voluntarily sending their children to a formerly black school. J. J. (Jake) Pickle endorsed this approach, fearing chaos in the Austin desegregation plan. Even this modest, southern-sponsored amendment was defeated quickly, 202–185.[64]

The Senate was not yet ready for such arbitrary action. The conference committee removed the Dingell amendment.

The idea of cutting off the gas continued to appeal to the House —it incorporated a similar proviso in a 1975 energy bill, though there was no current gas shortage. It was all reminiscent of Georgia Governor Lester Maddox's suggestion that the answer was to let the air out of the school bus tires. At any rate, the restriction was again quickly removed by the conference committee.

### Throttling Legal Services

Since the beginning of the Nixon administration, the legal services program, one of the most controversial remnants of the War on Poverty, had been threatened. As the climax approached it became entangled with the busing issue.

Neighborhood legal services had been in trouble ever since they stopped merely representing ghetto residents who claimed to have been cheated by local merchants and began to raise difficult test cases challenging basic legal assumptions. Governors in five states had attempted to veto funding for their offices. California's Governor Ronald Reagan was the leading critic, continually feuding with the California Rural Legal Assistance program. Senator George Murphy of California led unsuccessful 1967 and 1969 Senate battles to prohibit all test cases.[65]

An analysis of 2,050 of the program's test cases between 1967 and 1972 showed that less than 1 percent dealt with the field of civil rights. Few of these were school cases. Of the early northern and western school cases, only two in the small Southern California communities of Inglewood and Oxnard were litigated by legal services lawyers.[66] Legal services offices in larger cities, including Hartford, Springfield, Illinois, and Dallas, later initiated litigation. While these efforts consumed only a tiny fraction of the resources of the legal services program, they were an important addition to the meager legal means of private civil rights organizations. They soon provoked congressional anger. It is indicative of the extraordinary pressure of the race issue that it overshadowed all other legal services work in congressional debate.

Conservatives were particularly critical of the Harvard Center for Law and Education, one of a series of "backup centers" the legal services program created to do research and help manage important test cases. The Harvard center worked on many types of educational cases. When Marian Wright Edelman, a militant black integrationist, became the center's director in 1972, desegregation action accelerated. In the ensuing years, the center was involved in the litigation in Boston, Detroit, Indianapolis, Pittsburgh, and Dayton.[67]

The House had acted to forbid desegregation litigation by legal services offices in June 1973, even if only private funds were being used. (The only other categories of proscribed litigation were cases on abortion and the draft.) [68]

Representative Robert Drinan of Massachusetts, a former law professor, strongly objected. "Singling out" school cases, he said, might well be unconstitutional.[69] Senator Edward Kennedy said that any attorney "would have been professionally remiss to have ignored totally any requests for help" from victims of illegal segregation.[70] But the White House promised to sign the legal services bill only if the Senate eliminated the backup centers immediately. Under this threat the Senate acceded and the House happily agreed by a 2–1 majority.[71]

After years of confrontation on legal services, the President got just what he wanted. In fact, in the busing provisions, he got more than he had asked for. At a time when neither the Justice Department nor HEW's Office for Civil Rights was enforcing school desegregation requirements, the last public resources for enforcing the constitutional requirements had been closed off. The organizations could finish the cases they had begun, but nothing new could be initiated. This ban was renewed in 1977.

## EXTENDING THE ELEMENTARY AND SECONDARY EDUCATION ACT, 1974

The gasoline and legal services debates were minor sideshows compared to the long struggle in 1974 over the extension of the basic education programs in the Elementary and Secondary Education Act. The authorizing legislation was expiring and the President wanted changes. Even without the desegregation issue, Congress would have faced the necessity of rebuilding the old education coalitions by working out accommodations on major regional issues and disputes between the urban, suburban, and rural members over how money should be allocated. Democratic leaders saw the legislation as an opportunity to preserve the main educational programs of the Great Society at least through the 1976 presidential election and perhaps permanently.

The busing issue magnified the obstacles. Although the President's power had been sapped by Watergate, there was no doubt about the popularity of his attack on busing. He maintained the pressure, threatening to torpedo the entire $26 billion measure. Congress, caught up in the impeachment proceedings in the House and an expected trial in the Senate, strove to find a way to keep the school programs operating. The President, on the other hand, needed policies—like busing—that might help him hold his conservative support and prevent a two-thirds vote for removal.

After a year of debate, the House Education and Labor Committee cleared a new bill in February 1974, with only four Michigan members opposing because the committee had voted down antibusing language. This calm mood was not to last.

The real donnybrook came on the floor when Republican Congressman Marvin Esch of Michigan proposed a package of restrictions similar to those adopted by the House in 1972. Once again the opponents of desegregation were led by Michigan members. They insisted on absolute restraints on the courts. Efforts of a group of self-styled moderates to devise some kind of compromise were rejected both by civil rights supporters, who insisted that Congress had no right to restrain the courts, and by opponents of busing.

The "moderate" effort, led by Congressmen John Anderson of Illinois, Richardson Preyer of North Carolina, and Morris Udall of Arizona, failed to win black support. Their "National Equal Educational Opportunities" bill was introduced by Anderson, who said that Congress had been "derelict in its responsibility to take affirmative and constructive action in this sensitive area." [72] The bill called for ten years of federal aid to upgrade ghetto schools and to pay for "free choice" transfers of black students to white schools they wished to attend. It prohibited court orders sending children to "significantly inferior" schools. It said busing must not be ordered until the courts had considered other remedies first.[73] Preyer said the bill was an answer to "the most serious challenge to the political center we have ever had in this country." [74]

The effort got short shrift. Liberal Representatives Lloyd Meeds of Washington said that it "comes into conflict with what the Court has already said." Representative Esch dismissed it as "a probusing amendment." [75] The moderates' amendment was overwhelmingly defeated in a voice vote. The House then immediately passed the Esch amendment, 293–117.[76]

House Education and Labor Committee Chairman Carl Perkins and Representative Quie had appealed without success to the members to avoid a busing brawl that would endanger an extremely important education measure. Perkins said, "We are just fooling ourselves" by trying to "reverse Supreme Court decisions." He was sick of the whole issue:

> We have had busing amendments introduced in every appropriation bill, we have had busing amendments introduced in all the school bills, and to complicate the greatest school bill that we have in existence by adding an antibusing amendment at this stage of the game, in my judgment, would be doing serious harm . . . because we are going to have a great many problems in working this matter out with the other body.[77]

Quie urged the members not to "complicate the future of a good education bill" with amendments that were probably unconstitutional.[78] South Carolina Representative William Jennings Bryan Dorn said that tacking on antibusing amendments, trying to "set up a special arrangement for the northern metropolitan areas," was "an exercise in futility"; it was an attempt to preserve "the outmoded, outdated, segregated neighborhood school system of the past." [79]

The critics were ignored. The House added the perennial amendment barring the use of federal aid money for busing even when there was an "express written request of appropriate local school officials." It passed easily, 239–168.[80]

As was by now so typical, passage of the basic education bill was anticlimactic, its substance overshadowed by busing.

### The Senate Decides

The Senate got the bill in May 1974. Busing dominated the debate. The twentieth anniversary of the Brown decision found the Senate closely divided on various proposals intended to preserve segregation.

When debate began, the situation was ominous for the civil rights forces. The education legislation had only two months to run. School organizations urged action. Liberals had been able to manage a brief filibuster near the end of the 1972 session, but this year adjournment was months away. The Supreme Court's decision in the Denver case meant that many northern cities were vulnerable to court orders. Desegregation battles were raging in major cities of Massachusetts, Colorado, California, Ohio, and Michigan. President Nixon and the new vice-president, Gerald Ford, attacked congressional inaction.

The Senate Labor and Public Welfare Committee tried to head off further amendments by including language delaying the enforcement of court orders to achieve "racial balance."[81] A more controversial provision forbade federal civil rights officials to bus students to "substantially inferior" schools; this could be read as an affirmation of the "one-way" busing plans criticized by most minority leaders.

In the Senate debate, one side cited polls and argued for majority rule, the other argued for constitutional rights and judicial independence. Many members claimed that a fall 1973 Gallup poll showed 95 percent of the public as opposed to busing. (Actually, the question asked was whether people favored busing over other ways of achieving integrated schools, assuming that alternatives existed.) Most of the opposition to the bill was based squarely on the argument that it was unconstitutional.

Civil rights organizations sought to counter the criticism of busing. A series of reports by the Civil Rights Commission and materials prepared by the Washington Research Project and the Center for Civil Rights at Notre Dame University provided limited ammunition. The united position of the congressional black caucus and the determined leadership of the Senate's only black member, Edward Brooke of Massachusetts, were important in offsetting assertions that blacks opposed busing.[82]

The antibusing crusade was led by Senator Edward Gurney, who tried to get the House Esch amendment enacted. "It is interesting," Gurney said, "to note that the farther busing spreads, the closer the vote here in Congress on antibusing measures."[83]

Local problems strongly influenced some members. A case in point was the reaction of the senators from Colorado. Both conservative Peter Dominick, who was up for reelection in 1974, and liberal Floyd Haskell were critical of desegregation in Denver and supported a succession of antibusing moves.[84] Senator Robert Dole of Kansas described controversies in Wichita and Topeka. Wichita had responded to six years of threats of fund cutoffs from HEW with a plan busing 90 percent of the black children and about 1,200 whites, mostly volunteers attracted by special programs in the formerly black schools. In Topeka, the principal site of the original *Brown* case, children were still segregated in seven ghetto schools.[85]

Critics of the antibusing moves emphasized the costs of stirring up futile public hopes that desegregation would be reversed. Senator Claiborne Pell of Rhode Island said the bill would "lay bare wounds which have only recently closed." [86] Senator Harold Hughes of Iowa blamed the President for treating "legislation which goes to the heart of one of the most profound moral imperatives of our history" as "just another amendment." [87] Senator Alan Cranston of California, the state with the most desegregation experience outside the South, blamed the controversy on a deliberate decision by the administration to "stir things up."

> I find this situation especially saddening because so many communities across America—including California—have tried so hard to make these desegregation plans, including busing, work in the best interests of their children and in the interest of community cooperation and peace. It is appalling to me to think of disrupting the progress these good-spirited citizens have fought for and won.[88]

The most passionate denunciation of the Gurney proposal came from Senator Edward Brooke. He said the amendment was a direct encouragement for the "small minority" of whites and blacks favoring racial separatism who would "put us back decades" and foster resegregation where integration was working well. Congress, Brooke said, must not return to the separate but equal doctrine of *Plessy v. Ferguson.*[89] "I have never seen anything both separate and equal in this Nation."

> The hope for an end to racial division lies in our educational system. The opportunities we afford our young people determine the shape of our Nation's future. . . . If we perpetuate separate societies, divided by ignorance and suspicion, we risk an unsteady and uncertain future.[90]

Senator Philip Hart, the only prominent Michigan politician to steadfastly support desegregation through the Detroit panic, reminded members of their oath to support the Constitution, saying, "Some of these amendments . . . are dead wrong in terms of what the Constitution says we may or may not do." [91] Senator Robert Taft, Jr., of Ohio said: "I cannot in good conscience support an approach to this difficult problem that seems to me to be patently unconstitutional." [92]

A few members like Brooke and Hart were ready to risk their seats, if necessary, over a clear stand on the issue. Those who did, like Hart and Edward Kennedy, were able to survive antibusing opponents. Most of the other civil rights supporters, however, were looking for some constitutional way to show that they opposed "unreasonable" busing while they respected the courts. One senator to use this approach was Indiana Democrat Birch Bayh, who was facing a hard reelection battle from a strong GOP candidate, Indianapolis Mayor Richard Lugar, a critic of busing. With Indianapolis threatened by a metropolitan desegregation case, Bayh proposed a convoluted amendment forbidding busing unless courts found that "all alternative remedies are inadequate." It prohibited desegregation plans crossing city-suburban lines unless the lines had been created for discriminatory purposes or had the *effect* of fostering segregation.[93]

The Bayh proposal, which was more rhetoric than substance, infuriated the conservatives. Senator William E. Brock of Tennessee said it "does absolutely nothing to change the situation as it exists." Senator Gurney said it was a "probusing amendment." Bayh replied that Brock was trying to go "back to the old segregation system that we fought a civil war to prohibit." [94]

The Senate debate came to an end with Vice-President Ford waiting to cast the decisive vote against busing if the closely divided chamber deadlocked. By a single vote, the Gurney amendment was tabled, and the Senate promptly adopted the Bayh measure, 56–36. Bayh's proposal drew votes from a bevy of civil rights supporters, including Thomas Eagleton, Warren Magnuson, Mike Mansfield, Charles Mathias, Gale McGee, George McGovern, Gaylord Nelson, John Pastore, James Pearson, and Robert Taft, all of whom could now claim a vote against cross-district busing.[95]

The next day the Senate adopted another amendment forbidding the implementation of new desegregation court orders in the middle of a school year. Although this amendment flew in the face of the Supreme Court's unanimous 1969 decision, *Alexander v. Holmes,* which required immediate correction of unconstitutional segregation, the impatient members showed little interest in Senator Javits's effort to explain the constitutional principles. The amendment quickly passed, 71–20.[96]

## Another Compromise

As the debate came to an end on May 16, 1974, the balance of power seemed suddenly to switch to the opponents of desegregation. Senator Griffin made a last attempt to revive the House amendments without the controversial provision permitting the reopening of court orders. A liberal-moderate effort to table this proposal failed by a single vote. At this point, with the clear danger of strong Senate action against the courts, Senate Minority Leader Hugh Scott and Majority Leader Mansfield offered a less drastic substitute amendment prepared for such a contingency. The tactic worked. The conservatives failed by three votes to table the Scott-Mansfield amendment.[97] Once again the leaders combined forces to take the edge off antibusing efforts.

The substitute contained Griffin's text but added at various points language stating that its restrictions were "not intended to modify or diminish the authority of the courts of the United States to enforce fully the Fifth and Fourteenth amendments to the United States Constitution." [98] Scott said that the "only question" before the Senate was whether members would state that the Senate "does not intend to violate the Constitution of the United States." [99] Forty-six senators voted against it anyway.[100]

The Scott-Mansfield proposal passed, 47–46, without any serious debate. The complex document was laid on the Senate desks minutes before the vote. Although it appeared to leave the status quo largely untouched, it had a crucial provision that went unnoticed by both the Senate and the subsequent conference committee. It forbade not only the courts but also federal "departments or agencies" to order the busing of students beyond the next closest school. The language protected the courts but said nothing specific about HEW's powers. The Senate may have accidentally approved an amendment to the 1964 Civil Rights Act. With Congress contemplating legislative nullification of Supreme Court decisions, an attack on the century's most important civil rights law—a change that a few years earlier would have been considered a terrible defeat for civil rights—now went unnoticed. HEW, of course, did not fight to retain its authority.

Still more severe restrictions remained to be voted on. Senator William Lloyd Scott of Virginia, for instance, proposed altering the constitutional system by denying all federal courts jurisdiction over cases concerning public schools. This proposal was supported by twenty-five senators.[101] (Two years later it got more votes.)

As the Senate finished debate on the education bill, Senate leaders raised the muddled compromise. Hugh Scott called it "sound wisdom," but Senator James Pearson of Kansas pointed out that the Senate had substantially modified existing policy with a series of constraints on the courts, which meant that "busing can be used only as an extreme and last resort and as the only final alternative to the continuation of a segregated and, therefore, unconstitutional school system."[102] Whatever it meant, senators were glad to send it on to the conference committee. The bill passed, 81–5.[103]

Everyone knew that the conference struggle would be long and difficult. During the six weeks that the conference worked House members took the extraordinary step of voting three different times to instruct their conferees against compromise on busing.

All those involved reported that the conference committee negotiations were contentious and sensitive. The busing issue, said Senator Pell, consumed "endless days and hours of debate. The language the Senate brought into the conference was totally unacceptable to the House. . . . Nevertheless, the Senate conferees held to the belief that there were also certain House provisions that were totally unacceptable to them. The final language is a melding of the two."[104]

The conference bill was attacked, said Pell, by both liberal and conservative senators. Senator Javits, for instance, thought the compromise might well be unconstitutional but the best obtainable in the face of House antagonism.[105] He said that the conferees had "sat into the small hours of the morning" until they hit upon an agreement to modify the tradition of continual judicial supervision of desegregation plans by allowing the termination of court orders in certain circumstances.[106]

Later, House Democratic and Republican leaders told a similar story. "We have scraped the bottom of the barrel," said Representative Carl Perkins of Kentucky. "There is no way where we can get anything further. These are all of the antibusing provisions we will get, and we will not get any more this year." [107] Perkins's Republican colleague, Albert Quie, said that the conferees had accepted all the major House provisions, adding only the Senate language that Congress intended to "conform to the requirements of the Constitution." [108]

Just exactly what the conference agreement meant was not clear. Most of the floor debate was on whether the package was tough enough. There was little serious analysis of the compromise.

The fifty-nine sections of the new law incorporated a miscellany of overlapping and contradictory provisions, most of which had not been discussed at all on the floor. A few of the sections actually were advances in civil rights laws. Many others attempted to constrain the process of devising desegregation plans while proclaiming Congress' intention to avoid encroachment on the authority of the judicial branch.

A major new area of discretion for federal judges was provided. Since 1954 desegregation cases had remained open for many years. Judges retained jurisdiction and litigants could file new motions asking that the old orders be tightened. Southerners in cities with rapid outward movement of whites wanted the urban court orders limited to a single decision that would, by legal definition, correct the vestiges of de jure segregation. Then the court could relinquish its jurisdiction, leaving new segregated schools invulnerable to legal attack. In a society where the average family moves every five years and residential segregation is pervasive, such a policy would normally guarantee resegregation of schools. Although judges already had the power to terminate cases, the amendments encouraged the courts to use it.

The provisions of the law most directly in conflict with the courts had become familiar in earlier legislative fights. It said that neighborhood school assignment practices did not violate students' rights unless they were designed to intentionally segregate students. One passage read: "No court, department, or agency of the United States shall . . . order the implementation of a plan that would require the transportation of any student to a school other than the school closest or next closest to his place of residence which provides the appropriate grade level and type of education for such student." [109] The Esch language included a list of remedies the courts must consider before ordering busing.

The net effect of the antibusing language on the courts was probably minor. Congress clearly recognized that the restrictions on the courts would not apply when they limited the constitutional rights of minority children. Since the courts generally ordered busing only when there was no other way to achieve desegregation, judicial compliance with the provisions of the act presumably would involve only a recitation of this fact and a declaration of the preeminent requirements of the Constitution. This is just what happened in several cases after the legislation was passed.

The most important changes were the possible political and legal effects of the act on HEW's desegregation enforcement program. Since HEW had not seriously enforced the fund-cutoff provisions of the 1964 Civil Rights Act since mid-1969, little attention had been paid to its role. The department, however, had powers of great importance. It had been found guilty of failing to enforce the 1964 law by a federal court and had been ordered to act promptly against segregation in scores of southern and border state school districts. HEW officials used the existence of a law forbidding it to order systems to carry out busing plans as a defense against compliance with the court order. The really serious constraint on HEW under this policy came when a court order required HEW to enforce the 1964 law in the big cities.

The law could be construed in ways that would eliminate its restrictive effect on HEW. In actual practice, HEW provides guidelines; it never "orders" the implementation of a desegregation plan; it does not have the authority to do so. The department's enforcement policy, when it uses it, is merely to withhold funds from or recommend the initiation of litigation against school systems that refused to comply with constitutional requirements for desegregation. [110]

## Final Passage

The compromise held. The vote came first in the Senate, where many members asked the body to consider the educational issues in the bill for a change. The dominant desire was to get the bill enacted. It rapidly passed, 81–15. [111]

The real battle was expected from antibusing forces in the

House. Their leader, Congressman Esch, opposed the entire bill. The language on the supremacy of constitutional requirements, he said, "raises a cloud over the effectiveness of the rest of the Esch amendment." He asked that the bill be sent back to conference. Louisiana Congressman Joe Waggoner, Jr., insisted that "the vote on the conference report is a busing issue vote." [112]

Representative Marjorie Holt, whose district included two large Maryland school systems with busing problems, called the compromise "nearly worthless, because the Federal courts are expressly invited to continue imposing racial quotas requiring mass busing." [113]

The debate, however, was neither as long nor as passionate as the earlier ones. When the final vote came on July 31, 1974, in Nixon's chaotic last days, the House voted to accept the conference committee report, 323–83—almost four to one.[114]

When President Ford suddenly took office he found the education bill on his desk awaiting action. In his first address to Congress he announced that he would sign the bill. "Any reservations I might have about its provisions . . . fade in comparison to the urgent needs of America for quality education." [115] He later added that he was still unsatisfied with the busing provisions.[116]

## SEPARATE, NOT EQUAL

Congressional action on the ESEA bill showed that, though Congress and the President were ready to restrain desegregation, they were not disposed to provide additional resources for improving education in ghetto schools. Nixon and Ford had frequently proposed upgrading inner city education as an alternative, but both consistently submitted education budgets proposing yearly cuts in school programs (after allowing for inflation). And the House Education and Labor Committee reported a bill raising school aid for suburbs and southern and rural states, sharply cutting funds for New York City, Los Angeles, and Chicago, and somewhat reducing funds for many other cities.[117]

The New York delegation, with the support of other urban members, attempted to amend the bill to reverse New York City's loss of almost $50 million under the new distribution formula. They pointed out that it would give Montgomery County, Maryland (one of the wealthiest U.S. counties), 44 percent more money while the District of Columbia would lose 12 percent.[118] The

New York proposal was buried in an avalanche of opposition, losing 87–326.[119]

Some suburban members of the House urged still greater redistribution to the suburbs. Michigan Democrats James O'Hara and William Ford, antibusing leaders, proposed a plan that would give $5.6 million more to the two Detroit suburban counties, both among the nation's twenty richest, while taking $4.4 million from nearly bankrupt Detroit, $2.4 million from Baltimore, and some from other central cities. This proposal was too overt. The amendment went down, 103–312.[120]

As passed, the House bill cut funds to forty-one of the country's largest cities at a time of rapid inflation. The biggest losses came in some of the cities with the largest ghettos—New York, Chicago, Los Angeles, Philadelphia, Cleveland, Newark, and Washington.[121]

Nor was the Senate interested in channeling more money into ghetto schools. The Senate committee bill had protected funds for the big cities. On the floor, however, Senator John McClellan of Arkansas moved to substitute the House formula. It was adopted, 56–36.[122]

Futile efforts were made by two Senate moderates, Lowell Weicker, Jr., of Connecticut and Lawton Chiles of Florida, to enact large compensatory education programs for ghetto children. Chiles proposed a $2.5 billion program that would give any neighborhood school with more than 40 percent poor children additional funds equal to at least two-thirds the national annual average total per-pupil costs. Chiles said he thought people were ready to pay to avoid the "tremendous discombobulation" of the busing controversy. His measure did not even come to a vote.[123]

Weicker's "Quality School Aid" bill would have more than doubled federal compensatory aid. He asked senators to commit themselves to raising taxes sufficiently to cover the costs of eliminating "inferior schools with inferior teachers and opportunities." Weicker did ask for a vote. He lost, 4–83.[124]

Thus in the end Congress responded to the financial problems of big city schools by diverting some of their funds to the suburbs and the South.

Senator Brooke later described the issue well:

> We have many debates on the Senate floor about whether we should go forward with integration . . . or whether we should try to

make the segregated ghetto and barrio schools more equal. . . .
Our decisions about investing money in education show that Congress has rejected both approaches. Each year we are providing less assistance, in dollars of constant value, both for helping the integration process work better and for compensatory education.[125]

Brooke supported his contention with statistics showing that the compensatory education program had one-seventh less money than three years earlier and that the desegregation aid program had shrunk 30 percent (see Table 3).

## The Holt Amendment

Before the 1974 session ended, there was a final skirmish. Another previously obscure member injected the issue into the debate in a new way. As congressional adjournment neared, Congresswoman Holt tried to eviscerate what remained of the 1964

*Table 3: Appropriations for Selected Federal Education Programs, Fiscal Years 1965-76*

Thousands of 1965 dollars[a]

| Fiscal year | Title I, ESEA[b] | Emergency School Aid Act[c] | Title IV, Civil Rights Act[d] |
|---|---|---|---|
| 1965 | 0 | 0 | 6,000 |
| 1966 | 1,161,118 | 0 | 6,109 |
| 1967 | 993,666 | 0 | 6,164 |
| 1968 | 1,084,258 | 0 | 7,738 |
| 1969 | 976,355 | 0 | 8,041 |
| 1970 | 1,103,083 | | 9,885 |
| 1971 | 1,175,416 | 58,771 | 12,538 |
| 1972 | 1,196,780 | 56,187 | 10,938 |
| 1973 | 1,298,110 | 178,580 | 15,563 |
| 1974 | 1,143,841 | 157,319 | 14,435 |
| | 1,129,476 | 129,444 | 16,075 |
| 1975 | 1,081,507 | 122,391 | 15,198 |

Source: Calculations by Congressional Research Service, *Congressional Record* (daily edition), May 27, 1976, p. S8154.

a. The appropriations are stated in constant dollars to show the real purchasing power of the programs from year to year.

b. Title I of the ESEA is designed to aid "target" schools with high concentrations of children from poor families.

c. The Emergency School Aid program is designed to facilitate the transition from segregation to desegregation and to provide aid for schools in central cities that remain segregated.

d. Title IV is a small program of technical assistance and staff training for desegregation.

Civil Rights Act as it applied to education. She offered an amendment that would have prohibited withholding federal aid funds to force school systems to carry out desegregation plans and would have stopped the collection of records and statistics HEW needed to determine the extent of segregation.[126] Her amendment, she said, would end the government's "obsession" with "racial quotas." Without data, enforcement was of course impossible.

Although the provision was narrowly defeated on the Senate floor, the conference committee accepted the Holt language in the final days of the Congress. The *Washington Post* described the situation:

> HEW Secretary Caspar Weinberger is among those who have seen this deceptive language for what it is—an attempt to terminate the federal government's pursuit of its duty to enforce the Civil Rights Act of 1964 and related laws. . . .
>
> There has been an almost haphazard, not to say irresponsible, note to the way the legislators in both sides of Congress have let this momentous bit of legislation come so near to passage.[127]

Once again Majority Leader Mansfield and Minority Leader Scott joined forces at the last minute to head off disaster by persuading the Senate to reject the conference report. Pressing toward adjournment, senators swept aside a conservative filibuster, cut off debate, and voted down the Holt measure.[128]

The House soon followed suit. Once the Senate majority made its position clear, the initiative shifted. House members knew that getting programs funded and adjourning the session now depended on accepting the Senate position. The House agreed in a 224–138 vote.[129]

The victories against the Holt amendment were unexpectedly swift and decisive. The 1974 election was over and there was less pressure for action against busing.[130]

## DESEGREGATION IN DELAWARE, DEFEAT IN WASHINGTON

Any hope that the worst was past proved to be illusory in September 1975. After a year of little discussion of the issue, the publicity accompanying desegregation in Boston and metropolitan Louisville revived political debate. The sudden intervention of President Ford, who claimed that the courts were requiring unnecessary busing without looking for better alternatives and thus violating the provisions of the Esch amendment, added to the pressure.

Attitudes crystallized in a sudden Senate reversal, probably the most important move against school integration in the upper chamber at any time. An amendment attempting to end any authority to require busing remaining in HEW was offered by a young progressive senator from Delaware, Joseph Biden. For the first time, such an amendment had the support of northern liberal Democrats, including Majority Leader Mansfield.

Senator Biden's leadership was the direct result of community reaction to a pending lawsuit in Wilmington. After the 1974 battle, when Biden had voted with the civil rights forces, he was denounced by leaders of the influential New Castle County Neighborhood School Association.[131] Publicly challenged to speak about his future votes on the issue, Biden was condemned as "the number one phony in Delaware" by the head of the suburban antibusing organization.[132] Realizing that he could be harassed for the next four years, he agreed to discuss the issue at a public meeting on July 9, 1974, in the suburbs,[133] where he faced a hostile crowd for two hours of questioning. Although he told the audience that his "liberal friends" were criticizing him and promised to support a constitutional amendment that would forestall the court-ordered metropolitan racial-balance for Wilmington, he won little support. He said he still favored busing when it was necessary to correct intentional local gerrymandering for segregationist purposes.[134]

But as the antibusing movement grew in the Wilmington suburbs in 1975, Biden again raised the issue, which he now saw as a "domestic Vietnam." He led the liberal turnabout, received favorable national press attention as a tough-minded realist, and restored his white political base in the state.

Nor was Senator Biden the only one to receive national attention from the media; Minority Whip Robert Byrd came up with a similar amendment of his own. He had been a leading opponent of the 1964 Civil Rights Act, one of the few nonsouthern members of the Democratic party to oppose the legislation. He had then joined the southern filibuster with a long speech about biblical justification for segregation.[135] Now, eleven years later, he won Senate passage of an amendment repealing part of the 1964 law.

After days of parliamentary in-fighting and heated public statements, the Biden and Byrd amendments came up for final votes in late September. Both passed.

The amendments, which required HEW to follow a neighborhood school policy, had little immediate significance, since HEW was not requiring any urban school desegregation anyway except where specifically ordered to act by federal court decision. The votes were symbolically important, however. Senator Humphrey said of the Senate's shift:

> The message is that the Senate, the last bastion of civil rights support, has now joined the President and the House in opposing desegregation of towns and cities across the North and West. The message to segregated children is that Congress is ready to destroy the only existing machinery for systematic enforcement of their constitutional rights, even though the machinery has not been used for 6 years and was severely limited by legislation just last year. . . . The symbolic power of congressional action is immense, often more important than the specific legislative action. . . . The action can only encourage supporters of segregation and increase the already immense pressures on the Federal courts.[136]

When the bill went to conference, the conferees struck the confusing Biden amendment but retained the Byrd restrictions, which became law in early 1976. The last redoubt of defense for urban school desegregation seemed to be crumbling on Capitol Hill.

## AN ELECTION YEAR LULL

As the 1976 election year approached, another round of battles over busing seemed likely. After a year of relative quiet, President Ford began to speak out against busing in speech after speech.[137] Protests and violence in Boston and Louisville during the fall of 1975—the worst fall since 1972—were widely publicized.

At the National Democratic Issues Conference in November, Democratic presidential candidates confronted three thousand demonstrators from an antibusing group led by labor union activists. The issue fragmented the candidates. Senator Lloyd Bentsen of Texas attacked busing as a "bankrupt social policy," Representative Udall blamed Congress for failing to search for alternatives, and former nominee George McGovern delivered an emotional speech calling racial equality a "transcendent moral issue." "All of us," he said, "should warn any candidate who turns to the tactics of racial division and fear that in conscience we cannot support him even if he is the nominee." [138] A poll showed that the party activists were deeply divided.[139]

If the Democrats were divided, the Republican candidates were strongly united on the popular side of the issue, debating merely which tactics should be used to fight busing. The President attacked the courts just as Boston faced citywide implementation.[140]

The Democratic campaign opened as expected, but it soon took a new direction, in part because of the emergence of an unexpected leading candidate, Jimmy Carter. The busing issue was most prominent in the Massachusetts primary, where Senator Henry Jackson fought George Wallace for the support of voters aroused by Boston's turmoil. Jackson won the primary after running large ads announcing "I am against forced busing" and outlining his plan to limit the remedy. Closer analysis of the Massachusetts results, however, showed, first, that Jackson had not been able to take the votes of strong antibusers away from Wallace, and second, that an antibusing stance could cost the party support among its many liberal and minority voters. Udall, the leading liberal contender, argued that politicians should "give the courts some help and not try to undercut them." [141]

The issue was turned against Jackson in Florida by Carter, who saw the primary there as vital to eliminating Wallace as the principal southern candidate. Running in the state with the most extensive busing orders in the country (most of the state had countywide busing on a racial-balance model), Carter claimed that Jackson was exploiting "racist" feelings. "I don't believe that a candidate is going to be successful in this country who concentrates on that kind of emotional issue, which is divisive, which is a negative issue. . . . I don't say he is a racist. . . . But he exploited an issue with racist connotations." [142]

Carter won the primary decisively, making himself the dominant political figure in the South and the leading contender for the nomination. Although busing was not popular in Florida, it was no longer a paramount issue. The key to Carter's victory was winning the votes of three-fourths of the state's blacks while holding moderate whites.[143]

Carter staked out a position on the busing issue early and held to it throughout his campaign. Among other things:

1. He strongly supported integrated education, often calling HEW's enforcement of the 1964 Civil Rights Act the "best thing that ever happened to the South" and pointing out that his daughter Amy attended an integrated school with a black majority.
2. He stated his personal opposition to court-ordered busing and his preference for the arrangement in Atlanta, where the busing issue was dropped in exchange for increased black control of the school bureaucracy.
3. He promised to oppose antibusing amendments to the Constitution and to support the desegregation orders of federal courts.

But after the Florida primary had eliminated Wallace and damaged Jackson's campaign, little was heard of the busing issue during the remainder of the Democratic campaign.

In contrast to the Republican platform, which promised the party would support an antibusing amendment to the Constitution, the Democratic platform strongly endorsed integrated education and reluctantly accepted the necessity for some busing. It was adopted without any floor fight.

> Mandatory transportation of students beyond their neighborhoods for the purpose of desegregation remains a judicial tool of last resort. . . . The Democratic Party will be an active ally of those communities which seek to enhance the quality as well as the integration of educational opportunities. We encourage a variety of other measures, including the redrawing of attendance lines, pairing of schools, use of the "magnet school" concept, strong fair housing enforcement, and other techniques for the achievement of racial and economic integration.[144]

President Ford attempted to reactivate the issue during the spring campaign. In May and June he made a series of widely publicized statements about busing and directed the Department of Justice to intervene in litigation to limit busing and to draft legislation for consideration in Congress. The result was the School Desegregation Standards and Assistance bill, which the

President sent to Congress with a message saying that some of the courts had "gone too far" and thus "slowed our progress toward the total elimination of segregation." [145]

The bill was designed to block busing unless there was school-by-school proof that segregation was intentional. It required the courts to ignore evidence that school segregation had resulted from de jure housing segregation, stipulated that desegregation orders should terminate after three to five years, and instructed the courts to ignore resegregation that emerged in the meantime.[146] It would have limited desegregation to temporary orders integrating schools near the ghetto or barrio line, concentrating the burden of change on lower-income whites and probably accelerating racial transition in the affected neighborhoods.

The most interesting thing about the bill was the contrast between its fate and that of the Nixon proposal four years earlier. The Nixon bill produced a major fight and was blocked only by a Senate filibuster. The Ford bill was sent to committee and never heard of again in either house.

There were, of course, other skirmishes over busing during the year, but the results showed a gradually changing mood. Except for the final enactment of the Byrd amendment early in 1976, no antibusing amendment was passed by Congress during the election year. A Senate that had been ready to directly attack the courts four years earlier now defeated a number of far more limited antibusing measures by substantial votes.

One of the perennial proposals—by Senator William Scott, to end the right of lower federal courts to hear any cases dealing with education—surfaced again. This was tabled by a better than two to one majority. A related proposal, limited to busing, was also quickly defeated.[147]

A more serious proposal, sponsored by Senators Dole and Biden, would have imposed limitations on civil rights litigation by the Department of Justice. The 1964 Civil Rights Act had given the department broad authority to initiate or intervene in civil rights cases, and Justice had been an important participant in many school cases. The Dole-Biden amendment would have prohibited any Justice Department participation in busing cases unless the department intervened against civil rights groups. Dole said that the goal was to bring Justice in line with the policy imposed on HEW by the Byrd amendment. This was tabled by a 55–39 vote.[148]

After the national conventions, busing received no serious discussion in the presidential campaign. The issue was never raised in the televised debates between Ford and Carter, and the few desegregation plans that took effect in September were carried out peacefully.

There were signs of probusing action in Congress. Some southern senators expressed their refusal to support amendments designed to prevent the changes the South had already lived through from reaching the North.[149] Senators Javits and Brooke attacked the premises of the antibusing forces in a series of statements culminating in a January 1977 conference in the Senate Caucus Room, the first major meeting supporting school integration on Capitol Hill in years. Congress enacted a modest civil rights bill, providing fees for lawyers bringing civil rights cases.

One sign of the changing mood was the leadership of Senator John Glenn of Ohio. Representing a state where virtually all of the major cities were involved in the most concentrated campaign of urban school litigation ever launched by the NAACP, Glenn refused to join the antibusing forces. He proposed legislation granting funds to districts for providing better education through the development of "magnet schools" offering special programs to encourage voluntary integration. Glenn's amendment did nothing to restrict the power of the courts; it simply gave local school systems more educational options. The amendment received wide support in the Senate and passed easily.[150]

## A NEW ADMINISTRATION

The election of President Carter and the transition to a new administration made the future of the school desegregation issue uncertain. The 1977 session of Congress was the first in years without executive branch support of some kind of antibusing legislation. Nor did the administration push desegregation—in fact, the new attorney general, Griffin Bell, and his deputy, Peter Flaherty, were criticized by congressional liberals during their confirmation hearings for a history of opposing urban desegregation. On the other hand, civil rights groups were pleased with appointments in HEW and with the selection of the black attorney who had desegregated much of Florida, Drew Days III, as assistant attorney general for civil rights. In his first year in office, President Carter sent Congress neither negative nor positive proposals; he said nothing about the issue. When HEW made a modest attempt to revive desegregation enforcement, the White House did not intervene, nor did the President say anything when Congress promptly passed an amendment quashing the attempt. Although polls showed continued public opposition, for the moment it seemed possible that the worst was over.

## REFERENCES

1. During this period Hispanics were only beginning to emerge as a major force. They were never clearly integrationist and many espoused goals of cultural and linguistic separatism.

2. House Committee on the Judiciary, *Civil Rights Act of 1963*, House Report 914, 88:1 (GPO, 1963), pp. 44, 85.

3. *Congressional Record*, June 4, 1964, pp. 12715–17.

4. Ibid.

5. *Bell v. School City of Gary, Indiana*, 324 F.2d 209 (7th Cir. 1963), *cert. denied*, 377 U.S. 924 (1964). The Gary case was repeatedly mentioned in both committee and floor consideration. Although it is improper to infer any judgment on the substance of a case from the Supreme Court's refusal to hear it, the fact that a denial of review left standing a lower court's finding that the de facto segregation was constitutional was often seen as Court support for this proposition.

6. 78 Stat. 241, Title VI, 42 U.S.C. §2000(d).

7. The 1965 school desegregation guidelines developed by the U.S. Office of Education are reprinted under the title "General Statement of Policies," in *Guidelines for School Desegregation*, Hearings before a special subcommittee of the House Judiciary Committee, 89:2 (GPO, 1966), pp. A20–A24.

8. See *Integrated Education* (December 1965–January 1966), pp. 10–35, for text of complaint submitted by Chicago's Coordinating Council of Community Organizations.

9. *Congressional Record*, August 9, 1966, pp. 18703–10.

10. Ibid., pp. 18717, 18721.

11. Ibid., pp. 18701, 18715.

12. Letter from the southern caucus to President Johnson, May 2, 1966.

13. *Congressional Record*, October 14, 1966, pp. 26922, 26927.

14. 80 Stat. 1257.

15. *Congressional Record*, October 6, 1966, pp. 25573, 25578.

16. *Congressional Record*, October 20, 1966, pp. 28207–15.

17. *Congressional Record*, December 4, 1967, pp. 34964–80.

18. *New York Times*, December 12, 1967.

19. Theodore H. White, *The Making of the President 1968* (Pocket Books, 1970), pp. 429–36.

20. Regional television broadcast from Charlotte, North Carolina, reported in *Washington Post* and *New York Times*, September 13, 1968.

21. Public Law 90–557 (1968), §410.

22. Interview with William van den Toorn, Office of Civil Rights, May 1, 1974.

23. Interview with OCR Atlanta Regional Director Paul Rilling, July 3, 1969.

24. 396 U.S. 19 (1969).

25. "Statement about Desegregation of Elementary and Secondary Schools, March 24, 1970," *Public Papers of the Presidents: Richard Nixon, 1970* (GPO, 1971), p. 305.

26. Congressional Quarterly, *Civil Rights Progress Report, 1970*, pp. 39–41.

27. Gallup poll, April 5, 1970; reprinted in *Congressional Record*, April 8, 1970, p. 10908.

28. 84 Stat. 121.

29. The committee published thirty-six volumes of hearings on the major issues involved in school desegregation, more than a dozen special studies, and a final report, *Toward Equal Educational Opportunity*, 92:2 (GPO, 1972).

30. Earl Browning, Jr., "Emergency School Assistance: Financing the Desegregation Retreat" (unpublished paper, 1971).

31. "The Emergency School Program—An Evaluation," a report prepared by a coalition of civil rights organizations including the NAACP Legal Defense Fund, the American Friends Service Committee, and the Washington Research Project (1970; processed); Report of the General Accounting Office, 1971.

32. *Swann v. Charlotte-Mecklenburg Board of Education*, 402 U.S. 1 (1971).

33. *Bradley v. Milliken*, 338 F. Supp. 582 (E.D. Mich. 1971).

34. *Washington Post*, February 15, 1972.

35. *New York Times*, February 16 and 17, 1972.

36. *School Busing*, Hearings before Subcommittee No. 5 of the House Committee on the Judiciary, 92:2 (GPO, 1972), pp. 1877–78, iii–xii.

37. *New York Times*, March 17, 1972.

38. Analysis of voting records by Orfield, in *School Busing*, Hearings, p. 734.

39. *Time* poll reported in *Integrated Education* (November–December 1976), p. 24.

40. *Washington Post*, November 20, 1975.

41. *Gallup Opinion Index* (May 1975), p. 22.

42. *Alexander v. Holmes*, 396 U.S. 19.

43. *Congressional Record*, November 4, 1971, pp. 39317–18.

44. *Washington Post*, January 6, 1972; *Congressional Quarterly*, March 18, 1972, p. 585.

45. *Congressional Record*, March 8, 1972, pp. 7554, 7562; May 11, 1972, pp. 16841–42.

46. *Congressional Record*, March 1, 1972, p. 6276.

47. *Congressional Quarterly*, May 27, 1972, pp. 1242–43.

48. *Congressional Record*, May 24, 1972, p. 18862; *Congressional Quarterly*, June 10, 1972, p. 1371.

49. "Statement on Signing the Education Amendments of 1972, June 23, 1972," *Public Papers of the Presidents: Richard Nixon, 1972* (GPO, 1974), pp. 701, 703.

50. Ibid., March 25, 1972, pp. 642–48.

51. *Congressional Record*, August 17, 1972, pp. 2888–2907.

52. His testimony appears in *Equal Educational Opportunities Act of 1972*, Hearings before the Subcommittee on Education of the Senate Committee on Labor and Public Welfare, 92:2 (GPO, 1972), pp. 1312–20. (Bork later became solicitor general in the Nixon administration.)

53. *Congressional Record*, August 17, 1972, p. 28906.

54. "The President's News Conference of October 5, 1972," *Public Papers of the Presidents: Richard Nixon, 1972* (GPO, 1974), p. 338.

55. *Congressional Record*, December 13, 1973, p. 41268.

56. Ibid., p. 41270.

57. Ibid., pp. 41270–71.

58. Ibid., p. 41271.

59. Ibid., pp. 41272–73.

60. Ibid., p. 41275.

61. Ibid.

62. Ibid., p. 41280.

63. Ibid.

64. *Congressional Record*, December 14, 1973, pp. 41701–03.

65. Earl Johnson, Jr., *Justice and Reform: The Formative Years of the OEO Legal Services Program* (New York: Russell Sage Foundation, 1974), p. 193.

66. *Johnson v. Inglewood Board of Education*, L.A. Super. Ct., No. 973669 (1969); *Soria v. Oxnard School District Board of Trustees*, 328 F. Supp. 155 (S.D. Cal. 1971).

67. *Congressional Record*, January 31, 1974, p. 1675.

68. *Congressional Record*, May 16, 1974, pp. 14995–15014.

69. Ibid., p. 15012.

70. *Congressional Record*, January 31, 1974, p. 1640.

71. *Congressional Record*, July 16, 1974, pp. 23543–48, 23359.

72. *Congressional Record*, March 26, 1974, p. 8274.

73. Ibid.

74. Ibid., p. 8276.

75. Ibid., p. 8275.

76. Ibid., pp. 8281–82.
77. Ibid., pp. 8279–80.
78. Ibid.
79. Ibid., pp. 8281–82.
80. *Congressional Record*, March 27, 1974, pp. 8505–06.
81. *Congressional Record*, May 8, 1974, p. 13740.
82. *Congressional Record*, May 14, 1974, pp. 14601–05.
83. *Congressional Record*, May 15, 1974, p. 14815.
84. Ibid., pp. 14850–51, 14909.
85. Ibid., pp. 14902–03.
86. Ibid., p. 14821.
87. Ibid., p. 14829.
88. Ibid., p. 14924.
89. 163 U.S. 537 (1896).
90. *Congressional Record*, May 15, 1974, pp. 14858–61, 14853–54.
91. *Congressional Record*, May 16, 1974, p. 15074.
92. *Congressional Record*, May 15, 1974, p. 14913.
93. Ibid., p. 14862.
94. Ibid., pp. 14864–65, 14866–67.
95. Ibid., pp. 14924, 14926.
96. *Congressional Record*, May 16, 1974, pp. 15069–70.
97. Ibid., p. 15078.
98. Ibid., p. 15076.
99. Ibid., p. 15078.
100. Ibid., p. 15079.
101. *Congressional Record*, May 20, 1974, p. 15424.
102. Ibid., pp. 15443–44.
103. Ibid., p. 15444.
104. *Congressional Record*, July 23, 1974, pp. 24772–73.
105. Ibid., p. 24775.
106. *Congressional Record*, July 24, 1974, p. 24891.
107. *Congressional Record*, July 31, 1974, pp. 26103, 26111.
108. Ibid., p. 26110.
109. *Congressional Record*, July 23, 1974, pp. 24543–44, text of bill sec. 215(a).
110. See Gary Orfield, *The Reconstruction of Southern Education: The Schools and the 1964 Civil Rights Act* (Wiley, 1969), pp. 47–150.
111. *Congressional Record*, July 24, 1974, p. 24926.
112. *Congressional Record*, July 31, 1974, pp. 26111–12.
113. Ibid., p. 26125.
114. Ibid., p. 26128.
115. *Congressional Quarterly*, August 17, 1974, p. 2211.
116. *Congressional Quarterly*, August 24, 1974, p. 2321.
117. *Congressional Record*, March 12, 1974, pp. 6339–42.
118. *Congressional Record*, March 26, 1974, p. 8237.

119. Ibid., p. 8243.

120. Ibid., pp. 8246, 8247.

121. *Congressional Record,* May 13, 1974, pp. 14333–34.

122. *Congressional Record,* May 15, 1974, p. 14838.

123. *Congressional Record,* May 20, 1974, pp. 15281, 15282.

124. Ibid., p. 15424.

125. *Congressional Record* (daily edition), May 27, 1976, p. S8153.

126. *Congressional Record,* October 1, 1974, p. 33364.

127. *Washington Post,* December 4, 1974.

128. *Congressional Record,* December 10, 1974, p. 39114.

129. *Washington Post,* December 15, 17, 1974.

130. The election showed that busing was still an important issue but not one that destroyed political careers. Florida's Governor Reubin Askew won by a landslide in spite of his defense of busing orders. Oklahoma's Senator Henry Bellmon, who was criticized by his opponent for opposing legislation attempting to override the Supreme Court on busing, was reelected. Birch Bayh won reelection over Richard Lugar, who strongly opposed busing. (*New York Times,* November 6, 1974.) Denver Congresswoman Patricia Schroeder, representing the first northern city ordered by the Court to desegregate, soundly defeated a challenge by a school board member who built much of his campaign around the busing issue (*New York Times,* September 9, 1974).

It was not that busing was popular. A Gallup poll published the day before the election showed the public opposed by a majority of 68 to 32 percent (*Baltimore Sun,* November 4, 1974). On the question of busing across city-suburban lines, an NBC poll taken on election day showed 77 percent opposed (*Washington Star-News,* November 6, 1974). The issue, however, was not decisive. Perhaps, as later surveys would show, people no longer believed that elected officials could do much about the problem. At any rate, it was still possible to support desegregation and survive politically, at least in some parts of the country.

131. *Wilmington Morning News,* June 15, 1974.

132. *Wilmington Evening Journal,* June 28, 1974.

133. Ibid., June 29, 1974.

134. *Wilmington Morning News,* July 10, 1974.

135. *Congressional Record,* June 10, 1964, pp. 13207–09.

136. *Congressional Record* (daily edition), September 26, 1975, p. S16905.

137. *New York Times,* August 20, 1975; *Education Daily,* August 21, 1975; *Washington Post,* September 17, 1975.

138. *Washington Post,* November 23, 1975; *Washington Star,* November 23, 1975.

139. *New York Times,* November 24, 1975, reporting findings of Peter Hart poll.

140. *Boston Globe,* August 27, 1975.

141. *Washington Post,* March 1, 1976.

142. *New York Times,* March 4, 1976.

143. Robert Reinhold, "Voting Reflects Shifts in Florida," *New York Times,* March 11, 1976, interpreting a statewide poll.

144. Democratic platform reprinted in *Congressional Record* (daily edition), July 2, 1976, p. S11580. Republican platform summarized in *Congressional Quarterly,* August 21, 1976, p. 2296.

145. "The President's Message to the Congress Transmitting the Proposed School Desegregation Standards and Assistance Act of 1976," *Weekly Compilation of Presidential Documents,* vol. 12 (June 28, 1976), p. 1080.

146. Ibid., pp. 1081–82.

147. *Congressional Record* (daily edition), April 1, 1976, pp. S4831, S4837.

148. *Congressional Record* (daily edition), June 24, 1976, pp. S10398–403.

149. See remarks by Senators Dale Bumpers of Arkansas and Robert Morgan of North Carolina, ibid., pp. S10403–04.

150. Glenn's speech introducing the amendment appears in *Congressional Record* (daily edition), April 14, 1976, pp. S5733–36; debate and passage in ibid., August 27, 1976, pp. S14773–86.

*Under the provisions of the Supreme Court's 1971 Swann decision the city-county school system of Charlotte-Mecklenburg, which covers more than 500 miles, was ordered to begin a busing program in order to eliminate segregation in its schools. In this article Mark Nadler, education reporter for* The Charlotte Observer *and winner of the North Carolina Association of Educators' School Bell Award, details the way in which this Southern city has adjusted to busing.*

# Charlotte-Mecklenburg

## MARK NADLER

The suburban housewives were gathered around the coffee and pound cake, exchanging the strained small talk so often heard among neighbors who are strangers. Feeling a sense of civic duty, or curiosity, or just plain boredom, they had come to the campaign coffee for Ashley Hogewood Jr., a candidate for the Charlotte-Mecklenburg Board of Education.

As the candidate was ushered about the living room by his hostess, the conversation around the dining room table gradually progressed from the weather to calories to schools. It didn't take long for the mothers to get around to one of their major concerns —the pupil assignment plan, Charlotte's version of court-ordered busing.

What bothered the parents of this upper-middle class community was that children living in the same subdivision attended four different elementary schools. "It's ridiculous," drawled one fashionably dressed woman, who had decided to attend the coffee at the last minute after rain washed out her tennis date. "The kids are bused across town all day and come home and don't even know the children across the street." There were murmurs of assent, followed by personal anecdotes, many of them recounted in angry tones.

The exchange was interrupted by the formal introduction of the candidate, who quickly launched into his well-practiced patter, expressing fervent support of "quality education" and unwaivering faith in the sanctity of "public input."

But no mention of busing. No criticism of the pupil assignment plan, or the judge who ordered it, or the school board that supported it, or the superintendent who told the board he'd rather quit than undermine it. No criticism of the plan responsible for bus rides of up to two hours each day for more than 20,000 of the system's 78,000 children. Nor was the subject brought up by the attentive mothers whose children are shuttled miles away each morning to elementary schools surrounded by the bleak bungalows and stark projects of Charlotte's black communities. Instead, they wanted to know about reading programs, the quality of cafeteria lunches, and the consequences of competency tests.

But no busing. And in a community torn eight years ago by fear and violence, the routine campaign gathering gained special significance. So did the election results two weeks later, on May 2, 1978, when the candidate easily won election to the board along with three others who support the principle of busing to maintain racial balance in Charlotte's 109 schools.

Charlotteans are proud of their school system, the largest in the Carolinas and certainly one of the most progressive. And while they may not like court-ordered busing, they're proud of the way they accepted it without the massive turmoil of a Louisville or Boston. Most consider it an unavoidable evil, like taxes or traffic jams. There is dissatisfaction, balanced by resignation.

In early 1978, the school board ordered selected reassignments to bring eight schools back into compliance with the 1970 U.S. District Court order banning predominantly black schools. On two separate occasions—both times by a 7–2 vote—the board blocked attempts by antibusing stalwarts to ignore the violations and go back to court to fight the order.

When the plan was adopted, ordering reassignment of 4,850 students in the fall of 1978, parents took little notice of the event except in the outlying suburbs of southeastern Mecklenburg County, where whites had built $80,000 and $90,000 homes in secluded subdivisions with quaint names like "Providence Plantation." And in May, when four of the nine school board seats were up for election, busing was never an issue. Only one of the 14 candidates—an insurance company personnel manager and former junior high school teacher—based his campaign on opposition to busing. He placed a distant eighth, winning only two of 109 precincts—his own and the neighboring precinct in southeast Mecklenburg.

Of the four winners, one was an incumbent who has substantially softened his opposition to busing. During the campaign he discussed the issue only when pressed and suggested that with the percentage of black students increasing by one percent each year—it's now nearly 37 percent—the court order should be changed in the future to a more flexible formula that would still require substantial busing.

Hogewood, a lawyer, also avoided the busing issue whenever possible, merely reiterating he was "not hell bent for leather to go back to court." The third candidate chaired the citizens group that developed the current busing plan in the early 1970s. And the fourth, a minister, became the third black ever elected to the board, giving the body two blacks for the first time. He too, avoided the busing issue, devoting his speeches to such innocuous non-issues as "the need for community involvement."

All in all, it was an uninspiring campaign. It was calm, polite, and totally lacking in controversy—just the way Charlotte normally likes its politics. And judging from the surface evidence— the dull campaign, the relatively muted reaction to the new pupil assignments—one could almost draw the conclusion that busing is a dead issue in Charlotte, where the official antibusing stance a decade ago resulted in the Swann case and the U.S. Supreme Court's first specific endorsement of court-ordered busing.

But the people who run Charlotte's schools aren't kidding themselves. "I have no doubt that if you put it on the ballot tomorrow, the majority of people would vote to end the pupil assignment plan," says superintendent Jay Robinson, taking a page from antibusing candidate David Rowe's campaign speech. "But I firmly believe that integrated schools are a sound, healthy educational environment. If we dropped the pupil assignment plan, we'd start sliding back into a segregated system over night."

The reason is simple. Charlotte-Mecklenburg, a consolidated city-county school system, covers more than 500 square miles. But

90 percent of the blacks live in northwest Charlotte neighborhoods, which make up less than nine percent of the school system's geographic area. The result is obvious: widespread busing, with most of Charlotte's 598 buses converging on the black communities each morning and scattering their children throughout the outlying suburban schools. Simple mathematics dictate that in a system where two-thirds of the students are white, black children are bused twice as often as whites.

For that reason, much of the limited opposition to busing these days is coming from the black community. Three blacks ran for the school board in May, and all three voiced concern that blacks shoulder an unfair burden in keeping the schools integrated. All three, while affirming the need for busing, suggested that black students be allowed to attend local schools through the third grade. The argument that most educators believe integration in the primary grades to be crucial made little difference to them—theirs was a popular position in the black community.

But no one has yet come up with an acceptable solution to the problem. During the school board's deliberations on the 1978 reassignments, representatives of the local NAACP chapter's Education Committee expressed the same concern in combative terms. But when asked for a solution, the group's leaders told the board, "If I had the answers, I'd be up there. That's your job." The board was not impressed.

The complexity of the busing problems was illustrated once again the day after the election, when 45 young business and professional people, tapped by the Charlotte Chamber of Commerce as the "Leaders of Tomorrow," presented reports on their 10 weeks of work in small task forces. The task force assigned to develop ways to decrease school busing came up with three recommendations, and of these the committee admitted one was illegal and the remaining two unworkable. "The report is a joke," muttered a young insurance executive who served on the committee. "We couldn't even agree on the supporting data. We were so fragmented we couldn't elect a chairman."

The complexity of the busing plan is what bothers so many Charlotteans, including those who support the philosophy behind it. It is a difficult, time-consuming process eating up the energy and attention of school administrators and board members, who put aside other important matters for the first four months of the current school year while they wrestled with the new assignments. Night after night, the board met before a back-drop of floor-to-ceiling color-coded maps, as top administrators shuffled through mountains of computer printouts looking for ways to keep 15 first graders closer to their homes. "It's so damn complicated," the board was told one night by Clyde Pope, the pupil assignment director. "It's like a game of dominoes. You put 20 black students in this school, and it changes the ratio, so you have to take 20 blacks and send them somewhere else, and then it starts all over again."

It's that kind of logic—and that is the logic of busing in Char-lotte—that angers those who think the schools have done more than enough to carry out the Supreme Court's mandate. "We've done what we were supposed to do," says board member Tom Harris, a leader of the antibusing movement when first elected to the board in 1970. "The Supreme Court does not require us to continually police the schools to maintain artificial racial bal-ance."

Busing opponents speak of the need for "quality education" and angrily resist any charge of racism. Their arguments are that time spent on a bus is not only lost time but dangerous time, con-sidering a spate of school bus fender-benders early in the school year. Reassignments are emotionally shattering experiences for young children who must leave their friends, the parents say, and the crazy-quilt pattern of school assignments ruins community spirit and eliminates traditional neighborhood support for a neighborhood school. "This ratio business is for the birds," busing opponent David Rowed said during his unsuccessful school board race. "Our community has an integrated system and no longer needs artificial racial guidelines. Now the emphasis should be put on ensuring that all of our schools have equal teachers, facilities, and materials."

The parents speak with feeling about the kind of education they want for their children, and it would be a grave mistake to discount them as racist rednecks. But it would also be foolish to completely discount bias—social as well as racial—as a factor. Late at night, as antibusing meetings would become more emo-tional and the heat and fatigue would melt away the coating of civility that enveloped the early-evening speeches, the gut-level feelings would begin to surface. "When we moved down here from Albany, we bought a house out here in Providence Plantation so we could get our kids out of inner-city schools," a young mother complained, her nasal upstate New York accent sounding incongruous in the antebellum church hall. "But dammit, you got us anyway."

The woman and her audience illustrated the newest phenomenon in Charlotte's antibusing movement. The most vocal and highly organized opposition comes from suburbs filled with transplanted Northerners transferred to Charlotte by large corporations shifting their operations to the Sunbelt. The parents are disappointed with what they consider an inferior Southern school system, and their irritation is compounded by the forced busing many had expected to leave behind in Northern cities. These parents have formed the nucleus of a new group called Parents for Quality Education and Stability Today (Parents QUEST). By mid-May, the group had between 1,000 and 1,500 members, and organizers claimed to have raised enough money for a prolonged court battle, if necessary, to seek an end to Charlotte's busing.

"Our only interest is quality education," says Darryl Myers, a leader of the group and an executive for the Carowinds theme amusement park south of Charlotte. "The Charlotte-Mecklenburg schools used to be head and shoulders above the rest of the state, but I'm afraid that's not the case any more. The school board is more concerned with numbers than education."

Myers has already enrolled his nine-year-old daughter in one of Charlotte's most exclusive private schools for next fall, although he claims to be "a firm supporter of the public school system." In fact, even if the busing situation doesn't change, he plans to send his son to public schools so he can take advantage of sports programs and have a better shot at a college athletic scholarship.

Myers isn't the only parent turning to the private schools, although there has been no stampede in that direction by any means. But the affluence of the current crop of busing protestors, along with their Yankee accents, has cooled the ardor of native Charlotteans and working class parents who might otherwise join the movement. There's a feeling that the "carpetbaggers"—and that's a term that's actually used—have come down from the North, are putting down the local schools, opposing busing without having lived through its difficult years, and are saying they're ready to pay private school tuition of up to $2,000 a year if the schools won't change the rules more to their liking. To local parents, that smacks of arrogance and elitism, and relatively few long-time residents have shown much interest in Parents QUEST.

Those parents, and school officials, are more interested in the questions of how well integration has worked in the local schools and whether busing has produced benefits that outweigh the burdens. Not surprisingly, there are no easy answers.

School officials point most often to the academic progress made by black students as indicated by standardized test scores. The schools with the highest percentage of blacks consistently rank lowest when the test scores are released. But there has been undeniable progress, with dramatic improvements starting with children who entered the first grade the year Charlotte's full-scale busing began. While average scores for children in higher grades often lagged two full years behind national norms, the children who grew up with busing perform on the average right at national norms.

School officials are also encouraged by results they see in testing children for talent development classes, accelerated programs for the system's top students. Federal guidelines require racial balance in those classes, and in the past entrance requirements for black students were two stanines below the minimum required of white students who took the same standardized tests. This year, the gap closed to one stanine, and officials estimate that within two years, whites and blacks will have to meet identical standards.

And there are visible signs that the children and their parents have accepted integration and are trying to make it work. Six years ago, policemen patrolled the high schools, and swarms of patrol cars streaked to a school each time a fight broke out in a cafeteria. There were constant fights, widespread vandalism, and threats of boycotts by whites.

Today, the single policeman assigned to each school is called a "resource officer," whose main job is giving lectures on law enforcement and the courts. There is vandalism, to be sure, and pushing matches still erupt in the cafeterias, but little of the trouble can be traced to race. Parents who bitterly opposed busing in the early 1970s now help paint classrooms and run carnival booths for PTA fundraisers at schools miles away from their homes.

But that's only one side of the picture. You can see the other side at Bruns Avenue Elementary School, where two fifth-grade math classes are merged into one. At one end of the room is the advanced groups, where children easily whip through rows of long division problems on the blackboard. At the other end are the slower learners, where children stand befuddled at the blackboard, the multiplication tables in their hands, pathetically trying to multiply 12 by 6. All but one of the advanced students are white. The entire group at the other end of the room is black.

You see the other side of the picture at West Charlotte High School, where the journalism classroom is divided into six rows of desks, all pointed toward the center of the room where a wide aisle bisects the room. All the students in the three rows to the left of the aisle are white, as is the teacher whose desk is on their side of the room. The right side of the classroom is black. You see it when you drive up to the school, where students—all of them white—lounge around the lawn or play touch football. On the grass behind the main building, more students—all of them black—are doing the same thing.

You see the other side in the results of the system's competency test, given to all tenth graders for the first time in the fall of 1977. More than twice as many blacks as whites couldn't pass the test based on sixth-grade reading and math skills.

You see it in the drop-out rate, the retention rate, the suspension rate. Blacks simply are not succeeding in school at the same rate as whites, and school officials, particularly the superintendent, are concerned.

This school year—superintendent Jay Robinson's first in Charlotte—he assigned top aides to begin a comprehensive education audit, going into each school and analyzing statistics dealing with dropouts, suspensions, retentions, test scores, and practically anything else that indicates what's going on in the school.

"I know we've got some real problems, and I'm sure that black students are not receiving the same treatment as whites in all cases," says Robinson, an informal, almost folksy educator from the North Carolina mountains whose hillbilly accent and down-home mannerisms are found disarming by all but his most severe critics. "I think our biggest problem is one of expectations," he says. "A lot of white teachers just don't expect much of black students, and the students sense that. We're going to have to find better ways to overcome some of these attitudes. But first we've got to take the steps of finding out exactly what our problems are and letting people know what they are. If we try to hide them and say they don't exist, we're just fooling ourselves, and nothing will change."

After more than a decade as superintendent in rural Cabarrus County, N.C., where he led the fight for integrated schools and stepped-up hiring of black teachers and administrators, Robinson has found himself caught in an unfamiliar dilemma: on one hand, he is trying to convince whites of the benefits of integrated schools, while at the same time growing numbers of blacks are saying they'd rather attend all-black neighborhood schools than endure the hardships of busing.

Some blacks argue that the court ban on predominantly black schools attaches a stigma to all schools with large numbers of blacks. And some, including younger teachers whose memories may be clouded by childhood perceptions, contend that black students received more attention and achieved better results when taught only by black teachers "who really cared."

"All that 'Let's go back to the good old days of segregation' stuff is bull," says one of Charlotte-Mecklenburg's top administrators, who taught and served as principal in the all-black school system in the 1950s. "We had no books in the library. All our furniture was picked up from the warehouse after the white schools were finished with it. We didn't have enough textbooks, we didn't have musical instruments, we didn't have money. When the kids needed to use the john, they had to use a two-holer out back behind the school."

Some vestiges of the dual school system remain and demonstrate why Robinson and others are adamantly opposed to seeking an end to busing in the foreseeable future. The point is made most clearly, perhaps, in the year-end audit of school activity funds, made up for the most part by money raised from PTA and school fund-raising activities. The figures are consistent: by and large, schools in the wealthy white suburbs raise three, four, even five times as much money during the school year as schools with the highest percentages of blacks.

The activity funds are not insignificant; they're spent on much more than band uniforms and end-of-the-year picnics. Charlotte schools, like others in North Carolina, continue the old practice of expecting parents to pick up the tab for many critical school expenses not funded by tax revenues. For example, many schools are almost entirely dependent upon activity funds and PTA contributions for library reference materials. The impact of parent contributions is felt even more directly in classrooms. In most cases, the school system will purchase basic texts, but it's up to each school to come up with money to buy workbooks for every student. It is no exaggeration to say that even without the field trips and school carnivals and the array of activities that bring parents into the schools, parents' organizations have a significant effect on the quality of education in the schools, and the strength and effectiveness of those organizations varies drastically in nearly direct proportion to the percentage of black students.

This reason alone, superintendent Robinson insists, shows why Charlotte-Mecklenburg cannot afford to abandon court-ordered busing, and there are those in Charlotte, including many busing opponents, who recognize the validity of that argument. The answer, they say, is a system of compensatory education through which the formal school budget would compensate for variations in parent support. And Robinson agrees, up to a point. But the idea raises two major concerns: compensatory aid might discourage parents who are actively working for their schools, parents who might see an inequity in other schools being given the money they worked hard for in their own; and secondly, with a return to a segregated system, support for compensatory aid might dry up among white parents, who are the majority of voters.

Obviously, the problem is a difficult one. Without question, parents are tired of busing and would like to see an end to it, but barring court action arising from a potential suit from antibusing parents, there's no reversal of current policy in sight, particularly in light of the recent school board election.

What the board has recognized is the possibility of lessening the busing plan's disruptive impact on the community. But neither the board nor the administration, preoccupied with other issues ranging from competency tests to budget problems, have taken any steps in this direction. However, there is increasing understanding that constant monitoring of the schools, and immediate reassignments in cases where schools slip over the 50 percent line, will eliminate the necessity of periodic wholesale shake-ups of the entire system. School officials realize that even though the numbers involved in systemwide readjustments are relatively low —only about six percent are involved in next fall's shifts—the psychological impact of months of hearings, debates, squabbles, and protests magnify the conflicts and resurrect the old divisions.

"The ideal situation would be to make these reassignments

completely routine," says one board member. "Everybody understands that when the number of children in a neighborhood changes, you need reassignments. So when you have a shift in the racial make-up of a school, it should be the same thing—reassignments. It should be done routinely, every summer, as one of our normal responsibilities, just like approving a budget and setting a calendar. Nobody likes busing, but I think this community could live with that."

*Unlike the Charlotte-Mecklenburg busing plan, the one ordered by the Supreme Court to eliminate segregation in Detroit does not extend beyond the central city. In this account William R. Grant, education writer for the Detroit Free Press, shows the problems of carrying out a busing plan in a system in which over 80 percent of the students are black and wealth and power have fled to the suburbs.*

# Detroit

## WILLIAM R. GRANT

In early 1970, civil rights lawyers made what proved to be a major breakthrough when they convinced the federal courts to apply the same scrutiny to segregated schools in the North that had been applied to Southern school systems. Four years later the nation's highest court, by then substantially reshaped by President Nixon, ruled in a Detroit case that lower federal courts grappling with the problems of urban school segregation could not reach out into the white suburbs that ring many of the nation's cities in order to develop a remedy.

Detroit now finds itself trapped in this cul-de-sac of the law. The city has been required to make changes in its public schools in an effort to overcome a history of racial discrimination, but it is prohibited from involving the suburbs to which many of the city's white families have fled to escape blacks and other perceived ills of big city life. "It is both a joke and a hoax," said the late C. L. Golightly, a black professor of philosophy who until 1976 was president of the Detroit Board of Education, "that a school

An earlier version of this article appeared in *Urban Review* (Summer, 1975). It is revised and enlarged here with permission of the editors of *Urban Review*.

**321**

board with a majority of black members is required by law to integrate a minority of white students into a majority of black students in order to bring those black students into the mainstream of American life."

The fight over busing in Detroit is nearly a decade old and is expected to continue for some time. It began when a liberal majority of the Detroit school board voted in April 1970 to begin a modest integration plan in high schools. The board members who voted for the plan were recalled from office, and the state legislature blocked implementation of the changes. That action prompted the federal court suit, which in 1976 finally brought about a small measure of integration in some city schools.

U.S. District Judge Robert E. DeMascio, who took over the case in 1975 after the death of the original judge, Stephen J. Roth, ordered even this limited desegregation plan with great reluctance. Judge DeMascio was a conservative, a Nixon appointee. Unlike Judge Roth, also a conservative but who during the initial hearings on the case abandoned his hostility to integration, Judge DeMascio remained steadfastly against busing. His orders are filled with antibusing rhetoric, and his final desegregation plan was shaped in an effort to avoid white opposition.

The plan, which involves less than half of the city's schools and buses less than 10 percent of the students, is one of the nation's most limited. In 1976 the U.S. Court of Appeals for the Sixth Circuit rejected Judge DeMascio's view that desegregation in a majority-black school system could be accomplished by simply desegregating the majority-white schools. The appeals court ordered Judge DeMascio to develop a new plan, but so far the judge has failed to comply.

The Supreme Court rejected the metropolitan desegregation plan in mid-1974. Judge DeMascio held numerous hearings during 1975 as he developed his busing order. The plan was implemented on January 26, 1976, at the beginning of the second semester of the 1975–76 school year.

The development of the desegregation plan came at a time when Detroit was in serious trouble in several ways. A poll taken by the Detroit Free Press at the end of 1974 indicated that six out of every ten Detroiters believed the city had become a worse place to live during the previous year. The poll, based on interviews with 587 persons in a carefully drawn sample, showed that almost half of the city's residents—55 percent of the whites and 43 percent of the blacks—would move out of Detroit if they could.

The city's residents were sick with the fear of crime. In 1974, 801 people were murdered in Detroit, a new record for the city that had set new homicide records for each of the three previous years and called itself the "murder capital." Handguns were everywhere; even the mayor sometimes carried one. Each Detroiter had one chance in 464 of being shot in 1974. A close examination of the murder statistics shows that a substantial proportion of the killings result from family arguments or arguments between friends. Typically, a gun is handy, and a shooting occurs when without the weapon there might have been nothing more than a fistfight. These facts do not lessen people's fears, however, and in the 1974 year-end poll, 36 percent of the blacks and 26 percent of the whites interviewed by the *Free Press* gave crime as the reason they wanted to leave the city.

Detroit has been affected more than many other areas by the downturn in the United States economy. Unemployment in the city in January 1975, when Judge DeMascio began considering the desegregation case, was 13.7 percent, compared with a nationwide average of 8.2 percent. There were more people out of work in the city that month than in any other period in the 20 years during which the Michigan Employment Service Commission has been keeping data. Unemployment among the city's blacks was 30 percent and on the increase. Mayor Coleman A. Young, who was then in his second year as the city's first black mayor, said "Detroit has no recession. This is a depression."

The years since 1974 have seen a reduction in crime and an increase in employment, and there are some indications that Detroiters feel better about their city. Both crime and unemployment continue to be serious problems, however, and improved crime statistics have not removed fears that paralyze many neighborhoods.

The crisis in Detroit's economy overshadowed, at least for a time, the racial tensions that long marked the city. Detroit was the scene of the nation's worst race riot in 1943, and in 1967 Detroit experienced the worst of the series of urban disorders that swept eastward from Watts.

Black migration to Detroit continued even after it had slackened in other cities. It was accompanied by the movement of whites to the scores of suburbs that surround the city. In the decade of the 1960s, the city lost 344,093 whites, while it gained 178,205 blacks. That means that on the average day during the decade the city lost 94 whites as 48 blacks moved in. Detroit was 43.7 percent black at the time of the 1970 census. There is now evidence that migration both in and out of the city has slowed substantially, but the population is now estimated to be 55 to 60 percent black. In the 1977–78 school year, Detroit's public schools enrolled 228,771 students, 81.8 percent of them black, 16 percent white, and 2.2 percent other minorities.

Most Detroiters would probably say that the condition of the public schools is even worse than the condition of the city itself, even though that assessment may be unduly harsh. The system is, like all other big city school systems, filled with contrasts. It has serious problems but is rich in many resources. Talented teachers and administrators work side by side with incompetents.

Inside the schools crime is as big, or an even bigger, issue than it is on the streets outside. In early 1975, the school board agreed to the stationing of armed police in the high schools and in some junior highs as a response to the murders inside different schools of two students in a three-day period late in 1974.

The Detroit school system is a traditional one that makes few attempts at innovation in organization or curriculum. Money from the federal Elementary and Secondary Education Act and a similar state of Michigan program appears at least to have helped stop the decline in student achievement test scores, if not even improve scores slightly. Detroit, with an average elementary class size of 35, operates larger classes than most big cities and than virtually all of the city's surrounding suburbs. The special federal and state money has reduced class size to 25 in many schools in low income neighborhoods. This improving picture of achievement has been widely discussed by school officials and in the media, but it appears to have made no difference in the poor attitudes of Detroiters about their schools.

Many of these perceptions about schools are related to racial attitudes, of course. What continues to decline in Detroit schools is the percentage of white students. While parents of white children in schools whose student body is becoming more black outwardly express concern about declining achievement, one suspects that the underlying concern, recognized or not by the parents themselves, is that something must be done to stop the movement of black families into the city's remaining white neighborhoods. Judge DeMascio lives in suburban Grosse Pointe, and his children attended parochial schools. But his concern for preserving Detroit's white neighborhoods was every bit as real as those who had a more direct stake in the matter.

Before the desegregation plan was implemented, there was remarkably little integration in Detroit's classrooms, despite the racial mix of the students citywide. In the 1973–74 school year there were 158 schools—a little more than half of the schools in the city—that were 90 percent or more black. There were 27 schools that were 90 percent or more white, and another 46 that were 65 to 89 percent white. Only 43 of the more than 300 schools had a racial composition at or near the racial mix citywide. The Detroit system was, in fact two systems—one very large majority black school system operating alongside a small number of largely white schools. Black Detroit was virtually out of sight, if not out of mind, for parents and students in many white neighborhoods.

Judge DeMascio's desegregation order was designed to change as little of this as possible. In only a few instances did it call for busing white students out of their neighborhoods into black neighborhoods. DeMascio believed, although the court of appeals later rejected the notion as unconstitutional, that he could satisfy the legal requirement for desegregation in Detroit simply by improving the percentage of black students at the heavily white schools. He made no attempt to deal with the overwhelming number of all black or nearly all black schools.

Much of the busing required by the plan is one-way busing of blacks into white neighborhoods. In one case a new and well equipped majority black junior high school was cleared of most of its students—who were sent to a converted elementary school with no advanced facilities of any kind—so that hundreds of whites could be assigned to the better building.

The statistics for the 1977–78 school year reflect how little things changed inside the schools after the court order, despite the fact that the proportion of black students citywide had climbed to 81.8 percent. There were in 1977–78 still 147 schools that were more than 90 percent black. The smaller number compared with the 158 schools that were 90 percent or more black in 1973–74 reflects the school closings made by the Board of Education during those years and not an increase in the percentage of whites at any heavily black school. The main impact of the court order, just as Judge DeMascio had intended it to be, was to increase the proportion of black students in white neighborhoods. In 1977–78 there were no schools more than 90 percent white. There were still 17 majority white schools, however, and another 30 that were at least 40 percent white.

For a brief period beginning in the mid-1960s, a liberal Detroit school board tried to meet the growing demands of the city's blacks for better treatment in the schools. The board named an integrationist superintendent who hired more black teachers and promoted blacks into administration.

Little was done about student integration, however, until 1970, when the board voted to change the attendance boundaries of 11 high schools in order to increase integration. The plan, which would have sent about 9,000 students to different schools than they normally would have attended, stirred many of Detroit's white residents unlike anything the board had previously done. Their successful campaign to remove the school board's majority from office and legislative intervention that blocked implementation of the plan prompted the NAACP in August 1970 to file a federal court suit demanding integration of the Detroit schools.

The lawsuit was filed just as the federal courts were starting to look seriously at cases of school segregation outside the South. The U.S. Supreme Court's 1954 school desegregation decision in *Brown v. Board of Education* had been aimed specifically at the 17 Southern states and the District of Columbia, which required blacks and whites to attend separate schools, and at the four others that permitted segregation by local option.

Ironically, some of the earliest school desegregation cases were fought in the North, including an unsuccessful one in Boston, which preceded the adoption of the Fourteenth Amendment. By the time of *Brown,* however, segregation had come to be regarded as a Southern problem. It was not until the early 1960s that the NAACP attempted to use the federal courts to break up segregation in Northern school systems.

Because states affected by the 1954 decision all had laws requiring or permitting segregation, cases in those states did not require the presentation of proof that state-imposed segregation actually existed. Southern cases thus began with discussion of what to do to bring about an end to this segregation. In the North, though, most states no longer had a segregation law on the books, although some, like Indiana, had repealed segregation legislation only a brief time before the *Brown* cases began to make their way through the courts. Some states, like Michigan, even had statutes that prohibited segregation.

Robert L. Carter, then the NAACP's general counsel, read into the sweeping language of the *Brown* decision an invitation for lower federal courts to rule any kind of school segregation illegal without first looking at whether or not the segregation resulted from state or local government actions. School attendance figures in most big city systems in the North showed that blacks and whites were, for the most part, attending separate schools. Carter formulated an argument that held, basically, that school desegregation was wrong regardless of its cause because it denied blacks an equal educational opportunity.

Carter won at least partial success with this position in the New Rochelle and Manhasset, New York, cases and in Springfield, Massachusetts. But when he took his argument into the Midwest, Carter suffered a series of defeats that seemed at the time to end any chance of getting federal court orders in states where there were no laws requiring separate schools for blacks and for whites.

In 1963 in Gary, Indiana, U.S. District Judge George N. Beamer concluded that Gary did not have "segregated schools . . . but segregated housing." The decision, which was endorsed by the U.S Court of Appeals for the Seventh Circuit, set the tone for decisions that followed in Kansas City, Kansas, and in Cincinnati, Ohio. The decisions in these cases created the troubling legal distinction between *de facto* and *de jure* segregation. The effort to extend the requirement for integrated schools in the North continued, but it was 1970 before a breakthrough came in the courts.

In February 1970, U.S. District Judge Damon J. Keith virtually ignored the distinction between *de jure* and *de facto* segregation in his decision regarding the Pontiac, Michigan, schools. Judge Keith was faced with two local NAACP attorneys who argued a straight equal educational opportunity case that the national office considered so flimsy that it refused to provide financial aid. Judge Keith wondered if the time had come for the federal courts to accept Robert Carter's theories. He decided that it had not. "One day that will be the law," he said later in an interview, "but it is not yet."

Instead, Judge Keith took a handful of decisions concerning school boundaries and the construction of new schools made by Pontiac school boards over a 15-year period and ruled that they gave proof of a pattern of de jure segregation. The Pontiac board, he said, had acted in "such a way as to perpetuate the pattern of segregation in the city."

U.S. District Judge Manuel Real followed a similar course in Pasadena, California, at virtually the same time. He issued a short, unexplained decision in January 1970 and followed it with a more detailed opinion in March. Judge Real, even more firmly than Judge Keith, outlined what he believed to be a school board's responsibility to overcome segregation. "Racial imbalance" in the Pasadena schools resulted mainly from the "failure [of the local school board] to carry out [its] announced policy of integration," Judge Real ruled.

There have been a growing number of federal court desegregation orders issued in the North since the Pontiac and Pasadena decisions. Most have followed the pattern set by Judge Keith and Judge Real, and in 1973 the U.S. Supreme Court gave its endorsement to this legal standard for evaluating the guilt of the Northern school boards in its decision in the Denver case.

Although these decisions potentially affect far more school systems than did the Brown decision, they have generally received little attention. Pontiac made the front pages not because it was a legal turning point, but because ten school buses were bombed on the eve of the beginning of a busing program in September 1971. Boston was the focus of continuing news coverage during its first two years of desegregation because of the protests and violence that made it the first real battleground for integration in the North. Despite this occasional media attention on the issue of busing, there has been virtually no reporting—and there is certainly little public understanding—of the larger evolution in the law that has made student assignment policies of the school systems of the North subject to judicial review.

This extension of federal court scrutiny to school systems in the North left one major barrier to integration, however. "In the 20 years since Brown," William Taylor, director of the Center for National Policy Review at Catholic University argues, "it has become clear that the major remaining obstacle to integration of the public schools is the segregation we find in urban areas between the city and its suburbs."

Judge Stephen Roth concluded, in issuing his September 1971 opinion on school segregation in Detroit, that the city's schools had been segregated by a variety of state and local actions. His opinion cited incidences of schools being built in segregated neighborhoods, school attendance lines being shifted as neighborhoods turned black so that blacks and whites remained in separate schools as long as possible, and blacks being transported from overcrowded black schools to other black schools even though there were white schools with space available nearby.

It also became clear to Judge Roth during the four months he heard evidence in early 1971 that Detroit would in a matter of a few years have a school system that was virtually all black. A permanent solution to school segregation in Detroit, he concluded, would have to link the city and its overwhelmingly white suburbs.

The U.S. Court of Appeals for the Sixth Circuit upheld Judge Roth's city-suburban integration order and observed that letting the wall between the city and the suburbs stand would "evoke haunting memories" of the "separate but equal" doctrine overturned by the Supreme Court in the *Brown* decision. A Supreme Court reversal of Judge Roth's order "would prove in time to be the *Dred Scott* decision of this century," one of the appeals court judges glumly predicted in a private conversation.

The increasing isolation of blacks in the core cities of the nation raises serious doubts about how much integration there can be if school desegregation orders must stop at the city limits. In 1954, 70 percent of the nation's blacks lived in states where separate schools for blacks and whites were required by statute. By the 1970 census, nearly half of the nation's blacks were living outside the South. The 1972 racial survey by the U.S. Department of Health, Education, and Welfare showed that about half of the nation's 6.8 million black school students attended school in the 100 largest school systems. About one-fifth of the nation's school children who were black attended classes in just five cities— New York, Chicago, Los Angeles, Philadelphia, and Detroit. The U.S. Commission on Civil Rights warned in 1967 that "the rich variety of the nation's urban population is being separated into distinct groups, living increasingly in isolation from each other."

At the time of the 1970 census, 87.2 percent of the blacks in the three-county Detroit metropolitan area lived inside the city limits of Detroit, and 78 percent of the remaining blacks lived in six heavily black suburbs. Of the 275,000 people living in Detroit's middle-class suburbs of Birmingham, Bloomfield Hills, Farmington, Southfield and the five Grosse Pointes, only 261 of them, or less than one percent, were black. The argument that an increase in the education and income level of blacks will open a pathway for them to the suburbs simply doesn't hold in metropolitan Detroit, if, indeed, it does anywhere. Albert Hermalin and Reynolds Farley, writing in the October 1973 issue of the *American Sociological Review,* found that a smaller percentage of blacks earning between $15,000 and $29,000 annually live in the suburbs than do whites earning between $5,000 and $7,000. They wrote, "If Detroit area black families were represented in the suburbs to the same extent as whites with comparable incomes, then 67 percent rather than 12 percent of the blacks would have a suburban residence."

The Supreme Court majority remained blind to the implications of such data, however, and on July 25, 1974, the four Nixon appointees were joined by Potter Stewart in ruling that the wall between Detroit and its suburbs could stand. Chief Justice Warren Burger's majority opinion did not reject outright the possibility of city-suburban integration, and indeed a few such plans have evolved in recent years. But the tone of the court's opinion makes it clear that most of the justices are prepared to approve busing across school district lines only in unusual cases.

The court did not back away, however, from its commitment to integration in those school systems where a link between board actions and segregation can be made. That will mean continuing pressure on Northern school systems and more desegregation orders. But the decision dashes the hopes of a quick, if revolutionary, attempt at confronting the race problems of Detroit and the other majority black big cities.

Following the Supreme Court's decision, the attorneys for the NAACP asked, as they traditionally ask in any desegregation case, for a court-ordered plan that would make the racial composition of each school in the system reflect the racial composition of the system as a whole. That would have meant in 1975, when the issue was before Judge DeMascio, about 71 percent black students and 26 percent white students in each school. (Three percent were other minorities, mostly Spanish Americans.)

The prospect of such a plan put local leaders and the school board in a dither. Editorial writers for both daily newspapers thundered at the NAACP, and even some influential black leaders tried to persuade the civil rights organization to retreat from its position. The board of the Detroit NAACP said it would stand behind the national legal staff, and the national NAACP board took the position that to back away from busing in Detroit just because the school system was three-fourths black would jeopardize the NAACP's position in every other case in the country. If the NAACP had decided it would not pursue desegregation in Detroit despite the finding of *de jure* segregation, then every other local school board faced with a similar court ruling would come up with reasons why it too should be spared a remedy for its wrongs.

The attempts to force the NAACP to recant its support for a Detroit busing plan were founded on the belief that busing—especially busing that creates heavily black schools in every neighborhood—would cause many of the city's remaining whites to flee. Implicit in this argument is the reverse belief that no busing—continuation of a policy that permitted a small majority white system to operate inside a large majority black system—would cause the whites to stay. Nothing that has happened in the 1970s suggests the likelihood of that. But the argument was doubtful at the outset. White flight existed in Detroit before there was a busing case. In fact the greatest degree of flight came in the late 1950s and the early 1960s when the schools were most rigidly segregated.

But of far more serious concern is the impact of the Detroit case for all cities. The message from the Supreme Court, whether Chief Justice Burger intended it or not, is that whites who choose to remain in Detroit and other majority black cities can expect to have their children educated in heavily black classrooms, regardless of whether or not they have settled in a largely white neighborhood. At the same time, however, a few miles away and across the city line, the all-white suburban schools find themselves getting a Supreme Court pledge that they will be left alone. This opinion can only serve to reinforce the feeling of many that a move from the city to the suburbs represents an effective escape from the city's problems. The court's decision poses not only a serious threat to school integration, but to the future of big cities as well.

That is, of course, not intended as an argument that a majority black school cannot be a good school or that a majority black city cannot govern itself. The NAACP has never made that sort of claim. The civil rights organization faced a similar dilemma when it decided to pursue the cases that led to the *Brown* decision. In most of those cases the NAACP would have had little trouble in proving that the black schools were not equal to the white schools, as the law then required. But the NAACP decided not to seek financial or physical facilities equality. It chose instead to make a frontal attack on segregation itself. In cities, counties, and states controlled by whites there seemed little likelihood of getting permanent equity for separate black schools. One way to assure an equal educational opportunity for minority children is to have them attend school with white children—not because blacks and other minorities must sit next to whites in order to learn but because it is the parents and grandparents of the white children who control the school boards and the state legislatures that run the schools. For these practical purposes and for deeper emotional and philosophical reasons, the U.S. Supreme Court accepted in 1954 the argument that separate schools can never be equal.

The wisdom of that decision is now being underscored in cities like Detroit. The city has a black mayor and a majority black school board. Yet what power do these officials have over the future of the city and its schools? Mayor Young's administration is deeply dependent on the policies of the national government and finds itself having to turn to the state legislature for any change in taxing power. The school board learns daily that the legislature has more real control over the schools, particularly the school budget, than does the local board. Having a black school board in Detroit in charge of a black school system may be an uplifting thought to black Detroiters, who were long denied their share of political power, but it is a hollow victory. Wealth and power have fled to the city's suburbs, and the Supreme Court has reinforced this flight by excusing the wealthy and powerful from helping to solve the problem of racial isolation in the city's school system.

The impact of this court decision may fall most directly on those cities like Detroit, where white flight is all but completed. But it applies to other cities as well. Even though Boston, San Francisco, and scores of big cities still have black minorities, they too cannot help but be affected by the Supreme Court's statement that school integration will follow white families only so long as they remain inside the city limits. This is a proposition almost calculated to start white flight in those cities where there has been little of it. As long as the Supreme Court's decision remains unchanged, it stands as a promise to whites who want to live in isolation from blacks that they can find a sanctuary in the suburbs.

*When court-ordered busing first came to Boston, the city reacted as though it were about to become the Little Rock of the North. It did not continue on that destructive course, however, and Howard Husock, staff writer since 1974 for* The Boston Phoenix, *explains why.*

# Boston

## HOWARD HUSOCK

It was autumn, 1974, and Boston was unpleasantly surprising much of the nation. Three months earlier, federal Judge W. Arthur Garrity, ruling on a suit brought by the NAACP, had ordered the desegregation of the nation's oldest public school system. In September, the first bus loads of black students were arriving at formerly all-white South Boston High School, the aging brick building on the top of a hill in the middle of the blue-collar Irish neighborhood whose name was about to join Little Rock and Selma as symbols of resistance to desegregation. The buses arrived under police escort, and more police—including Justice Department observers—awaited them. So did network television crews. And so did mobs of South Boston residents. Some had written signs, some graffiti—"Southie Says Never." "Niggers Suck." "Stop Forced Busing."

In the first few weeks of court-ordered integration, the arrival and departure of the few bus loads of blacks attending the place known as Southie High was seldom uneventful. Crowds would rock the hated yellow symbols of the federal "tyrant" who had ordered what local school officials had long promised would never happen. Police eventually began to plot a variety of escape routes for the buses, in order to avoid the mobs. On a day in mid-October, when the buses successfully sneaked out of South Boston, the waiting crowd seized instead on a black Haitian immigrant, a French-speaking bakery worker on his way to pick up his wife at work, oblivious to the crisis. The man was dragged from his car, his head pummeled with a hockey stick. The film and photos of the event were shown nationwide. The image was nothing less than that of a lynch mob, only blocks from the historic site where George Washington had massed troops and forced the British to depart Boston. Irony abounded, and the nation seemed genuinely wondrous. It simply did not expect such goings-on in the capital of the only state to vote for George McGovern in 1972, in the birthplace of the Abolition movement, in the "cradle of liberty." George Wallace, after carrying the city in the 1976 presidential primary, would crow that he had won "liberal Boston."

How could it have happened? When a similar question was put by a reporter to Boston Mayor Kevin White at the height of the busing crisis, White, his national image as the leader of a liveable city slipping away, snapped, "Are you from out of town?" It was dark, but appropriate humor. For, in fact, the crisis of school de-segregation came as no surprise to Bostonians. Far from being the beginning of racial strife in the city, the events of autumn 1974 —and nearly two years after—capped some 11 years of tension. They were years in which race in general—and busing for the purpose of school integration in particular—had become the city's dominant political and social issue.

It remained so until the fall of 1977, when its decline was symbolized by the defeat at the polls of City Councilor Louise Day Hicks who, as a member of the city's School Committee in the early 1960s, had built a career on vows never to end what she and her political progeny contended was a system of "neighborhood schools." By the time those vows were revealed as both hollow and cynical, the public schools in a city that is about 20 percent black had become majority non-white. Large groups of white students had boycotted school for three years. All-white private academies had been established, and almost all white Catholic schools had boomed. The city's trauma had inspired ambivalence about busing even in the most liberal quarters.

By 1977, too, however, the city had changed to the point that two bus loads of white students from South Boston would voluntarily ride buses daily to an innovative new high school in black Roxbury. A new political order—including the election of a black member to the Boston School Committee for the first time in this century—had shown signs of emerging. The city had seen the end of what had been—perhaps more blatantly so than in any other northern city—a deliberate policy of school segregation. And, without a doubt, the events that peaked in autumn 1974 had introduced the nation to a city it hadn't really known.

That Boston is not the city of prestigious universities and innovative public school systems often associated with its name. The city of Boston proper, with a population of some 650,000, is a small part of a three million-plus metropolitan area. Neither Harvard nor M.I.T. are within the city limits, nor are the widely praised school systems of suburban Brookline and Newton. Boston was, even more so in the early 1960s than today, a poor, generally white working class city, with a long history of ethnic rivalries. That history dates from the frosty—and exploitive— relationship between New England's nineteenth century Yankee gentry and the first waves of immigrant Irish. The city was the scene of Civil War riots when poor Irish resisted the imperative of affluent Yankee abolitionists for whom they worked to fight for the freedom of Southern blacks. Before Louise Day Hicks, Boston had supported the right-wing ministry of Father Coughlin in the 1930s and the McCarthy witch-hunts of the 1950s. When the race issue emerged in the 1960s, median income in parts of the Irish enclaves of South Boston and Charlestown was as low as that in black Roxbury. South Boston's D Street public housing project was—and is—among the city's worst. Even those parts of the city that were not poor were—with the exceptions of the remaining Yankee bastions of Beacon Hill and Back Bay—hardly affluent. Dorchester, the city's largest single district and predominantly white in the early 1960s, is a sea of three-family frame homes, many of whose residents watched enviously as neighbors who could afford to do so were heading for suburbia. The Italian North End and East Boston were still communities with immigrant atmospheres whose residents felt largely alienated from the dominant Irish political structure.

It was this unstable cauldron of a melting pot into which significant numbers of blacks, mainly from the Southeast and other large cities on the East Coast, came in the late 1950s. Boston had had a black community dating back to Colonial days. (Crispus Attucks, killed in the Boston Massacre, was one member.) But it traditionally has been small—perhaps five percent—and quietly lower middle class. The blacks who would swell the city's minority population to its present level were poor by comparison. They were drawn to the city, ironically, by its liberal tradition, never anticipating a day when it would be viewed as a Mississippi of the North.

The chain of events that brought racial confrontation to Boston leads back specifically to May, 1963. It was then, in the heyday of the Southern civil rights movement, that a group of blacks approached the Boston School Committee, the elected five-member board that runs the city's school system, with a series of modest demands. Among those who made the approach were Paul Parks, a civil engineer who is now the Massachusetts Secretary of Education, Ruth Batson, a Boston University psychologist, Mel King, later to be an M.I.T. faculty member and a state representative, and Kenneth Guscott, a businessman who headed the local NAACP chapter. Calling themselves the NAACP Education Committee, they were a generally middle-class group of long-time Bostonians trying to represent the aspirations of their poorer brethren. They asked the School Committee to, first, acknowledge that *de facto* segregation existed in the city—that there were identifiably black schools—and that those schools were in need of help.

It is unclear, in retrospect, whether the blacks were more concerned with quality of education or segregation. Ruth Batson, in fact, would later recall that, "I had to sell my own committee on the idea that *de facto* segregation was bad." One can only wonder what might have happened had the black parents somehow been able to see beyond the Southern model—in which white schools were, almost without exception, superior to black—and sought an alliance with whites to improve schools throughout poorer sections of the city. Both white and black schools were, in fact, plagued by poor reading achievement, low percentages of students going on to college, aging physical plants (the newest school in the city had been built in the 1930s) and faculties whose members often got jobs—and promotions—through political patronage.

An alliance between blacks and whites may well have been impossible, given the tradition of mistrust among Boston's ethnic groups. Certainly asking blacks to attempt to forge it was to ask for more than white Bostonians would have done for them. In any event, what happened after a series of seemingly conciliatory meetings was that the School Committee, spearheaded by Mrs.

Hicks, a Boston attorney and member of a well-known political family, began to espouse the attitude that would eventually lead to the involvement of the federal court in the Boston school system. If there were inferior schools in the city, said Committee member William O'Connor, they were the result of "an inferior type of student." If there were racially identifiable schools in the city, maintained Mrs. Hicks, it was only because they reflected the neighborhoods around them. The city had "neighborhood schools."

The black parents did not really dispute the latter point. They did not, at this point, charge that the School Committee had fostered segregation. They only wanted the Committee to go on record saying that segregation was socially undesirable. But Hicks would not do this. Integration, she in effect said, was less important to her than preserving neighborhood schools. With this, the sides were drawn. A generation of white Boston politicians, mainly on the School Committee, would focus on desegregation as a political bogey man. In the name of neighborhood schools, Boston would set up a system in which school assignments, the federal court would find, were based on race rather than residency.

What motivated Mrs. Hicks and those who followed her example? One can only speculate as to her true racial attitudes. But even if she were less a bigot than an opportunistic politician, she would have been drawn to the desegregation issue. Black parents were, given the Boston electoral system, a tailor-made political punching bag. Alienating them posed little risk and great potential for political gain. To understand why, one must look at the system by which Boston chooses its School Committee.

The five Committee members are winners of an election held "at-large," that is, citywide. There is no provision that various sections of the city have representation on the Committee. Most, in fact, do not and have not. Committee members have traditionally relied on one voting block—that of Boston's heavily voting, white Irish-American majority. For the most part, winning the Irish vote—more so in the early 1960s than later—meant winning an election. Thus, Hicks et al. had no political reason to be interested in blacks, but every reason to rebuff them.

Blacks were clearly useful as a symbolic menace. The School Committee, if it did nothing else, could win favor merely by seeming to protect its constituency from blacks. As the 1960s wore on and Northern riots supplanted freedom rides in the public mind, the strategy was reinforced. Hicks would go on to play the role of the mother-protector to the hilt. She would, for instance, attend, despite being asked not to, a graduation ceremony at an all-black school. As she sat quiet and long suffering on stage, she was berated for a half-hour by a firebrand black minister— unwittingly serving her political ends.

It is important to note, too, that service on the Boston School Committee is not the kind of part-time, low-profile, pro-bono endeavor sitting on such boards often is in other cities. Although members are unsalaried, they wield extraordinary control over the school system budget, which approached $100 million in the 1960s and is $200 million today. Committee members vote on the smallest of contract and personnel matters. Even today, a teacher cannot get a maternity leave without beseeching the Committee. Such power has traditionally been parlayed into political patronage. The full range of school employees—from truant officer to superintendent—have found it necessary to have political patrons. In return for employment, employees have traditionally made sizeable contributions to the election campaign funds of School Committee members. The result: ready-made political organizations.

These organizations have not been insignificant. Because Committee members do run citywide, election to the board marks one as a political power. The Committee had a reputation as a political steppingstone. One-time Boston Mayor Maurice Tobin ascended directly to the mayoralty from the Committee. And Louise Day Hicks similarly attempted to capitalize on the visibility she gained from her anti-desegregation stand on the School Committee. Starting in 1964, she ran for other offices 12 times in 13 years, seeking such diverse posts as Congresswoman and City Councilor —which she won—and mayor and state treasurer, which she lost.

The system of School Committee patronage politics was one from which blacks were excluded, and it was one black parents threatened, not so much by their request that the city endorse the goal of an integrated school system as by their focus on the quality of public education. Education had been an afterthought in the Boston public schools. Making it a priority threatened a cozy relationship between politicians and school employees. So it was that Louise Day Hicks and others found it far more useful to concentrate on the bugaboo of desegregation.

The political payoff was quick. Hicks, who had been a relatively minor candidate when first elected in 1961, became the top
vote-getter among School Committee candidates in November,
1963. She did the same in 1965, establishing herself as a strong
mayoral candidate in 1967. But just as significant as the showing
of Mrs. Hicks was an action taken by the state of Massachusetts
in 1965. It was in that year that the state legislature took aim at
the Boston public school system, passing something called the
Racial Imbalance Act, a statute without counterpart anywhere in
the nation. The law effectively mandated what Boston black
parents had asked the School Committee to agree to. It required
communities to attempt to phase out segregated schools. The state
suggested that attendance districts be drawn and new schools
situated toward that end, and the law gave the appointed State
Board of Education power to withhold funds from school systems not complying with the act.

The state's action was to prove a key and unique element in
the Boston busing saga. Rather than forcing an end to the type of
racial politics the School Committee had begun to practice, the
law served to encourage it. Hicks and company now had a new
improved villian against which to protect their constituents. Had
the law not been passed, the busing issue might well have faded
in Boston. The federal government, it should be noted, had made
it clear at the time that it was not about to withhold educational
aid on the basis of *de facto* segregation. Thus the Racial Imbalance Act effectively imposed a standard on the Boston schools
unlike that on any other big city school system. What's more, it
provided city politicians with new antagonists: "hypocritical" suburban liberals who were accused of asking the city to live up to a
standard of racial justice from which overwhelmingly white suburbs were immune. This argument, although clearly self-serving,
had significant elements of truth. The law aimed at Boston would
not reach the municipalities of most legislators who had voted for
it. More important, however, its passage provided city politicians the opportunity to tap deep historical resentments held by
the immigrant Irish against the landed gentry, the Yankees associated with the new law. (Among them was Mary Parkman Peabody, civil rights activist and mother of then Governor Endicott
Peabody.) As Boston journalist Alan Lupo has pointed out in his
book *Liberty's Chosen Home*, this class resentment, complete

with its racial component, paralleled the Irish reaction to the Civil War, in which the poorly paid Irish servants of Yankee families were asked to risk their lives in the cause of Abolition. Indeed, just as the law of that era allowed the wealthy to hire stand-ins to fight, so did twentieth century political boundaries protect affluent, suburban Bostonians from the demands of the Racial Imbalance Act.

Ultimately the School Committee's resistance to the Racial Imbalance Act would not avert busing, but make it inevitable. To keep their promise to avoid integration, officials had to take direct, *de jure* actions to keep the races apart. This long series of actions, which began seriously in 1966, was aimed particularly at high schools. It included redrawing school district lines, expanding overcrowded white schools but leaving seats vacant in black schools, and eventually establishing a system by which blacks went to high schools whose student bodies were drawn from throughout the city (or at least from all black neighborhoods) while most whites retained the right to attend neighborhood schools, unless they lived too close to a black neighborhood. Judge Garrity would write:

> A dual system of secondary education was created, one for each race. Segregation could not be maintained without complex changes being made (in the school enrollment system). The defendants made such changes for the purpose of promoting racial segregation and accomplished their purpose.

To understand why such complex changes were necessary, one must understand the demographics and geography of Boston. Unlike Chicago, Detroit, or Cleveland, the black community in Boston, although concentrated in select areas, is not isolated from, but contiguous to, white neighborhoods. There is no Boston equivalent to Chicago's South Side or Cleveland's East Side. Blacks and whites are separated by a series of shifting dividing lines—hills, main streets, parks. If the school district and enrollment system of the early 1960s had been left unchanged, some degree of integration would have occurred naturally. It would have come even to all-white South Boston, a peninsula whose closest neighboring community—the next peninsula south—is the site of the predominantly black Columbia Point public housing project. To avoid sending Columbia Point students to South Boston High, school officials had them *bused* miles across town to the predominantly black English High School.

The 1974 federal court decision would in large part be a compendium of deliberate contortions that school officials, reflecting the wishes of elected officials, went through in order to maintain segregation. The state Board of Education, with its power to withhold state aid, was simply no match for the city pols of Boston. The most famous demonstration of the relationship between the state and city came following the construction of a new Boston middle school—the Joseph Lee—built with state aid on the condition that it would open as a racially balanced school. Since it was built on the border of white and black Dorchester neighborhoods, that seemed a likely prospect. Further, the May before the school was set to open in 1971, the School Committee affirmed its prospective integration through student assignments. But by fall of that year, the Committee—specifically member John Craven—had flip-flopped. Seeking to move to a position on the City Council, Craven had fared poorly in the September preliminary election. As an apparently direct consequence, he, along with Committee members John Kerrigan and Joseph Lee, voted to allow students at a white school, many of whom were slated to attend Lee, the option instead of remaining at the white school. So politicized was the atmosphere surrounding the decision that the Committee held the meeting at the white school affected. Judge Garrity, later reviewing the minutes of that meeting, would describe it as a "political rally." Craven was praised by a host of politicians—including then member of Congress, Louise Day Hicks, there for the occasion. The Lee School opened as a black school.

John Craven did not go on to a particularly successful political career. But there is no doubt that opposition to busing continued to pay political dividends in Boston. Its power was demonstrated particularly in School Committee elections. The 1967 election saw, for instance, the emergence of a successor to Hicks, who left the board to run for mayor. Dorchester attorney John Kerrigan, who is said to have entered politics after a bet that he could capitalize on his name (one John E. Kerrigan was a popular long-time City Councilor), would become the most explicit race-baiter of all. In contrast to Hicks, who couched her sentiments in code words and spoke in a girlish voice, Kerrigan delighted in crude characterizations of blacks. An effective demagogue, Kerrigan added to the Hicks formula for political success by linking the "liberal media"—specifically the *Boston Globe*—to pro-desegregation forces and, on that basis, attacked the press. The *Globe* was a useful target: it is owned and edited by affluent, suburban Yankees. Kerrigan's press-baiting prompted *Globe* political columnist Martin Nolan later to dub the school Committeeman, who hails from Dorchester's Ashmont section, the "Ashmont Agnew."

It seems clear that Kerrigan acted out of desire to capitalize on the race issue as much as any genuine prejudice. An incident that particularly reveals his attitude was related by one-time School Committee member Paul McDevitt. In the wake of Roxbury riots, which followed the assassination of Martin Luther King, McDevitt proposed that a Roxbury middle school be renamed in honor of the slain civil rights leader. The school was, in fact, so named. Kerrigan, McDevitt later recalled, cautioned his colleague as a result. "This is going to hurt you, this being up-front and appearing to be pro-black," Kerrigan said. "You are going to jeopardize your re-election so long as you are up front on this issue. Try to make some conservative statements so white voters will not get the perception that you have been leaning toward pro-busing." McDevitt did not do so and failed to win re-election in 1969.

Politics and busing, then, were inextricably intertwined. They would remain so even after 11 years of campaign promises failed to deter a federal court. The city's leading busing resistance organization, formed after the court order and called ROAR (Restore Our Alienated Rights), was founded and in part led by Louise Day Hicks's City Council staff aides. (Hicks became a Council member in 1973.) In 1975 ROAR gained even new strength with the election of Elvira "Pixie" Palladino to its East Boston Chapter.

Nonetheless, as early as 1967, there was a clear sign the antibus ride had a limit for Boston politicians, a limit that would also apply to the city's resistance to the 1974 court order. That limit emerged when Louise Day Hicks failed in her bid to become mayor of the city. One can only shudder to think of what fate might have befallen Boston had she won. One of the nation's most delicate and explosive eras of race relations was in progress, and indeed, following Martin Luther King's assassination, riots came to Roxbury as they came elsewhere. Hicks had given a hint, in her campaign, of how she might have handled the situation. In reaction to promises of restraint during rioting by her opponent, then, Massachusetts Secretary of State Kevin White, Hicks said she would order police to "use the weapons they have" to quell a disturbance. She was not to have the chance to give such orders, however. Although the School Committeewoman had topped five candidates in the September mayoral primary election—a run-off that determines the final two contenders—she had received as many votes as she would get in November. There was, the city found, a hard-core Hicks constituency, but it was not a majority of the electorate. Her strength, it turned out, was in poor white sections where most families rented. In wards of heavy home ownership, her totals dipped. She was too extreme for the mayor's job, voters in such areas apparently felt. Their distaste for Hicks was shared by Italian, black, and the city's few liberal voters. Kevin White, son of a well-known city politician but a comparative unknown, parlayed anti-Hicks sentiment into victory and set about casting himself as a Lindsay-style liberal.

A pattern of Hicks' defeats—important reflections of the city electorate—had been set. Hicks never, in her long career, won an election against just one opponent. In School Committee and City Council contests—where voters have five and nine votes to distribute respectively—she triumphed. But in 1971, as in 1967, she was defeated by Kevin White in her bid for the mayoralty, and in 1972, after a term in Congress (she won the seat in a three-way race), she was defeated for re-election by John J. Moakley, a city councilor from South Boston who capitalized on the black vote in a district that includes Roxbury. Even in 1976, when busing fervor had again climbed as a result of the court order, Hicks failed to win a one-on-one race for the obscure post of Suffolk County Register of Deeds.

Similar limits to the city's willingness to resist school desegregation would eventually emerge when the long-feared "forced busing" became a reality in 1974. There were, however, days when it seemed as if there were no limit to the crisis engulfing the city. It was a crisis the magnitude of which the city had not experienced since a wave of lawlessness followed the famed 1919 police strike. Once again, it seemed as if the fabric of social order was endangered. Blacks and whites alike were accosted as they wandered through the others' neighborhoods. High schools were equipped with airport-style metal detectors. A black businessman was attacked by a group of South Boston teenagers who had attended an anti-busing rally on City Hall Plaza. They attempted to spear him with a pole on the other end of which hung an American flag. (A photograph of the event won a Pulitzer Prize.)

In retrospect, Mayor Kevin White and his Police Commissioner Robert DiGrazia must be credited with seeing the city through the siege. DiGrazia, a California native, was the only well-known city official who dared label violent busing resisters "hoodlums" and cast their actions as blatantly racist. White and DiGrazia, it can fairly be said, played the role that Robert Kennedy and Nicholas Katzenbach played in Alabama in 1963, at a time when the sympathies of the federal government had, in fact, shifted. (Gerald Ford pointedly criticized the Boston desegregation order at an October, 1974 press conference.) White's triumph in maintaining some semblance of order came, ironically, while his own ambitions for national office were being dealt a fatal blow by the bad publicity the city suddenly received.

There is obvious reason for the depth of resistance to the court's desegregation order: the city's voters had been promised for more than a decade that such an eventuality would not come about. Their will, many believed, had been overturned by a non-elected judge—a judge who lived in affluent Wellesley. But there were other reasons for the chaos that engulfed the city. The court order itself was not the best-designed. Students living in integrated neighborhoods were bused to integrate schools in all-white areas. Such assignments perplexed those who felt neighborhood schools in integrated neighborhoods were ideal. In addition, the School Department, not unexpectedly, contributed to the confusion. Many students found their school assignments late in arriving, and school officials sometimes named persons with avowed anti-busing sympathies as aides charged with keeping schools calm.

Perhaps most significantly, however, was the absence of moral certainty about the busing order that had accompanied similar orders in the South. Blacks themselves were ambivalent about their victory. To end a policy of deliberate segregation in which they were victimized, they were asked to brave rocks so as to integrate schools of poor quality. A black aide to Kevin White later said that his first reaction upon entering South Boston High with the first bus load of black students was, "All this trouble to get into this dump?" What is more, the Boston area's nationally known liberal community was constrained during this crisis. Its own house was not in order. Liberals were, after all, concentrated in white suburbs. As never in the South, the confusing issues of race and economic class crossed in Boston. Although it was the segregative actions of the School Committee that had created the necessity for busing, this became a subtlety forgotten by many. What was more obvious was the fact that less affluent whites and blacks were being ordered to co-exist peacefully, while more affluent members of both races were insulated from the consequences. That insulation seemed to be constantly underscored. Senator Edward Kennedy, suddenly persona non grata with the Boston Irish because of his support for the court order, told this writer, in a published interview, that if he lived in Boston he would send his children to private school. Columnist Jimmy Breslin, in town from New York, pointed up the contrast between South Boston High and Milton Academy, a bastion of privilege only a few miles to the south. Such contrasts provided powerful fuel for the busing resistance.

The impact of the court order on the city's schools, in fact, gave pause even to those committed to racial justice. Although token presences of blacks and whites appeared in previously segregated institutions, many schools remained identifiably white or black. It is difficult to know how much of the much-ballyhooed white flight occurred from the city. It does not appear to have been widespread—many whites could not afford suburbia. What did undeniably take place, however, was a withdrawal of the middle class from the public schools in large numbers. Parochial schools, long a major alternative system in the city, enjoyed a renaissance notwithstanding an admonition from Humberto Cardinal Medeiros against their use as "havens." (Medeiros, of Portuguese extraction, has little influence over the Boston Irish.) Private schools profited from the crisis as well, drawing the support of both white liberal parents from the city's Beacon Hill, Back Bay, and South End sections and black parents, many of whom did not want to thrust their children into what they saw as a dangerous situation. Black parents in addition continued to avail themselves of a program in which black students are bused in small numbers to affluent suburbs. The net result was—and is— a non-white, overwhelmingly poor Boston public school system.

But if the court order did not accomplish all it may have been designed to do, neither could it be said, overall, to have been a failure. It has, in fact, set in motion what may well be long-term improvements in the Boston schools, improvements that almost incidentally include integration. As part of the court order, there has been established a series of "magnet schools"—the court called them the "magic" in its plan—whose innovative curricula, including arts and vocational courses, have drawn students, black and white, from throughout the city. Many have been strikingly successful against all odds. Roxbury's Martin Luther King School, with its symbolic name and location in one of the city's poorest black neighborhoods, has been able to attract enough white students to remain open. (All magnet schools must be racially balanced.) It did so after extraordinary efforts by faculty members, many of whom went door-to-door in white neighborhoods in recruiting efforts. Such effort by teachers was almost unknown before desegregation. Parents, too, have become more involved in the school system, in part because of a court-established system of elected parent councils for every school. The court's supervision has also been responsible for the hiring of innovative administrators, most notably at South Boston High School. Owing to School Department recalcitrance, the court assumed direct control over the school and brought in a crew of Minnesota administrators to run it. It is safe to say none would have ever had a chance of being hired in Boston in the days before the court's involvement in the schools.

Led by headmaster Jerome Winegar, however, the court-appointed staff has not only calmed the school—plagued by suspensions the first year of busing—but completely shaken up the faculty and encouraged unusual programs. Business students, for instance, have, with the help of advice from the staff of the Boston Federal Reserve Bank, operated a store in Boston's well-known Fanueil Hall Market. Such "pairings" have been set up by the court throughout the city. Major businesses, universities, and museums now conduct programs in many of the public schools, haltingly bringing together the Boston of national repute with the city as experienced by its residents.

But busing has always been as much a political as educational issue, and, in that context, too, there is cause for fledgling optimism about race relations in the city. The November, 1977 elections especially provided reason for tentative hope that race is fading as the city's dominant political reality. Those elections saw the defeat of the three incumbent members of the City Council and School Committee who had based their careers on opposition to busing: Elvira Palladino, John Kerrigan and, most surprisingly, Louise Day Hicks. At the same time, voters elected the first black School Committee member since the five-member board was established in 1896. He is John O'Bryant, a career educator whose credentials, including a master's degree in education, make his presence on the board as unusual as does his race.

The scenario of 1967 has been replayed. The majority of the city, while still opposed to busing, has accepted it as inevitable and rejected what had come to be viewed as extremist resistance. Behavior that was condoned in 1975 alienated the majority of Bostonians two years later. Even more heartening, though, was the fact that candidate O'Bryant was able to attract significant numbers of votes in what have been viewed as conservative white areas. His election also reflected increased black voter sophistication. Many blacks had "bulleted" for O'Bryant, marking only his name and not using their four other votes. This strategy, long practiced in politically sophisticated parts of the city, made white politicians take notice after the election. It seemed to indicate that the day in which the black community could be discounted politically, a key element in anti-busing politics, had ended. Indeed, just as Vietnam has made foreign intervention by the United States unimaginable today, so the busing crisis, having passed, has made it impossible to imagine a major Boston politician rising on the race issue today. An exorcism of sorts has occurred.

Boston is not the same city that began the road to busing in 1963. It has changed demographically and in its thinking. An influx of young, middle-class professionals, many suburban-bred, into what were parochial white neighborhoods has created the makings of a greater liberal constituency. So, too, have attitudes held by the new generation of native Bostonians, whose parents catapulted Mrs. Hicks into prominence. The city's new generation of Irish politicians reflects this change. Absent are the old demagogues. Younger officials show an ability and a willingness to discuss the city with sophistication. Among the new politicians is David Finnegan, current head of the School Committee and a graduate of Boston University Law School, who has made halting steps toward dismantling the patronage system that has dominated the School Department. The likelihood appears strong that he, as part of a reform School Committee majority that also includes John O'Bryant and three-term member Kathleen Sullivan

Alioto (wife of former San Francisco Mayor Joseph Alioto), will hire the first school superintendent in Boston history not to have risen through the ranks of the school system. Finnegan speaks plainly about the need to draw the city's middle class back to the public schools.

The city has come a long way in 15 years from the time when black parents called for improvement and desegregation of the schools. It has travelled a long, dead-end path of resistance, which culminated in crisis. And it has only begun to pursue the road it shunned in 1963. There is cause for regret but cause, too—at long last—for optimism.

*Despite having what the NAACP has described as the "most classically segregated" school system it has ever encountered, Chicago has not had to deal with a court-ordered busing plan. A limited number of the city's black students have, however, been bused to less crowded schools in white neighborhoods, and in this report David Moberg, staff writer for* In These Times, *explores the angry reactions this move has caused and what they suggest about Chicago's ability to face court-ordered busing in the future.*

# Chicago

## DAVID MOBERG

It was the first day of school on Chicago's far Southwest Side. Outside of Sawyer elementary school, in a homey working class neighborhood of the just barely prospering sons and daughters of immigrants, there was a cluster of grim looking mothers.

Near the corner of the school, two blond boys, Chris, 11, and Ralph, 9, were watching the action. They had no intention of going to school that day, but they did want to see the bus pull up with the anticipated 29 black students.

The bus riders were coming to underused Sawyer from overcrowded Henderson school. It was only minutes away by bus, but the gulf of experience—symbolized by Western Avenue, the current dividing line between black and white in that part of town—made it seem like a vast distance.

Then a nervously smiling, white-haired minister greeted the two boys as he approached their corner.

Part of this article appeared in different form in *In These Times* (Sept. 28–Oct. 4. 1977) and is reprinted here with permission.

"You here to give the black kids their final blessings?" Chris asked.

No, he said, but he did want to tell the boys that some of the black students on the bus came from a Methodist church, just as they did. He'd met them a couple of weeks earlier while eating dinner at the nearby black Methodist church.

"You mean you ate with them?" Ralph asked incredulously. Then, with a mixture of snide self-assurance and genuine curiosity, he probed further, "What did they eat? Soul food?"

"They eat just like you," the clergyman said, "except they don't have Polish sausages and sauerkraut."

"Well," Chris warned, despite the near bridge of humanity— *sans* sauerkraut and a Polish sausage—"if they take refuge in your church, the white kids are going to bomb it."

Later the preacher found signs of hope in the conversation. Chris had only said "the white kids" would bomb the church, not that he would. It was a day when such little signs were taken as blessings.

Despite the tensions, despite the fears beforehand, a few white kids had black kids in class with them for the first time. And the earth did not open up and swallow the city whole.

## SEPARATE AND UNEQUAL, CHICAGO-STYLE

September 7, 1977, both was and wasn't the start of desegregation in Chicago public schools. The "permissive transfer" plan that brought kids from Henderson to Sawyer had been operating since 1963 to relieve "critical overcrowding" in some schools. But in 1977 its level of operation changed. Fifteen critically over-crowded elementary "sending" schools were matched with 51 "receiving" schools. Buses, instead of tokens for public transportation, were provided for the youngest students. The total of eligible students was expanded to 6,500, a tiny fraction of the more than a half million students in the Chicago public school system. Ultimately, only about one-sixth of those eligible spots were filled with transfers, and in many cases the transfers were of black students from one overcrowded, segregated school to another less crowded but still segregated building. In short, nothing very dramatic happened. However, for the first time a few black students transferred into elementary schools that feed into Bogan

High School in the all-white Ashburn neighborhood on the south-west fringe of the city.

Since 1963 a strident, determined band of women, commonly dubbed "the Bogan broads," had blocked every effort to permit blacks into the schools in their area. They became a convenient ex-cuse for politicians and educators who also had no interest in de-segregating schools in Chicago, the most segregated major city in the country according to standard indices of racial separate-ness.

In theory the school board, appointed by the mayor, and school administrators have long-standing promises on record to de-segregate schools. However, like the politicians who ultimately control the nominally autonomous school board, these officials have not only bowed to existing residential segregation and racial bigotry but also deliberately furthered segregation in the schools. Such conscious segregation continued even in recent years while the city has been under numerous legal compulsions to move in the opposite direction.

Chicago politicians had long acted to defend racially discrimi-natory covenants in the private housing market, to build public housing in a way that concentrated poor blacks in the traditional ghetto, and to maintain a dual, discriminatory labor market in both the private and public spheres. The pattern was set in the 1920s and has been maintained without breach by the city's leaders ever since. Even Mayor Ed Kelly, boss of Chicago from 1933 to 1947, was not reslated by the Democratic party when he broke with the tradition and supported open housing.

Over and above that, the school board intensified the segrega-tion within the public schools. Especially in the decades after World War II, Chicago expanded schools in crowded black neigh-borhoods rather than send black children into empty classrooms in nearby white schools. Sometimes new schools were built, but often the black schools were expanded with supposedly tem-porary mobile units in the school playgrounds, some of which are still in place. District lines were gerrymandered to increase seg-regation. The faculty was highly segregated in its assignment, in-creasing identification of schools as all black or all white. Voca-tional education for the skilled trades was literally 99 percent white in 1962 and little has changed a decade later. All these de-liberately discriminatory policies have since been verified in court cases or other public reviews. Along with this racial division came discrimination in spending. Even in 1976, according to a study by The Chicago Reporter, white elementary schools received 7.3 percent more money per student than black schools.

The legal mandate to Chicago schools should have been clear. There were not only the 1954 Supreme Court decision against school segregation and the Civil Rights Act of 1964 but also the 1963 Illinois statute, the Armstrong act, which outlawed school segregation. Despite two official studies in 1964 that documented the segregated patterns, recommended some measures to reverse such division, and warned that the problem would only worsen with delay, Chicago continued to perpetuate rigid segregation, especially of blacks and whites, slightly less with Latinos. On a scale where 100 indicates total separation of races, Chicago's black-white segregation index in 1977 was 91, virtually unchanged from a decade before. While other cities were forced to desegregate under court order, usually as a result of NAACP lawsuits, Chicago was spared. However, since the late 1950s the local NAACP had been dominated by blacks loyal to Mayor Richard Daley, and the national organization—which renewed its threat to sue the city in the spring of 1978—has said that it did not have the $750,000 to $1 million needed to fight Chicago in the courts.

Finally the Justice Department told the city to end discriminatory assignments of teachers. Despite efforts to delay or circumvent the order, school administrators began in the spring of 1977 to shuffle 2,000 teachers and principals around the system, but often in extremely awkward ways that led critics to suspect that administrators were trying to stir up further resentment at the desegregation orders. At the same time the state board of education put the city schools on probation for a year. Chicago had not met student desegregation guidelines issued four years earlier. By March 1978 the school board was expected to present a plan to meet the state guidelines, which specify that all schools should have student populations within 15 percent of the racial proportions of the district. In 1977 the system's enrollment by racial category was 60 percent black, 23.2 percent white, and 15.1 percent Latino.

Although a poll in the fall of 1977 showed that nearly four-fifths of Chicagoans expected more desegregation to come eventually—and peacefully—attention turned to the diehard opponents in the Bogan area. However, in some other white neighborhoods parents and PTA leaders actually welcomed black students. They wanted to keep up dwindling enrollments to preserve programs that might otherwise have been cut. Even the isolated opposition in the Bogan area was less hostile than feared.

When the anti-desegregation forces were rebuffed in their request for a three-year moratorium on desegregation of their neighborhood schools, they announced plans for school picketing and boycotts on opening day and every Friday afterwards. That quickly provoked fears of violence, especially when a policeman from the Ashburn area told the August school board meeting that white policemen would get "blue flu" rather than protect black school children. Black leaders, including Rev. Jesse Jackson, called on the city police to abandon their plans for a "low profile" on opening day. The city responded with pieties about the need for a peaceful start to school—but no defense of desegregation—and promised adequate police protection.

Opponents of the transfers called off their opening day pickets, citing fear of pro-integration "radicals," but first day attendance was off by 80 percent in Bogan area schools—much, but not all, indicating support for the boycott. (In neighboring Marquette Park, by contrast, the school turnout was down by only 20 percent.) Attendance in the targeted schools soon returned to normal, however. The Friday boycotts were dropped, although routine picketing continued at some schools for a couple months. However, a September 11 antibusing rally of 1,000 turned disorderly when a speaker without a park permit was arrested. Rocks were thrown at passing black motorists. One black driver struck three demonstrators as he tried, according to his account, to flee a mob attacking his car.

Although Mayor Michael Bilandic urged protection of the students in the transfer program, he contributed to the intransigence of the desegregation opponents by expressing his doubts about the merits of busing after meeting with the hard core leaders from the Bogan area. Newspaper editorialists, black leaders, and the head of the regional office of the U.S. Commission on Civil Rights stepped up their criticism of the mayor's leadership, which had been vacillating at best.

During the fall a City Wide Advisory Committee, drawn from school districts and community organizations throughout the city, worked on proposals for desegregation of schools, despite what members described as Superintendent Joseph Hannon's thoroughly non-cooperative attitude. They were assisted by a special outside advisor, Edward A. Welling, who had gotten off to a bad start with a proposal for preliminary integration through closed-circuit television, presumably in color.

CWAC eventually advocated a largely voluntary program—permissive transfers, open enrollment in general high schools, expansion of magnet schools and academic interest centers, elimination of the mobile units at crowded schools, and clustering elementary schools to cover a wider area and greater ethnic variation. After a long, see-saw discussion, they eventually agreed to include a provision for a mandatory back-up if the voluntary means did not bring about sufficiently swift change.

State guidelines require that a voluntary program include a mandatory back-up. The Chicago school administrators had always avoided any sign of compulsion, pleading with the state to trust their "goodwill." But the goodwill of the city school board has frequently been called in question and not only by their delays on desegregating schools. Following Hannon's lead, they also refused in 1978 to target special state aid for disadvantaged children to poverty areas and instead included it in the general budget. It was not a sign of concern about redressing the inequities in Chicago's schools. Instead, it indicated the problem of trusting the existing powers to produce "quality education for all," often offered as an alternative to desegregation.

Having gone through the formalities of soliciting citizen opinion, Hannon and his staff then drew up their own plan, "Access to Excellence." Just as he had promised, it was entirely voluntary, specifically rejecting any mandatory back-up. It did not even include the CWAC proposal for clustered elementary schools. On nearly every other point, "Access to Excellence" scaled down the ambitions of the CWAC proposal, which had itself decided that the strict state guidelines for desegregation were too rigid for the huge, divided city. However, Hannon substituted a very weak standard: schools would be considered desegregated if they had at least 10 percent white or black students in a school that was otherwise predominately the other race.

Critics immediately assaulted "Access to Excellence" as a potentially well-meaning but extremely fuzzy proposal for some educational innovations that contributed virtually nothing to desegregation. Welling, who was absent when Hannon presented the plan, later urged that a mandatory back-up be included. Welling also calculated that the plan would increase the number of "full-time equivalent" students in desegregated settings by a maximum of 4.23 percent over the current 13–14 percent. The "full-time equivalent" figures were themselves an overly generous estimate of the program's impact. Many of Hannon's proposals involved bringing together black and white kids for part of a day, a few weeks, or some other brief period. Most integration experts did not consider that meaningful segregation. Welling's criticisms apparently were not well received. He was fired shortly after making them.

A committee of educational experts reporting to the state board of education was even less impressed with "Access to Excellence." The state Technical Assistance Committee slashed Welling's estimate of the number of students likely to be affected by more than half and soundly rejected the part-time or even summer school integration as meeting legal requirements or educational standards for desegregation. Moreover, they calculated that the costs under the plan were staggering—$18,000 to $40,000 for each child desegregated full-time for five years. "These costs would be so high, of course," the committee wrote, "because most of the money requested for this program has nothing to do with full-time desegregation, or even any desegregation at all. It is an effort to transfer to state and federal funding, under the rubric of 'equal opportunity,' a wide range of educational programs Chicago school officials wish to support." Straightforward busing would have been far cheaper.

The committee couldn't have been much blunter in its final conclusion: "The plan submitted by the Chicago Board of Education will not, in its present form, produce substantial desegregation as required by state law and the Constitution." Moreover, it wrote, the city and school district had long violated rules intended to reverse their status as the nation's most segregated school system and had "produced little or no increased desegregation" with any of their actions. A voluntary plan simply would not work, it said, but a voluntary plan with a mandatory back-up could work, since many parents would take advantage of options such as magnet schools if they realized that the alternative was busing to some school not of their choice.

Finally, the committee suggested that true desegregation would have to be undertaken on a metropolitan basis. The record bears them out. Segregated housing patterns have been extending into the suburbs in recent years, and even without increased "white flight," the percentage of blacks and Latinos in the Chicago public schools will probably reach 85 percent within the next decade. The city schools alone cannot provide significant integration under those circumstances. Moreover, the suburban schools are nearly one-fifth empty now, and many have had to close for lack of students. In addition there is the situation of Chicago's Catholic schools. Nearly two-thirds as many white children in Chicago attend Catholic schools as the public schools, providing a needed population for integration of education. Although the Catholic schools are less segregated than the public schools, the Archdiocese has shown little evidence of interest in helping blacks or in promoting desegregation. At the close of the 1977–78 school year, for example, a highly successful Catholic school serving black students was shut down, continuing a trend toward abandonment of inner-city Catholic schools.

Despite the criticisms and a unanimous "no" vote by the state board's Equal Education Opportunity Committee, the Illinois state board accepted the Hannon plan if certain "deficiencies" were corrected by December 1, 1978. But the "deficiencies" went to the heart of the Hannon plan: more full-time desegregation, a change in the city's definition of desegregation, more vocational education desegregation, and a mandatory back-up plan. Ultimately the board and state Superintendent Joseph M. Cronin could have used their strongest sanction: withhold money. They didn't, and most observers expect that they never will, thus permitting Chicago to shuffle along with a desegregation plan that doesn't desegregate. Why? The legislature would most likely immediately step in to make the state superintendent of schools elective again rather than appointed, to repeal the Armstrong act, or to amend the act to prohibit busing.

Meanwhile, Chicago's political leaders have no desire to proceed with desegregation. They do not see any immediate threat to their power if they don't budge. Latinos have taken little interest so far in desegregation. Blacks, who often are lukewarm about certain forms of busing, are politically divided. Many black votes are still controlled by the machine. Otherwise the turnout in recent elections has been low enough that a black rebellion at the polls doesn't seem to worry the powerful Democratic machine.

The primary political agenda for the machine is not desegregation or improving the conditions of the black and Latino majority in the city but rather revitalization of the downtown area, expansion of middle-income housing in the area around the Loop and along the shore of Lake Michigan, and seduction of white professional and middle-class families away from the suburbs and into the city. School board member and University of Chicago education professor Edgar Epps maintains that "Access to Excellence" was designed to attract these whites through the provision of magnet schools that would have high standards of admission and classical schools that would appeal to middle-class whites. "The kind of plan Hannon proposed is probably an accurate reflection of his own philosophical position," Epps said, "and I think it's also his reading of the political situation."

Part of that situation is the Bogan neighborhood. "The school board needs Bogan terribly," Meyer Weinberg, editor of *Integrateducation,* said. "They would be in trouble if Bogan didn't make the school board appear middle-of-the-road. Bogan plays a necessary role, but a symbolic role, since it really has no power."

How has this one small neighborhood become every politician's excuse for not desegregating education? The answer has to do with far more than schools.

### "OUR MISSISSIPPI"

To many Chicagoans who are liberals, sympathetic to the idea of integration, or in some way appalled by racism, the Southwest Side is an embarrassment—"our Mississippi."

In 1966, for example, Martin Luther King was stoned when he led an open housing march into the area east and slightly north of Ashburn, commonly known as Marquette Park. The American Nazi Party set up its headquarters there shortly afterwards with hopes of finding receptive ears for their virulent "white power" message. Homes of black families moving into the fringes of the area, but still east of Western Avenue, have suffered the by now predictable assaults of everything from bricks to firebombs. Blacks passing through the Marquette Park area are often physically attacked.

In June 1976, a tiny, obscure group calling itself the Martin Luther King, Jr. Movement attempted to march into Marquette Park. Led by three black ministers, lacking any community base or backing from most other black organizations, the group had vaguely articulated demands, no clear strategy, and tactics unthinkingly lifted from the civil rights movement of the 1960s. Usually blocked by police and the courts from marching, they succeeded in leading 125 to 150 supporters into Marquette Park in July 1976. They were pelted by bricks, stones, bottles, beer cans, and other missiles thrown by an outraged mob of at least 1,000 angry whites.

In the summer of 1977, several white mobs raged through the streets attacking black motorists when a King Movement march, which they had been anticipating, was called off at the last minute.

All this gives a picture of the Southwest Side as deeply racist, inclined to violence, and open to rightwing politics. Although true of some people, it is neither complete nor fair as a sketch of the neighborhood. Most of the people living in the Marquette Park and Ashburn areas are relatively skilled blue-collar workers, lower-level white-collar workers, small businessmen, and city employees, including many policemen. A bit above average in income and below average in unemployment, it is a neighborhood where people are struggling to pay off mortgages on their brick bungalows or two- and four-flat apartments. Hard work, frugality, connections, and a white face have given these skilled workers from twentieth century immigrant families a small margin of affluence.

The Catholic church is strong, and people often think of themselves as living in a parish, St. Rita's or St. Nick's, for example, rather than Chicago Lawn, the official name of the Marquette Park area. Although many families have been rooted in the neighborhood for many years, there is also a large and influential bloc of people who have moved there within the last decade to escape from neighborhoods to the east that were becoming all black. The change of their neighborhood generated great bitterness. Some people lost money on their hurried sales. Although blacks were usually blamed, the disruption and rapid resegregation was in large part a result of the actions of powerful financial interests.

Panic-peddling and solicitation by realtors were commonplace. Savings and loans institutions that were filled with neighborhood money redlined white neighborhoods near black communities, refusing or setting difficult terms for mortgages or home improvement loans. Unscrupulous mortgage bankers sold houses in bad repair to blacks who could not afford to keep up the house or payments. Mortgages were quickly foreclosed, and the buildings abandoned to vandalism, while the mortgage holders collected their guaranteed profits—the problem worsened after Federal Housing Administration loan requirements were greatly loosened in 1968.

Nobody makes money from a house with a mortgage already paid off, but everybody in the real estate business could take a cut out of the rapid circulation of houses through the frightened market.

Meanwhile, savings and loan institutions were investing the money of Southwestsiders in a massive overbuilding of suburban housing. Young whites, who might otherwise have settled in their home city neighborhoods, found it easier to get housing out in the suburbs, where their liberally spent dollars went to new shopping centers rather than the commercial strips of the Southwest Side.

Across the racial divide, the black population was growing with immigration from the South. The housing stock available in the center city was shrinking. Landlord neglect of old buildings, highway construction, and urban renewal laid waste to large sections of land. City and private money then, and now, went to redevelop desirable parcels of that land to attract middle-class whites to the city. In the process, blacks were pushed to compete with white workers on the south and west sides of the city for moderate-priced housing. Whites on the Southwest Side now look at poor black neighborhoods where many of them once lived and see boarded-up buildings, vacant storefronts, and a neighborhood in desrepair. They rarely see the black neighborhoods on the South Side that are as neat as theirs, with blacks cleaning gutters on Saturday afternoons and worrying about mortgages just as they do.

They fear crime, and when they hear "black," they think of crime. This tension is worsened on the Southwest Side by an unfortunate juxtaposition. The white neighborhood has one of the lowest crime rates in the city. Englewood, the adjacent black neighborhood, has one of the highest incidences of crime in the city. In addition to this situation, there are also deep hurts and angers among individual whites. Especially on the Southwest Side, rumors spread and amplify bad individual white experiences with racial conflict into firmly believed myths of black savagery. Hatreds flow back and forth, at times erupting into violence from both sides.

Many Southwest Side whites resent government at all levels. They feel that unresponsive politicians dictate how they should live, take away their "rights" (with the "neighborhood school," for example, becoming a virtual constitutional right), and give everything to blacks at their expense. Anti-desegregationist leader Connie Schaeffer, president of the Bogan Community Council, for example, attacks the protective guard for bused-in kids as setting up a "police state" in Ashburn.

Most neighborhood people share an intense version of the American credo that everyone can and should pull him or herself up by the bootstraps. "I think it's good that people have to struggle to get ahead, have to work hard," says Francine Fatima, wife of a policeman and one of the anti-busing leaders. A vast number of Southwestsiders also see blacks as lazy welfare parasites. They reject any government action to eliminate poverty, arguing that they or their parents could make it. Why can't blacks?

Wouldn't full employment for blacks in the city also benefit whites by strengthening and stabilizing black communities? "Niggers don't want to work," is the standard answer.

School desegregation triggers a whole complex of anxieties. Outside of some Southwest Side elementary schools on the first day of school, neighborhood women and teenagers voiced many of the common obsessions: "They get you through the schools. . . . We're hurt—hurt by the way the government is running the country. . . . They'll want to live close. That's the next step. . . . We're going to be forced to sell our houses. . . . If they want better education, why don't they improve their schools instead of wrecking ours? . . . How many homes are going on sale today? . . . Why can't they keep the schools like they used to be? . . . The school board is using our kids as pawns just to get state and federal money. . . . If the schools go broke, why are they spending money on these buses? . . . It's our tax money that built these schools. Now they want to take them away from us. . . . Our backs are to the city wall. Where can we go?"

Yet one young mother, who shared many of these worries, also added, "No one is objecting to these little kids coming and getting a good education. They're worried about their houses. There are a lot of narrow-minded people here just worried about their money. "People here will accept it (transfers). There really wasn't much of a showing against it. They feel it won't do any good. They have no confidence in their politicians."

I noted a number of "Nigger Beware" signs plastered about by the Nazis. "I hate it," said Linda, who had brought her son to school despite the boycott call. "I tell him to avoid kids like that, kids who mimic that kind of language. It's difficult in this neighborhood to teach him to be a decent human being when you have to fight off kids like that." Yet Linda, like so many moderates in the neighborhood, felt that she was in a minority. She keeps quiet.

Those fostering a hostile race consciousness have been most vocal. Many of the leaders are actively involved with numerous "new right" issues, politicians, and organizations. Francine Fatima, a local leader of the new National Association for Neighborhood Schools, was pleased that the ethnic rivalries of Poles, Irish, Lithuanians, Italians, and Germans were declining. "We have a growing consciousness of ourselves as white people," she said, "just like the blacks with their 'black power.' "

Other themes and tactics from the black movement have also been self-consciously picked up, turned around, and distorted by the Bogan protestors, including the pleas for community control by the powerless and race pride. "There will always be racially identifiable black schools," Connie Schaeffer told the Bogan Community Council. "But we are not allowed to have racially identifiable white schools. Think about it. We are not allowed to have our homes, our families, our community."

While the Bogan protests were going on, another side of the neighborhood showed itself in a more subdued way. Nearly 100 local business people gathered one evening of the second week of school at the Royalty Restaurant on West 63rd Street, a major shopping area in Marquette Park. The new development commission of the Southwest Parish and Neighborhood Federation, the largest and best-organized community group, had invited them to talk about revitalizing the neighborhood economy, using city money to make the shopping area more attractive, and keeping old businesses in the neighborhood while attracting new ones to any vacant spaces. There was a sense of urgency in many of the local merchants' questions. Most of the men and women there were concerned, as one man said, to "keep Western Avenue viable and closed off from the element you don't want in."

Virtually nobody in the area counters anti-black sentiment head-on. Another community organization, the Southwest Community Congress, tries to defuse some of the more racist reactions and looks forward to stable integration of the neighborhood sometime in the future. Partly because of its moderate stand on radical issues, however, it remains weak. The Federation focuses on redevelopment, also a major effort of the SWCC, in an effort to direct neighborhood energy toward strengthening the community. If there is ever a chance of integration succeeding somewhere down the line with the neighborhood, it will require whites committed to staying there, improving the community, and pouring their money and work into it. Unfortunately, the Parish Federation not only does little to challenge racism in its bailiwick, it also rides the waves of racial fear to build its organization and program. Despite its origins with organizers who had come out of the civil rights movement, the Federation has become increasingly trapped within the prevailing consciousness in the community as a result of its narrow Alinsky-style vision of community organizing.

However, the Federation has succeeded in turning the community's anger more toward banks, savings and loan institutions, and downtown politicians and slightly less toward blacks alone. It has also encouraged more constructive outlets for neighborhood fears: reconstruction and rehabilitation, in particular. Without that development drive, a push for open housing alone, for example, would mean almost certain racial turnover and resegregation as well as more conflict. Realtors, bankers, and other speculators would profit. Blacks would inherit a neighborhood stripped of capital, services, commerce, and the amenities of a decent city life.

In 1977 the Federation, working with the Illinois Public Action Council, helped to push through a new state law restricting mortgage banking abuses. They also collected signatures of neighborhood residents who wanted to take advantage of a 1971 state law enabling people to stop realtors from soliciting them to sell their homes.

Although the desegregation controversy has sparked a little more activity and unity in Chicago's fragmented, weakened black movement, blacks remain disorganized. A majority of blacks probably favor some form of desegregation, but there are doubts about it. One group of black leaders even attacked school desegregation in favor of black community control of black schools.

Even more typically, many blacks see full desegregation of Chicago schools as an impossible goal. Judson Hixson, education director of the Urban League and a member of the Citywide Advisory Committee, said that full desegregation would require busing 100,000 of the system's 125,000 white students. He prefers to talk about developing a plan for quality education for black and white students. Desegregation through various mechanisms would be only one way of bringing that about. He looks to a recent Supreme Court ruling in the Detroit busing case as opening up a new strategy. The Court required the state of Michigan to help pay for schooling to compensate for past damages of school segregation.

Hixson's belief in the appeal of "quality education" and his awareness that it might win a number of white moderates away from the most militantly anti-integration forces has not, however, made him give up on desegregation. He remains firmly committed to desegregating the schools, even if other blacks waver, either out of antipathy toward the hostile whites or out of a desire for black pride and community control. "For a system to be desegregated, not every school has to be desegregated," he says, "but the pattern of school attendance has to be altered. Hannon's plan says for a few people in isolated instances, we will let you escape the school for a short period. For Hannon the interest of the white students and parents is of paramount importance. If blacks or other minority students benefit, it is purely accidental. You can't do anything with the Bogan bigots, but I take the position that they don't own the schools. They can't translate their personal prejudice into policy that restricts access to public institutions.

"Desegregation is a necessary prerequisite to access to quality education. The same persons and political forces that created the tragedy of Chicago public schools are still in power. To think that they would treat all-black and minority schools equally is unbelievable. Black schools, as long as they're separated out, won't get the same access and the same quality. There's always the question of why do those forces want to keep you out of certain schools? Becoming educated is a social process, too. We live in, whether people like it or not, a multiracial society and a multiracial world. To the extent that we educate black, white, brown, and Asian students in separate schools, they're unprepared to work in this world."

Epps, one of the three black members of the 11-member school board, stresses the symbolic value of integration. "As long as there are segregated schools," he argues, "they are symbols of exclusion, of apartheid, a class society. As long as policy-makers fight against desegregation, they are delivering a message that, 'We do not believe you deserve the best quality education this society has to deliver.' It seems to me that these symbols are more important than the educational substance. We all know that all-black schools can be excellent."

Increasingly blacks are concerned that the issue, whatever the form of desegregation plan adopted eventually, is the "segregation of power," in the words of Rev. Jesse Jackson. Without greater power over the schools, blacks can even be harmed by desegregation plans that bus only black kids (and often into hostile white neighborhoods), that fail to make a strong effort to improve black-white relations in the schools, or that deprive blacks of positions, power, or programs that they already have. For example, Hixson criticized the "Access to Excellence" plan for terminating a very successful middle school in a black neighborhood in order to convert the new building into a magnet designed to draw both blacks and whites.

Power, however, remains segregated, that is, in the white hands of the Democratic machine. Faced with a decision on three school board positions in the spring of 1978, Mayor Bilandic ignored the advice of his citizen advisory committees and reappointed two whites who have been consistently opposed to desegregation rather than increasing the representation of blacks on the board. This guaranteed that for the near future Hannon would have control of the board with six votes, and the opposition would continue to consist of the three blacks, one pro-integration white, and the off-again, on-again vote of the one Latino.

That leaves desegregation advocates discouraged. "Until some federal district court orders this system to desegregate, we aren't going to get anywhere," black school board member, Henry McGee, a former postmaster, told an NAACP meeting in the fall of 1977. The prospects had changed little in the following year. Yet court-ordered busing would probably be much worse for the city than the reasonable plans city leaders could pursue if they were willing to break from the Daley mold of government. To be really effective, however, they will have to tackle the devastating effects of racism on all fronts. They will have to fight both private and public abandonment of the city economy to the ravages of real estate speculation, runaway factories and offices, continuing forms of bank and insurance redlining, and development only for the sake of downtown businesses and upper-income whites.

The Bogan area resistance to desegregation of schools is a gloomy cloud on Chicago's horizon. There are, however, whites— even on the Southwest side—who are willing to accept de- segregation, especially if they could also improve the quality of education for their children at the same time. Unfortunately the last place anyone searching for signs of hope should look is the first place they should be able to look—the offices of the city's political leaders in city hall.

# Index